THE LOWLAND MAYA POSTCLASSIC

The Lowland Maya Postclassic

EDITED BY ARLEN F. CHASE AND PRUDENCE M. RICE

UNIVERSITY OF TEXAS PRESS, AUSTIN

Requests for permission to reproduce material from this work
should be sent to Permissions, University of Texas Press,
Box 7819, Austin, Texas 78713.

Library of Congress Cataloging in Publication Data
Main entry under title:
The Lowland Maya Postclassic.
   Bibliography: p.
   Includes index.
   1. Mayas—Antiquities—Addresses, essays, lectures.
2. Indians of Mexico—Antiquities—Addresses, essays,
lectures.   3. Indians of Central America—Antiquities—
Addresses, essays, lectures.   4. Mexico—Antiquities—
Addresses, essays, lectures.   5. Central America—
Antiquities—Addresses, essays, lectures.   I. Chase,
Arlen F. (Arlen Frank), 1953–   II. Rice, Prudence M.
F1435.L86   1985   972.81'01   84-13168
ISBN 0-292-74643-1

For reasons of speed and economy, this volume has been
composed from computer files prepared by the editors.

Contents

Preface

This collection of essays represents a "state of the art" attempt by current researchers to interpret and explain a portion of Maya prehistory that, until recently, has been the subject of little archaeological investigation and much speculation. Many of the scholars whose work is represented in this collection also seek to answer questions which either led to or arose during their investigations into the archaeology of the Maya Postclassic period. Ten of the essays in this volume were originally presented in December 1979 at the American Anthropological Association meetings in Cincinnati, Ohio. This session was convened in order to bring about an exchange of information and perspectives among lowland Mayanists who were closely involved in research bearing on the Postclassic period. Later the volume was expanded to include essays tying together work outside the traditionally defined Maya lowland area.

The book has been organized into three "areal" sections: the Northern lowlands, the Southern lowlands, and the peripheries. Our geographic divisions (for example, the "periphery") may be somewhat at odds with traditional areal breakdowns. That this is so is partly because contacts, emphases, and foci of cultural development are different in the Postclassic as compared to the Classic period. It may still be argued, however, whether or not Ball's essay on the western Gulf Coast is correctly subsumed in a "peripheral" role. Preceding each regional section, we have included a short introduction and summary of data not covered by essays in the accompanying sections, in order to place the contributions into a larger context.

Although we do not claim that all recent data on the Maya Postclassic are discussed in this volume, we are secure in the fact that many questions concerning this ill-defined time period have been raised and hope that some answers have at least been hinted at, if not established. The Postclassic period can at minimum be described as an enigmatic period of Maya history. We hope that this volume begins to fill a void in our knowledge of the Maya civilization and that its selections prove worthwhile in stimulating further research into a difficult but fascinating period of time.

INTRODUCTION

"Decline, decadence, and depopulation" are three terms that have long been used to describe the Maya Postclassic. Recent archaeological data, however, are casting into doubt the validity of this traditional characterization. The myth concerning the Postclassic Maya has its roots in the early 1920s, when researchers began to glorify a "peaceful, non-warlike" Classic Maya society. Although a later doctoral thesis by Robert Rands (1952) demonstrated that the Classic Maya did engage in war, the fairytale of the Classic Maya "peaceable kingdom" persisted, with profound effects on reconstructions of Maya culture history. One of its most telling roles was that of depicting the succeeding Postclassic Maya as "warlike and militaristic." This apparent contrast with the Classic period provided the basis for the view of Maya "decadence" and "decline" during the Postclassic. Equally overplayed is the concept of Postclassic "depopulation," which arose out of the romantic notion of a cataclysmic lowland Maya "collapse." While an argument may be made for reduced Postclassic populations in some areas such as the central Peten of Guatemala (Cowgill 1964) and the central part of Campeche (Ball, this volume), this is not true for all regions, the Northern lowlands being a major exception. In sum, the most commonly used terms for describing the Maya Postclassic are exaggerations or misconceptions, and the majority of the essays in this volume serve to illustrate this fact.

Defining the Postclassic

Attempting to define the Postclassic is a chicken-and-egg endeavor. The definition depends on the date chosen for its beginning, but the date chosen to begin the period depends on how the Postclassic is defined. For the purposes of this book, particularly in consideration of the fact that our knowledge of the lowland Postclassic is still in its nascent stages, the Postclassic is defined in both a temporal and processual way. The "Postclassic" is an interval of time beginning roughly A.D. 909 (10.4.0.0.0.) in the Maya lowlands. This date marks the end of the erection of monuments with Long Count dates in the Southern lowlands; the demographic, sociopolitical, architectural, and ceramic changes characterizing the "collapse" are largely a *fait accompli*. Thus, while the Terminal Classic period is not temporally included in the Postclassic, its demographic shifts, alteration (or removal) of elite power structures, decline in monumental construction, and changes in the ceramic corpus are processually important to an understanding of the succeeding temporal era. The role of the Classic-to-Postclassic transition in developing the nature of the Postclassic period is in no way denigrated. Rather, an additional perspective is gained that is advantageous both in emphasizing the emergence of new patterns and themes and in stressing the real and significant continuities from the Classic. The period is not forced into the subsidiary posture of being merely "Post-" something else. In fact, the Maya Postclassic may be viewed as a fresh start on a new and untried trajectory.

What is archaeologically known of Maya prehistory indicates that a population that can in some way be called "Maya" was apparently present in the lowlands by 2000 B.C. (Hammond et al. 1979). Whether the "Maya" can be identified with an occupation back to 9000 B.C. as recently claimed (MacNeish, Wilkerson, and Nelken-Terner 1980: 61) is not known. The period between 2000 B.C. and A.D. 250 witnessed a vibrant Maya culture and the development of an advanced civilization. Most Maya research in the last few decades has focused on the Classic civilization from A.D. 250 to 900, with its spectacular architecture, carved stelae, and complex social and economic organization. Sometime around A.D. 900, following the 11.16.0.0.0. correlation, the Maya culture of the Southern lowlands experienced a major reorganization: the people disappeared, abandoning their stela cult and focus on monumental architecture (see Sharer 1977). This termination of the Classic Maya civilization, its so-called "collapse," has had a special, almost mystical place in Maya studies.

Recognition of this break in the archaeological record led S. G. Morley (1947; with Brainerd 1956; with Brainerd and Sharer 1983) to hypothesize the existence of "Old" and "New" Maya Kingdoms: the "new" kingdom began when the people of the "old" Southern lowlands kingdom migrated to northern Yucatan to found a new Maya society in the Puuc sites. In Morley's synthesis, the Southern low-

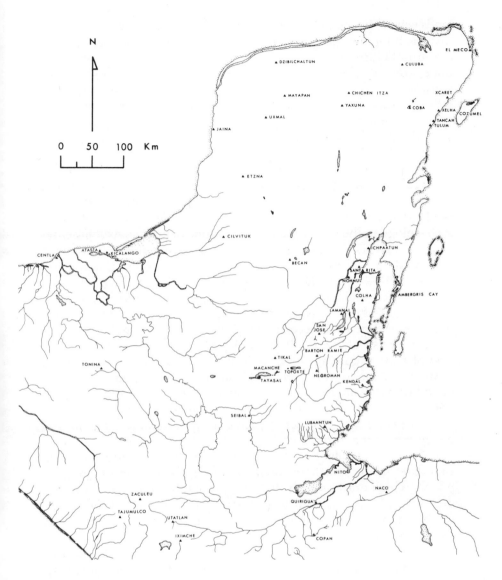

Fig. 1. Map of the Maya area showing location of sites discussed (prepared by D. Z. Chase).

lands were believed to be a void after the Classic period, despite ethno-historic references to the contrary. This view may have been partly a result of Guthe's (1921, 1922) work at Tayasal, Peten, Guatemala, under the auspices of the Carnegie Institution of Washington. His work was part of an original Carnegie scheme for defining the Post-classic. When Guthe's excavations at Tayasal did not produce the expected large amounts of Postclassic materials, Morley must have seen the data as confirming his suspicions of the enormity of the Southern lowland collapse.

Subsequent decades saw the reconstructions of a "declining, decadent, and depopulated" Postclassic Maya period reinforced, and near validation of the Morley model of Old and New Kingdoms in the lowlands in standard prehistory texts. The reigning paradigm in archaeology in the 1940s and 1950s was one of static developmental stages which also gave tacit support to the Morley model. It has been very hard for Mayanists to emerge from the cocoon of this precon-ceived framework. In fact, it was not until the early 1960s, with work at Tikal (Adams and Trik 1961), Barton Ramie (Willey, Bullard, Glass, and Gifford 1965), and Flores (Cowgill 1963), that a viable Postclassic period was recognized for the central Peten.

Strictly speaking, the Postclassic refers to no more than the pe-riod of time following the Classic period. This simple statement, however, glosses over a number of important issues, plus a great deal of additional denotative and emotive baggage that continues to ad-here to the concept of the Postclassic. Perhaps the most misunder-stood aspect of the Postclassic period is its chronology. The formal beginning of the Postclassic has been a source of controversy, not only from the standpoint of terminology, but also in terms of its ac-tual date. In the Northern lowlands, it begins after the Florescent period, which until recently (Ball 1979a, 1979b; Andrews IV and An-drews V 1980) was viewed as following the "collapse" of the South-ern lowlands. In the Southern lowlands, some investigators include the Terminal Classic or Tepeu 3 events within the Postclassic, while others do not. Within subregions of the Southern lowlands, this transition is viewed as occurring at differing times: earlier at Uaxac-tun than at Tikal; later at Altar de Sacrificios than at Seibal.

Temporal subdivisions within Postclassic sites have proved diffi-cult to recognize because Postclassic remains are often found dis-tributed horizontally over a landscape; they are not usually found in vertical strata as are the remains of Classic period precursors. It is therefore difficult to obtain a multiple-facet stratigraphy based on a single locus excavation. Postclassic peoples also seemed to find it easier to shift site locations than to build on top of an already existing one. Consequently, good stratigraphy has not often been recovered for this era. Even at Mayapan excavated lots were generally assigned to three categories: Late (usually surface), Middle (generally core or sealed deposits), and Early (usually non-Postclassic). The sequence for Mayapan was partially established because of Roys' (1976, originally 1933) readings of the Books of *Chilam Balam* in relation to Mayapan (Smith 1971: I: 19). In the most specific sense, then, the Mayapan sequence is relative and not absolute. Close readings of other Postclassic sequences show much the same situation or reveal that they are cross-referenced to another site sequence (often that of Mayapan). The fact emerges that there is no absolute time control within the Postclassic period.

Just as the beginning of the Postclassic cannot be fixed with surety, but varies from site to site, the end of this time period is also exceedingly difficult to place. This is partially a consequence of an apparent reluctance on the part of the Maya to accept European trade items or at least to deposit them in the archaeological record. Negroman–Tipu, Belize, is a partial exception to this statement as Spanish olive jar sherds have been recovered in association with the construction fill for Maya–style buildings. In general, however, the presence of the Spaniards in the Maya lowlands is not clearly detectable in the archaeological record until the nineteenth century. The Maya continued to live much as they had prior to the Spanish arrival, with major changes occurring primarily as a consequence of population declines or movement due to introduced diseases and Spanish settlement policy.

Postclassic Themes

Several themes of Postclassic lowland Maya culture have been developed out of recent archaeological and ethnohistoric work. Replacing the earlier views of a declining society, these new themes underscore the strength and complexity of Postclassic culture, in terms of both economic and social adjustments (Erasmus 1968; Rathje 1975; D. Chase 1982a). Like the earlier Postclassic characterizations, however, they say as much about the research orientations that produced them as about Postclassic society itself. It is very likely that they too will be modified, expanded, or negated by future work.

A major theme of Postclassic Maya society is its involvement with long–distance trade. Reconstructions of the importance of trade in the Postclassic are based on two kinds of data: ethnohistoric accounts, and the traded goods themselves. Observations of Spanish priests and explorers give insights into commercial activities of the sixteenth through eighteenth centuries, providing us with glimpses of patterns that may extend back several hundred years. Much of the trade appears to have been carried out along coastal routes around the Yucatan peninsula (Sabloff and Rathje 1975a, 1975b), probably extending as far as Central America and perhaps into the Caribbean, if Columbus' early reports of huge trading canoes are any indication. Apparently trade throughout much of the Postclassic was dominated by Acalan (Scholes and Roys 1948) on the Gulf Coast, which was in a convenient location to mediate trade between the Maya and the Aztec, with their establishment at Xicalango. Some of this trade is likely to have passed overland through the Peten, and thence to the Caribbean; Roys (1943: 52) notes the specific existence of overland routes from the Yucatan area south to the northern part of Belize. After the demise of Acalan, occasioned by Spanish activities, the eastern littoral trading emphasis appears to have continued through the seventeenth century (G. Jones 1982). Among the most significant of the goods being circulated in these exchange networks were cacao, salt, cotton cloth, and obsidian, the latter indicating the importance of extra–regional ties. Other goods mentioned in ethnohistoric documents or found in archaeological contexts include: shell, ceramics, vesicular basalt, jadeite and greenstone, copal incense, slaves, honey, feathers, skins, dyes, and probably a large variety of foodstuffs.

A second major characteristic of the Postclassic lowland Maya is a coastal or riverine settlement focus. This is by no means an exclusive orientation (witness the land–locked position of Mayapan and Chichen Itza); however, it is certainly true for the east coast of Yucatan and Belize. It is possible to connect this focus of settlement with the economic realities of trade as described above. Water–based coastal trade is obviously facilitated by coastal settlement. In addition, two of the major economic goods enjoying wide circulation in the Postclassic period, salt and cacao, were produced in these environments. Northern Yucatan was one of the major salt producing areas in Mesoamerica (A. Andrews 1983) while cacao grows best in swampy or moist fertile riverine soils. In the Southern lowlands, the settlement focus appears first along both rivers and lakes (at least in the Late Classic/Early Postclassic transition) and then appears to shift solely to lacustrine locations for the duration of the Postclassic period. At all these locations an aquatic subsistence emphasis is likewise indicated by the presence of aquatic fauna and notched sherds or net weights, which are found in abundance in Postclassic archaeological assemblages.

Militarism is another pervasive theme in reconstructions of Postclassic lowland Maya society. It has been invoked as an explanation both for the new organizational nature of Postclassic society and for the changes that occurred within Maya society at the end of the Classic period; warfare is in fact one of the hypothesized causes of the collapse (Sabloff and Willey 1967; Cowgill 1964; D. Chase and A. Chase 1982). Data from Altar de Sacrificios and Seibal have supported a non-Maya invasion hypothesis on the western periphery of the lowlands (Sabloff and Willey 1967; Adams 1971), although recent evidence from the eastern coast has indicated a much more complex picture of thrust and counter–thrust (D. Chase and A. Chase 1982). Militarism has also been used as an explanation of the construction of the east coast Yucatan walled cities, and, together with trade, to account for the rise and fall of Northern lowland merchant elites and their leagues and alliances (Rathje 1977). The bow and arrow may have first appeared in warfare at this time, because small arrow points are common at Postclassic sites. In the central Peten, the densely populated island settlements may have been so located for reasons of defense, as Cortes makes several references to protracted hostilities between the Itza and their neighbors as he marched through Peten on the way to Honduras. Walled, palisaded, and moated sites were apparently common, as were alliances and uprisings between their inhabitants in the early sixteenth century.

Defensive posturing may have been enhanced in the Postclassic because of a series of possible migrations-cum-invasions in the lowlands, movements that are both internal and external. The earliest Postclassic migration, that of the "Toltecs" to Chichen Itza (Tozzer 1957), may be intimately intertwined with the Classic Maya "collapse" and, without a doubt, had major implications for later Maya prehistory (see Thompson 1942; Rands 1954; D. Chase and A. Chase 1982; Lincoln n.d.). An internal migration of the Itza from the Northern to Southern lowlands is recorded in the Books of *Chilam Balam*, and is probably responsible for the architectural and ceramic stylistic similarities between the two areas (Bullard 1973; A. Chase 1982, this volume). It is also possible that the Arawak occasionally harassed the east coast of the Yucatan peninsula, as did buccaneers of the historic period. The identification of these population movements has been attempted archaeologically (Tozzer 1957; Sabloff and Willey 1967; A. Chase 1976, 1982; D. Chase and A. Chase 1982), but is still speculative due to the nature of the remains. It is clear, however, that population movements did profoundly affect the entire Maya area in the Postclassic period.

Archaeologists' understanding of the nature of the six centuries of the lowland Maya Postclassic period continues to evolve. Mayanists are still searching for patterns and structure in order to improve their concepts and interpretations. When the field problems and non-chronometric dating difficulties, as discussed above, are combined with the perpetually troublesome correlations of Maya and Christian calendars, interpretive issues are even more difficult to resolve. This volume surveys some aspects of current research into the Maya Postclassic, suggesting further questions for research and attempting to begin to synthesize an answer of what the Maya Postclassic period is or was. At minimum, the volume serves as notice that research into the Maya Postclassic period has come of age.

Postclassic Temporal and Spatial Frames for the Lowland Maya: A Background

ARLEN F. CHASE AND DIANE Z. CHASE

Temporally, the Maya Postclassic period begins with the "Maya collapse" at approximately 10.3.0.0.0. in Maya long count notation and ends during the sixteenth through seventeenth centuries with the arrival of the Spaniards. The date for the beginning of the Postclassic period is dependent upon a correlation of the Maya and Christian calendars. Although the generally accepted 11.16.0.0.0. correlation would place the collapse at A.D. 889, other correlations alter this date and the length of the Postclassic period by intervals of 256 years. Attempts to place the Maya calendar into an absolute time frame related to the Gregorian calendar have focused on native chronicles (Brinton 1881; Nicholson 1955; Thompson 1937; Vaillant 1935; Wauchope 1947), the Books of *Chilam Balam* (Brinton 1882; Morley 1911; Roys 1933 [1976], 1960; Valentini 1880; Weitzel 1931), and scientific methods such as radiocarbon dating (Satterthwaite 1956; Satterthwaite and Ralph 1960; Stuckenrath, Coe, and Ralph 1966; Satterthwaite and Coe 1968). In addition to the 11.16.0.0.0. (Thompson 1927, 1937) correlation, the principal proposed correlations include the 11.3.0.0.0. (Escalona Ramos 1940; Vaillant 1935; Thompson 1941a, 1941b; Wauchope 1947; A. Chase n.d.) and the 12.9.0.0.0. (Spinden 1924; Andrews IV 1965a, 1965b). Unfortunately, no one correlation fits all the data and, as has been pointed out in the past by Satterthwaite (1956), Deevey, Gralenski, and Hoffren (1959), Kirchoff (1950), and more recently Kubler (1976) and A. Chase (n.d.), the correlation question has not yet been settled. That the Spaniards did not penetrate all of the Maya area at the same date adds further confusion to the picture. The general lack of early historic trade items in the archaeological record and the elusive nature of contact sites make it difficult to fix the end of the Postclassic period temporally.

Dating within the Postclassic period is further complicated by a number of factors: (1) lack of monuments with long count dates as in

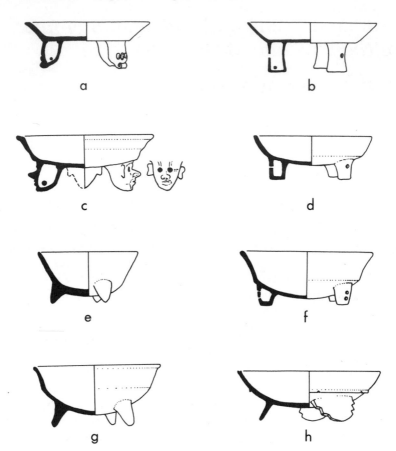

Fig. 1. Redware bowl forms of the Postclassic Maya lowlands (diameter of "a" is approximately 22 centimeters; all other vessels are drawn to the same scale)

a.   Augustine Red (Peten)
b.   Paxcaman Red (Peten)
c.   Undesignated Type (Lamanai)
d.   Topoxte Red (Topoxte)
e.   Mama Red (Mayapan)
f.   Payil Red (Tulum)
g.   Rita Red (Santa Rita)
h.   U Fine Orange (Atasta)

the Classic period; (2) the scarcity of deeply stratified Postclassic deposits, and until recently, (3) the small sample of Postclassic sites excavated. Because of these problems, Postclassic Maya archaeology is frequently dependent upon ceramic analysis to provide the relative dating of excavated materials. In the past, this dating was limited both by the small number of excavated samples and by a seriation of sherds without much contextual data. The increase in excavated Postclassic samples has now allowed for a broader understanding of Postclassic ceramics. There are, however, almost as many different ceramic sequences and types (fig. 1) as there are excavated sites, thus making wider interpretations difficult. While recognizing these limitations, it is useful to relate the various sequences and areas to each other in an effort to gain a temporal overview of the lowland Maya Postclassic.

Yucatan

The Yucatec sequence (fig. 2), which serves as the foundation for most current work on the Northern lowland Postclassic, was formulated by R. E. Smith (1971) and builds on the earlier work of Andrews IV (1943: 74–79) and Brainerd (1958). As developed by Smith, the sequence had several unstated assumptions. The chronology was primarily derived from Roys' (1933, 1976) interpretation of the ethnohistoric Books of *Chilam Balam* and appears to subsume their linear seriation by Morley (Morley and Brainerd 1956; Pollock et al. 1962). Smith may also have followed an unstated assumption that ceramic complexes generally had a "life–span" of approximately 200 years. Following earlier interpretations of the *Chilam Balams*, Smith accepted that the occupation of the Puuc area was earlier than that of Chichen Itza, which was in turn earlier than that of Mayapan. Mayapan and the Tases ceramic phase were both viewed, on the basis of interpretation of information in the native chronicles, as ending promptly at A.D. 1450. Smith (1971: 4) noted that "no possible stratigraphy was found for the pottery earlier than the Hocaba ceramic complex of the Middle Postclassic Period" at Mayapan and that "without stratigraphy there resulted a confusing mass of sherds which of necessity had to be classified typologically in an effort to determine which types were associated with each of the different periods." The limited archaeological stratigraphy present at Mayapan led Smith (1971: 4) to incorporate the prevalent linear paradigm for the interpretation of Yucatec history (Roys 1962) into the formal Postclassic ceramic sequence for the site. The Cozumel sequence (Connor 1975: 115; Sabloff and Rathje 1975a: 3), as now defined, ap-

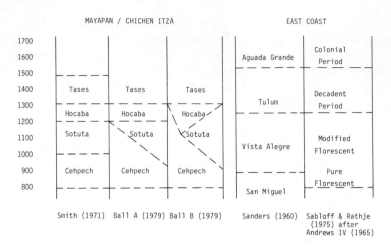

Fig. 2. Various schemes for ceramic complexes of the Postclassic Yucatan Peninsula.

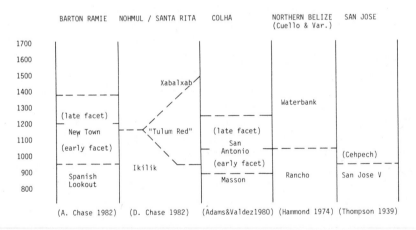

Fig. 3. Various schemes for ceramic complexes of Postclassic Northern Belize.

parently accepts Smith's (1971) presentation of this time period and conjoins it with Sanders' (1960) east coast sequence.

Recently, however, Ball (1979a, 1979b) has argued that this original sequence is not correct, especially in regard to the linear arrangement of Cehpech (Puuc sites), Sotuta (Chichen Itza), and Hocaba (Mayapan) in the 1971 R. E. Smith arrangement. The basic argument, as presented by Ball (1979a, 1979b), is that Maya ceramicists have been confusing spatial variation with temporal change. Ball suggests two alternate schemes: partial overlap of the sequences or complete overlap of the sequences. Three chronological schemes are, therefore, now proposed for northern Yucatan. The first can be defined as "sequential" or "linear" and was propounded by Smith. In the second, or "partial overlap" scheme, Sotuta and Cehpech are seen as overlapping and prior to the Hocaba ceramic complex. In the third "total overlap" scheme, Cehpech, Sotuta, and Hocaba are at least partially coeval. This last scheme finds some confirmatory evidence in northern Belize (D. Chase and A. Chase 1982; D. Chase 1982b). Ball's complete overlap scheme also necessitates a review of the applicability of the 11.3.0.0.0. correlation to Maya chronology as it suggests that the temporal dimension allowed for the Postclassic period needs to be foreshortened (see A. Chase n.d.).

Belize

Barton Ramie (Gifford 1965, 1976) was the first site in Belize to generate a recognized Postclassic ceramic sequence (fig. 3). Gifford (1965: 384) viewed the Postclassic ceramics recovered there as having little, if any, relationship to the Classic material which preceded it and as being a relatively short term phenomenon restricted to the earlier part of the Postclassic period. The formal definition of this sequence (Sharer and Chase 1976), however, delineated an early and a late facet of the New Town phase, the whole of which was thought to be representative of continuous occupation of the Cayo District of Belize. The Augustine ceramic group (fig. 1a) was placed in the earlier facet and the Paxcaman ceramic group (fig. 1b) in the later facet. The well-represented Daylight ceramic group is still not securely placed in either facet although it was suspected to belong to the earlier facet. The Daylight Orange ceramics may in fact be derivative from the Late to Terminal Classic Taak ceramic group of northern Belize (D. Chase 1982b). Daylight Orange finewares, which did not occur at Barton Ramie, may be present at Lamanai (fig. 1c; A. Chase personal observation). Recent review of the New Town phase has suggested that the late facet extends no further than the Middle

Postclassic at Barton Ramie (P. Rice 1979: 80–81; A. Chase 1982) while the New Town ceramic sphere has a Late Postclassic manifestation at the site of Tayasal in the Peten of Guatemala (A. Chase 1979, 1982, 1983, 1984).

Thompson (1939), in his early excavation of San Jose, found little that he ascribed to a Postclassic horizon although he did postulate that Cehpech-related (Yucatec) material was later than his San Jose V complex. Excavations at Nohmul (D. Chase 1982a, 1982b; D. Chase and A. Chase 1982), however, produced a Yucatec-inspired architectural assemblage and, more importantly, yielded a single-unit refuse deposit containing a mixture of San Jose V, Cehpech, Sotuta, and Hocaba-related material, indicating some temporal overlap between these complexes (or, at a minimum, problems in their original definition). Other excavations at Nohmul have suggested that Terminal Classic materials were possibly directly overlain and continuous with Tulum Red ware materials (Hammond 1974: 184–185) although more recent analysis has clouded this point (Hammond 1977a: 57–58).

Tulum Red ware (fig. 1f) has long been suspected as belonging to the later part of the Postclassic period in the Northern lowlands. This suggestion was first formulated by Andrews IV (1943: 74–79), who combined Mayapan and Tulum into a single period which he dated as lasting from about A.D. 1350–1450. Lothrop (1952: 6) took umbrage at this dating and, while accepting that the two redwares belonged to a single period, argued that this period "began earlier, at least at Tulum where there were three or more different and successive architectural periods, two or more successive styles of frescos, multiple coatings of plaster, repairs to sagging roofs and crumbling walls, and other evidence of long occupation." Lothrop's (1952: 6) revised dating of the "Mayapan–Tulum Period" was from A.D. 1204 to 1450; this period was preceded by a "Tula–Toltec Period" (A.D. 987 to 1204) and followed by a "Mixteca–Santa Rita Period" (A.D. 1450 to 1550). Recent excavations at both Colha (Hester 1979; Hester, Eaton, and Shafer 1980) and Santa Rita (D. Chase 1981, 1982a, 1984, n.d.) would suggest that Tulum Red ware makes an even earlier appearance in northern Belize, as it is present at Colha during the early part of the Postclassic (Adams and Valdez 1980) and at Santa Rita by the middle part of the Postclassic (A. Chase and D. Chase 1981; A. Chase n.d.). It should be noted additionally that the paste for Late–Terminal Classic Kik Red ware is extremely similar to that of Tulum Red ware (D. Chase, personal observation). It may in fact be that Tulum Red ware originated in Belize, but this cannot yet be determined with certainty because of dating problems. Pendergast (1981a, 1981b), however, has suggested on stratigraphic and chronological grounds (radiocarbon dating) that the Mayapan style Postclassic redwares and censers, common in northern Yucatan (fig. 1e), may have had their origin in Belize.

Investigations at Santa Rita have uncovered both Terminal Classic and Late Postclassic materials. Although Late Postclassic deposits directly overlay a Terminal Classic deposit in one case, no absolute indication of continuities between the two ceramic complexes has been recovered at the site. A Late Postclassic Rita ceramic group (fig. 1g) has been established for Santa Rita (D. Chase 1982a, 1984). Although sharing modal similarities with Tulum, Mayapan, and to some extent Topoxte (fig. 1d), it appears to be completely distinct and possibly later than the Tulum Red as illustrated by Sanders (1960). Tulum Red and modeled effigy incensarios are found in construction fill at Santa Rita, overlain by primary Rita Red ceramic deposits; this would imply that the Rita material, which is most similar to Tases complex materials at Mayapan, postdates Tulum–related ceramics in northern Belize (at least at Santa Rita Corozal). The ceramic stratigraphy between Tulum–related and Mayapan–related redwares is not as clear at Lamanai. As at Santa Rita, however, it is difficult to establish at Lamanai just how late these redware traditions continued in Northern Belize. A long occupation is certain (see Pendergast 1977).

Peten

The Postclassic period in the central Peten is just as complex as elsewhere (fig. 4). Early, Middle, and Late Postclassic periods have been identified for Tayasal (A. Chase 1982, 1983, 1984, n.d.). Presently, there is a general consensus that the Paxcaman ceramic group (fig. 1b) is one of the most long–lived in the Peten although its absolute cessation date is still unknown. It probably was in existence in some form through the seventeenth century. Some plainware material (Chilo Unslipped), which may be even later, has been recognized in the Tayasal–Paxcaman zone (A. Chase 1979: 101) and in the Macanche area (P. Rice n.d.a, n.d.b; D. Rice and P. Rice 1981). Topoxte (fig. 1d) is another ceramic group which appears in the east-central Peten and which is not firmly placed in time. Bullard (1973: 229, 231) believed that it dated to the Middle Postclassic. P. Rice (1979, n.d.a) has suggested that it first appeared in the Early Postclassic and continued through the Late Postclassic period. On the basis of data from the Lake Peten area, it would appear to be largely contemporaneous with late Paxcaman Red ceramics (A. Chase 1979, 1983,

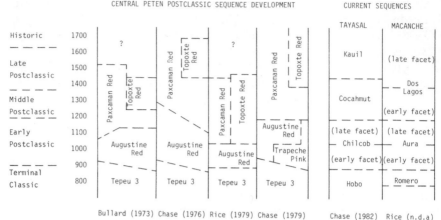

CENTRAL PETEN POSTCLASSIC SEQUENCE DEVELOPMENT

CURRENT SEQUENCES

Fig. 4. Various schemes for ceramic complexes of Postclassic central Peten.

1984, this volume). Again, its date of cessation is not known. While P. Rice (1979; G. Jones, Rice, and Rice 1981) argued that the group was largely indigenous, A. Chase (1976, 1979, 1982) has suggested that the group was intrusive to the region and representative of the "Itza."

On the basis of the Tayasal data, the Augustine ceramic group (fig. 1a), defined at Barton Ramie (Sharer and Chase 1976: 291–294), can be placed stratigraphically earlier than Paxcaman. A possible transitional Terminal Classic–Postclassic group, the Trapeche Pink ceramic group, has also been defined (A. Chase 1979: 104–115). At Tayasal this group appears to be ancestral to the Paxcaman group. P. Rice (n.d.a, n.d.b) has reported new varieties of this group from Macanche, where it begins in the Early Postclassic and continues through the Late Postclassic. It would appear that at least some of the Macanche Trapeche Pink is probably later than that at Tayasal and may exhibit some linkage to the San Joaquin Buff group at Mayapan. The Topoxte group also contains a late dichrome with red and cream decoration (Chompoxte Red-on-Cream) that has possible Yucatec parallels (P. Rice 1979: 40; n.d.a). The ceramic censer "typology" for the central Peten is nebulous although variants of Chen Mul Modeled censerware do exist in this region. P. Rice (1979: 50–56; n.d.b) has designated new effigy censer types, Idolos Modeled and Patojo Modeled, for the censer materials in the eastern lakes region; the censer material from the central Lake Peten area differs from that to the east and has been included within the types Nohpek Unslipped or Puxteal Modeled (A. Chase 1983, 1984).

A Tentative Overview

Through increased excavation and contextual analysis of ceramics and artifacts, Postclassic Maya archaeology is beginning to comprehend the variability in ceramic remains as well as overcome the recognized temporal-spatial problems. Reanalysis of the sequence and time depth for Northern Yucatan (Ball 1979a, 1979b) together with the implications of Yucatec influence in Terminal Classic northern Belize (D. Chase and A. Chase 1982) imply that the presently accepted Maya-Christian calendrical correlation should not be taken for granted. In fact, the new data suggest that the 11.3.0.0.0. correlation (A. Chase n.d.) may be more applicable than once was thought, as it would lessen the time gap between the Classic and Late Postclassic and probably more accurately reflect the recovered stratigraphic relationships.

Interpretation of the Postclassic Maya is now advancing toward a model of intensive and extensive regional variation. This accords well with ethnohistoric accounts of distinct Late Postclassic territorial units (Roys 1957; D. Chase n.d.) as well as historically derived divisions (Thompson 1977; G. Jones 1982). At least five broad, but distinct, regions can be recognized archaeologically for the Postclassic (fig. 5). The borders of the defined archaeological regions vary somewhat over time, but in general are fairly cohesive. Similar regional subdivisions proposed for the southern lowlands of the colonial period (G. Jones 1982: 279) may be viewed as deriving from Late Postclassic forerunners, yet the time depth involved is unclear. Surely, the broad lumping of categories into a single widespread "Chan Maya" territorial and cultural unit, temporally extended back to the Classic-Postclassic period transition (Thompson 1977: 3, 40–41), does not find confirmation in the extant archaeological diversity.

REGION I

The westernmost archaeological region can be characterized as *The Western Campeche Postclassic Tradition* and is paralleled by Jones' (1982: 279–280) Putun Acalan region of the colonial period. Archaeologically, it is visible in the works of Andrews IV (1943) and Ruz (1969) and, while exhibiting ties to the Maya lowlands, also reflects events occurring to its west. This region plays an important role in both the Early and Late Postclassic periods and acts as a boundary or sieve for much of the rest of the Maya realm. The Early and

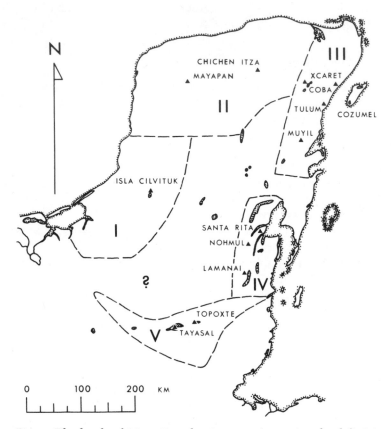

Fig. 5. The lowland Maya Postclassic: tentative regional subdivisions:
   I. Western Campeche Postclassic Tradition
   II. Northern Plains Postclassic Tradition
   III. Eastern Yucatec Postclassic Tradition
   IV. Northern Belize Postclassic Tradition
   V. Central Peten Postclassic Tradition

Late Postclassic ceramics (Ruz 1969) of the region are characterized by a mixture of Postclassic traits and by the extensive use of fine paste wares (fig. 1h), many of which occur as trade items in other parts of the Southern lowlands. The Late Postclassic for Region I may be characterized by the island site of Isla Civiltuk (Andrews IV 1943), noted for its buildings with beam and mortar roofs, a characteristic also found on the east coast of Yucatan.

REGION II

The Northern Plains Postclassic Tradition refers primarily to Tases-equivalent and possibly Hocaba material, which may be dated to the Middle and Late Postclassic periods. During this time the League of Mayapan bound the larger part of this area together in a Postclassic manifestation amply documented architecturally by Pollock and others (1962) and ceramically by Brainerd (1958) and R. E. Smith (1971). The Northern Plains Postclassic Tradition also binds together a melange of complexes which had existed previously in the area during the Early Postclassic (Ball 1979a, 1979b). The earlier part of the Postclassic period in the Northern Plains may be architecturally typified by the somewhat anomalous site of Chichen Itza (Ruppert 1935, 1952; Morris, Charlot, and Morris 1931; Bolles 1977; Lincoln n.d.). Although Chichen Itza evinces close ties to the indigenous architectural traditions which occur in the Puuc (Pollock 1981) and elsewhere in the Yucatan (Lincoln n.d.), the site also sports foreign (and probably introduced) architectural plans such as the patio-quad (D. Chase and A. Chase 1982).

REGION III

The Eastern Yucatec Postclassic Tradition is largely contemporary with that of its Late Postclassic western neighbor, yet differs stylistically in its ceramics and architecture (Lothrop 1924; Sanders 1960; Andrews IV and Andrews 1975; Sabloff and Rathje 1975a; Miller 1982) from the interior area. It is possible that this tradition slightly predates that of the latter part of the Northern Plains. In general, the amount of architectural construction crowded along the east coast north of the Xcalac Peninsula is representative of a large population.

REGION IV

The Northern Belize Postclassic Tradition (Pendergast 1967, 1981a, 1981b, 1981c; Sidrys 1976; Pring 1976; D. Chase 1981, 1982a, 1982b, 1984, n.d.) presents perhaps the most complex area of all the regions. Several temporally different manifestations are evident in this area and it is possible that the origins for the northern redwares (possibly Mayapan and probably Tulum) lie in Belize (Pendergast 1981a, 1981c). Data pertaining to the Early Postclassic indicate the existence of at least three regional traditions (Adams and Valdez 1980; A. Chase n.d.; Pendergast n.d.a), ultimately influenced by what may be interpreted as an outpost of Chichen Itza at Nohmul (D. Chase and A. Chase 1982). The late manifestation of this tradition, as evident at Santa Rita (D. Chase 1981, 1982a, 1984, n.d.), evinces ties to both Regions II and III, but is independent of both. On a slightly later temporal horizon and on the basis of colonial period data, G. Jones (1982: 282–285) has also segregated this area into a distinct unit called the "Belize Missions subregion."

REGION V

The Postclassic material culture of the southernmost region has previously been included under the label *The Central Peten Post-classic Tradition* (Bullard 1973; Sharer and Chase 1976). On the basis of an array of disparate data, Thompson (1977: 3) attempted to include the entire colonially known Southern lowland area into a single "Chan Maya region"; he (1977: 36–41) also argued that there was cultural continuity for this group back into the Classic period. It would appear, however, that neither archaeological nor ethno-historic data support this suggestion. In fact, G. Jones (1982) has sub-divided Thompson's area into three separate subregions for the colonial era. The first of these three subdivisions, the "Belize Missions subregion," found at least a partial identity with the Northern Belize Postclassic Tradition defined for Region IV. The region included here within the Central Peten Postclassic Tradition is similar in areal extent to the "Central Lakes subregion" defined by Jones (1982: 280–281) for the colonial period. Jones' (1982: 285) third division, the "Cehach subregion," has no known archaeological parallels, and it may be that this area was largely unoccupied prior to the advent of the Spaniards (or at least their associated diseases) in the Maya low-lands (cf. Ball, this volume).

The region of the Southern lowlands manifesting the Central Peten Postclassic Tradition shows much unity throughout its boundaries during the Early and Middle Postclassic periods. The earlier part of the Postclassic in the Southern lowlands is primarily represented by the appearance of the Augustine and Trapeche ceramic groups, while the Middle Postclassic is typified by the widespread occurrence of the Paxcaman ceramic group. There is more variability during the Late Postclassic with the trade and assimilation of the Topoxte group (P. Rice 1979, n.d.a) into the indigenous complexes of the Belize valley and central Peten (A. Chase 1982). Striking architectural remains, which include features similar to those of the Late Postclassic Northern lowlands (Bullard 1970: 273–276, 304), exist on Topoxte Island in Lake Yaxha. These Yucatec–like architectural assemblages extend from Lake Yaxha on the east as far west as Lake Salpeten, but do not occur on the Tayasal peninsula and have not been noted from the Lake Peten area or farther west around Lake Sacpuy. Besides the research done by Cowgill (1963) and Bullard (1970, 1973) on the Peten Postclassic, other work has been undertaken in an attempt to derive an understanding of the region and the recovered data have provoked a vibrant discussion (A. Chase 1976, 1979, 1982, 1983; P. Rice 1979; G. Jones, Rice, and Rice 1981).

Summary

On the basis of the present state of archaeological knowledge, five regions have been identified in a tentative spatial breakdown of the wider lowland Postclassic area. Undoubtedly, further research will refine these subdivisions. Many of the similarities visible between the various regions may be credited to an "international style of the Late Postclassic" (Robertson 1970). In spite of the superficial gloss created by this style, there is significant diversity in Postclassic material culture, primarily along regional lines. This is not surprising given the ethnohistoric descriptions of distinct Late Postclassic polities. Recent analysis of the variability evident among regions and sites within the Postclassic Maya area does not, for the most part, suggest significant temporal or sequential change within specific locales, but rather spatial variation between locales caused by situational and flexible cultural boundaries imposed by the Postclassic Maya themselves. In past research, such spatial variation has often been mistaken for temporal differences.

The areal diversity evident within the Postclassic lowlands dictates that local Postclassic sequences be established before wider processual interpretations can be made. The simple determination of spatial and temporal differences within a single Postclassic site is, in itself, a difficult task due to the prevalence of non-stratified remains for this period; determination of variability between regions is only compounded by the lack of serious work undertaken until recently on Postclassic sites. While spatial boundaries may be affected by trade, warfare, and alliance, they also appear to be correlated archaeologically with certain regional capitals. By identifying and excavating such foci, a definition of both temporal and spatial variation within the Postclassic archaeological record may be achieved. With continued excavation and comparisons, it should become possible to distinguish between temporal and spatial distinctions within the wider Postclassic record. This would allow for the archaeological identification of ethnohistorically known Late Postclassic territories, a definition of the relationships between these regions, and the application of the direct historic approach to Postclassic Maya archaeology to determine the processes behind, first, the Postclassic-to-Historic transition and, second, the Classic-to-Postclassic transition. It is research along these lines that should allow for more exact delineation of lowland Maya Postclassic spatial and temporal frames.

# THE NORTHERN LOWLANDS

The term "Northern lowlands" is used here to contrast with "Southern lowlands," the two regions being distinguished by differences that are ecological (climate and vegetation) as well as cultural. One major point of distinction between them is in the Classic to Postclassic transition: a tongue-in-cheek definition of the Northern lowlands may be that it is "that region where a 'collapse' did not occur." While definite replacement and change took place in ceramic complexes of the Northern lowlands between the Regional and Florescent periods, clearly the major transformation characterizing the transition in the Southern lowlands did not take place. Instead, the situation appears to be one of successive replacement of competitive spheres, as first pointed out by Ball (1974, 1979a, 1979b), and finally replacement by a generalized Postclassic complex. These changes may correspond to the political events taking place in this area: the Postclassic Northern lowlands were integrated into a widespread federation of eighteen territorial provinces by about A.D. 1400 (Roys 1943: 11). The political integration implied by the "League of Mayapan" was paralleled by a corresponding homogeneity of general ceramic and architectural styles that extends from the northern shores of Yucatan to the modern territorial division separating Guatemala and Mexico and thence through the heartland of northern Belize. It is because of these similarities that we have taken the step of including northern Belize within the Northern lowlands rather than, as is customary, within the Southern lowlands. Ceramic and architectural linkages suggest closer ties to the north than to the west.

Postclassic sites in the Northern lowlands exemplify the features noted in the "Introduction" to this volume as being characteristic of the Postclassic, as well as hinting at greater variability than may have previously been supposed. For example, with the exception of Chichen Itza and Mayapan, many Postclassic sites in the

Northern lowlands have a decidedly coastal or riverine focus. The ethnohistoric works for this region, however, note large inland settlements, so this preconceived focus may be the result of more work having been done on the architecturally impressive east coast of Yucatan. Walled cities are also common in northern Postclassic settlements, being found at Xcaret, Xelha, Tulum, Ixpaatun, and Mayapan (see Noguera 1940 and Andrews IV and Andrews 1975 for east coast material). That they are not the only form of cities found in the Postclassic, however, can be seen from Cozumel, Lamanai, and Santa Rita.

Trade seems to have been a major Postclassic economic pursuit in the Yucatan peninsula, and involved salt, honey, cacao, feathers, and a multitude of other goods. Canoes plying the waters around the peninsula, as well as overland movement of goods through the "neck" of the peninsula led to the extension of the Maya economic networks to Mexico, Central America, and perhaps into South America (D. Chase 1982a: 258–259, 299).

Historic and ethnohistoric records have provided a great deal of information on the nature of the contact between European and Maya civilizations in this area. As early as A.D. 1511, and perhaps as early as A.D. 1506, the Maya of the coastal area of Yucatan experienced (albeit by accident) the initiation of a sustained and painful contact with the Spaniards. The first formal Spanish visits to northern Yucatan did not occur until the years A.D. 1517, 1518, and 1519, when Spanish forces under Hernandez landed in Ecab and Grijalva, and Cortes stopped at Cozumel. Cortes learned that several Spaniards had already been shipwrecked on the peninsula. One of these individuals, Jeronimo de Aguilar, became Cortes' interpreter while the other, Gonzalo Guerrero, became a Maya war chief (*nacom*) and was instrumental in preventing the Spanish capture of Chetumal in A.D. 1528. This latter event effectively stalled the Spanish conquest of the Yucatan peninsula until Montejo's onslaught in A.D. 1542. That the Yucatec Maya were never completely subjugated can be seen in the Caste Wars of the nineteenth century (Reed 1964).

Concise information on Yucatec Maya culture, social organization, political institutions, commerce, and religion at the time of the Spanish Conquest can be found in the various works of Roys (1943, 1957, 1965) as well as in Friar Diego de Landa's *Relacion de las Cosas de Yucatan* (Tozzer 1941) and the *Relaciones de Yucatan*. Unfortunately, much of what Landa records is archaeologically unverifiable (D. Chase n.d.; this volume). Additional information has been garnered concerning the pre–contact history of the Yucatan peninsula through the Books of *Chilam Balam* (Roys 1962,

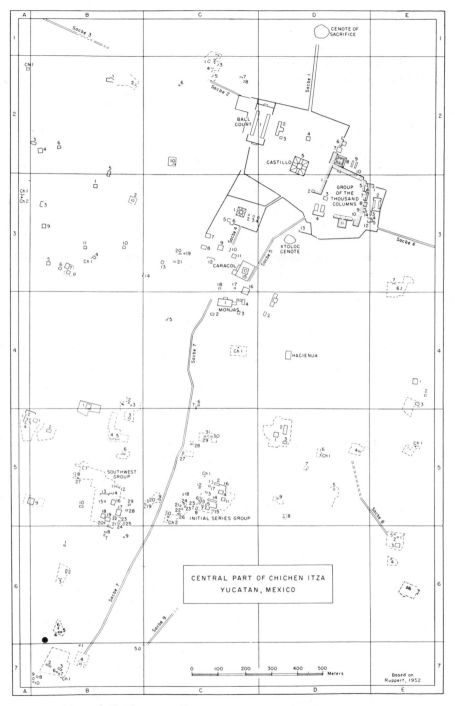

Fig. 1. Map of Chichen Itza (from Tozzer 1957: fig. 1).

1976; Edmondson 1982). These books are most likely Spanish transcriptions of earlier Maya codices, most of which were burned by Friar Landa in an attempt to erase what he perceived as teachings of the devil. They provide a tentative outline of important events in the Postclassic Maya history of northern Yucatan, but unfortunately the relative chronologies in these books cannot be placed with absolute certainty into the Christian calendar (A. Chase n.d.).

Much of the original archaeological research into Postclassic Yucatan was carried out by the Carnegie Institution of Washington, first at Chichen Itza and then at Mayapan. Chichen Itza (fig. 1) is crucial for understanding the onset of the Postclassic period in the Northern lowlands and probably in the Southern lowlands as well. From what has been published concerning the Institution's work at Chichen Itza, it would appear that the site has an unusual Terminal Classic occupation and a Late Postclassic reoccupation (Brainerd 1958: 34–45). Archaeological data suggest that Maya and "Toltec" groups coexisted at Chichen (Tozzer 1957), which survived the Southern "collapse" and became a dominant force in the Northern lowlands until finally challenged by neighboring Coba and succeeded by Mayapan. The Andrews and Robles paper deals with events surrounding this transitional time period in Maya prehistory.

Following the Chichen Itza excavations, the Carnegie Institution began work at Mayapan (fig. 2), the known capital and unifier of the various Maya city–states. This material has been fully published both in preliminary form (C.I.W. Current Reports series, 1952–1957) and in final form (Pollock et al. 1962; R. E. Smith 1971). Although investigations at Mayapan revealed a complex and planned settlement covering a large area, comparisons of the architecture and ceramics of Mayapan with those of earlier sites led to the notion of the "decadent" Postclassic (Proskouriakoff 1955; Rathje 1975). This concept, although superficial, was influential in clouding the view of this Maya period in the popular literature (Morley and Brainerd 1956; Thompson 1954), and has only recently been seriously reconsidered (D. Chase 1981, 1982a).

Additional work was carried out under the Carnegie Institution auspices at Tulum and along the east coast of Yucatan by Sanders (1960). Although the murals and architecture of Tulum had been extensively documented by Lothrop (1924) in the 1920s, it was not until Sanders' publication that the differences between Mayapan and the east coast became apparent. The east coast chronology was deemed roughly equivalent to that at Mayapan although the exact relationships between the two complexes could not be defined. Miller's paper addresses the temporal faceting of the different classes

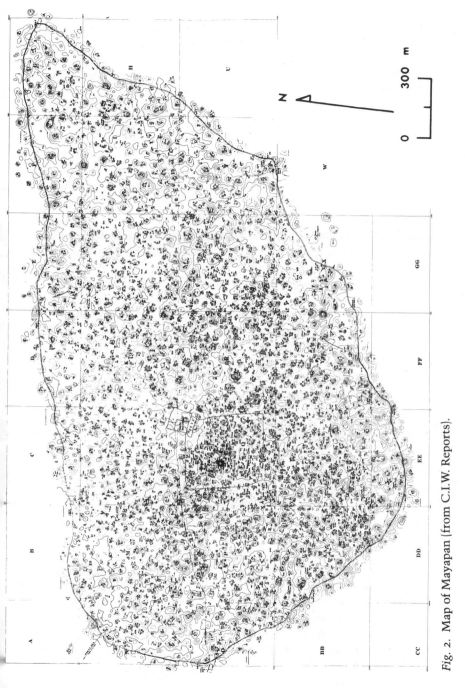

Fig. 2. Map of Mayapan (from C.I.W. Reports).

of Late Postclassic remains at Tulum and Tancah, while Barrera Rubio's paper presents some of his recent excavation results at Tulum in terms of the site's subsistence economy.

Farther to the south, recent work in Belize has revealed that the Postclassic remains in the northern river basins are interwoven with the sequence in northern Yucatan. It would appear that Nohmul (fig. 3) may have witnessed the presence of a Chichen Itza–related outpost at the onset of the Postclassic period in northern Belize (D. Chase and A. Chase 1982). Present data further suggest that northern Belize is a prime candidate for the origins of the Postclassic complexes visible in the Northern lowlands (Pendergast 1981a). Loten's paper is a statement on the Postclassic architecture at Lamanai while Pendergast's paper presents a synthesis of the general picture of the Postclassic period that has been gained from continued excavations at Lamanai. Lamanai has produced Postclassic pottery that is related to ceramics found elsewhere in northern Belize (Thompson 1939; D. Chase 1982b) as well as ceramics that are more akin to complexes found at Mayapan and Tulum. Pottery relating to these latter two categories, which are late in the Northern lowlands, occurs at Lamanai on what appears to be an earlier horizon (as well as a later one); similarly, Tulum–like ceramics are clearly visible at Colha in the early part of the Postclassic period (Adams and Valdez 1980). At Santa Rita, Tulum–style ceramics appear to be supplanted by a later regional redware. The paper by D. Chase presents archaeological and ethnohistorical data from Santa Rita which are crucial to understanding organizational aspects of the Late Postclassic period.

Postclassic events in the central part of the Yucatan peninsula are difficult to reconstruct. Ball argues that the south-central spine of the Yucatan peninsula was largely unoccupied, with the possible exception of isolated censer deposition, during the later part of the Postclassic period. He also suggests that non-pottery–making or –using populations may have been sparsely represented during the later part of the Postclassic in western Campeche. Fry's paper deals with what he sees as a Postclassic revitalization movement in the interior of the Yucatan peninsula. He argues for this phenomenon in the Uaymil area on the basis of recovered evidence of massive architectural modifications and associated ceremonialism; similar evidence of grandiose and elaborate ceremonialism in association with burial rituals during the Postclassic has been archaeologically uncovered at both Lamanai and Santa Rita. Importantly, Fry ascribes an earlier dating to the Postclassic events in the Uaymil interior than that argued by Harrison (1979).

Most of the present understanding of the lowland Maya Post-

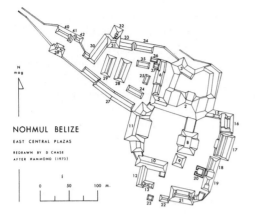

NOHMUL BELIZE

EAST CENTRAL PLAZAS

REDRAWN BY D CHASE
AFTER HAMMOND (1973)

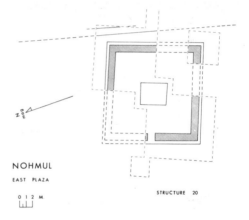

NOHMUL

EAST PLAZA

STRUCTURE 20

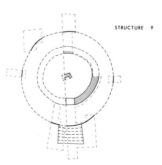

STRUCTURE 9

Fig. 3. Map of Nohmul and detail of Structures 20 and 9 (from D. Chase and A. Chase 1982: figs. 1 and 2).

classic social organization derives from ethnohistorical and archaeological information coming from the Northern lowlands. Our comprehension of this information will surely change with further research into less well-known areas and sites. What is now known, however, suggests that—as one would expect from ethnohistoric data—the Postclassic period in the Northern lowlands may be described by two contrasting characterizations: it exhibits extensive regionalism, but this is manifest in archaeological complexes demonstrating overarching similarities.

The Postclassic Sequence of Tancah and Tulum, Quintana Roo, Mexico

ARTHUR G. MILLER

It goes without saying that the culture history of an archaeological site or region must be understood before processual questions can be meaningfully asked: the "what" and "where" is needed before the "how" and "why" can be broached. And it is equally obvious that the significance of processual issues is directly dependent on the completeness of the historical record. Chronology, then, is not the mere ordering of man—made traces from the past, but rather forms the very basis of effective inquiry into the specific characteristics of that past.

Understanding Postclassic chronology on Yucatan's east coast is complicated by the reality that different classes of material culture change there at different rates. For example, what does it mean if ceramic assemblages change twice, architecture three times, and murals four in the Tancah—Tulum region during the Postclassic period? It should come as no surprise that the change charted out through the Postclassic period for different classes of material culture was not the same and, therefore, that these differing rates of change were in themselves suggestive of the region's culture history and process. Ceramics, architecture, and murals are not, of course, encountered archaeologically prepackaged, but are inextricably interwoven through time and with other man—made things.

This essay presents the distinct and differing Postclassic chronological developments of three classes of material culture at Tancah—Tulum: ceramics, architecture, and murals. While the analysis of mural and architectural data is my own, I have relied on J. W. Ball's ceramic evaluations of the Tancah material collected during the course of stratigraphic excavations carried out at Tancah in 1974 and 1975 (Ball 1982). The chronologies of these three material classes from Tancah—Tulum, while they all change at different rates

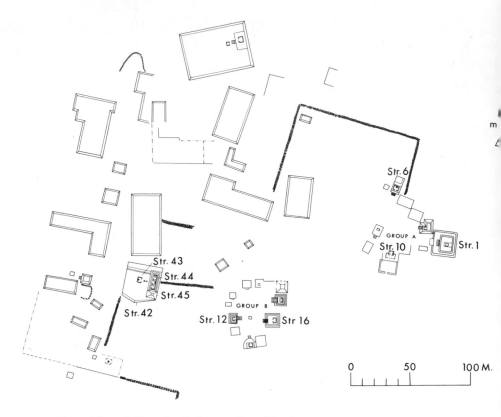

Fig. 1. Plan of Tancah, Quintana Roo, Mexico.

during the Postclassic, suggest together that the Postclassic period in this eastern coastal lowland Maya region begins as early as A.D. 770, when distinct patterns of external influences cause major re-orientations in Maya life.

Mention should be made at the outset that the prehistories of Tancah (fig. 1) and Tulum (fig. 2) are inextricably interrelated. While Tulum was not founded until well into the Early Postclassic, ca. A.D. 1200, Tancah has an uninterrupted history dating back at least as early as the Late Preclassic. And while there is evidence that after A.D. 1400 Tulum dominated Tancah, it is also evident that shortly after 1521, Tulum was abandoned and Tancah became the colonial site of Tzama until it, in its turn, was abandoned in A.D. 1668 (Miller and Farriss 1979; Miller 1982).

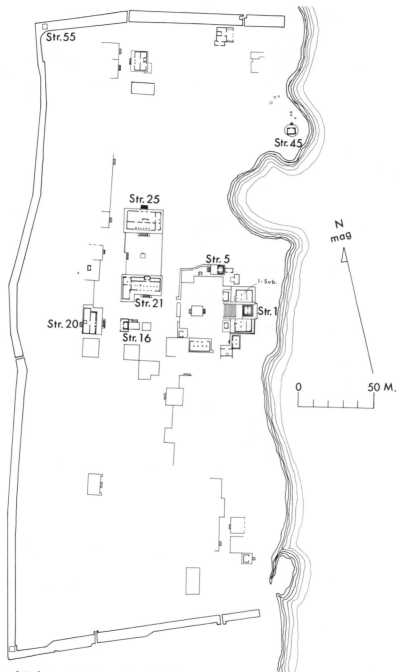

Fig. 2. Plan of Tulum, Quintana Roo, Mexico.

Postclassic Ceramic Chronology

Trenches cut into the platform supporting Tancah Structure 44 itself revealed a sequencing of platform architecture containing building fill and a series of burials dating the constructions from 250 B.C. to A.D. 1350 (fig. 3). The platforms of interest to us here are the last two: Structure 42–2nd and Structure 42–1st, dated ca. A.D. 900–1000 and A.D. 1000–1100 respectively, primarily on the basis of burial deposits and their ceramic fill. Two burials associated with the Structure 42–2nd platform, Burials 9 and 7, provide the most conclusive dating evidence based on ceramics.

Ceramic material from the upper excavation levels of the Tan-

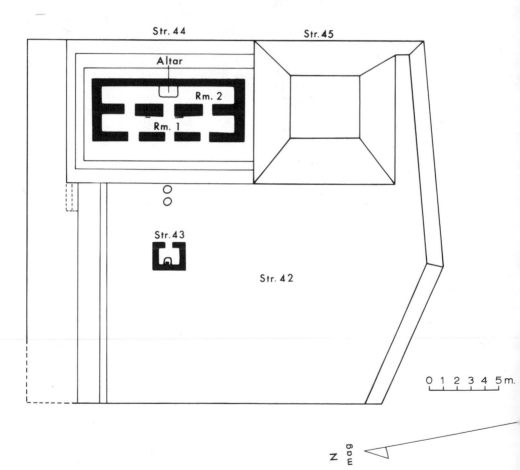

Fig. 3. Plan of the Structure 44 complex at Tancah.

cah Structure 44 complex (figs. 3 and 4) came from both burial deposits and building fill. Three burials (8, 9, and 7) were found directly associated with Structure 42–2nd, the penultimate construction stage of the Structure 42 platform (fig. 4). The first is Burial 8, which was partially disturbed by the laying down of a subsequent mortuary feature, Structure 42: Unit 1, containing Burial 7. Fortunately, Burial 8's direct dating evidence, a Sayan Red-on-Cream vessel (fig. 5b), survived the disturbance. Considered an excellent marker for the last gasp of the Classic period, this type is dated to the end of the eighth or beginning of the ninth century. It is clear, however, that this Sayan Red-on-Cream vessel was extremely worn before interment, suggesting that it may have been included in Burial 8 sometime after the period associated with the manufacture of this vessel type. It is therefore probable that some period of time passed from the date of manufacture of the vessel and its subsequent incorporation into Burial 8. On the other hand, the Teabo group Puuc Red ware (fig. 5d), associated with Burial 9, which was intrusive into Structure 42–2nd, showed no evidence of wear whatsoever. Teabo group Puuc ware is dated from A.D. 800–1000, later than Sayan Red-on-Cream. In view of the fact that the Sayan vessel was worn upon interment, a date of A.D. 800–1000 for both Burials 8 and 9 is possible on the basis of ceramic evidence.

The ceramic contents of Burial 7 probably indicate the period of latest use of the Structure 42 platform. Burial 7 was found inside the small mortuary platform designated Structure 42: Unit 1, which had been added onto the floor of Structure 42–2nd (fig. 4), and clearly postdates the laying down of the Structure 42–2nd floor itself. Burial 7 was a secondary multiple burial containing a red-on-orange bowl of Puuc Red ware, its rim decorated with painted chevrons (fig. 5a). It is like the vessels belonging to the Copo 2 complex at Dzibilchaltun. The worn rim of the vessel indicates that it was already old when interred. Another bowl, Vessel 2 from Burial 7, is an example of the Slate Muna group specifically identified as a Chumayel Red-on-Slate basal break dish. The vessel has solid slab supports and exhibits several repair holes (fig. 5c). Ball (1982: 109) states that neither the Chumayel Red-on-Slate nor the red-on-orange bowl of Puuc Red ware can be precisely dated at present. Nevertheless, it is clear that the vessels were deposited in Structure 42: Unit 1 after Burials 8 and 9, which were both intrusive into 42–2nd. In view of the fact that both vessels in Burial 7 show unmistakable evidence of excessive wear before interment (the Chumayel Red-on-Slate vessel had been repaired many times and the rim of the red-on-orange bowl of Puuc Red ware was very worn), it is probable that the period of ceramic

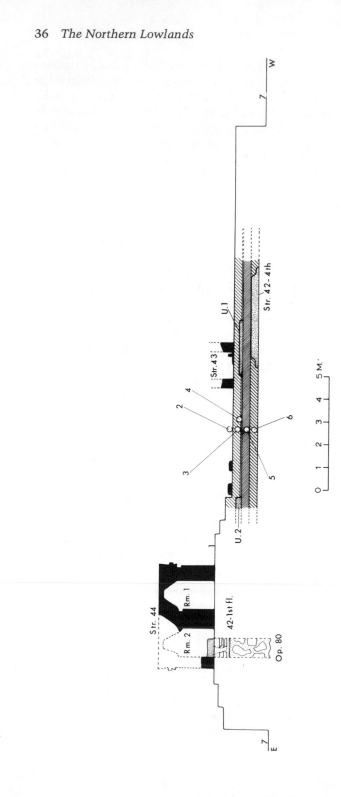

manufacture of these vessels does not date the mortuary feature in which it was found. In any case, the ceramic evidence from Structure 42: Unit 1, when combined with the ceramic data from Burials 8 and 9, does suggest an A.D. 800–900 date for Structure 42–2nd.

Construction fill including pottery sherds associated with the Structure 42–2nd platform provides secondary chronological data based on ceramics. Ball's evaluation (1982: 109–110) of the incensario fragments sealed between the Structure 42–3rd and 42–2nd floors suggests that they span an A.D. 800–1200 period. One type, Tepakan Composite, Ball (1982: 109) dates on the basis of R. E. Smith's (1971: 28–29) Mayapan work to A.D. 800–1000. Ball (1982: 109) does not accept Smith's (1971: 24) dating for the Cehac Hunacti Composite type at A.D. 1200; sherds of this censer type were found inside the Structure 42–2nd fill. Citing the association of a Cehac Hunacti Composite incense burner in direct contextual association with Ticul group Thin Slate ware at Becan, Campeche, Ball states that this suggests a somewhat earlier placement for this type "than currently is assumed" (Ball 1982: 109).

No burials or caches were found sealed between the floors of Structure 42–2nd and 42–1st. Indeed, the 42–1st floor was largely eroded away and the ceramic material collected from the fill below it undoubtedly included admixtures from final surface debris which found its way into the final humus layer. Although great care was taken to separate the material from below the Structure 42 floor from its obvious surface debris, the poor condition of the Structure 42–1st stucco floor and the destructive root action near the surface of this lowland tropical locus makes this collection a contaminated one indeed. Nevertheless, it is worth noting that sherds of what Ball calls fully developed Xcanchacan Black-on-Cream, Cehac Hunacti Composite, Tepakan Composite, Ticul Thin Slate, Muna Slate, Chumayel Red-on-Slate, and transitional Puuc Slate–Peto Cream ware material were found below the Structure 42–1st floor and above the 42–2nd floor. Ball's evaluation (Ball 1982: 109–110) confirms that the ceramic material from below the 42–1st floor produced no examples of Mayapan Red ware, Matillas group Fine Orange paste ware, Tulum Red ware, or Chen Mul Modeled effigy censers. These

Fig. 4. (opposite page) Composite section drawing of Structure 44 complex excavations at Tancah: (1) Structure 44 terrace; (2) Structure 44–1st floor; (3) Structure 42–1st platform fill; (4) Structure 42–2nd replastered floor; (5) Structure 42–2nd platform fill; (6) Structure 42–3rd platform fill; (7) stucco floor abutting Structure 44 complex.

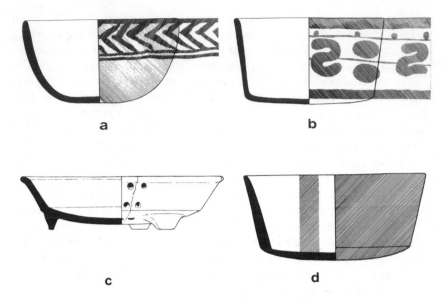

Fig. 5. Burial ceramics from Tancah: (a) Vessel 1 from Tancah Burial 7 (Puuc Red ware); (b) vessel from Tancah Burial 8 (Sayan Red-on-Cream); (c) Vessel 2 from Tancah Burial 7 (Chumayel Red-on-Slate); (d) vessel from Burial 9 (Teabo group Puuc Red ware).

ceramic wares were encountered, however, in the above–floor room fill and on terrace refuse associated with Structure 44 itself.

Neither burials nor caches were found pertaining to time spans later than the period indicated by the ceramic contents of the Structure 42: Unit 1 mass burial. None of our collections from between these floors produced Tulum Red ware or Chen Mul Modeled type sherds, which can be seen as diagnostic of the major ceramic break that characterizes the Late Postclassic period of the east coast of Yucatan, beginning ca. A.D. 1400.

Xcanchakan Black-on-Cream is the latest ceramic material found beneath the Structure 42–1st floor, upon which Structure 44 and its terracing were subsequently constructed (fig. 4). Conspicuous in the lots below Structure 42–1st is the absence of Tulum Red sherds. Further, Chen Mul Modeled censers are notably absent, while Xcanchakan Black-on-Cream is present along with filleted censer wares. A similar situation was encountered while dismantling wall sections of Structure 44 during its consolidation. Lots collected from undisturbed, above–floor surface debris from the collapse vault of Room 2 each produced a Matillas group Fine Orange paste ware sherd (which Ball dates anywhere from ca. A.D. 1150 to the Early Colonial period) with stucco mortar still adhering to one of them, strongly suggesting that the Matillas sherd was indeed included as part of the Structure 44 building fill. Admittedly this is equivocal evidence, but sealed beneath Structure 42–1st in Operation 80 (where the 42–1st stucco floor was found intact) we found Xcanchakan Black-on-Cream, which Ball believes to persist as late as A.D. 1400.

In summary, the ceramics from the Tancah Structure 44 complex excavations fall into two temporal periods, broadly defined as an A.D. 800–1200 group and an A.D. 1000–1400 group. The duration of the Matillas group Fine Orange paste ware sherds into the Early Colonial period and the problematic dating of Tulum Red wares does little to indicate chronology in the Tancah locus with any precision. Nevertheless, a temporal designation of Structure 42–2nd as having been constructed ca. A.D. 900–1000 and Structure 42–1st ca. A.D. 1000–1100 does not seem impossible, given the ceramic evidence. The ceramic data for dating Structure 44 itself, which was constructed sometime after the laying down of its Structure 42–1st supporting platform, is too inconclusive to be convincing. Fortunately, comparative chronological data of masonry technique and architectural and mural styles from the Tancah–Tulum region does help pin down the date of Structure 44 with more precision than the ceramic data alone would allow.

Postclassic Architectural Chronology

Stratigraphic excavations in the Tancah Structure 44 complex revealed a sequencing of Postclassic platform architecture. Following the Carnegie Institution nomenclature adopted by Sanders (1956, 1966) in his work at Tancah, these buried platforms were designated as "structures." The first is designated as Structure 42–2nd and the second is labeled Structure 42–1st. The differences of fill technique between these two sequential platforms are quite marked: the earlier platform is filled with stones averaging 10 centimeters in diameter and then gradually graded from smaller stones to pebbles as the platform reached the top, where it is capped with a substantial layer of stucco (fig. 4). In contrast, the later platform is composed of enormous boulder fill, averaging 50 centimeters in diameter; there is no gradation of stone size just under the stucco floor of the platform (fig. 4). This sequential distinction in fill technique has been noted by Robles at Xelha, just 10 kilometers to the north of Tancah. On the basis of ceramic fill material associated with these distinctive construction techniques, Robles (personal communication, 1982) has suggested that they may be diagnostic of the construction differences between what Robles calls Hocaba and Tases phase platform architecture at Xelha. Although platform construction technique is hardly a diagnostic chronological trait, in the contexts of its association with the ceramic fill Robles found at Xelha and with the burial deposits and ceramic fill associated with Tancah Structures 42–2nd and 42–1st discussed above, the platform construction change noted at both Xelha and Tancah has chronological implications which are sequentially secure, at the very least.

Standing architecture of the Tancah–Tulum region can be classified into three periods, probably having chronological values. The first exhibits the use of pecked masonry and boot–shaped vault stones embedded in rubble hearting, combined with pyramidal bases and roofcombs. Andrews V (personal communication, 1982) considers the appearance of boot–shaped vault stones to be highly diagnostic of an A.D. 770 date for northern Yucatan (marking the beginning of the Florescent period there). If a similar date can be assigned to the use of boot–shaped stones in their proper vault context for the east coast, then some period of time would have had to have elapsed for vaults to be disassembled and their masonry reused in other con-

Fig. 6. Tancah Structure 6, illustrating the extensive use of pecked masonry (drawing by K. Grootenboer).

texts, such as in vertical walls as in Tancah Structure 10. I would suggest that the reuse of boot–shaped stones takes place at Tancah–Tulum during the same period that Structure 42–2nd was constructed, i.e., on the basis of associations discussed above, from A.D. 900–1000. Pecked veneer masonry dominates in the construction of buildings during this period of Tancah–Tulum (see fig. 6) and is gradually replaced by percussion–and–spall masonry, until virtually all construction is composed of percussion–and–spall masonry covered by a thick layer of stucco, as is the case in the latest buildings of Tulum.

I suggest that there are chronological implications in the changes evident in masonry techniques of the Tancah–Tulum region. I would characterize that change as the following, in sequential order: (1) exclusive use of well–cut pecked veneer masonry, boot–shaped vault stones, and rubble hearting fill; (2) pecked veneer masonry combined with percussion–and–spall masonry; no boot–shaped vault stones in vault contexts; occasional reuse of boot–shaped vault stones in lower walls; and (3) predominant use of percussion–and–spall masonry with slab vaults and flat mortar and rubble roofs; occasional reuse of pecked veneer masonry and boot–shaped vault stones in lower walls.

The mixing of reused pecked masonry with percussion–and–spall masonry in the construction of Structure 44 itself defines a stage intermediate between the exclusive use of pecked masonry and the almost exclusive use of percussion–and–spall masonry of the Late Postclassic period. Combinations of these two types of masonry are found in several buildings near Structure 44, probably representing a group of coeval buildings at Tancah.

Other examples of the long, low range–type buildings similar to Structure 44 are not known at Tancah, but I have seen several at neighboring Xelha, and Tulum Structure 1–Sub is of this building type. While Lothrop (1924: 169) and Sanders (1960: 227) assigned the columned "palace" exclusively to the Tulum or Late Postclassic period (Structures 20, 21, and 25), the fact that Structure 1–Sub is distinguished by a colonnade places this architectural trait as early as A.D. 1200, in view of the distinctive Early Postclassic mural style painted on its walls (discussed below). The colonnade of Structure 1–Sub is reminiscent of those at Mitla in Oaxaca, yet it is earlier by 300 years. Also reminiscent of Mitla are the inset panels above doorways, yet their limited distribution outside the east coast suggests origins in eastern Yucatan; inset panels are found on Late Postclassic buildings at Coba and Okop (Stromsvik, Pollock, and Berlin 1955: 173). The only other Maya site with which I am familiar that possesses the inset panel is Topoxte in Peten (Bullard 1970: 266).

Lothrop's (1924: 171) seriation of inset panels that touch the lower moldings (i.e., the articulated upper facade) as being earlier than examples that "are from 2 to 6 inches *below* the molding" may indeed be correct, but if so, the earlier insets that touch moldings have a duration lasting from Terminal Classsic times to as late as A.D. 1450, and Late Postclassic buildings show both types of moldings occurring together. I see little possibility of any chronological value to inset panels and their relationship to lower moldings.

The most distinctive architectural forms standing on the east coast of Yucatan are sequentially the latest and, not surprisingly, the most abundant. These structures, which are the latest preconquest constructions in the Tancah–Tulum region, are marked by the introduction of new construction forms and a dramatic increase in the quantity of those forms; the masonry technique is almost exclusively percussion–and–spall with occasional reuse of Terminal Classic pecked masonry that never exceeds 10 percent of the total masonry content. Buildings are proportionally dwarfed, and flat ceilings replace vaulted interiors, although vaulting is still found during this late period.

It is noteworthy also that the physical situations of this latest architecture of the region differ from those of the two preceding types. Whereas earlier structures are situated inland from the sea, these late buildings are more often than not prominently situated on high ground overlooking the sea. Other common locations for this architecture are the beaches and the rocky promontories that jut out into areas difficult for coastal navigation, such as at Punta Tulsayab, just north of Tancah. An exception to the tendency for earlier Tancah–Tulum structures to be built back from the sea is Structure 1–Sub at Tulum which, although constructed on a bluff facing the sea, had a low profile which would not have been easily noticed from the sea. This contrasts with the prominent, vertically oriented later addition to that structure known as Tulum Structure 1, commonly referred to as the Castillo.

A new architectural form introduced during this late period is the so-called shrine–within–a–shrine complex, or the three–in–one or four–in–one building. This type consists of smaller and smaller buildings encapsulated by larger buildings, all representing single period construction, and is best represented by Structure 16 at Tulum (fig. 7).

Surface architecture in the Tancah–Tulum zone is also marked by the proliferation of small shrine–like structures; these are often isolated from other buildings and are characterized by a flat roof and

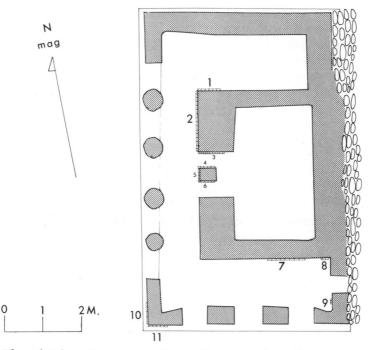

Fig. 7. Plan of Tulum Structure 16 showing location of murals.

single doorway. Such shrines are situated on rocky points, inlets, or reef–protected bays, and it is probable that they served as coastal navigation markers, as lighthouses do today. These structures, much too small to allow even the small-statured Maya to stand in them, are totally absent during earlier periods. Standing architecture also includes types exhibiting the battered basal molding and outward–sloping walls best illustrated by Tulum Structures 16 and 5. Upper facades with vertical niches enframing high–relief figural sculpture are introduced during this period, and corner masks become new elements of architectural design.

    In summary, there are chronological implications in the three discernible masonry techniques during the Postclassic period in the Tancah–Tulum region. The first architectural construction technique and style bears many of the traits associated with the Puuc architecture of western Yucatan: roofcombs, boot–shaped vault stones, and distinctive pecked masonry being among the most salient. This period of architecture marks the appearance of colonnades, conspicuously evident in Tulum Structure 1–Sub. But this first architectural style suggests a period of time between the initial introduction of the style and reuse of its characteristic traits, such as boot–shaped vault stones reset in vertical walls. The second style is best represented by Structure 44, and incorporates a combination of earlier pecked masonry with percussion–and–spall masonry. The third style is constructed of mostly percussion–and–spall masonry and is characterized by several new architectural forms such as small shrines, shrines–within–shrines, basal moldings and battered walls, and architectural sculpture incorporated in upper facades.

Ceramic data associated with architecture indicate that the three changes in masonry technique and architectural styles span the period from ca. A.D. 770–1400. The dates at which these three changes occurred are not evident in the constructional and architectural data alone, nor can associative ceramic data specify architectural time spans, because the ceramic data are even less sensitive as chronological markers than is architecture.

Postclassic Mural Chronology

Murals in the Tancah–Tulum region are found on the earliest architecture at Tulum, those having been painted on the east wall of the colonnaded portico of Structure 1–Sub (Miller 1982: fig. 84, Pls. 13–21). Related to the earlier murals from Tancah Structure 12, their more linear style suggests a period of time between the two murals, yet predates the appearance of the highly linear style of the Late Postclassic. The flat colored areas of the Structure 1–Sub paintings tend to be filled in with wide, hesitantly drawn lines; these interior lines are seen as prototypically leading to the kind of interior linear treatment associated with the murals of Tancah Structure 44's first painting layer. The differences are particularly evident on two counts: first, the thickness of the interior lines (up to 7 millimeters, as opposed to 2.5 millimeters in the Late Postclassic murals) and, second, their hesitant awkwardness.

Variations in the Structure 1–Sub murals can be seen as differing because of lighting conditions. Where paintings would have been viewed in almost full light (the area now covered by the staircase of Structure 1), the black interior and framing lines are relatively thin, averaging 4 millimeters. But the murals of the side rooms, deprived of direct illumination, have their interior lines eliminated and the large color areas are bounded by outlines averaging 8 millimeters wide, so that the images would be more visible in the dim light of the lateral chambers. In a like manner, the simplified colored areas that are devoid of interior lines and bounded by the thick outlines in

Fig. 8. Mural on interior of Structure 12, Tancah (drawing by F. Davalos).

the mural of Tancah Structure 12 may be a stylistic adaptation to the dim interior light (fig. 8).

Taking into account the variations of style determined by such architectural contextual considerations as the natural light available for perception of the murals, a clear stylistic patterning through time emerges for the relationship between the Tancah Structure 12 mural, the Tulum Structure 1 – Sub mural, and the Tancah Structure 44 murals. Increasing linearity marks time. The simple broad flat areas of color are earlier, followed by the inclusion of thick interior lines, followed by a multiplicity of thinner interior lines. This stylistic progression is confirmed by an independent seriation of architecture, based in part on stratigraphic contexts of Tancah Structure 44, and by the fortuitous representation of ceramic forms shown in the murals which have been ordered chronologically.

The murals of Tancah Structure 44, stylistically dated to A.D. 1350, are a modification of the preceding style of murals represented by those of Tulum Structure 1 – Sub, stylistically dated to A.D. 1200. In addition to the increased linear treatment in the rendering of figures, this succeeding period of mural style in Tancah Structure 44 can be seen in the reduction in scale. The most salient stylistic feature of the Structure 44 murals is the segmentation into vertical and horizontal divisions of the painted surface, reminiscent of the page layout that is typical of Maya codex painting. The crude application of the blue and red colors that overlap onto black outlines of the main design is so similar to that of the Codex Madrid that I call this the "codex–style." There is good evidence to suggest that the entire east wall of Room 1 was painted anciently in this segmented, codex–style manner. Although only three fragments of the original mural are now visible, showing black outlines painted directly on

Fig. 9. Mural detail from interior of Structure 44, Tancah (drawing by
K. Grootenboer).

plain stucco with areas of blue and red, there are indications that
more of the original painting survives underneath the protective
layer of calcium carbonate that now encrusts the wall.

The next development in mural painting in the Tancah–Tulum
region comes as a radical innovation. This new painting style is
visible in the second painting layer in Tancah Structure 44 (fig. 9),
and most notably at Tulum. The post–A.D. 1400 murals of Tulum
Structure 16 and Structure 5 are the finest examples of mural painting in the region and are stylistically unrelated to the earlier paintings. A comparison of the lower legs shown in profile view in the
Tulum Structure 1–Sub murals with those shown in any figure of
Tulum Structure 5 illustrates the unexpected changes found in Late
Postclassic murals (fig. 10). Most noticeable is the substitution of a
monochrome palette for the earlier polychrome one. These late murals are also the richest in terms of artistic complexity. The control
of draftsmanship and the intricate painting technique, probably involving the use of bird feather brushes, make clear that a first–rate
workshop was responsible for these paintings.

Fig. 10. Mural on the east wall of the interior of Structure 5, Tulum (drawing by F. Davalos).

The most salient stylistic characteristic of these murals is the evenly controlled and distributed linearity of the figures and objects: there appears not to be a center of focus. The inside fill lines of a figure's face, when compared with his lower leg, for example, attract the eye equally because the linear treatment of each is the same, resulting in a tapestry–like effect over the entire surface of the wall. The black background of these murals, also an innovation, serves two functions: it unifies the disjointed body segments and the interchangeable parts of costume and ritual paraphernalia, and it "freezes" the implied notion of gesticulating limbs. While the disjointed design would tend to make one's eye concentrate on body parts and costume details rather than on the whole figure, and the suggested movement would tend to break up the compositional regularity of the figures, the black background unifies the various forms filling in every available space into an insistently flat, coherent, and static visual whole.

The final development of mural painting at either Tancah or Tulum can be found on the columns of Tulum Structure 1. The origin of the motifs shown in the painting fragments clearly lies in the murals on the east wall of Structure 16 interior. Enough of the Structure 1 paintings survive to indicate that the composition consisting of upper sky band, middle band of confronting figures, and a lower underworld band derives from the compositional framework of Structures 5 and 16. The monochrome palette is similar in both styles, but the differences between the masterful style of Structure 5 and 16, and the Structure 1 style, can be seen in the hesitancy of drawn lines, rendering the figures and forms in a manner one would expect of an ill–trained copyist. The elaborate jaguar pelt band, separating the middle and lower register of the Structure 5 and 16 murals, is in the column paintings simplified into a row of circles alternating with J–motifs; instead of showing an underworld, underwater scene as in the murals of Structures 5 and 16, those of Structure 1 are plain solid black. These stylistic differences denote a later workshop than the one responsible for the Structure 5 and 16 murals.

In summary, the murals in the Tancah–Tulum region undergo four stylistic modifications. The first style, represented by the murals of Tancah Structure 12 and Tulum Structure 1–Sub, can be seen as clumsy artistry, characterized by the use of broad flat areas of color outlined and partially filled by thick, black outlines painted on a stucco ground. The second stylistic change (A.D. 1350), seen in the first painting layer of Tancah Structure 44, is marked by a decrease in scale and an increase in the linearity of the figures and forms rendered. The model for this kind of painting is seen as the "codex" tradition of the Codex Madrid, and it is probable that a Maya codex served as a "model book" with even the page subdivisions transferred onto a wall. The third stylistic change (A.D. 1400) marks the beginning of the Late Postclassic period, and is represented in the murals of Tulum Structures 5 and 16, indicative of cultural florescence. The murals of this period are stylistically innovative in the region: a monochromatic palette, the adoption of fine lines to fill in drawn areas, consistent flatness to convey meaning clearly, and a *horror vacui* are the salient new stylistic features. The fourth modification (A.D. 1513) is represented by the derivative paintings that decorate the columns of Structure 1 at Tulum, probably painted by local artists who were commissioned to copy the style of Tulum Structures 5 and 16, but who were not up to the sophistication the style demanded.

Conclusions

While ceramic assemblages significantly change twice and architecture changed three times during the Tancah–Tulum Postclassic time period analyzed in this essay, mural painting undergoes four distinctive stylistic and iconographic modifications of differing degrees. The Tancah–Tulum mural tradition exhibits a more rapidly changing developmental sequence than those of architecture or ceramics.

Although the absolute date of change in each of the material classes discussed in this paper is far from secure, that they do not change at the same time, and that some change more frequently than others, seems certain. On the basis of the evidence presented here, and in view of the fact that different classes of material culture change at different rates and at different times, what then is the Postclassic sequence of the Tancah–Tulum region? This question, of course, begs the obvious one: what sequence? There is no single chronology for the region. Time can only be reflected in the rates of change in traces left behind. In the case of Tancah–Tulum, these traces have been arbitrarily designated as ceramics, architecture, and murals. That any one class of material culture could be used to define a regional chronology would present a biased picture at best.

Because ceramics survive more consistently than painting and architecture in more sites and regions, providing a data base for comparison, this slowly changing class of material culture has been used as the basis for regional chronologies not only in the lowland Maya Postclassic, but throughout Mesoamerica, for all periods.

Littoral-Marine Economy at Tulum, Quintana Roo, Mexico

ALFREDO BARRERA RUBIO

The intensification of commercial maritime routes on the east coast of the Yucatan peninsula during the Late Postclassic was the consequence of sociopolitical factors and changes, most probably induced by the fall of the Itza of Chichen Itza. This event occurred during the transition from the Terminal Classic to the Early Postclassic between A.D. 900 and 1250 (Sabloff and Rathje 1973). The loss of Itza hegemony over the area impeded the continued use of traditional commercial land routes and marked the decline of sites, such as Coba, which had exercised commercial control over the area from the east coast toward the center of the peninsula during the Classic period (Benavides 1976: 190–191). During the Postclassic period, coastal sites that could control long distance sea routes emerged in importance. Like sites on the northern coast of Quintana Roo, the island of Cozumel had an unexpected boom of commercial activity which was combined with religious pilgrimages, as in former periods (Scholes and Roys 1968: 33). Similarly, Tulum, a major coastal site in the central region of Quintana Roo, was not only one of the principal centers of commercial exchange during the last part of the Postclassic period, but also an area of religious influence as seen in the birth and rebirth of cults (Miller 1974).

Trade patterns have been of considerable interest in recent research at Cozumel (Sabloff and Rathje 1973; Sabloff and Freidel 1975; Sabloff 1977), Cancun (Mayer 1977), and Xelha (Robles 1978), reflecting the fact that commercial activities were a crucial factor in the development of Postclassic communities along the east coast. The material base which sustained internal relationships, however, has received less attention at these sites. Littoral–marine resources provided the ancient population with a means of subsistence, commercial products for exportation, raw materials for the manufacture of artifacts, and the surplus required for the maintenance of nonproductive activities necessary for the consolidation of the ruling class. The objective of our recent analysis and interpretation of excavated material at Tulum is to understand the local economy and social relationships.

Analysis of the ceramics from Tulum reveals that its occupation began between A.D. 1100 and 1200. The first ware of importance is Peto Cream (Xcanchakan Black-on-Cream type), which represents the transition from the Early Postclassic to the beginning of the Late Postclassic. This ceramic ware, found early in the history of Mayapan, is an indicator of the simultaneous emergence of the two sites. At Tulum, it is found associated with eight structures: the majority from the central nucleus of the walled–in area; in a cave under Structure 1; in Burial 1; and at the deepest level of Test Pit 1 (fig. 1), located on the platform of Structure 25 (Barrera 1977: 46–60). This material slightly modifies the chronology of the site formulated by Sanders (1960: 226). Ceramic evidence indicates continuous occupation of Tulum from this initial period up to the Spanish conquest. The following wares are present: Tulum Red ware, Matillas group of Fine Orange ware, Mayapan Red ware, and Mayapan Unslipped ware, especially the types Navula Unslipped and Chen Mul Modeled, which occur as censers.

During the Late Postclassic, Tulum reached its apogee. It is interesting to observe that Mayapan and Tulum simultaneously maintained direct commercial relations with two distant points of the most important trade route of that time: Tabasco and Honduras. For example, the report that one of the Cocom rulers of Mayapan, absent

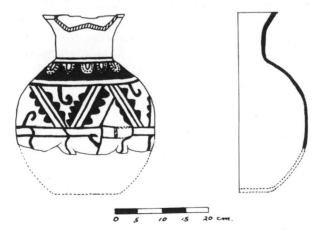

Fig. 1. Peto Cream ware: Xcanchakan Black-on-Cream type jar. This example was recovered from Test Pit 1, layer 6, at Tulum.

during an insurrection that destroyed the city, was at that time trading in the Ulua region of Honduras (Tozzer 1941: 32–39) indicates intensive commerce in that direction. Relations with Tabasco are indicated through ethnohistoric reports, which state that "Mexican mercenaries" were brought to Mayapan from the region of Xicalango and Tabasco over a period of time. Also indicative of this commerce is the presence at Tulum of the Matillas group of Fine Orange, which was probably manufactured in Tabasco (Noguera 1975: 47).

Obsidian Trade on the East Coast of Yucatan

Trade was clearly important to the economy of Tulum, and probably involved exchange of such exotic items as obsidian, jade, cacao, feathers, and metals. Obsidian is of particular significance in delineating prehistoric trade patterns in Mesoamerica, because chemical analysis of the materials and sources, as well as study of the techniques of artifact manufacture, have helped clarify the commercial routes. Study of obsidian found on the peninsula and in the Peten has revealed changing patterns of trade from the Middle Preclassic up until the Late Postclassic, Guatemala being the principal source of supply and the Mexican highlands a less important source. Analysis of 27 samples from Cozumel shows that during the Late Classic, the principal supply source was El Chayal (100%). During the Early Postclassic there was a gradual change from El Chayal (25%) to Ixtepeque (50%), and with a smaller amount (25%) from Zinapecuaro, Michoacan. Finally, during the Late Postclassic, 90% originated in Ixtepeque with the remaining 10% divided between El Chayal and Pachuca (Nelson and Phillips n.d.). Obsidian from other sites in the eastern region of Quintana Roo (Coba, Cancun, and Tulum) has been the object of recent analysis by x-ray fluorescence. Coba received obsidian from El Chayal throughout all of the Classic period, as did the majority of the centers in the Peten. Ixtepeque was the only supplier to both Cancun and Tulum during the Late Postclassic (Nelson, Phillips, Robles, Mayer, and Barrera n.d.).

Sources for obsidian conform to a homogeneous pattern in the Late Postclassic: from the principal source of supply, Ixtepeque, the obsidian was probably transported to the Motagua River and from there to the Caribbean sea, whence it could have been sent around the peninsula. The small percentage from El Chayal could have been transported in the same way, while the obsidian from the Mexican highlands arrived by way of the Laguna de Terminos whence it was carried along the coast to the eastern region (Hammond 1976).

Part of the obsidian trade to Tulum surely served to satisfy the

Table 1. Results of Analysis of Obsidian Artifacts from Tulum, Quintana Roo, Mexico, for the Late Postclassic (A.D. 1250–1550) Period

Sample No.	Provenience	Rb ppm	Sr ppm	Zr ppm	MnO %	Fe$_2$O$_3$ %	TiO$_2$ %	Ba ppm	Na$_2$O %	Obsidian Source
785	Terrace 1, Terrace 2	86	163	141	.067	1.44	.230	1071	4.01	Ixtepeque
786	Terrace 1, Burial 3	89	164	158	.067	1.47	.229	1061	4.02	Ixtepeque
787	Test pit 1, layer 1	84	163	130	.067	1.45	.228	1070	3.99	Ixtepeque
788	Test pit 1, layer 1	91	167	149	.067	1.45	.228	1070	4.02	Ixtepeque
789	Test pit 1, layer 1	92	166	168	.068	1.41	.230	1068	4.00	Ixtepeque
790	Test pit 1, layer 1	90	168	135	.068	1.45	.230	1074	4.01	Ixtepeque
791	Test pit 3, layer 1	86	164	155	.067	1.44	.226	1064	3.93	Ixtepeque
792	Test pit 3, layer 1	88	166	153	.067	1.45	.230	1053	4.04	Ixtepeque
793	Test pit 3, layer 1	85	161	150	.067	1.51	.234	1059	3.97	Ixtepeque
794	Test pit 2, layer 1	90	167	156	.067	1.45	.229	1058	2.39	Ixtepeque

SOURCE: Nelson, Phillips, Robles, Mayer, and Barrera Rubio n.d.

demand of other regional sites in the interior of the peninsula with which economic ties were maintained. The presence of fragments of obsidian cores, generally with their striking platforms having been smoothed with sand, along with flakes from the worked surface, indicates that the obsidian was worked on the site by knappers. Altogether, 135 blades of gray obsidian were found in seven different structures.

Local Utilization of Littoral–Marine Resources

The principal activity of most of the population of Tulum was apparently the utilization of the sea, fishing being one of the inhabitants' chief occupations. Fish and mollusks formed an important part of the native diet, and conch shell, coral rock, bone, and silex were used for manufacture of artifacts.

Remains of fishing tools were plentiful at Tulum: 401 clay sinkers used to give weight to the nets and lines were encountered in eleven different structures. These sinkers were generally made from sherds of Tulum Red ware, most often pieces of broken pottery with grooves added on the rims where the lines could be tied. The slip on the central part of the artifact is better conserved due to the protection given it by the thread that covered the area.

In the seventeenth century, Nicolas de Valenzuela observed the use among the Cholti-Lacandon of this type of sinker with their nets: "and in two of said houses large nets were found . . . with their floats and for weights clay [balls] well sewn on . . ." (cited in Hellmuth 1977: 426). Archaeological evidence for this type of sinker on the east coast of the Yucatan peninsula has been reported at Cancun, Xcaret, Tancah, and Cozumel (Andrews IV et al. 1974: 188–190; Andrews IV and Andrews 1975: 73; Mayer, personal communication; Miller 1977: 100–101; Phillips 1979: 2–18). They have also been noted on the northern coast of the peninsula (Eaton 1976: 231–243, 1978: 56). Their widespread frequency demonstrates the importance of fishing and confirms the sixteenth and seventeenth century references, such as those describing the area of Tulum-Tancah as a fishing center (*Relaciones de Yucatan* 1898–1900: Vol. 2: 197). Sanchez de Aguilar (1937: 151) reports that in the province of Chahuac-ha, "tienen sus redes y chinchorros y sus barquillos, que llaman canoas los que viven en la costa . . ." Further emphasis to the importance of fishing is given by the discovery of remains of fish in Structures 18, 20, and 21 (according to Lothrop's 1924 classification), and in Test Pit 1, where they were associated with a hearth (Barrera Rubio 1977).

Fishing is an activity that can be carried out individually or in groups, the latter requiring either simple or complex cooperation. Most of the production was probably to satisfy the needs of the majority of the population and for trade, made possible by preservation techniques known to have been used for seafood (Landa 1941: 190). Fish was also a tribute item demanded by the governing class (Roys 1972: 69). The ruling class had its own boats and slaves who worked on them, according to reports from the provinces of Ah Canul and Chakan (in the Codice de Calkini, Barrera Vasquez 1957: 111; Roys 1972: 69).

Mollusks consitute another important marine resource that was not only utilized for subsistence needs and trade but also for the fulfillment of religious ceremonies. The fact that they represent earth, the underworld, and the realm of the dead helps explain their frequent appearance in offerings and burials (Thompson 1970: 49). In Tulum, 25 edible species were identified in archaeological context; *Strombus gigas* was apparently the most esteemed for food. Its shell

Table 2. Archaeological Shell from Tulum, Quintana Roo

Species	Whole	Frag-ments	Arti-facts	Archaeological Occurrence
Gastropoda: Edible				
Strombus gigas	31	98	8	S. 1, 7, 8, 13, 19, 20, 21, 22, 25, 27, 29 Cave under S. 1, Test pit 1, 5
Cittarium pica	9	2		S. 1, 4, 20, 25, 38, Test pit 1, 5
Strombus costatus	4	1		Test pit 1
Cypraecassis testiculus	4			S. 3, 8, 20, 25
Melongena melongena	3			S. 20, Test pit 1, 8
Columbella mercatoria	2			S. 25
Turbinella angulata	1	4		S. 20, Test pit 1
Cypraea zebra	1	2		S. 8, 25
Polinices lacteus	1			S. 25
Nerita tessellata	1			S. 21
Nerita versicolor		1		S. 25
Astraea phoebia	1			S. 25
Cypraea cervus	1			S. 20
Oliva sayana	1			S. 25
Conus mus	1			S. 25
Thais deltoidea	1	1		S. 25
Fasciolaria tulipa	1	1		S. 20, Test pit 1
Gastropoda: Not Edible				
Fissurella barbadensis	70		1	S. 20, 21, 22, 25, Test pit 1, 2
Oliva reticularis	11		9	S. 1, 21, 22, 25, 38, cave under S. 1
Acmaea pustulata	8			S. 25
Fissurella fascicularis	7			S. 21, 25
Bulla occidentalis	3			S. 1
Acmaea leucopleura Jamaicensis	1			S. 21
Turbo castanea	1			Cave under S. 1
Pelecypods: Edible				
Spondylus americanus	5	5	1	S. 1, 20, 23, 25
Codakia orbicularis	4	4		S. 1, 20, 25
Chama sinuosa	2			S. 25, Test pit 1
Arcopagia fausta	2			S. 1, 25
Chama macerophylla	1		1	S. 1, Test pit 1
Arca imbricata	1			S. 25
Lyropecten nodosus		3		S. 1, 25
Tellina radiata		1		S. 13

Table 2 (*continued*)

Species	Whole	Frag-ments	Arti-facts	Archaeological Occurrence
Pelecypods: Not Edible				
Chama congregata	2			S. 25
Pteria colymbus		1		S. 25
Chione cancellata		1		S. 25
Barbatia cancellaria	1			Test pit 1

often was used for tools and utensils, as well, and less frequently for ornaments. The conch shell also appears associated with burials; for example, one was found in an interment within the west stairway of Tulum Structure 20 (Velazquez 1974). Shells of edible conchs generally had a perforation in the apical base to facilitate the extraction of the mollusk. Those encountered are common to the east coast, and only two of the thirty-six identified species, *Cypraea cervus* and *Strombus costatus*, are more frequent to the north coast.

The coastal sites on the Yucatan peninsula present a great quantity of artifact remains of conch and shell, as shown in the reports of sites on the north and west coasts (Eaton 1974; Eaton 1978; Andrews IV 1969; Pina Chan 1968) as well as in reports concerning sites of the east coast, such as Cancun, Tancah, El Meco, and Cozumel (Andrews IV et al. 1974; Mayer 1977; Vokes 1978). The prevalence of these artifacts demonstrates the ready adaptation of the ancient dwellers to the local abundance of raw materials.

From the analyzed material from Tulum, we find six implements which served as tools to satisfy local needs. This sample, although small, gives us an idea of the daily activities for which they were once used. *Strombus gigas* was the preferred shell, as it was in other coastal sites. One of these local artifacts is a scoop (figs. 2a, 2b, and 2c); among its functions may have been the mixing of dyes. This type of artifact had a wide distribution on the north and west coasts of the peninsula, where it has been reported at Jaina, La Alegria, and Chuburna (Pina Chan 1968: 71; Eaton 1978: 59) and on the east coast at Cozumel (Vokes 1978: 2–3). The technique used to make this artifact consisted of making a transversal cut through the columella and half of the outer surface of the shell, first by chipping and then by abrasion.

Shell perforators were other locally made tools; two were found in Structure 1 at Tulum (figs. 2d, 2e, and 2f). Eaton (1978: 58) reports a similar one from Jaina, which they classify as a celt with a spe-

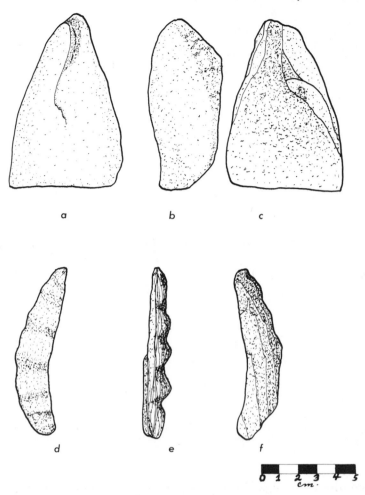

Fig. 2. (a–c) scrapers, recovered from Tulum Structure 13; (d–f) celts, specialized in function, from Tulum Structure 20.

cialized function. Its arched form, suited for use with or without a handle, was obtained by cutting off the exterior lip by chipping and abrasion.

A scraper with a diameter of 6.5 centimeters was also found; it consisted of a concave disc with irregular edges and one section worn by use (figs. 3a, 3b, and 3c). Apparently it functioned as a scraper for soft surfaces, its concave form easily held in the hand; this instrument was obtained by cutting through the surface of the *Strombus*. A knife (?) (figs. 3d, 3e, and 3f) was also produced by the same technique; its rough and irregular borders indicate that it was shaped

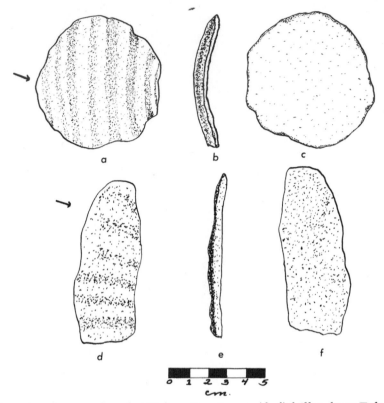

Fig. 3. (a–c) scoops found at Tulum Structure 2; (d–f) driller, from Tulum Structure 1.

solely by chipping. The left lateral edge of this artifact is worn in such a way as to indicate a cutting function. It could have been manipulated with or without a handle. Eaton has classified similar artifacts found on the north coast as celts (Eaton 1974). Shell fishhooks were apparently less commonly used than were fishing nets. The only hook found (fig. 4b) was made from the apex of the *Strombus*.

Other local materials, although not as extensively used for tools as shell, were coral rock and silex. Four coral rock manos were found, and a number of chips, core debris, and the base of a silex point were recovered.

Adornments made from shell were most probably manufactured for local use and for trade. In our recent investigations at Tulum, nine pendants made from *Oliva reticularis* were found, cut in one of two ways. The apex might be cut transversally by chipping,

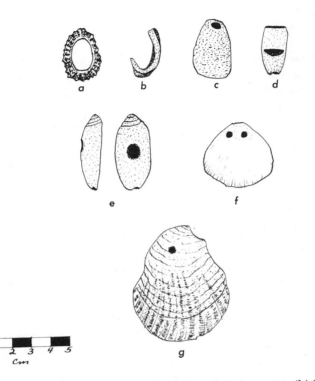

Fig. 4. (a) *Fissurella barbadensis* bead, Tulum Structure 25; (b) fishhook
from Tulum Structure 25; (c) tinkler from Tulum Structure 27; (d and e)
Oliva reticularis tinklers; (f and g) *Spondylus americanus* and *Chama
macerophylla* pendants from Tulum Structures 20 and 1.

with a circular or lenticular perforation in the middle (fig. 4d), or the
middle might be shaved longitudinally across the axis of the coil,
with a circular perforation placed in the center (fig. 4e). The *Oliva*
has a long tradition of ornamental use from the Preclassic period
through the Postclassic (Andrews IV 1969: 17) as well as a ceremonial function, having been encountered as offerings in burials in
Tikal and Cozumel (Moholy-Nagy 1963: 79; Vokes 1978: 4). Its archaeological distribution was widespread through Mesoamerica
(Kidder et al. 1946: 147–149), and it was a highly prized article of
exchange.

Pendants were also manufactured from other species. One from
Tulum was fashioned from the spine of a *Strombus*, with a perforation in the apex; it was then detached from its surface by a diagonal
cut (fig. 4c). One from *Spondylus americanus* had two perforations

in the upper part of the shell for its suspension, while one from *Chama macerophylla* had only one perforation in the same area (figs. 4f and 4g).

In one rather uncommon case, we found a bead made from *Fissurella barbadensis*, which has been reported once before in archaeological context (Andrews IV 1969: 5), although not as an artifact (fig. 4a). It was shaped by shaving off the top of the shell, leaving the oval contour as an ornament. Two other worked pieces of shell were found but neither was identifiable because of heavy polishing. One is a pendant with two perforations, and the other one is a polished plaque of approximately rectangular shape.

Social Relationships

The development of the coastal sites during the Late Post-classic, principally on the east coast of the peninsula, cannot be explained by the commerce and trade routes exclusively. The problem is more complex, because it implies an integral vision of the economic activities of the prehispanic communities, including local production and the social destination of the products. It is also important to mention the historic circumstances of that time, such as the strategic location of Tulum in the center of the Quintana Roo coastline. This location on the peninsular coastal trade route (from Tabasco to Honduras) was responsible for integrating Tulum into the most important maritime route of that period.

The archaeological evidence and the ethnohistoric sources have shown the importance of littoral–marine resources on the coasts of the peninsula and particularly at Tulum, because its principal productive activities are intimately related to the sea and marine life. The excavations in Tulum have shown that the subsistence base of the population, their most important productive activity, their tools and utensils, objects of adornment, commerce, and tribute are found in the utilization of these sources.

Ethnohistoric sources have demonstrated the importance of certain agricultural and apicultural products and local fauna as part of the tribute paid to elites. The social tributary relationship permitted the accumulation of goods and services in the hands of the ruling class, which concomitantly allowed them to control the commercial activity. The exchange of local products for imported goods allowed consolidation of their political and economic dominion. For this reason, the ports of exchange were strategic points of economic control, and they were generally protected by palisade walls or other fortifications, as in the case of Tulum, Potonchan (Roys 1972: 37), and

Ichpaatun. At Cozumel, Sabloff and Freidel (1975a: 376–377) have shown that although San Miguel was the commercial port, the administrative center for the island was San Gervasio, a site protected by its inland location.

Besides serving as an element of defense in Tulum, the wall served to separate the elite who lived within the walled–in area from the majority of the population who lived on the outside. In this outlying area, a series of structures and systems of walls have been located which define the area as a habitation zone (Velazquez 1976: 59). These surveys of a small (90 meters by 90 meters) area south of Tulum revealed a system of single and double walls with an average height of 90 centimeters. This network of walls forms an interlacing of quadrangular patio–like spaces with small circular, quadrangular, and oval structures. According to the classic sources for the history of Yucatan, such as Landa (Tozzer 1941), Cogolludo (1867–68), and the *Relaciones de Yucatan* (1898–1900), at the time of the arrival of the Spaniards, there still functioned a tributary system on the peninsula that had had its peak during the hegemony of Mayapan. Besides fish, mollusks, shells, and those other artifacts discussed above, other perishable tribute products were circulated, but these leave no archaeological evidence. Among these, historic sources mention products such as blankets of cotton, wax, honey (*RY* 1898–1900: 197), corn, beans, and hunted animals (Chamberlain 1974: 42). Slaves, feathers, cacao, metals, obsidian, and other products also moved through the network, but may have been traded primarily to meet the needs of the elite class. Spanish domination of the Yucatan peninsula did not destroy all these ancient Maya forms of social and economic organization, but adapted them to their own political system, thereby encouraging them for their own economic gain.

Acknowledgments

The Tulum Project was under the direction of Arqueologo Norberto Gonzalez Crespo, director of the Centro Regional del Sureste del Instituto Nacional de Antropologia e Historia. The field research was carried out in 1974–1975; since then I have had access to the material excavated by others as well as my own, which has allowed me to synthesize data and make inferences relative to the site. I thank Dr. Peter Schmidt for his comments and suggestions and Dr. Anthony P. Andrews for the classification of the majority of mollusks. I also thank Marcial Lewandowski for the translation from Spanish and Joann M. Andrews for the editing.

Chichen Itza and Coba: An Itza-Maya Standoff in Early Postclassic Yucatan

ANTHONY P. ANDREWS AND FERNANDO ROBLES C.

The last six hundred years before the arrival of the Spaniards were trying times for the Maya of northern Yucatan, times of political turmoil and war that saw the rise and fall of numerous small city states, as well as the foiled attempts of large regional polities to impose their control over the entire region. Several studies of the last decade have attempted to unravel the complex series of events that gave rise to the Postclassic culture of northern Yucatan (Roys 1966; Thompson 1970; Ball 1974, 1977a, 1977b, 1978, 1979a, 1979b; Sabloff and Rathje 1975a, 1975b; Miller 1977a, 1977b; Shuman 1977; A. Andrews 1978b; Andrews V 1979, 1981). While our understanding of Postclassic Yucatan has transcended the "traditional" view of the 1960s (cf. Andrews IV 1965a), we still have much to learn, and fundamental problems remain unsolved.

Foremost among these is the present state of our understanding of the Terminal Classic and Postclassic chronology of northern Yucatan. While most scholars now reject the traditional scheme of pan-regional, non-overlapping sequential stages (Terminal Classic–Early Postclassic–Late Postclassic), and prefer more flexible nonlineal schemes that allow varying degrees of overlap in different regions (cf. Andrews V 1979, 1981; Ball 1979a, 1979b; Robles 1980), these new sequences are still being worked out, and an integral chronology for northern Yucatan still eludes us.

Another fundamental problem is our adherence to quasi-historical sequences of events which offer felicitious, but somewhat simplistic, accounts of the arrival of foreign groups in northern Yucatan in the ninth and tenth centuries of the Christian era. Because such reconstructions fail to clarify the archaeological record, we must assume that a far more complex series of events took place. In this respect, we are not alluding to the old Quetzalcoatl–Kukulcan migration myth, but rather to the more intricate "Putun models" proposed in the early 1970s (Thompson 1970; Ball 1974). These models offer only a superficial explanation of the social, economic, and political processes underlying the events, and fail to deal adequately with the interaction between foreign groups and local polities in the course of those changing times. This inadequacy is especially clear in the case of the large polity of Coba in eastern Yucatan, long assumed to have been abandoned by Terminal Classic times. This paper addresses some of these problems.

Los Hijos de Putun

Who were the Putun? Available evidence suggests that the Putun were the sixteenth century Chontal Maya of eastern Tabasco and southwestern Campeche (Scholes and Roys 1948; Roys 1957; Thompson 1970). The meaning of the word "Putun" is not clear; Roys (1957: 167) notes that the only viable translation is found in Chol, in which dialect "Putun" means "peaceful." The word "Chontal" on the other hand, derives from the Nahuatl *chontalli*, "foreigner" (Thompson 1970: 5). In view of recent reconstructions of Putun history, the translations of their two names provide a most curious juxtaposition.

Sir Eric Thompson (1970) has suggested that these people controlled a circum–peninsular maritime trading network. We do have evidence that one of the main Putun groups, the Acalan, had an elite merchant class actively engaged in a trading network which spread from the Gulf Coast of Tabasco to the Gulf of Honduras, across the base of the peninsula; we also have good reason to believe that the Acalan traded with northern Yucatan via the west coast (Scholes and Roys 1948: 59–60). There is, however, no solid evidence of a more extensive Putun–controlled network at the time of conquest (but see Sabloff and Rathje 1975b for a summary of evidence for earlier ties between the Chontal and Cozumel). In fact, beyond the prominent status as long–distance merchants, very little is known of the language, social and political organization, or religion of the sixteenth century Putun peoples (Thompson 1970: 8–10).

Despite these shortcomings, in 1970 Thompson published his landmark study of Putun prehistory, in which he traced Putun ancestry to the eighth century, and held them responsible for almost every major political event of the following eight centuries of Maya history. His detailed reconstruction need not be recounted here; suffice it to say that he presented a vision of ancestral Putun sea–going merchant–warrior groups, the "Phoenicians of the New World," who expanded out of their homeland on the Gulf Coast, exacerbating the tensions already leading to the Classic Maya collapse of the Southern lowlands, and then laying the foundations of a New Empire in the north.

Thompson's "Phoenician" model is an intricate tour de force, overwhelming in its marshalling of the historic, ethnographic, and linguistic data. His basic premises have been widely accepted, and only a few scholars have expressed reservations about some of his assumptions (Adams 1973; Miller 1977a). The principal objection of these critics is that it is difficult to accept the notion that a single ethnic group was responsible for so much. As Miller (1977a: 222) notes, the Putun "loom as supermen" in the recent literature, when in fact they may have been constituted of several related, yet competitive, Gulf Coast groups rather than a single unified people. We would tend to agree with this view and, until more data are at hand, we would prefer to refer to these groups as "Gulf Coast peoples."

Another problem with Thompson's vision of Putun migrations is the primary focus on historical events, rather than larger socioeconomic processes (Sabloff 1973); this focus is due in part to Thompson's primary reliance on ethnohistoric sources and his efforts to find a "fit" between the data and the migrations of the Quetzalcoatl–Kukulcan myth. While not denying the likelihood that such events have a historical base, the archaeological evidence suggests that the so-called "migrations" or "invasions" were gradual deployments of Gulf Coast peoples along the west and north coasts of the peninsula, rather than sudden historic events; if in fact the mythical *entradas* occurred, they would have merely been noted as the culmination of the gradual process of deployment (A. Andrews 1981).

Moreover, A. Andrews (1978b) has argued that the development and eventual conquest of northern Yucatan in the tenth century should be seen as the outcome of economic and political processes that were the result of competition over trade networks and foreign exploitation of the weakening political structure in the interior of northern Yucatan, factors that will be further discussed below. The following scenario attempts to place these new considerations in proper perspective. As was Thompson, we are also somewhat biased, and if some of our arguments border on speculation, they do so only in the spirit of provoking further discussion.

Western Yucatan: A.D. 700–900/1000

This period, known as the Terminal Classic or Pure Florescent, saw the emergence of the Puuc cities of northern Yucatan. Ceramic, architectural, and radiometric data suggest that this Puuc style originated in northern Campeche, spread to and flourished in the Puuc hills and later in northeastern Yucatan, where Puuc architecture and ceramics are found at the sites of Chichen Itza and Culuba (Andrews V 1979). While the distribution of Puuc architecture appears to be limited to western and northeastern Yucatan, Puuc ceramics, collectively representing the "Cehpech sphere," are found throughout most of the peninsula, as far south as Champoton, the Rio Bec area, and northern Belize (Ball 1979a; D. Chase and A. Chase 1982).

The origins of Puuc architecture and ceramics can be traced to three different basic components: (1) indigenous developments in northern Yucatan; (2) architectural influence from the Chenes and Rio Bec regions; and (3) foreign ceramic and architectural influences from the Gulf Coast and central Mexican highlands. These latter influences are of central concern to this paper, as a growing body of evidence now suggests that Gulf Coast ceramic styles and architectural ties to Central Mexico form a major component in the development of the Puuc "style" (Ball 1974, 1979b; Andrews V 1979; Sharp 1981). Moreover, recent survey data attest to a gradual deployment of Gulf Coast trading groups along the west and north coasts of the peninsula during this period; these groups selected sites of high strategic value for trading and military purposes, such as islands, promontories, and entrances to waterways (A. Andrews 1977, 1978a, 1978b; Eaton 1978; Garza T. de Gonzalez and Kurjack 1980).

The relationship that existed between these Gulf Coast peoples and the inland Puuc peoples is not entirely clear. We suspect an uneasy alliance of sorts, in which the former group provided a powerful medium for the exchange of goods and ideas between Yucatan and distant regions to the west and south; through this medium Yucatan acquired architectural stylistic features from Veracruz, Morelos, and Oaxaca, as well as ceramics from the Gulf Coast–Usumacinta basin region. The architectural similarities are so strong, in fact, that it seems likely craftsmen were moving both into Yucatan and out; witness, for example, the Puuc–style masonry and vault found on Structure A–3 at Seibal on the Pasion drainage. In addition to craftsmen and traders, other groups may have also been moving about; it has been suggested that the foreign warriors depicted on relief sculptures on two door jambs at Kabah may have been early Toltec immigrants or mercenaries (Proskouriakoff 1950: 170; Roys 1966: 154). Similar depictions are found on Terminal Classic stelae at Uxmal, Edzna, and Oxkintok (Proskouriakoff 1950, 1951).

The gradual deployment of "westerners" along the west and north coasts may also have been a response to internal conditions in northern Yucatan. Several lines of evidence suggest that a gradual deterioration of sociopolitical structures set in, particularly after A.D. 900. Data from the recent I.N.A.H. *Atlas* surveys attest to overwhelming population growth in Late and Terminal Classic times; these data, along with the recent discovery of fortifications at several Terminal Classic sites, raise the possibility of increasing competition over limited land resources (Kurjack and Andrews V 1976; Webster 1979; Barrera Rubio 1980). And, unlike their southern neighbors, the people of northern Yucatan had no way of intensifying their agricultural production (save planting orchards of *ramon* trees, a matter worth investigating). If this scenario is accurate, then, the subsequent events of the tenth and eleventh centuries were clearly the logical outcome of the inevitable interaction between aggressive "outsiders" and the disintegrating politics of the interior.

Eastern Yucatan: A.D. 700–900/1000

An issue commonly ignored in recent discussions of political events of Terminal Classic and Postclassic Yucatan is the role of the Coba polity in those developments.

Investigations conducted at Coba during the last decade by numerous researchers under the direction of the Instituto Nacional de Antropologia e Historia have revealed quite conclusively that Coba was one of the largest urban centers of the Maya area. The city itself covers an area of more than 70 square kilometers, and drew on the agricultural surpluses of satellite communities as far away as 20 kilometers. In fact, there is good reason to believe that its political domain spread from the western terminus of the Yaxuna causeway to the adjacent east coast, where it probably maintained a port at Xelha. Moreover, it is likely that Coba served the role of a middleman in the trade which flowed between north Yucatan, the east coast, and points south (Benavides and Robles 1975; Benavides 1976, 1977; Robles 1976, 1977, 1980; A. Andrews 1983).

Another important result of the recent investigations was the establishment of a continuous ceramic sequence from Late Formative to Late Postclassic times (Robles 1977, 1980); this was based on the ceramics from architectural excavations as well as ceramics recovered from more than 130 test pits from all areas of the site. These data clearly indicate that, contrary to previous beliefs, Coba was not abandoned during Terminal Classic times; rather, this was a period of further growth, which continued well past A.D. 1000. Thus, while the Puuc cities were experiencing considerable internal and external stress, Coba was emerging as a state polity of unparalleled scope in Yucatan history.

East and West, A.D. 900–1200: An Early Postclassic Standoff

This period begins with the further deterioration of the northern cities and the eventual irruption of the "westerners" into the interior. As A. Andrews (1978b, 1980, 1983; cf. also Medizabal 1929; Ball and Eaton 1972) has argued elsewhere, taking over the north coast salt beds and their related long-distance trade networks was a critical part of this process, enabling the outsiders to deliver an economic coup de grace to the already weakened interior.

The events that followed are well known: the intruders, today known as the Itza, moved inland, established their capital at Chichen Itza, and from there consolidated their control over most of northern Yucatan. They also strengthened their position on the coast, monopolizing the salt beds and the long–distance trade networks; their main port was probably located at Isla Cerritos, at the mouth of the Rio Lagartos estuary (figs. 1 and 2; A. Andrews 1978b). As a result of this consolidation and the subsequent management of the new economic order, Chichen Itza grew to be one of the largest and wealthiest capitals of Mesoamerica.

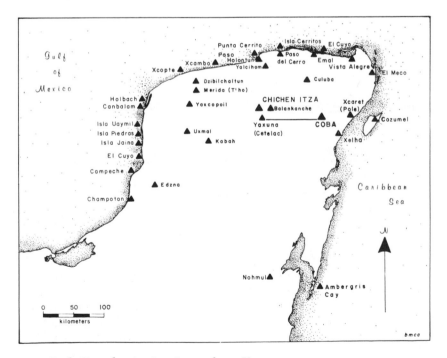

Fig. 1. Early Postclassic sites in northern Yucatan.

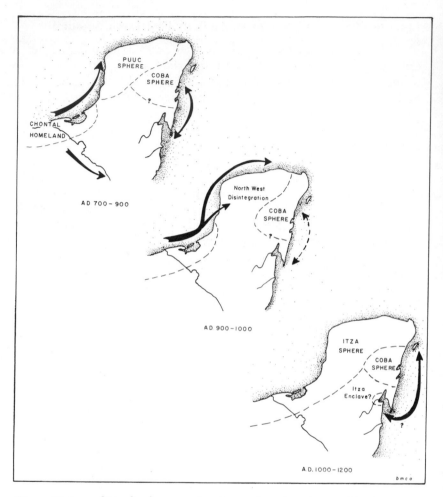

Fig. 2. Major political spheres and major trade, migration, and/or invasion routes of Terminal Classic and Early Postclassic Yucatan, ca. A.D. 700–1200.

That the Itza economy relied primarily on coastal resources and long–distance trade is clearly corroborated by the distribution of Itza–related ceramics and architectural remains. In many coastal sites of the period, the Itza–related remains are the major component; in fact, many of the sites have only Sotuta sphere remains. In the interior, evidence of an Itza presence is limited to a few sites where Itza–related remains are sparse. It seems likely that these remains are the traces of Itza garrisons and/or administrative groups, who were responsible for looking after the interests of Chichen Itza (fig. 1; N. Gonzales, personal communication).

The final military campaign by the Itza in northern Yucatan, which purportedly took place in A.D. 987, is believed to have been recounted, in legendary fashion, in the Hunac Ceel epic of the *Chilam Balam de Chumayel*. According to the chronicle, the Itza disembarked at Pole (Xcaret), proceeded across northern Yucatan into the Puuc heartland, and then back across again to central northern Yucatan, eventually arriving at Cetelac (Yaxuna). The account of what happened at Cetelac is unclear. We know only that the Itza and the ruler of Cetelac had some differences, as the account notes, somewhat euphemistically, that "they agreed in their opinions." The account records that the ruler of Cetelac subsequently agreed to pay a tribute to the Itza, who then moved north to Chichen Itza, where they established their capital (Roys 1933: 72–75).

The Itza campaign clearly skirted the northern border of the domain of Coba. Moreover, the events at Cetelac may have been purposefully garbled by Itza historians. It is more likely that the Itza encountered massive resistance at Cetelac, the western frontier of the Coba polity, and withdrew. A standoff resulted in which the Itza were able to consolidate their control over western and northern Yucatan, but were unable to assert their control over the eastern Coba polity.

The near total absence of Sotuta sphere ceramics at Coba and Yaxuna (Robles 1980), a good indicator of Itza presence elsewhere, adds support to the notion that the Itza were unable to enter the domain of Coba. Such a notion is reinforced by recent analysis of the ash temper of Terminal Classic and Early Postclassic ceramics from several sites in northern Yucatan. Chichen Itza and the western sites had a type of ash temper that is markedly distinct from that of Coba and Yaxuna, suggesting separate sources of supply; moreover, the use of ash temper at Coba may have declined throughout the period (Simmons and Brem 1979). The continuity of Cehpech ceramics at Coba well into the Early Postclassic period also hints at a certain degree of isolation.

While the present data suggest that two competing political spheres emerged in northern Yucatan after A.D. 1000, or perhaps even earlier, the boundaries of the two spheres have yet to be mapped out. On the basis of the known distribution of Sotuta phase ceramics, we can surmise that the Itza controlled the territory spreading from Tabasco and western Campeche across northern Yucatan to the northeast coast of Quintana Roo, at least as far south as El Meco, where significant quantities of Sotuta phase ceramics have been recovered (A. Andrews and Robles n.d.).

The nature of the Itza presence on the east coast is at present poorly understood. The Sotuta sphere ceramics at El Meco appear late in the Early Postclassic, in deposits that also contain Peto Cream ware (A. Andrews and Robles n.d.). Further south along the coast, Sotuta sphere materials are scarce; very small quantities have been recovered at Xcaret (Andrews IV and Andrews 1975) and Xelha (Navarrete 1974; Robles 1978). These data suggest that Coba retained control of the central east coast; that such a control existed still needs to be verified, however, for we have scant data on the Early Postclassic period of the east coast.

It is also unclear if the island of Cozumel was controlled by either sphere. Sabloff and Rathje (1975a) have argued that the island was an independent port of trade in Early Postclassic times, but the data generated from their work on the island have so far failed to substantiate their argument (Phillips 1979; A. Andrews 1983) and the final ceramic analysis is not yet available. Freidel (personal communication), however, notes the presence of Sotuta sphere ceramics at two sites on the island (El Cedral and Chen Cedral) and the existence of a large L–shaped platform at San Gervasio that is similar to those at Chichen Itza. Moreover, recent stratigraphic excavations at San Gervasio, directed by Robles, have revealed a strong Sotuta component there. Interestingly, the Sotuta phase materials are associated with Peto Cream ware which, as in the case of El Meco, suggests an Itza presence late in the Early Postclassic period.

Altogether, the available evidence would seem to indicate that the Itza established a strong presence on the northeast coast at El Meco and on Cozumel Island in the second half of the Early Postclassic period (ca. A.D. 1100–1200). Freidel (personal communication) suggests that Itza control of Cozumel would have allowed the Itza to bypass the central east coast. New data from northern Belize would tend to support this idea. Sotuta sphere ceramics have been found on Ambergris Cay (P. Schmidt, personal communication; Hammond 1976), and the Chases (D. Chase and A. Chase 1982; D. Chase 1982b) have argued, on the basis of ceramic and architectural evidence, that the site of Nohmul, in northern Belize, was an early Itza outpost. Whether or not the Itza maintained contact with Nohmul via the Caribbean or overland is not clear, but the presence of Sotuta sphere ceramics at Ambergris Cay would clearly suggest a Caribbean link–up with Cozumel. The Itza may have also utilized the overland route via Bacalar, however, which was an important trade artery between Chetumal Bay and central Yucatan at the time of the conquest (Roys 1957: 159). If such were the case, it would appear that the Itza managed to encircle the Coba polity and take over the

Caribbean networks that Coba had traditionally controlled from its home port of Xelha.

As an aside, it is perhaps worth noting Ciudad Real's report (1932: 35) of an Itza port on Ascension Bay, which has never been verified, either historically or archaeologically. If such a port existed, then the Itza may have controlled the southern east coast, from the Ascension and Espirito Santo Bay area down the Xcalac peninsula to Ambergris Cay, and the encirclement of Coba would have been considerably tighter. Because this area has yet to be surveyed, however, the issue of an Itza presence is, at best, mere speculation.

In sum, the emerging picture is one of economic competition between Chichen Itza and Coba. While the Itza were probably unable to penetrate the domain of Coba, they were able to cut off its trade arteries to the northwest and south, undermining its traditional role as a north-south middleman. Its older ties with the now—abandoned cities of the southern lowlands were gone; the eventual deployment of Itza trading enclaves on Cozumel and in northern Belize was likely the final blow, and Coba was faced with economic strangulation.

The archaeological evidence from Coba appears to corroborate this scenario. After A.D. 1100, the construction of public works ceased at Coba; the satellite communities and sites at the terminal of the *sacbe* system were abandoned, and a serious decline in population occurred throughout Coba. How the Itza exploited this situation is not clear; the fact that they did not actually move into Coba to establish a strong presence there may be due to their concern with events elsewhere. After all, the Itza were also likely to feel the internal pressures that led to their own eventual collapse a few decades later.

With the collapse of Chichen Itza at the beginning of the thirteenth century came also the collapse of the entire network of outposts the Itza had established along the west and north coasts of the peninsula. Surface surveys of these Early Postclassic coastal sites have revealed little or no trace of Late Postclassic habitation, save at Champoton, Emal, El Cuyo, and Vista Alegre (Eaton 1978; Ball 1979a; A. Andrews 1978b). Such a situation leaves no doubt that the coastal economic network created by the Itza collapsed along with Chichen Itza. This does not mean that the coast was abandoned; historical records note that Mayapan and many other communities continued to exploit the salt beds (A. Andrews 1983) and other coastal resources, while the east coast witnessed a major cultural renaissance of unprecedented proportions, accompanied by vast increases in population, the growth of many established communities and the appearance of new ones, as well as a resurgence of the trade networks of the Caribbean. And while the east coast flourished, the economic order of the west and north coasts collapsed along with the capital of the Itza.

Conclusions

This brief reconstruction of Terminal Classic and Early Postclassic events in northern Yucatan suggests that the cultural developments of the period are best understood in the light of economic and sociopolitical processes rather than isolated historical and semimythical events. Still, the reconstruction presented here is, at best, a preliminary and tentative sketch, which raises a host of new questions.

Many of the questions call for further basic research. A large part of our argument hinges on the assumption that Yaxuna (Cetelac) was an integral part of the Coba polity, a matter that is far from certain; the need for stratigraphic excavations and ceramic analysis at that site is all too obvious. Also needed are surveys of the east coast, an area of which we know next to nothing. An even more serious deficiency is the lack of a ceramic sequence at Chichen Itza; such a sequence may hold the key to the Postclassic chronology of the northern Maya lowlands.

Some questions raised here may take years to answer. For example, the nature of the Itza presence on the east coast remains a puzzle: did the Itza establish political control over part of the coast, or was their presence merely a commercial one? Did they control Cozumel? Finally, and more importantly, a study of the causes that led to the fall of Chichen Itza and foiled the Itza attempt to establish a pan–Yucatecan state would be of critical value to our understanding of the Maya Postclassic.

Acknowledgments

While we take full responsibility for the ideas herein expressed, we would like to express our appreciation to the many colleagues and friends whose aid, comments, suggestions, and outrageous disbelief both encouraged and tempered our thinking: Norberto Gonzales, Antonio Benavides, Peter Schmidt, Joseph Ball, Arlen and Diane Chase, E. Wyllys Andrews V, David Freidel, Edward Kurjack, Grant Jones, and Robert Kautz. Many of the ideas presented here were derived from recent research conducted under the auspices of the Centro Regional del Sureste of the Instituto Nacional de Antropologia e Historia. Andrews would also like to acknowledge the support of the National Geographic Society (Grant No. 1555). Finally, we would both like to thank Barbara McClatchie Andrews for editing the text and drafting the illustrations.

The Postclassic That Wasn't: The Thirteenth- through Seventeenth-Century Archaeology of Central Eastern Campeche, Mexico

JOSEPH W. BALL

Archaeological remains of possible Middle Postclassic through Proto-historic date (ca. A.D. 1200–1700) have been identified only rarely in the Rio Bec architectural zone of central eastern Campeche. Monumental architecture assignable to the era apparently does not exist. Lithic implements, almost certainly present had there been any contemporaneous occupation, have yet to be recognized and described convincingly (see Rovner 1975: 224–226). Even ceramic remains, generally so ubiquitous in the Maya lowlands, are so scarce as hardly to justify the establishment of a ceramic complex representing the period for the region (see Ball 1977a: 136). Superficially, the archaeological record is such as to raise the question whether the area supported any resident population at all during the thirteenth through seventeenth centuries, and I have noted previously that the Mayapan-style incense burners occasionally found at the feet of Classic period stelae in the region could as easily owe their presence to deposition by transient "pilgrims" as to importation by local inhabitants otherwise lacking access to pottery vessels (Ball 1977b: 175).

Between 1967 and 1975, archaeological investigations were carried out in central eastern Campeche by several different institutions with the financial support of the National Geographic Society.[1] Final reports detailing the findings of these separate projects now largely have been completed and published or are in press; scrutiny of them reveals the existence of a small and heterogeneous, but definite, corpus of data having to do with settlement in the region during the centuries following the fall of Chichen Itza and other contemporaneous cultural historical events, among which, I suggest, was the virtually total abandonment of the central eastern Campeche Rio Bec zone.

Originally these data appeared so disparate that fruitful discussion of them seemed neither warranted nor possible. I no longer believe this to be so, and here present the relevant data together with a brief attempt to evaluate their significance in light of what is known of contemporary remains and events in neighboring areas.

Ceramic Remains

Most readily identifiable of lowland Maya Postclassic remains are "Mayapan-style" effigy censers or fragments thereof. These are present, but rare, in central eastern Campeche, the only verified occurrences being at the site of El Chorro where they were found on and within the platform of a reset stela (no. 2) by National Geographic Society–Middle American Research Institute personnel during 1969.[2] An intact example of one such incensario allegedly from El Chorro was purchased in the lumber town of San Antonio Soda and currently forms part of a private collection in Merida which I examined during 1974. In stylistic appearance and paste characteristics, it is essentially identical to the fragments from the El Chorro stela platform, and very well could derive from that site or a near neighbor.

Previously, I had classified the El Chorro materials as Chen Mul Modeled (Ball 1977a: 113), but P. Rice (1979) recently has defined a new type/group/ware set from Topoxte, northeastern Peten, to which they are far more clearly and closely related. Thus, the only Middle Postclassic to Protohistoric effigy censers currently known from central eastern Campeche are from El Chorro and can be classified as Idolos Modeled (variety unspecified), a member of the Idolos ceramic group otherwise known from Topoxte and Cante Islands on Lake Yaxha.

Better represented are non-effigy censers of the simple perforated bowl and hollow pedestal base type still widely used in religious ceremonies by the Yucatec Maya of today (personal observations, 1972–1974). The known central eastern Campeche examples most probably are correctly classified as varieties of Thul Applique and/or Cehac Hunacti Composite (R. E. Smith 1971: 23–24, figs. 30g, 31a–31c), thus demonstrating closer affinities to the north and northeast than to the south. In addition to isolated sherds and scatters, complete non-effigy censers were recovered from the bases of Stela 5 at Becan, Stela 1 at Xpuhil III, Stela 6 at Lagunita, and from the floor of a small, presumably reused Late Classic residential structure located about 215 meters north-northeast of Causeway VI at Becan (Thomas 1891: Map 5, Structure 5G–5).

Other isolated ceramic finds, most probably representing post-twelfth-century ceremonial paraphernalia, were a crudely made

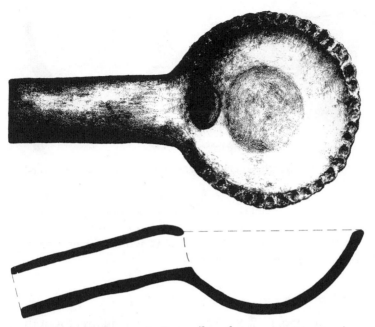

Fig. *1*. Postclassic ladle censer, Becan (length is 23.3 centimeters).

ladle censer (fig. 1; Ball 1977a: 94−97) and a small hourglass censer
(fig. 2; Ball 1977a: 113). Both were recovered at Becan Structure IV,
the ladle censer on the surface at its southwest corner, and the
hourglass-shaped vessel amidst the collapse debris filling Room 2−5
(see Potter 1977: fig. 9). The ladle censer is essentially nondescript
with respect to extraregional affinities, but the hourglass-shaped
piece is highly reminiscent of specimens from along the Quintana
Roo coast at such sites as Xcaret and Xelha.

Contemporary domestic pottery from central eastern Campeche is represented by a single intact vessel found atop the Terminal
Classic/Early Postclassic (Xcocom phase) refuse piled up in Room
4−1 of Becan Structure IV (see Potter 1977: fig. 6). The vessel is a
wide-mouthed, low-necked jar with rounded bottom (Ball 1977a:
10). Extensive fire blackening on both its exterior and interior surfaces presumably reflects its use for cooking. The exterior surface is
unslipped but roughly smoothed; the paste is coarse textured, heavily tempered with calcite, and extremely friable. While I had previ-

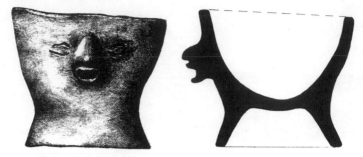

Fig. 2. Postclassic hourglass censer, Becan (height is 9.0 centimeters).

ously left the piece unclassified, I am now inclined to place it in Rice's Pozo Unslipped type as defined from Cante Island. Thus, its area derivation and temporal placement would be comparable to those of the El Chorro effigy censers.

Structural Remains

In April of 1970, R. E. W. Adams, then Field Director of the National Geographic Society–Middle American Research Institute Becan Project, cleared and excavated what were thought to be the foundations of a Classic period nonelite residence. The unit, designated Structure 6F–1 (Thomas 1981: Map 8), is located approximately 35 meters south-southeast of Causeway I, Becan. It lies in an area of low, clayey bajo which throughout much of the rainy season is converted into a watery mire. At the time of its discovery, the structure appeared to be a low limestone rubble platform. Excavation revealed it to be of rectangular plan, measuring approximately 11.5 meters in east-west length by about 3.5 meters in north-south width (fig. 3). The arrangement of the basal row of foundation stones and the distribution of the overlying rubble suggest a building consisting of a single long room and a transversely parallel "porch." The room would have enclosed an area of some 10.8 by 1.8 meters, or about 19.45 square meters of roofed space. Its walls, which had completely collapsed, originally probably comprised two or three courses of dry-laid, limestone blocks surmounted by a superstructure of poles or poles–and–mud, and roofed with palm or grass thatch. Many of the stones forming the basal foundation row were finely cut and smoothed on one or more surfaces. They had, with little question, been removed from more elaborate nearby structures of Late Classic (ca. A.D. 550–800) date. There is a central doorway opening onto the "porch" in the north wall in the room. Judging by the debris, the "porch" also

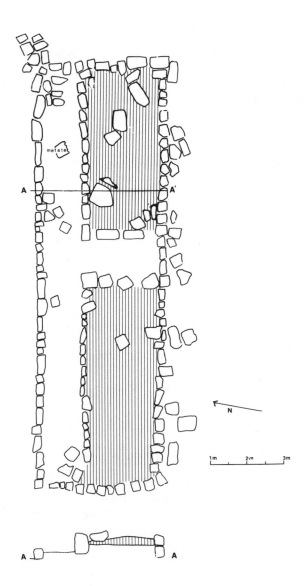

Fig. 3. Plan and section of Structure 6F–1, Becan; parallel lines indicate a deposit of cut and uncut stone and flint nodules.

was walled along its sides and roofed over. It seems, however, to have been left open along its front (north) side. Measuring 10.8 meters by one meter, it represents an additional 10.8 square meters of roofed space. The floors of both "porch" and room were raised above the surface of the ground outside the unit. The floor of the "porch" was about 10 centimeters above adjacent ground level; that of the room was stepped up yet another 20 centimeters above the "porch" floor.

Not a single trace of pottery was encountered during the excavation of Structure 6F–1. Not only were sherds absent from above the floors of both "porch" and room (itself an almost inconceivable situation in the excavation of a lowland Maya residential unit), but even from within and beneath the tamped earth of those surfaces. Ceramically, the locus of this building was genuinely sterile. Importantly, however, it was not otherwise lacking in cultural remains. On the floor of the "porch," just to the left (east) of the doorway, rested a *pila*–type limestone metate. The floors of both "porch" and room were littered with chert cores and flakes, probably representing a domestic assemblage and its associated debitage (Adams, personal communication, 1970). Stoltman (1974) has pointed out the potential role of such unretouched, secondary percussion flakes as cutting implements in the tool inventory of the central eastern Campeche Maya.

The implications of these data seem clear: the building concerned was constructed and inhabited by members of a group which apparently neither made nor used pottery vessels to meet household demands.[3]

Adams noted the ruins of a second, seemingly identical building about five meters to the west of 6F–1 (personal communication, 1970). This unit was neither cleared nor tested. During the course of their 1973 field season, members of the National Geographic Society–University of Tennessee Becan settlement pattern survey project recorded the remains of yet two more structures of similar type. Both had low, dry-laid rubble foundation walls, tamped earth floors, and a dearth of ceramic remains (Thomas 1974, personal communication). Finally, among the household clusters probed by members of the 1973 National Geographic Society–University of Wisconsin Rio Bec ecological survey project was one situated on a hillside about 14 kilometers east of Becan whose morphology closely approximates that of the other presumed Postclassic constructions. Its excavator noted that:

> The building walls are . . . finished on the exterior with carefully cut (but poorly fitted) blocks and veneer slabs . . . taken from some nearby formal building. This is the only house recorded to date that is faced . . . with reused cut stones. . . . Covering the floor was about 30 cm. of surface humus, and under this was a thin layer of gray dirt. The entire room was excavated, but not a single sherd, or other cultural materials, was found. . . . Sub–floor trenching produced a small collec-

tion of potsherds, some of which seem to belong to Chintok ceramic phase. This is a later phase in the Late Classic period (ca. A.D. 730–830). (Eaton 1975: 66, fig. 8)

Albeit primarily on negative evidence, I suggest that all of the foregoing structural units date from the Middle Postclassic/Proto-historic era. Given the abundance of ceramic debris in virtually all other cultural contexts investigated in the Becan area, the complete absence of even incidental sherd inclusions either amidst the sur-face living debris or within the tamped earth floor–fill of any of them, together with their shared structural similarity, suggest roughly con-temporaneous construction, habitation, and abandonment either prior to the Acachen ceramic phase (ca. 600+ B.C.) or following the Xcocom (ca. A.D. 1100). Logically, a pre–Acachen dating is un-likely, while a Classic or Postclassic one tends to be supported by the locations, construction materials, and preservation states of at least Strs. 6F–1 and Eaton's hillside unit, the only two intensively investigated.

Areal excavations carried out during 1973 by several members of the Rio Bec Ecological Project demonstrated that from Early Clas-sic times on through the Terminal Classic, nonelite families in the Becan area enjoyed a comparatively "high" standard of housing (as well as of overall material culture measured artifactually) which in-cluded such features as hard, lime–plaster floors and mortar–set, block masonry walls (see Eaton 1975). A variety of floorplans and building designs were employed, but among these were none resem-bling those of the structures noted above in either aspect. The ram-shackle nature of Structure 6F–1 is particularly striking in terms of its proximity to the major concentration of civil-religious, public, and elite residential private architecture comprising the Becan cen-ter. Clearly perceptible anomalies of location, design, and construc-tion separating the former from the latter all tend to suggest a Post-classic rather than earlier dating for the unit. By extension, the light scattering of other structurally comparable "dateless" units might also best be dated to that time.

Discussion

The overall impression conveyed by the foregoing data is that of an archaeological "grab bag." To see their actual collective signifi-cance, it is necessary to review the archaeological and ethnohis-torical information now available for the regions adjoining central eastern Campeche. In their light, the data do provide some new in-formation about the Postclassic-Protohistoric cultural history of the

southern Yucatan peninsula, albeit of a limited and highly specialized kind.

SOUTH CENTRAL QUINTANA ROO

Harrison (1974, 1979) has described a Postclassic-Protohistoric
cultural complex from an extensive area to the immediate northeast
of the Campeche Rio Bec zone. It is characterized by:

> . . . an architectural style of simple platforms that do not sup-
> port masonry buildings; differential destruction of Classic pe-
> riod buildings as preparation of a core for the platforms; the
> possible association with Mayapan-like censers, but no other
> ceramics; and the virtual absence of Classic period monu-
> ments, which may have been destroyed by the bearers of the
> phase. (Harrison 1974: 8)

Also present are:

> . . . simple house foundations, . . . in both rounded and rec-
> tangular forms standing at ground level. They are constructed
> of loosely piled stones of irregular shape. Occasional "dressed"
> blocks were used to mark corners or door jambs. . . . Occa-
> sional fragments of manos, metates, and chipped chert tools
> were found on the surface in association with these founda-
> tions at several sites. (Harrison 1979: 194–196)

Harrison believes these houses to postdate the other remains
significantly, possibly by as much as from one to three centuries. He
places the primary occupation in the late fifteenth–early sixteenth
centuries on ethnohistoric grounds.

Apart from the simple house foundations, the point of greatest
apparent similarity between the south central Quintana Roo and
central eastern Campeche Postclassic archaeological configurations
would seem to involve the presence in each area of a ceremonial ceramic subcomplex unassociated with virtually any domestic pottery.
In fact, however, the two manifestations differ radically in both composition and distribution.

The Quintana Roo subcomplex comprises Mayapan–style full–
figure effigy censers. With one exception, the Campeche censers are
of noneffigy kinds. The Quintana Roo censers consistently occur in
contexts suggesting their employment in public, "temple–top" ceremonies carried out on the summits of platform structures (Harrison 1974: 5, 1979: 196). Those from Campeche appear in situations
implying private or personal activities generally involving standing
or re-erected Classic period stelae. Finally, incensarios in general ap-

pear to be abundant in the Quintana Roo zone; in eastern Campeche, they are decidedly rare.

The behavioral and ideological disparities which the foregoing suggest appear to be reenforced by the ways in which Classic period monuments were treated in the two zones. Diagnostic of the Quintana Roo Postclassic was the deliberate destructive modification and incorporation or "cannibalization" of Classic structures as cores for platforms (Harrison 1979: 189–194). "The people who destroyed Classic period structures may also have destroyed Classic period monuments," notes Harrison (1974: 8), referring to the dearth of stelae or altars in the area other than as smashed, eroded fragments. In contrast, the Postclassic inhabitants of central eastern Campeche appear not only to have refrained from such activities, but actually, as at El Chorro, to have reset some toppled Classic period stelae.

Further, the distinctive Lobil–style architectural "treatment" (Harrison 1974, 1979) is at least rare, if not absent, in eastern Campeche. Harrison (1979: 203) cites two possible examples of structures modified in the Lobil fashion at Chicanna, Campeche. I am doubtful regarding these, but even if legitimate, they would appear to be very rare exceptions in a region generally characterized by well-preserved, unmolested Classic period architecture.

In sum, the central eastern Campeche and south central Quintana Roo Postclassic configurations reflect presumably contemporary groups which, while superficially similar in their possession of ceremonial pottery subcomplexes unassociated with domestic ceramic assemblages, were fundamentally different in behavioral, cultural, presumably ideological, and even ethnic compositions.

CENTRAL CAMPECHE

All too few remains are known pertaining to the archaeology of the historically important *lagunas* region of central Campeche. In general, however, there is scant evidence to link the Postclassic–Protohistoric inhabitants of the zone to those of contemporary central eastern Campeche. Obvious differences include the presence of a well-developed Postclassic architectural tradition and an apparently heavy distribution of Postclassic structures and centers in the *lagunas* zone (Andrews IV 1943). Also important were full–figure ceramic effigies and effigy censers closely related to the Chen Mul Modeled style but unlike anything known from eastern Campeche. Private collections from the *lagunas* region in Escarcega and Campeche City also indicate the existence of a full Postclassic domestic pottery assemblage.

In short, even the superficial knowledge of central Campeche archaeology now available indicates the existence of radical differences between the Postclassic culture of the area and that of the central eastern zone. Equally major disparities, in my opinion, separate the central Campeche *lagunas* and west central Quintana Roo Postclassic configurations, Harrison's (1979) suggestions to the contrary notwithstanding.

NORTHEASTERN PETEN

Only one other contemporary configuration proximate to central eastern Campeche currently is known archaeologically. Work on Topoxte and Cante Islands, Lake Yaxha by Bullard (1970) and other investigators (P. Rice 1979) has provided a reasonably good picture of Middle Postclassic–Protohistoric material culture in that zone. As elsewhere, well-developed architectural, sculptural, and ceramic traditions belie any substantive cultural identity between the area and central eastern Campeche, but, as noted, evidence does exist to suggest that persons from the Lake Yaxha zone did visit or supply goods to the former region at some time during the period under discussion.

Summary

Reviewing the foregoing, I think it clear that a light, scattered population was present in the central eastern Campeche area during thirteenth century or later times. The upper temporal limits of its presence are difficult to establish, but by the end of the nineteenth century and probably long before, the region was all but totally depopulated (see Maler 1910: 137–162; Ruppert and Denison 1943: 1–3; Scholes and Roys 1968: 68–69; Thompson 1970: 58–72).

The material record of this occupation is meager, but is sufficient to set the population concerned apart as something other than a simple hinterland extension of the more vital expressions of Middle Postclassic–Protohistoric culture neighboring it to the east and west. At the same time, occasional contacts with the Peten Maya of the Lake Yaxha zone do appear to have occurred, but whether these involved a northwards trickle of material goods, persons, or both remains unclear.

In essence, the dry, forested, hilly uplands of central eastern Campeche seem to have formed a largely vacant buffer zone separating and delimiting the territories of central Campeche *lagunas* zone peoples from those of southern Quintana Roo and, to a lesser extent, the northern Peten during and after the thirteenth century A.D.[4] The Middle Postclassic–Protohistoric archaeology of the region is, however, more than merely an exaggerated example of vacant terrain research for the purpose of territorial boundary definition. Beginning in the second half of the sixteenth century and continuing on through the seventeenth, it served as a refuge zone for Yucatec Maya from the northern and western portions of the peninsula fleeing the burdens of tribute, forced labor, and *repartimiento* as well as the religious and administrative control of their Spanish conquerors (Scholes and Roys 1968: especially 305–315 and 336–347).

In the impoverished shreds-and-patches character of the Postclassic central eastern Campeche archaeological record we have an opportunity to examine a phenomenon relatively rare in the Mesoamerican area, the material culture of a certainly identifiable fugitive social group.[5] A comparable, but temporally and historically distinct, episode has been recognized in south central Quintana Roo (Harrison 1979: 204–206), and in combination with further data from these two regions could yield considerable information on the lifeways of relocated refugee populations. Within the context of present-day events, such would seem imminently worthwhile.

Notes

1. The 1969–1971 National Geographic Society–Tulane University program of research in central eastern Campeche, directed by the late E. Wyllys Andrews IV of the Middle American Research Institute at Tulane, was undertaken with financial support from the National Geographic Society and the Ford Foundation. The National Geographic Society also supported subsequent research in the area by the University of Tennessee under the direction of Prentice M. Thomas, Jr. (1972–1973), and by the University of Wisconsin at Madison under the direction of Richard E. W. Adams of the University of Texas, San Antonio. All work was carried out under contract with the Instituto Nacional de Antropologia e Historia de Mexico. This report forms one of the final series of studies on the eastern Campeche Rio Bec program of the Middle American Research Institute and the University of Wisconsin at Madison. I am grateful to Richard E. W. Adams, Prentice M. Thomas, and Jennifer T. Taschek for making available material contained in their unpublished field notes. The accompanying illustrations were prepared by J.T. Taschek.

2. Fragments of several Chen Mul Modeled–style effigy censers were also obtained by project personnel during 1969 from an engineer who had encountered them while directing microwave tower foundation excavations at the archaeological site of Sakik. Not physically identified until late 1978, this now–destroyed site was located in the central Campeche *lagunas* region some 120 kilometers west of Xpuhil, and so does not, in fact, properly pertain to the zone here under discussion.

3. Arlen Chase has pointed out to me that this absence could be a result of functional rather than temporal factors, and the reader should keep this very real possibility in mind. Given the consistent failure of ce-

ramic remains to appear either in association with specific non-Preclassic or Classic contexts or among the general surface/subsurface materials collected by the several eastern Campeche projects, however, I remain inclined to interpret it in the manner presented.

4. A consideration of the various factors possibly responsible for the severe depopulation and continued subsequent avoidance of the zone is beyond the scope of this report. Changing ecological conditions in combination with technological limitations are obvious possibilities, but twelfth-century shifts in commercial patterns, transportation routes, political situations, or other socioeconomic conditions also could have been involved. Further archaeological, as well as ethnohistorical, research will be necessary to resolve this.

5. Several otherwise seemingly anomalous aspects of the post–twelfth-century central eastern Campeche archaeological record quickly acquire clarity and significance in this light. The apparent absence of domestic ceramics among a population presumably aware of and probably derived from others having lengthy traditions of pottery production is one example. Hastily fleeing refugees are unlikely to have burdened themselves with such bulky impedimenta as "easily replaceable" pottery cooking or storage vessels. Once in a new locale, however, ignorance of available resources might have stymied any immediate reemergence of this craft. At the same time, a ready availability of gourds and calabashes could have provided a very viable alternative media from which to produce required utilitarian vessels, as is clear from the material culture of early twentieth-century central eastern Quintana Roo Maya villagers (Villa Rojas 1945: 53–54).

Lamanai Postclassic

H. STANLEY LOTEN

David Pendergast and I began work at Lamanai in 1974. Now, after six seasons, it appears that the site has been more or less continuously occupied from at least as early as the Chicanel phase of the Preclassic right through to the conquest and beyond.[1] In A.D. 1640 the Christianized Maya desecrated the church that had been built in the sixteenth century and allied themselves with the citizens of Tipu, but Lamanai was still not entirely abandoned. Then, around the middle of the nineteenth century a sugar mill was established near the site. This operated until about 1880, when the site was finally completely abandoned as a permanent settlement. Although there were rumors in 1979 that the Belize government planned to locate a new agricultural village in the area, this has not yet come to pass; however, parts of the site of Lamanai have once again been reoccupied by refugees from El Salvador.

The strategic location of the site at the head of the New River lagoon, known in colonial times as the Dzuluinicob, or river of the "Foreign Men," no doubt explains this long continuity of occupation. But the question of when Lamanai reached its peak of population and in what fashion its fortunes shifted over time can only be answered with more reservations than assertions. We are just now completing one phase of investigation and starting another. Our understanding at this point naturally reflects the work that has been done. This tends to suggest that the high point for Lamanai was in the Preclassic and perhaps into the Early Classic periods. The largest structure that we have been able to date so far is from the Chicanel phase of the Preclassic. It is a pyramidal temple 30 meters high with the fully developed substructure form—system typical of Early Classic ceremonial architecture in the Peten, and may have had vaulted building components. It is not only large but architecturally sophisticated. Other structures comparable in size or even larger, as yet un-

Fig. 1. Sketch reconstruction of the front (north) elevation of a Lamanai building evincing architectural ties to the east coast of northern Yucatan.

tested, look very similar on the surface and may date from the same period.

Large scale construction continues through the Classic period and even into the Postclassic though at a much reduced level. But the Postclassic period, with one exception, basically appears as a cessation of monumental construction. The population may not have decreased very much and the ruins of the Classic period ceremonial structures continued to be used but the technical skills, organizational capacity, perhaps the access to resources, and maybe even the perception of a need for large scale monumental construction all have disappeared.

The site, or at least the area that we have defined for investigation, stretches four kilometers along the west shore of the lagoon. It covers six square kilometers and contains 718 structures visible on the surface. The largest structures form a fairly compact central zone outside of which both the scale and density drop off dramatically.

The sixteenth century *visita* church in the southern part of the site provides some historical period Maya artifacts that represent reoccupation after the church was burned in A.D. 1640. This material, which consists of domestic wares and censers, cannot be readily distinguished from Postclassic productions that date several centuries earlier. In other words, the material that we have been able to date stratigraphically to the early conquest period is not very distinctive stylistically. We may well have historic period settlement in other parts of the site but cannot separate it from Postclassic occupation.

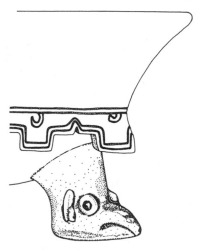

Fig. 2. Pottery effigy support in the form of a bird head (redrafted by A. F. Chase from an original slide).

A mound immediately south of the church had been used as a burial ground during the period in which the church functioned, from about A.D. 1570 to 1640. This mound could represent either a Postclassic Maya structure that had been razed and built over prior to the arrival of the Spaniards, or a structure in use at the time of arrival and demolished in the process of establishing the church. A masonry stair had been built against the debris–mound and dozens of burials, accompanied by very few artifacts, had been intruded into the core masonry. The structure, shattered in this process, was a small square building with a very crude three–element molding that ran around the top of its substructure component (fig. 1). The molding, though even more degenerate than anything at Tulum, clearly relates to architectural forms typical of northern Yucatan and certainly suggests the Postclassic rather than any earlier period.

To date, the most productive source of Lamanai Postclassic material is the southern part of the central zone of monumental construction. Here, right at the lagoon edge, a series of Postclassic residential structures appears to have been built on top of a long abandoned, mounded–over ruin of Classic period or earlier construction. The Postclassic structures are minimal house platforms of simple rectangular shape, only about 30 centimeters high, in one case with vertical slab facings. Large parts of the platforms have been destroyed by intrusive burials accompanied by pottery with both Mayapan and Tulum–related attributes. These include carved red wares with segmental flanges and tripod supports in the form of human and bird

Fig. 3. Pottery deity mask on a large Postclassic vessel.

heads (fig. 2). The period of occupation probably extends from Middle to Late Postclassic.

In the plaza to the west of these structures is a small rectangular platform representing three phases of construction, all Postclassic. Dedicatory to two of these were burials accompanied by large quantities of pottery, the later one in an urn that had been packed in and bedded on smashed Mayapan–related wares. The earlier of the three platforms had well–cut vertical slab facings.

The west side of the same plaza was formed by a much larger mound representing Postclassic construction on top of Classic period or earlier structures that may have been abandoned prior to Postclassic reoccupation. The Postclassic architectural development consists of three identical structures, one on top of the other, each with a single very large room, roughly 20 meters long by 10 meters

Fig. 4. Lamanai Postclassic monumental architectural construction.

wide. The roof structure must have been of timber and was supported on massive timber columns. Walls were thin, of wattle–
and–daub, plastered and painted with polychrome designs. The core
is a very distinctive type of dry–stone boulder construction found
elsewhere at the site only in one Terminal Classic structure. Facings
on the substructure are a mixture of horizontally bedded and vertical
flat slab stones, some merely split boulders. Inside the large room,
against its rear (west) wall was an interior platform around which
corn, beans, and other food crops had been burned in a way suggesting ceremonial rather than residential functioning. Dedicatory to
this structure is a rich burial dated by radiocarbon to the middle of the
twelfth century. Ceramics associated with the burial have Mayapan–
related attributes including elaborate deity masks (fig. 3).

Immediately inland from this structure, on the edge of a higher
plaza, is a large Postclassic midden that seems to consist entirely of
smashed ceramics and the remains of marine organisms and other
foodstuffs. The ceramic artifacts include ladle censers with croco-
dilian features. The midden seems to be a ceremonial rather than
residential one. It fills the southeast corner of the plaza and laps up
against the base of a large pyramidal temple that had been built in
the Early Classic period, modified frontally in the Late Classic and
again in the Postclassic. This is our one example of Postclassic monumental construction (fig. 4). Although only a frontal addition it is
still a large undertaking and in technical attributes is entirely Classic although the core contains Postclassic ceramics. At the time that

it was built the older Classic period structure had already started to collapse.

Farther north in the site evidence of Postclassic activity comes from scattered censer fragments in and on top of the debris of Classic period structures. Of four major Classic period temples two produced this kind of evidence. One of these produced fragments from perhaps 50 Mayapan–style anthropomorphic censers, all incomplete.

To summarize, a Peten orientation can be seen in both architecture and ceramics of Lamanai during the Preclassic and Early Classic periods. This becomes much weaker in the Late Classic, as the Peten area reaches a cultural peak, and disappears entirely in the Postclassic when affiliations, as seen in artifact styles, are with northern Yucatan. Attributes typical of Mayapan pottery appear at an earlier date in the sequence at Lamanai, indicating either a cultural flow from south to north or an expanded time depth for this material. We have evidence for both continuity and discontinuity between the Classic and Postclassic at Lamanai. This may mean nothing more than that different parts of the site were in use at different times. The size of the Postclassic settlement still remains to be investigated. In the start that we made during the 1979 season, testing in small structures outside the site center, we have already encountered Postclassic occupation. As this program continues we will surely find more and hope to be able to establish a complete Postclassic chronology.

Note

1. The text of this paper is essentially the same as that delivered at the American Anthropological Association meetings in Cincinnati in 1979.

Lamanai, Belize: An Updated View

DAVID M. PENDERGAST

One of the expectable results of long–term intensive investigation of a single site is that the understanding of events in the community's history will change, often significantly, from year to year. This sort of change is exemplified by the contrast between our knowledge of ancient Lamanai as presented by Stanley Loten after six seasons of excavation, and the knowledge we possess now, after completion of ten seasons of fieldwork. Because the picture of the Postclassic given in 1979 lacked several critical pieces that have been supplied by subsequent excavations, an update of that presentation seems desirable if readers are to be able to assess the full significance of Lamanai data to reconstructions of lowland Maya life from the tenth through the seventeenth century.

Among the facets of Lamanai's history about which little could be said in 1979, perhaps the most important, both to our view of internal dynamics at Lamanai and to our perception of the broad lowlands patterns of Postclassic development, is the transition from Classic to Postclassic. While Loten quite correctly alluded to the sense of both continuity and discontinuity that suffused the Lamanai data as of 1979, excavations of the past three years have strengthened the evidence for continuity to such an extent that the distinction between Classic and Postclassic has become as difficult to make on typological grounds as it is to fix temporally. It is now clear that the period traditionally seen as a time of decay and collapse was marked at Lamanai by construction and other activity on a scale at least equal to that in preceding centuries. During the period, which encompassed roughly the mid–ninth to early twelfth centuries, we can see what in fact we should expect in any functioning society: the maintenance of traditions alongside innovations, the sort of blending of old and new that is essential to orderly development.

Concentration in 1981 and 1982 on an assemblage of elite resi-

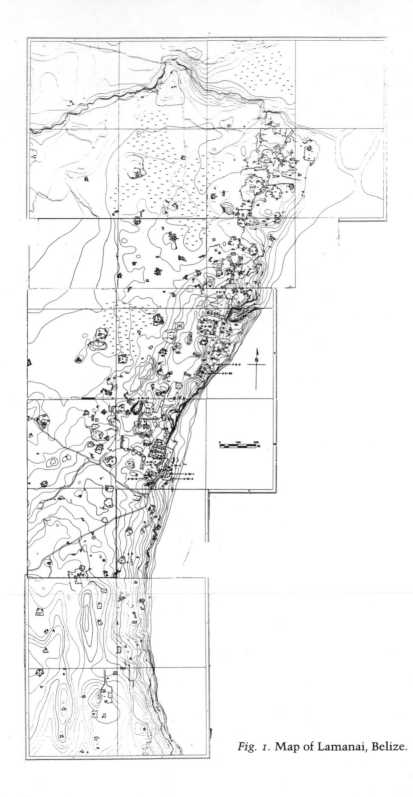

Fig. 1. Map of Lamanai, Belize.

dential structures (Plaza N10/3) north of the plaza bordered by Structures N10−7 and N10−9 (fig. 1), combined with examination of small−structure groups elsewhere in the southern portion of the site center, has given us a reasonably clear picture of domestic life in the transition years. This was a time in which, as Loten notes, the traditions of Classic ceremonial architecture were largely giving way to forms and techniques foreign to earlier centuries. In contrast, domestic architecture of the period is in most respects a continuation of earlier traditions, although with innovations both in form and in facade treatment that are of significance to our perspective on Postclassic building in general.

In its mid−ninth-century form, the elite residential group consisted of at least six structures, two of which appear to have rested directly on the surface of a large underlying platform, while the remainder were raised on two−terrace platforms. The three structures that formed the western end of the group had the distinction of sitting atop an unusual triple joined platform, a feature that prefigures Postclassic construction in northern Yucatan, but not at Lamanai as far as we are now able to determine.

An additional anticipation of Postclassic construction, both at Lamanai and elsewhere, may be present in the form of a partly colonnaded structure at the northwest side of the group, built during an extensive alteration of the assemblage in the late ninth or early tenth century. It is obviously impossible to characterize either the joined platform or the colonnade in terms of functional relationship to similar features found at other sites, especially as colonnaded buildings are known to occur in the Classic in northern Yucatan as well (Roys and Shook 1966: 5−11). The Lamanai features stand, rather, as part of the pattern of overlap and innovation that was clearly one of the community's strengths from Late Classic times onward.

At the northeast side of the assemblage is Structure N10−28, probably the last major addition to the group, constructed about A.D. 925−950. Plan and exterior surface features suggest that the structure did not serve as a dwelling, but rather may have functioned as a semipublic element in the group, perhaps with a combination of secular and ceremonial use. The structure originally boasted a highly elaborate upper zone, decorated with modeled stucco with very rich polychrome painting. Portions of the front panel of the upper zone stucco were recovered in 1981 from beneath core for later construction that concealed the partly demolished structure; these indicated that the decoration had included larger than life−size human and/or deity figures, set amidst panels of latticework and curvilinear motifs.

In 1982 we encountered most of the panel from the building's west side, dumped between the structure platform and the building immediately to the west. Conditions of recovery permitted reconstruction of significant portions of the panel, including a large center cartouche that contains a seated human figure. The excellent preservation of painted surfaces has enabled us to discern an extremely wide range of colors, among which are deep red, lighter red, pink, deep green, medium green, light green, light and dark yellow–green, yellow, dark blue, medium blue, light blue, blue–green, and black. Some, but not all, surfaces are highlighted with specular hematite, and a number of areas exhibit changes in modeling and in color in one or more additions. Although full reconstruction of the panels is not likely to prove possible, the material even in fragmented state constitutes a major contribution to our understanding of iconography and color symbolism in Terminal Classic and Early Postclassic Maya society.

In addition to its iconographic content, the general form and many of the individual motifs of the upper zone decoration permit the linking of this facade sculpture to examples from the Terminal Classic at Altun Ha (Structure E–7, 1st; Pendergast, n.d.b) and Seibal (J. Sabloff, personal communication, 1982). The appearance of such decoration in the early tenth century at several lowlands sites suggests an attempt at a strong visual restatement of religious precepts, perhaps in the hope of recapturing some of the vitality that had been lost in the preceding century or two. Though the contexts at Lamanai and Altun Ha differ in some respects, they both suggest a shifting of focus away from major temples as media for the expression of religious values, perhaps as part of the abandonment of large– structure modification in the northern and central parts of Lamanai's Central Precinct. In any event, the hopes bound up in the elaborate tenth-century stuccoed facades came to nought at other lowlands sites, while at Lamanai this new sort of public, or semipublic, iconography can be seen as part of a successful bridging of the transition period from which the community emerged with its strengths largely intact.

Perhaps almost contemporaneously with the erection of the stucco decorated structure came construction of the lone ballcourt at Lamanai, in a plaza north of the residential complex (fig. 1). Whereas the stucco facade seems a combination of introverted and extroverted approaches to the visual affirmation of faith, the ballcourt cannot have failed to be a fully public ceremonial statement, albeit in a setting that may already have been characterized by buildings in various states of neglect or decay. Together with the scale and nature of the construction, the presence of mercury, possibly from a Honduran source, in an offering beneath the center marker disc (Pendergast 1982b: 533, fig. 2) bespeaks the importance of the undertaking in the ceremonial life of Lamanai, just as it documents a trade link between the site and the Maya highlands.

Offerings in the elite residential complex, as well as midden dumped around a highly complicated dwelling (Structure N10–15) immediately west of the stucco decorated structure, add materially to the picture of persistence of Terminal Classic ceramic forms and surface treaments well into the Postclassic. This pattern is duplicated in small–structure groups both in the southern and in the northern suburbs, where we can see Terminal Classic vessel shapes in Classic wares, alongside San Jose V shape and surface treatment classes (fig. 2a–2g), accompanied by entirely new forms. Outstanding among the introductions that were joined with typical San Jose forms are remarkably tall blackware cylinders (fig. 3a and 3b) which, like some other ceramics of the period, seem to have had very short use spans. The ceramic data reduce the utility of some San Jose V vessel types as restricted time markers, but at the same time they tell us a great deal about the interplay of continuity and change in tenth- and eleventh-century pottery making.

In addition to data on the longevity of some ceramic techniques in the transition centuries, Structure N10–15 has yielded an almost unmanageably large body of information on a dwelling of the ninth to eleventh centuries that saw a greater number of modifications than any we have previously examined. While many of the alterations and additions to the building took standard forms, later changes were very frequently a matter of demolition followed by reconstruction of a bench, doorway closure, or other feature that duplicated what had just been destroyed. The data seem a persuasive argument for modifications dictated by ceremonial considerations rather than by practical necessity; this is something one can assume for earlier times as well, but its seeming intensification in the transition years might be seen as part of the increasing internalization of ceremonial practice suggested by other evidence.

Following the last modifications to the various structures in the elite assemblage, the entire two–level courtyard on which the buildings fronted was filled as part of an undertaking that transformed the multifaceted group into a single huge platform, atop which sat only a few single–terrace platforms that appear to have supported perishable structures. The courtyard filling, apparently begun in the late tenth century and carried on over as much as two hundred years thereafter, seems to have been part of a major reshaping of a large area that extended from the residential group northward to the south

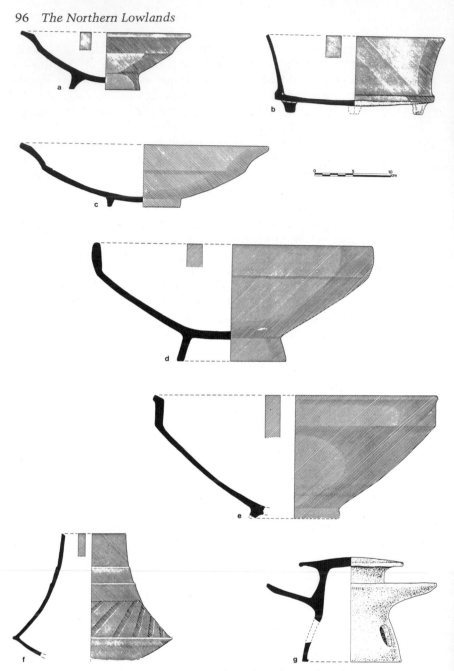

Fig. 2. Terminal Classic vessels from burial, cache, and surface contexts in the northern suburbs and southern site center. Vessels a–e are typical San Jose V forms; f is a variant of the San Jose V "bottle"; and g is a specialized "fire platform" from an offering in courtyard fill of Plaza N10/3.

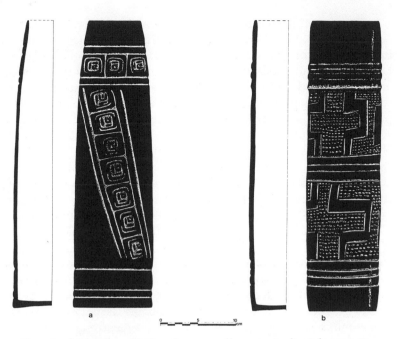

Fig. 3. Terminal Classic cylinders from small-structure burials near Structure N10–9 (a) and in the northern suburbs (b).

side of the plaza that contained the ballcourt. If all of the complex platforms in this area are in fact contemporaneous, as their forms and construction suggest, this tenth- to twelfth-century transformation of the southern site center embodied approximately 21,000 metric tons of core stone. This was clearly the work of a fully functioning community, and it probably exceeded the scale of any individual large construction effort of earlier times at the site.

By the twelfth century, the elite residential assemblage had been completely altered, but still served as the dwelling place for families whose rank in the Lamanai community we cannot judge at present. The occupants of houses here probably contributed to the large midden mentioned by Loten, which closed off the east side of the plaza south of the residential complex (fig. 1) and engulfed part of the base of Structure N10–9. The huge quantities of pottery from the midden appear to be of twelfth century and later date, but close checking of vessel fragment distribution in the meter–deep mass has shown that, as one should expect in a refuse accumulation, there is no stratigraphic basis for separating portions of the deposit, nor is there any solid evidence on the time depth represented.

The presence of the midden certainly indicates diminution of ceremonial activity related to N10–9, although the last major frontal modification of the structure occurred in the twelfth century or later, and minor construction at the base of the building's center stair continued until perhaps as late as the fifteenth or early sixteenth century. By or before the twelfth century, the principal focus of ceremonial activity in the site center had shifted to the area described by Loten (Structures N10–1, B10–2, and B10–4; see fig. 1), where it was apparently to remain until late in the Postclassic. At the same time, ceremonial and residential construction, as well as a range of non-construction activities, continued in various parts of the Central Precinct where abandonment of major buildings had taken place in Terminal Classic or Early Postclassic times.

By the mid– to late fifteenth century, the center of domestic life at the south end of the Central Precinct seems to have been the lagoon littoral, south of the abovementioned ceremonial structures. The margin of the lagoon is marked by an extensive midden as much as 50 centimeters deep, accompanied by burials that appear randomly placed at present, but were probably associated with small, perishable residences. The presence of unquestionably nonresidential construction beneath the midden documents a change in use of the lagoon edge from Classic to Postclassic; similar changes are in evidence in portions of the site center to the north and west, where domestic use of formerly ceremonial areas was revealed in 1983 excavations. In the absence of Middle and Late Postclassic residential data from the western suburbs of the site, we cannot judge whether the shore area and neighboring material represents concentration of the bulk of Lamanai's population along the lagoon in the southern site center during the Late Postclassic; however, evidence recovered in 1983 suggests a strong lagoon–side focus for both domestic and ceremonial Postclassic life throughout the southern portion of the site.

By the time of establishment of the littoral residential area in the southern site center, all modification of N10–9 may have ceased. Yet in the vicinity of the N10–9 plaza, and within the plaza itself, ceremonial construction of a moderately ambitious nature was under way. At the plaza center, a large, low platform was constructed, perhaps to support a perishable structure; near its south end stood a small platform, its facings of masonry typical of the period, with a core deposit of fragments of a very large number of Mayapan–related figurines and censers. Accompanying this construction was a pair of stela platforms, just west of the old elite residential complex. The two platforms duplicated the masonry style of the plaza area struc-

ture, and the core of one likewise yielded large quantities of Mayapan–related ceramics, as well as a portion of a near life–size stone
mask of which a second fragment was recovered from the small
plaza structure.

Each of the two platforms supported an uncarved stela, but it is
not clear whether the monuments were produced as part of the construction process or were relocated, as were several Classic monuments (Pendergast 1981a: 51). The platforms are clearly part of the
continuing Postclassic focus on the south end of the site center.
Though unimposing, they document the interest of the fifteenth-
century Lamanai inhabitants in maintaining the traditions of earlier
times, and the ability of the community to marshal the labor force
necessary to translate that interest into concrete form.

While the southern portion of the site was the primary focus of
activity in the Postclassic, other parts of the site saw intermittent
ceremonial activity, some of which has previously been described
(Pendergast 1981a: 51). Construction at the base of Structure N9–56
(see fig. 1) is characteristic of the Late Postclassic, and vessels recovered from core of the main platform in the group (fig. 4b–4i) confirm the dating. Viewed against the background of events at the
south end of the site center, the northern construction can perhaps
be seen as a small scale attempt to revive former foci of ceremonial
activity outside of the main Postclassic zone. The attempt was considerably above the level of pilgrimages to abandoned centers, such
as may have occurred at Altun Ha just before this period (Pendergast
1982a: 140), though the ruined state of buildings like N9–56 must
have given the effort some of the appearance of just such a journey.

In the northern suburbs of the site, excavations in 1980 and
1981 revealed late Postclassic construction of residences and related
structures, over and around buildings of Preclassic and Classic date,
just beyond the northern limit of the Central Precinct. Work farther
north in 1981 showed abandonment of a residential complex not
later than the end of the eleventh century, with no subsequent construction or reuse of any structure. This may indicate general abandonment of the northern suburbs early in the Postclassic, with reoccupation centuries later only in limited areas nearest the site center.
The data now in hand do not permit judgment as to whether the
northern settlement was functionally separate from the southern
one, but ceramics from the structures (fig. 5c) make it clear that inhabitants of the north were not entirely cut off from the ceremonial
practices of their southern confreres.

South of the Central Precinct, in the area of the sixteenth- and
seventeenth-century Spanish-dominated community (see fig. 1), re-

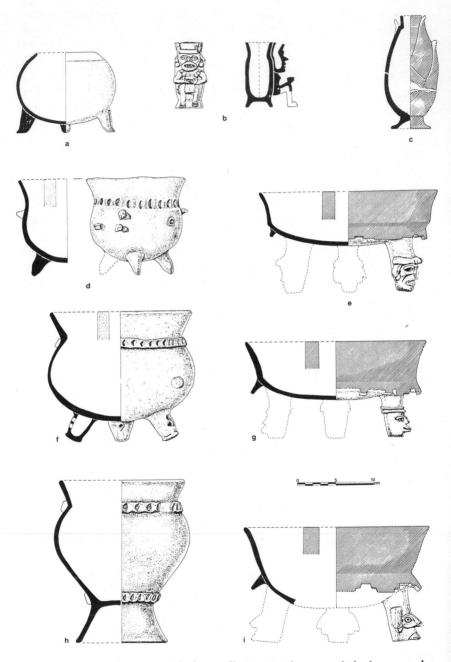

Fig. 4. Late Postclassic vessels from offerings in the core of platforms at the base of Structure N9–56.

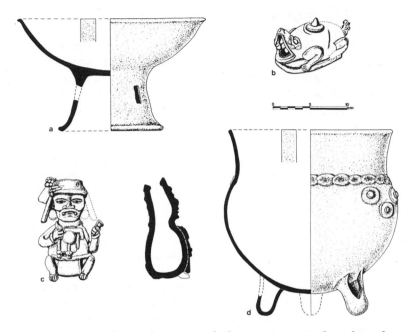

Fig. 5. Late/Terminal Postclassic vessels from an intrusive burial in a late Plaza N10/3 structure (a), an offering in a northern suburb residence (c), and post-A.D. 1641 vessels from a substela cache (b) and deposit through the chancel floor (d) at the church.

cent investigations have expanded our understanding of events at the close of the Postclassic and in the first century of the historic period. Excavations in 1982 and 1983 have revealed the existence of two Spanish churches, the earlier of which closely resembles that at Negroman-Tipu, in the western Cayo District of Belize. Archival evidence indicates that the earlier church is likely to date from A.D. 1568 (G. Jones, personal communication, 1983); the later, much more impressive structure may therefore have been built near the end of the sixteenth century. Within the platform of the first church are the remains of a Tulum-style structure that was demolished in preparation for construction of the Christian edifice; plaster from a similar structure, found in a great spread west of the sanctuary of the later church, indicates that at least two ceremonial structures stood on the site of the Christian churches, and presumably served as an important focus of Late Postclassic activity south of the Classic site center.

The church area has also yielded an impressive number of historic period offerings, as well as at least one burial and one small shrine that must, from their contexts, postdate abandonment of the later church in 1641. The materials document continuing ceremonial activity in the ruins of the church, related to residential use of the building that followed its desecration. Loten has referred to the apparent impossibility of distinguishing ceramics of this period from those of immediately preceding centuries, and reconstruction in 1982 of a vessel recovered earlier from a deposit cut through the church floor (fig. 5d) underscores the prehistoric–historic continuities in pottery manufacture. No terminal date can be assigned to the domestic use of the church, but it is very likely that occupation and ceremonial activity extended to at least the end of the seventeenth century.

Investigation of the structure at the north side of the later church has substantiated the Middle Postclassic or later date expectable on grounds of proximity to the aforementioned Tulum–style structures; unfortunately, the ministrations of Dr. Gann to the building left us with no clear evidence regarding use of the platform, though midden at the structure's perimeter certainly documents domestic use in Late Postclassic and/or early historic times. Here and elsewhere in the church area we have recovered considerable numbers of sixteenth- or seventeenth-century Spanish jar sherds, as well as one fragment of a shallow bowl or dish. Maya-Spanish contact is otherwise not in evidence in the archaeological record save for a single European glass bead, probably of early historic date, recovered by a local settler during posthole digging in a platform that we have not been able to investigate. Burials from the earlier church, which now number more than 110, have thus far yielded very little cultural material, none of which could be securely identified as historic were it not for the context. The principle that applies here is the same as that recognizable in the case of ceramics from the later church: separation of late prehistoric and historic materials may prove impossible except in those cases in which context resolves the problem.

As I said at the outset, it is to be expected that continuing excavation will broaden one's perspective on a site's history. I have summarized here only the principal areas of knowledge of the Postclassic in which such broadening has occurred since Loten's presentation. While an increase in breadth does not necessarily foster an increase in understanding, it seems to me that discoveries since 1979 have gone a long way toward turning isolated collections of data into something that approaches a coherent picture of the Postclassic at Lamanai. From that picture we can begin to draw inferences regarding the lowlands Postclassic as a whole. One such inference may be that we should begin to view events at Lamanai as one of the several alternative courses followed by the Maya in Post-classic times, rather than as a marked aberration in the otherwise standard progression from the heights of the Classic to the depths of collapse. The experiences of the past few seasons at Lamanai should, however, teach caution in the drawing of inferences, whether within or beyond the site. We can expect that the changes in our understanding of the community's history that have occurred as a result of recent seasons' work will be paralleled by equally significant alterations of our wisdom as the excavation program enters its final stage, and that the picture of Lamanai life we are ultimately able to present will differ in many particulars from that outlined here.

Ganned But Not Forgotten: Late Postclassic Archaeology and Ritual at Santa Rita Corozal, Belize

DIANE Z. CHASE

Investigations at the site of Santa Rita Corozal were undertaken in order to garner a body of data concerning Late Postclassic period occupation. It was hoped that the material gathered by the Corozal Postclassic Project would provide information which could be compared with previously excavated and collected information concerning the Late Postclassic period in the Maya lowlands. The envisioned goal was to develop a data base from which temporal and spatial variation during the period, as well as possible reasons for this variation, could eventually be established. The site of Santa Rita was selected for excavation because of its known Late Postclassic remains (Gann 1900, 1918; Green 1973; Pring 1973; Hammond 1973; D. Rice 1974; Sidrys 1976, 1983) and the possibility that it functioned as the regional capital of Chetumal at the time of the conquest (Thompson 1972: 6; D. Chase 1981, 1982a).

The site map key (fig. 1) provides an indication of the extent of the site of Santa Rita; the shaded areas represent those portions of the site which have thus far been mapped. There appears to have been continuous occupation between mapped portions of the site; the area intervening between the north part of the site and the southwest portion of the site will be fully mapped once the Belizean government comes into possession of the land. There is evidence of Postclassic occupation, either from our own work at the site or from that of Thomas Gann, from all the known sectors of Santa Rita.

While the research thus far at Santa Rita has been oriented toward Postclassic occupation of the site, extensive earlier and some later remains have also been encountered. These include deposits and constructions dating from the Early Preclassic (Swasey equivalent) to the historic period. These are being analyzed by Arlen F. Chase and myself but will not be focused on in this essay. All these earlier remains are of interest, however, for their own value and as

comparative material to other nearby northern Belize sites such as
Cerros (Freidel 1978, 1979), Cuello (Hammond various), Colha (Hester 1979; Hester, Eaton, and Shafer 1980), Nohmul (Hammond 1973,
1974, 1975, 1977; D. Chase 1982a, 1982b; D. Chase and A. Chase
1982), Altun Ha (Pendergast various), and Lamanai (Pendergast various); they also provide data pertinent to more generalized lowland
Maya traditions and horizons.

Archaeological Research at Santa Rita

Santa Rita is located immediately to the north of modern Corozal Town in northern Belize. The site, first noted by Gann in 1894,
manifests a long history of occupation but is most conspicuous for
its Late Postclassic remains. In 1894, the site had already been partially destroyed to provide building material for nearby Corozal;
however, thirty-two of the original mounds were noted as surviving
intact. Gann (1900, 1918) roughly mapped the area of the site and

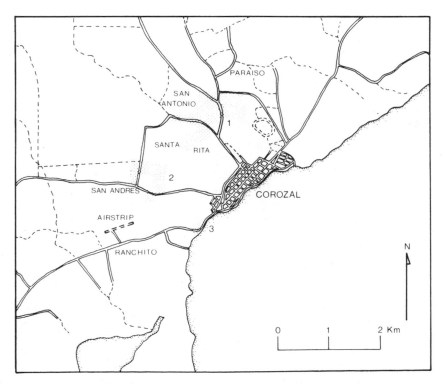

Fig. 1. Map key for Santa Rita Corozal.

subsequently excavated the majority of the structures he noted. His major contributions (1900: 662–663) to the archaeology of Santa Rita were his establishment of the site as Late Postclassic in date and his typology of mounds for Santa Rita: mounds constructed over buildings; mounds with a superficial deposit of pottery images and a deeper deposit of pottery vessels or a pottery urn; and mounds which could not be categorized or whose use was either unknown or doubtful. Although naive by modern standards, this represented the first attempt at functionally distinguishing Maya structures in northern Belize. Later excavations were carried out at the site by Green (1973), Pring (1973: 62–67; Hammond 1974: 24), and Sidrys (1976: 332–344; 1983: 124–159).

1979 SEASON

The 1979 Santa Rita reconnaissance and mapping program indicated that the site is much larger in both the number and the extent of mounds than had been previously realized, even given the great

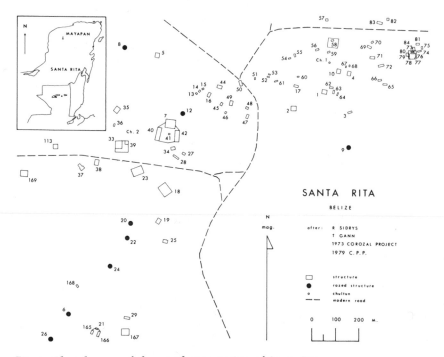

Fig. 2. Sketch map of the northern portion of Santa Rita.

amount of destruction at the site (see fig. 2 for a partial site map). Many of these mounds, however, are either low in height or outside the traditional site center. Occupation at Santa Rita also appears to blend geographically into that of the site of Aventura to the south, which is known to have large deposits of Terminal Classic pottery (Ball 1983; Sidrys 1976, 1983). It is probable that there was a shifting of occupation between Santa Rita and Aventura over time and that a clear understanding of population dynamics within the area (particularly during the Terminal Classic–Early Postclassic) will depend upon more information from both sites as well as from the area of lower mound density between the two sites.

All excavations undertaken in 1979 produced Postclassic remains; many produced evidence of earlier occupation as well. Investigation of Structure 7, which at 13 meters is the tallest remaining mound at Santa Rita, included trenching along with horizontal excavation. The recovered evidence of Postclassic activity consisted of an intensive censer deposit on the lower front stair. This deposit did not include other vessels generally found in Postclassic occupational refuse and may suggest the existence of a pilgrimage pattern of placement for some incensarios (see also Ball 1977: 175). Although the latest use of Structure 7 was during the Postclassic period, the latest building construction appears to have been considerably earlier, probably during the Middle Classic period.

Structure 58 excavations revealed a long low platform or terrace with outlines of a small structure above it. An almost identical construction has been illustrated for Dzibilchaltun (Andrews IV 1965: fig. 2) during the Late Postclassic period (Kurjack and Garza T. 1981: 292, fig. 11.2). The Postclassic Structure 58 and Platform 1 overlay earlier constructions. Late Postclassic deposits encountered during excavation included a modeled ceramic figure placed between an unslipped olla and a red-slipped tripod bowl (fig. 3). The modeled figure is a composite one. The head of a bearded man protrudes from the head of a horned jaguar, or possibly a bee. The body of the figure resembles a snail shell. The piece was originally stuccoed and elaborately painted, but only traces of color remain. Stoppered inside the vessel were two small flat pieces of turquoise and one jadeite bead. The cache was located on an axis to the platform in front of the small structure, just below the eroded floor level.

Postclassic burials were also uncovered in the excavation. These had been intruded through an earlier plaster floor. While many of these interments were devoid of associated objects, one woman was found to have been buried with a jadeite and *Spondylus* necklace as well as two copper rings. An irregular arrangement of stones located

Fig. 3. Modeled ceramic figure from the Structure 58 cache at Santa Rita, 10.7 centimeters high.

above the interment may represent an altar constructed above it. Another Postclassic burial of a decomposed individual also included a single copper bell. Although there was much Late Postclassic artifactual material on the surface of the platform, no primary refuse deposit was found in association with this complex. Historic occupation was located to the south of Structure 58 and what appeared to be a nineteenth-century privy was excavated within the platform itself; this neatly cut through the legs of two individuals occupying an earlier Late Postclassic grave.

Excavations in Structure 69 revealed a small, poorly preserved construction with a complex history of occupation. Artifacts and stratigraphy date the use of this area from Early Classic times well into the nineteenth century. The nearby Structure 70, even lower than Structure 69, was better preserved. Although no special deposits were found in association with Structure 70, artifactual remains and stratigraphy suggest that its construction and use took place only during the Late Postclassic period.

An areal excavation was undertaken of Structure 74, a low foundation marked only by lines of stone on the surface (fig. 4). This Late Postclassic structure had a double line–of–stone back wall and well-preserved interior plaster floors. Associated with it were interesting combinations of artifacts, including redware ceramics, ceramic beads, and lithics, but no burials or caches.

South of Structure 74 is the large low Postclassic Platform 2. It measures roughly 47 meters by 40 meters, is approximately one

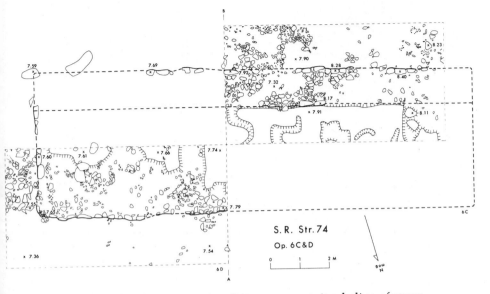

Fig. 4. Detailed plan of Santa Rita Structure 74, a simple line of stone construction with a double line of stone back wall.

meter high, and supports Structures 73 and 76 to 80. Excavations along the platform edges encountered extensive refuse deposits. In addition to the usual Late Postclassic pottery and lithics, these investigations produced faunal remains, ceramic beads, and a few pieces of green obsidian. The refuse deposit on the south side of Platform 2 also provided numerous examples of a modeled ceramic type called Cohokum Modeled. This unslipped ware resembles the better-known Chen Mul Modeled (Kol Modeled at Santa Rita) censerware in certain rim modes but can be easily distinguished from it; thus far, no Cohokum Modeled pieces have been found which show signs of burning. Cohokum Modeled also has a very limited distribution at Santa Rita; at present, it is known to occur only in the vicinity of Platform 2. An alignment of three stones, probably originally representing a low altar, was found near the southern extent of the platform; a multiple subadult interment was discovered immediately below this configuration and extending west of it. With the human bone were faunal remains and broken ceramics; the reconstructed vessels included a small unslipped tripod plate, unslipped cups with modeled faces (fig. 5), and a modeled foot–shaped cup. Further excavations were undertaken at this locus in 1980.

Fig. 5. Tlaloc "face cup" from Santa Rita, 7 centimeters high.

Structure 36, another small structure, had a relatively well–defined frontal terrace. Although there was relatively little Post-classic overlay, the construction proved to be entirely Late Postclassic in date with the discovery of a core cache of two modeled Postclassic vessels. The larger anthropomorphic vessel had the smaller one placed inside its mouth. While the outer vessel may represent an earth monster, the inner vessel was similar to the one encountered in Structure 58 and nearly identical to one found in Structure 81 in 1980.

Excavation of Structure 35 revealed a low, relatively large construction with a small structure on the western side. A sizeable Postclassic overlay was found on the surface of the platform, but the deposits within its core all dated to Terminal Classic times or earlier.

1980 SEASON

During the 1980 field season, the Corozal Postclassic Project resumed work on the transit map of the site and on the excavation of both known Postclassic structures and untested portions of the site.

Excavations were continued in the northeast sector of Santa Rita on Platform 2 and the overlying Structures 73 and 76 to 80. The trench through the north-south axis of the platform revealed buried Postclassic constructions and two Postclassic burials. Areal excavation at the southern extent of the platform was initiated in order to sample more of the unusual ceramic deposit located there in 1979 and to determine whether this deposit was distributed in spatially different patterns along the Platform 2 rear facing. This extensive deposit, which continued primarily to the east along the south platform wall, consisted of areas containing clusters of vessels, which possibly resulted from discrete activities. Nine face cups, resembling those located within the construction core of the platform during 1979 (see fig. 5 for one example of these cups; for similar examples recovered outside of Santa Rita see R.E. Smith 1971: figs.

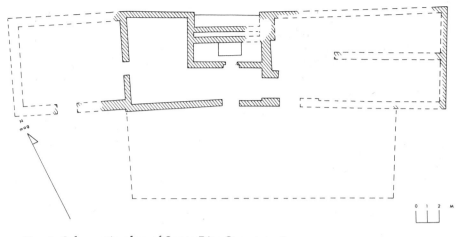

Fig. 6. Schematic plan of Santa Rita Structure 81.

31hh and 63), were recovered from within the deposit. Also in this deposit were faunal remains and a piece of sheet copper.

In addition to the refuse, seven distinct Late Postclassic interments were found south of Platform 2. All were flexed; the majority contained at least one object. Of these interments, two are of particular interest because of their associated artifacts. Both individuals were female. One had a copper ring on both hands. The other was buried with a quantity of ceramics, both red-slipped tinajas (water jars) and modeled redware pottery vessels. Most of the pottery had been smashed prior to deposition. One smaller tinaja had a kill hole in its base, a typical pattern in many Classic period burial vessels at Santa Rita.

Excavation in the looted Structure 77 provided a series of sealed Postclassic construction levels with associated artifacts. Pottery encountered in the deeply stratified deposits in this excavation has allowed faceting of the Late Postclassic ceramics at the site (D. Chase 1982a, 1984). Two interments were located west of the building below the level of the most recent platform floor. Ceramic beads, a stone turtle with traces of polychrome paint, and a large smashed red-slipped jar with an applied effigy head were located in the collapse of the latest construction. An alignment of three stones, possibly representing an altar, was also found west of Structure 77; a small headless pottery bird vessel was located beneath this feature near its presumed corner. Areal investigations were also made into other Late Postclassic structures on the summit of the platform, but

Fig. 7. Structure 81 Cao Modeled cache figure (15.2 centimeters in length).

they did not prove to have deposits associated with the terminal use of the platform surface.

One primary focus for excavation in 1980 was Structure 81 (fig. 6). This Late Postclassic building, located in the northeast part of Santa Rita, measured approximately 60 meters by 18 meters and proved to be the most elaborate Postclassic structure encountered in this portion of the site. Areal work revealed a multiroomed construction with a series of frontal doorways, an inner shrine, and many vessels smashed on the interior floor of the building. An axial trench encountered two caches and a burial. The latest cache consisted of two lip-to-lip unslipped vessels with a modeled and painted vessel between them. The inner vessel portrayed a bearded man with a horned jaguar head which protruded from a snail shell (fig. 7). The postfire paint was still intact on most of the piece, the colors being blue, white, black, and red. Within it were a number of smaller items: *Spondylus* beads, jadeite, and one thin piece of *tumbaga*. The earlier cache, located below the back wall of the shrine, consisted of a single black-slipped, double–spouted bird effigy vessel of nonlocal, possibly Peruvian, origin. An elaborate burial was found intruded into bedrock beneath the shrine–room altar; it contained the partially articulated remains of two adults enmeshed in broken ceramic vessels. Some of these vessels had apparently been smashed within the structure and had only been partially redeposited within the interment.

Earlier statements by Gann (1918) and Sidrys (1976) had noted that much of the coastal portion of Santa Rita had been encroached upon by the sea. A limited excavation in Structure 200, which had been largely washed away by waves from Corozal Bay, encountered human skeletal material. The recovered Postclassic deposit consisted of two skulls placed side by side and located directly above a flexed burial.

Ritual Indicators and Santa Rita

Determining the function of archaeological deposits has always posed somewhat of a problem. In the Maya area of Mesoamerica there appears to be a general agreement that the presence of particular types of material culture remains is indicative of ritual and/or ceremonial activity. These include special structure types, various types of altars, nonresidential or nondomestic pottery such as censers, and special deposits such as caches. During the Late Postclassic period, there are ritual associations between other artifact types (Proskouriakoff 1962b: 331–335) and architectural configurations (Proskouriakoff 1962a: 89–91). Most of these ritual indicators can be found at Santa Rita. We may ask, therefore, what the presence and/or distribution of these indicators suggests about ritual activity at Santa Rita during the Late Postclassic period.

ARCHITECTURE

Proskouriakoff (1962a) has dealt most extensively with defining Postclassic ritual buildings and assemblages. For Mayapan, she was able specifically to define two major configurations (1962a: 89–91). These were the basic ceremonial group, composed of a colonnaded hall, a raised shrine, and usually an oratory, and a temple assemblage, composed of a pyramid temple, one or more colonnaded halls, a shrine, a low platform in between the shrine and temple for holding stucco statues, and occasionally an oratory to the right of the temple. Twenty-six colonnaded halls are noted as existing at Mayapan; this building form is characterized by tandem long rooms with multiple front entrances, rear and side benches, and a central raised and square altar. Ten temples are noted to occur in epicentral Mayapan; this building form is characterized by a tall pyramidal structure supporting a small formal upper building (see Satterthwaite 1937 and 1944 for further discussion). A smaller ceremonial structure, the oratory, is also defined for Mayapan; this building form approximates a small temple, usually contains a bench, and is usually attached to other structures. Three kinds of shrines are defined for Mayapan: interior shrines, statue shrines, and raised shrines. Interior shrines are defined as enclosing altars, usually in a colonnaded hall. Statue shrines house a stucco figure and usually occur on stairways or on low platforms in front of temples. Raised shrines are defined as small buildings standing on independent substructures.

While prime examples of Proskouriakoff's temple assemblage and basic ceremonial group may have once existed at Santa Rita, the depredations of time do not allow for their formal definition. Because the known architecture of Santa Rita varies from that at Mayapan in form, however, it is suggested that even if such groups were present, they would not formally follow the defined Mayapan examples. The closest building form to that of the Mayapan colonnaded hall is Santa Rita Structure 81, but it differs from those at Mayapan in significant ways (i.e., no raised substructure, no tangent end rooms, and a nonsymmetrical plan). While no temples are presently noted from the site, save for possibly the earlier Structure 7, which was used by Postclassic people, there were elevated temple constructions during Gann's time at the site (specifically the mural–decorated Structure 1). At least one building may be identified as an oratory (looted Structure 77) based on the 1979 and 1980 work at the site; others no doubt existed. An interior shrine was recovered from within Santa Rita Structure 81, and Santa Rita Structure 58 may represent a raised shrine type of construction. No definite statue shrines have thus far been located at Santa Rita, although they likely existed.

ALTARS, CENSERS, AND CACHES

Smaller ritual indicators also exist at Santa Rita. Three specific altar types can be defined for the site. The first kind of altar consists of a rounded stone which is not formally attached to a building. The second kind consists of a formal square construction usually attached to the rear wall of an interior shrine. The third kind is a low, square line of stone construction set in open areas, often in front of other, larger buildings. The site also evinces a well-defined censer complex and a highly developed caching complex. Three stone altar figures, also noted for Mayapan in thirty-eight instances (Proskouriakoff 1962b), have also been encountered in disparate locations at the site.

Rounded stone altars were found in three locations in northern Santa Rita: on Structure 79, at Structure 75, and west of Structure 58. Santa Rita Altar 1 was formed from several stone blocks probably originally bonded together to make a round altar; it rests on the approximate center line of Structure 79. Structure 79, constructed from finely faced blocks, is the central building substructure on the western side of Platform 2; it exhibited no stone superstructure and apparently faced east. No censers, caches, or altar figures were found in association with either Structure 79 or Altar 1. Santa Rita Altar 2, associated with Structure 75, was composed of a single rounded stone. Structure 75 was unexcavated (and has since been bulldozed), but it was a relatively long substructure. It faced west and formed a group with Structures 81 and 74 north of Platform 2. Although it may have been associated with other material culture remains indicative of ritual activity, this is now impossible to ascertain. The complete rounded stone Altar 3, found west of Structure 58, was not associated with any construction or any censer deposition (at least as could be noted from the surface). It is probable that it was moved from its original placement on Santa Rita Platform 1, as no land–clearing activity was evident in the area near it which could account for a missing structure.

The only square architecturally constructed altar recovered from Santa Rita was encountered within the interior shrine associated with Structure 81. While no definite ancillary ritual indicators could be associated with the three round altars, the square architectural altar in Structure 81 is associated with two axial caches, a double burial, two smashed effigy censers (Kol Modeled), and a large number of other smashed ceramic vessels.

The third altar type at Santa Rita consists of a configuration of stones generally located on a platform exterior to any buildings. It is likely that these once formed small, slightly raised, square constructions. On Platform 1, an irregular composite stone feature had been raised above one of the Postclassic burials on an axis to Structure 58. On Platform 2, two such configurations were located; presently each consists of alignments of three or more stones and are located in front of Structure 77. Below and west of one of these was an interment of several disarticulated subadults; near the other a small headless bird vessel was found.

Late Postclassic censers at Santa Rita are of two distinct types. Kol Modeled censers are modeled effigy figures with an attached urn, similar to ones found at Mayapan (R. E. Smith 1971: fig. 32). Pum Modeled censers exhibit ring bases and are bowl or basin shaped. All Kol Modeled censers found thus far have been broken, but occasionally (and with much work) they may be nearly or completely reconstructed. At Santa Rita, Kol Modeled censers are found in pieces on abandoned buildings, in what may be formal groupings of two within buildings (such as in Structures 2, 5, 6, 17, and 81), and in refuse deposits. Pum Modeled censers apparently have a more limited distribution and are most clearly associated with Platform 2. Both of these censer types are found with evidence of burning and are associated with copal residue.

In addition to the two kinds of modeled censers discussed above, two other modeled ceramic forms also occur. Formally referred to as Kol Modeled face cups and Cohokum Modeled vessels, these do not appear to be domestic in function. These latter two vessel types are relatively common at Santa Rita but, like Pum Modeled censers, have thus far been encountered only in association with Platform 2. None of these four forms occurs within formal caches or is associated with the round kind of altar.

Caches at Santa Rita have thus far been encountered only on the axes of various structures at the site. Variation does, however, occur in the associated structure form and in the presence or absence of associated censers and square altars. The cache patterns encountered by the Corozal Postclassic Project are distinctive but also match surprisingly well with those illustrated and/or described by Gann (1900, 1918). This cache pattern usually includes one or more modeled ceramic figures or figurines encased in other ceramic vessels (see D. Chase 1982a for an extended discussion).

Patterning at Santa Rita

The archaeological materials thus far recovered from Santa Rita may be grouped into several patterns as follows:

1. Rounded, nonarchitectural altars appear to be found in association with buildings but do not appear to occur with other ritual paraphernalia.

2. Square, architecturally constructed altars occurring within interior shrines appear to be associated with censers, caches, and burials.

3. Alignments of stones located on platforms but exterior to buildings may form a third type of altar; these would appear to be associated with burials, and possibly with other types of special deposits, but are generally not directly associated with censer deposition.

4. Two kinds of censers occur, one of which may be found either in pairs within a building or purposely smashed on an abandoned building or in refuse deposits; the other kind appears to have a more limited distribution and occurs either smashed in burials or in certain refuse deposits.

5. Other nondomestic objects (i.e., Kol Modeled face cups and Cohokum Modeled vessels) have distinct spatial distributions at the site but appear in specialized refuse deposits.

6. Caches may be located in a variety of structural types but invariably appear to be set on an axis.

While it is not clear that these patterns will hold with further excavation, the two seasons of investigation thus far undertaken at Santa Rita by the Corozal Postclassic Project and the data available from Gann (1900, 1918) for the site indicate that this will be the case. Upcoming field seasons will attempt to test these defined patterns further. Even assuming that the patterns do hold, it is still necessary to attempt to ascertain what they mean in terms of the larger cultural configuration of the site. Except for the Santa Rita Structure 81 locus, a superficial examination of the newly recovered data shows no apparent correlations between the various classes of ritual indicators at the site.

The problem involved in the formal identification of ritual activity at Santa Rita is further amplified if one considers individual deposits of ceramics associated with a single structure. For example, in Structure 81, while paired censers, two caches, and a square architectural altar occur, other ceramic vessels are also present. While certain of these vessels are slipped, modeled, and somewhat extraordinary, others are inseparable from what might otherwise be interpreted as domestic or residential pottery. Whether this means that these latter vessels were any less ritual in nature cannot be stated with certainty.

A similar problem was encountered at Mayapan. R.E. Smith (1971) attempted to define what was ceremonial as opposed to what was domestic pottery and to use this distinction to suggest the function of various structures. He attempted to solve the problem of using the same pottery vessel forms for dissimilar purposes by considering the associated frequencies of vessel forms with certain structural types. This solution is viable, however, only when large, elaborate deposits of pottery are encountered; as such deposits are not often recovered, this method is clearly not a universal means for denoting structural or ritual function. In fact, it may actually be accurate only in those cases that can be classified as being clearly ritual or domestic by simple visual inspection; in other words, the ceramic frequency method for determining function is not particularly useful, especially for deposits associated with smaller, amorphous structures. Work at Santa Rita would, however, support certain findings suggested by R.E. Smith (1971); water jars (tinajas) are found primarily associated with domestic contexts, and censers and more elaborately modeled wares are likely to be associated with some sort of ritual function. These latter two points, however, are more readily recognizable archaeologically in reconstructible vessels than with sherds and sherd frequencies.

While the determination of function for structures and/or deposits is made difficult by the use of the same vessel forms in both ritual and domestic contexts, there is a similar problem with structures. These do not appear to have been utilized solely for one purpose or for a series of related activities. This is evident in the artifacts associated with Structure 81, one of the more ceremonial constructions at the site, by the presence of assorted flint tools and debitage as well as nested pottery vessels of probably primarily domestic function (Santa Crude) in one corner of the building.

Interpretation

Given the problems inherent in identifying ritual (or other) functions, the question of the interpretation of specified patterning is still present. As the site of Santa Rita is dated to Protohistoric times, based on the recovered archaeology and the known ethnohistory, it is suggested that the behavior responsible for the defined archaeological patterns may be elucidated through culling the available ethnohistoric sources relating to the early Historic Maya (see also D. Chase 1982a, n.d.). A brief review of the accounts pertaining to northern lowland Maya practices during early historic times, specifically those by Landa (Tozzer 1941), does in fact suggest that significant similarities can be found between the described behavior and the archaeologically defined patterns.

Three kinds of altars are described by Landa (Tozzer 1941: 119, 143): (1) stones of unspecified form associated with raised temples, (2) single round stones, and (3) piles of stones within a court; all were reportedly associated with blood sacrifice. Offerings of items, other than blood, appear to be primarily associated with idols rather than with altars (Tozzer 1941: 118, 147). No clear description is provided for altars actually being associated with idols, with the exception of the two heaps of stones found opposing each other at all four entrances to the town (Tozzer 1941: 139). It seems likely that the described rounded stone altar (possibly *acantun*) may be identified with the rounded single stones encountered archaeologically at Santa Rita. The third altar type described for Santa Rita, stone alignments, might be equivalent to one of the types of stone altars used in blood sacrifice, especially given their general proximity to shrines or oratories (and assumed proximity to temples, as at Chunyaxche) and their possible association with special deposits. The stratigraphic relationships for Santa Rita, however, indicate that interments possibly associated with these features were placed prior to their construction. At least one of these configurations (that in front of Structure 58) may be representative of the Postclassic practice, noted for high-

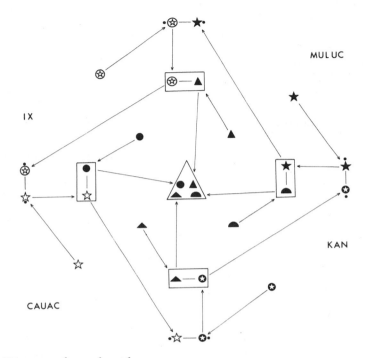

Fig. 8. Diagram of *uayeb* cycle.

land Guatemala, of erecting an altar above an important grave (see had a brazier for incense (called both an image and a statue; see Thompson 1939: 283–284; D. Chase 1982a).

Idols themselves were evidently made of wood, stone, and clay, although most were made of clay. According to Landa, numerous deities were portrayed in these idols (Tozzer 1941: 110). Many were actually effigy censers (Kol Modeled), "for it was the custom that each idol should have its little brazier in which they should burn their incense to it" (Tozzer 1941: 161). Idols have been described in several instances as the recipients of offerings, but two specific descriptions are of particular importance. In both cases, the presence of two or more idols is indicated.

During the *uayeb* (new year) ritual, a directionally rotating system for idols has been described (Landa in Tozzer 1941: 136–149; see also M. Coe 1965 for a review). These idols varied depending upon the year (Table 1, fig. 8), but generally at least two new idols, possibly representing different aspects of the same god, were made each year. One of these new images, which was made of pottery and

Table 1. *Uayeb* Rites and Their Various Associated Aspects

| Aspect | Dominical Letter | | | |
	Kan	Muluc	Ik	Cauac
Augury/ bacab	Hobnil	Cansicnal	Sac-sini	Hosan-ek
Image/ demon	Kan-uvayeyab	Chac-uvayeyab	Sac-uvayeyab	Ek-uvayeyab
Statue/ demon	Bolon tz'acab	Kinchahau	Itzamna	Vacmitun-ahau
Standard	Kante	Chacte	Sac-hia	Yax-ek
Dances	(Old women)	Batel-okot, Holcan-okot	Alcab-tan, Kam-ahau	Xibalba-okot
Stone	Kanal-acantun	Chac-acantun	Sac-acantun	Ekel-acantun
Evil idols	Itzamna-kauil	Yaxcoc-ahmut	Kinich-ahau Itzamna	Chichab-chob, Ahcanuol-cab, Ekbalam-chac, Ahbuluc-balam

Tozzer 1941: 139, 140), was set with an old idol on one of the piles of stones at the edge of the town, probably to effect a transference of power from the older idol to the newer idol. The new idol was then moved from the pile of stones to the principal's house, where it was set face to face with a newly made statue; besides the acceptance of various sacrifices by these two images, this act was also probably intended to effect the transference of power and knowledge between these two images. Following the particular *uayeb* rites, the statue was then moved to the temple and the idol was moved to another entrance to the town (Tozzer 1941: 142). It seems likely that older idols were being moved during these times as well; Tozzer reports (1941: n. 674) that certain of them remained in the principal's house. Occasionally, other idols were made during the *uayeb* rites.

It is the association with the principal's house as well as other aspects of these rites (discussed below in relation to caches) that indicate that this pattern may be directly related to Structure 81 at Santa Rita. The heaps of stones at the four entrances to the town have no known archaeological analogués at Santa Rita, unless they are not always at the edge of town, in which case Structure 7 would be one archaeological candidate for the final resting place of idols no longer in circulation. Given the frequent occurrence of broken censers throughout Santa Rita and elsewhere, it is possible that the images and idols were purposefully smashed, often in other locales, following their period of usefulness, possibly to destroy any stored power within them.

In addition to idols of the *uayeb* rites, idols were also made to represent the lords of each *katun* (Tozzer 1941: 166–169); it is possible that the characteristics of the *katun* and *uayeb* idols may have been merged into a single image.

> They had in the temple two idols dedicated to two of these characters. They worshipped and offered homage and sacrifices to the first, according to the count from the cross on the circle shown above, as a remedy for the calamity of their twenty years. But for ten years which remained of the twenty of the first idol, they did not do anything for him more than to burn incense to him and to show him respect. When the twenty years of the first idol had passed, he began to be succeeded by the destinies of the second and to offer him sacrifices, and having taken away that first idol, they put another in its place to worship that for ten more years. (Tozzer 1941: 168)

The *katun* idol pattern is an extremely appealing one to use in making an analogy to Structures 81, 2, 5, 6, and 17 (each building being associated with two recovered effigy censers). It is suggested as well, however, that it may have been merged with the *uayeb* rites and idols to form a more cohesive pattern.

Use of abandoned structures to make offerings is also indicated ethnohistorically; although deposition of censers is not specifically described, the burning of copal is (Tozzer 1941: 110). Structure 7 clearly fits into this category. Cups are also referred to in relation to a series of calendric rituals (Tozzer 1941: 147) and while they are never described, unless they were of perishable material, these were undoubtedly the Kol Modeled face and foot cups at Santa Rita. Cohokum Modeled vessels (fig. 9) do not appear to have any direct analogue in Landa's account, but their similarity to a depiction on page 46 of the Borgia Codex (Seler 1963; fig. 10) may be suggestive. The only occurrence of Kol Modeled face cups and Cohokum Modeled vessels at Santa Rita is south of Platform 2 and occurs with Pum Modeled censers and partial Kol Modeled effigy censers; this could indicate that this archaeological locale may have been the final resting place for used idols and other ritual paraphernalia.

Offerings made between two vessels are not only a common archaeological pattern but are also prevalent in Landa's account (Tozzer 1941: 143, 165). One ethnohistoric description of a ritual, which involves the making of an offering between two vessels, is particularly similar to archaeological deposits recovered at Santa Rita. In

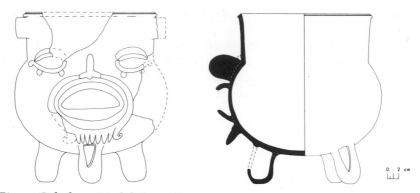

Fig. 9. Cohokum Modeled vessel.

the year described by Landa as indicated by "the dominical letter Kan" (p. 139) an "angel" was described as being part of the *uayeb* rites. These angels were "a sign of water" and were painted and "made frightful to look upon" (p. 141). As part of the traditional ceremonies for *kan* years, this angel was also a necessary component of rituals occurring after the new year ceremonies due to the occurrence of calamities.

> The manner of sacrificing in this feast was different, since they built in the court of the temple a great pile of stones, and they placed the man or dog whom they were going to sacrifice on something higher than it, and throwing down the bound victim from the height onto the stones, those officials seized him and took out his heart with great quickness, and carried it to the new idol, and offered it to him between two platters. . . . They said that an angel descended and received this sacrifice. (Tozzer 1941: 143)

The similarity and probable relationship between this description and many of the caches encountered during the various excavations at Santa Rita should be clear. This similarity may be further strengthened in the case of Structure 81. Page 69 of the Nuttall Codex (Nuttall 1902; fig. 11) reveals a figure which is reminiscent of the Cao Modeled cache figures of Santa Rita; this figure is depicted as descending to receive the heart of a sacrificed dog.

If caches at Santa Rita were primarily calendric in function, as seems likely given the above, then their distribution at the site in

Fig. 10. Vessel in the Borgia Codex similar to Cohokum Modeled vessel.

Fig. 11. Nuttall Codex figure thought to be equivalent to Cao Modeled vessels; see fig. 7.

different building types does not appear to be extraordinary; the frequent lack of association of the caches with other indicators of ritual activity is also explainable. The rare occurrence of these Cao Modeled cache figures outside of Santa Rita (in northern Belize at Laguna de On, Cerros, Lamanai, Douglas, and around Lake Bacalar; further north a related complex occurs at Mayapan) would be expected if Santa Rita were in fact a regional capital.

In summary, the various material remains recovered archaeologically at Santa Rita have a definite bearing on those described in the ethnohistory. The majority of the altars described by Landa are associated not with idols but with blood sacrifice, thus implying that no distinct material remains would be expected in archaeological association with them, with the possible exception of interments (Landa in Tozzer 1941: 120). The early historic "images," "idols," and "statues" very clearly include the archaeologically recovered pottery effigy censers. These censers appear to have been utilized for a number of purposes; at least two of them, those for the *uayeb* rites and those used as *katun* idols, are directly correlated with calendric as well as ceremonial activity. Censers, the prime archaeological indicators of ritual, have usually been associated by archaeologists with simple day-to-day religious activity or idolatry (Thompson 1970: 187–191); they may be more correctly associated with important rites associated with the cyclical passage of time. The ancient Maya practice of caching objects also appears to have analogues in early historic Maya activities, specifically in the making of an offering between two vessels. Certain cache patterns at Santa Rita may be correlated with practices undertaken during the *uayeb* rites, thereby suggesting that they are primarily associated with calendric ritual. Late Postclassic Maya caches may, in fact, have been deposited in a regular fashion in much the same way that the Classic Maya erected stelae.

Conclusions

Several implications may be derived from this comparison between archaeological and ethnohistoric patterns of ritual activity among the lowland Postclassic Maya. It is evident that an examination of ritual is one area where a correspondence may be found between Postclassic material culture remains, as excavated by the archaeologist, and descriptions of ceremonies, as recorded by the early Spaniards in the Maya area. While the defined archaeological patterns allow a tentative association to be established with ethnohistoric descriptions, the ethnohistoric detail provides further avenues for testing these patterns archaeologically. The presence of certain ritual indicators in diverse archaeological contexts may be taken to indicate the calendric nature of much ritual activity. From the archaeology, it is obvious that what would normally be considered to be ritual activity took place in contexts other than temples. This, however, is not interpreted as representing widespread, family–oriented, Postclassic idolatry as it has been in the past (Proskouriakoff 1955; A.L. Smith 1962: 268); it is instead interpreted as being indicative of the overall integration of Postclassic Maya society into a larger cohesive organization.

Acknowledgments

The major portion of this essay was presented at the 47th Annual Meeting of the Society for American Archaeology in April 1982 in Minneapolis. Sections of papers given in November 1979 in Cincinnati (78th Annual Meeting of the American Anthropological Association) and in May 1980 at Philadelphia (45th Annual Meeting of the Society of American Archaeology) have been juxtaposed with the more recent one to comprise the present article. Thanks are due to Arlen F. Chase for his encouragement and editorial comments as well as to all those who participated in or facilitated the field and laboratory progress of the Corozal Postclassic Project.

Revitalization Movements among the Postclassic Lowland Maya

ROBERT E. FRY

> There is an end to the misery of the Maya men when suddenly the men of Uaymil come to take vengeance on the world. (Roys 1933: 153)

Culture change is not always a gradual, uniform transformational process. Under certain conditions, change can involve drastic and rapid reorientation of ideology, social organization, and economic systems. Some of the most dramatic documented cases of major culture change involve revitalization movements: "deliberate organized attempts by some members of a society to construct a more satisfying culture by rapid acceptance of a pattern of multiple innovations" (A. F. C. Wallace 1970: 188). Only recently have archaeologists considered the possibility that some examples of rapid disjunctive culture change may be due to successful revitalization movements, rather than the traditional explanations of population replacement or massive "external" influence. Turnabaugh (1979) uses a revitalization model to explain the rapid adoption of calumet ceremonialism (but see Blakeslee 1981 for an alternative explanation). In the Maya area, Ashmore and Sharer (1975) and Dahlin (1975) used aspects of A. F. C. Wallace's revitalization framework to explain the reemergence of a powerful elite at the site of Tikal, Guatemala.

In this essay, I will examine some of the potential archaeological signals for revitalization movements. I will use this concept to explain an unusual pattern of architectural modification found by the Uaymil Survey Project in south-central Quintana Roo, Mexico. Finally, I will look for the potential origins of this common lowland Maya phenomenon in the turmoil following the disruption of Classic Maya civilization in the northeast Peten.

Revitalization Movements and Their Archaeological Recognition

Revitalization movements are most frequently generated by societies undergoing a high degree of internal stress, usually from contact or domination by a culturally different society. Personal dissatisfaction with the existing cultural framework or "mazeway" can stem from a variety of sources. Initial causes for dissatisfaction may be triggered by the impact of natural forces such as catastrophic storms or earthquakes, epidemic disease, or internal conflict. In most cases, however, these triggering forces merely aggravate a longstanding unease resulting from the perceptions of oppression by and/or inferiority to a dominant but foreign cultural tradition. When a sufficient number of individuals manifest this discontent, the result is a severe disorganization of the sociocultural system.

A. F. C. Wallace (1970) outlines a series of stages through which a successful revitalization movement passes. From a beginning steady state or moving equilibrium, there is a period of growing individual stress as the system increasingly fails to meet individual needs. If the system cannot maintain its equilibrium, there follows a period of cultural distortion in which both individual and institutionalized efforts are made to circumvent problems in the system, sometimes by violent means. This often leads instead to further social and cultural disorganization. In some cases, societies simply disintegrate; in others there are attempts by one or more groups to generate a social renewal or revitalization.

The period of revitalization begins with one or more movements, which are organized around a vision of a new utopian sociocultural organization, what Wallace calls a "goal culture." In large scale societies a number of such movements may appear almost simultaneously. In some cases this goal culture may be a uniquely new creation, in others it is a syncretic blend of "traditional" and superordinant culture, or it may be an idealized version of the traditional culture.

Revitalization movement codes specify new or unique patterns of social relationships, new or "renewed" ritual, and a shift in ideological orientation, i.e., a new world view. Followers of a movement often exhibit distinctive lifestyles in adhering to the new code, and may exhibit unique patterns of dress and deportment. Hostility to the established order can be seen not only in patterns of behavior in public as well as private contexts, but in many cases through reversals of "acceptable" dress style and public architecture. Alternatively, dress and behavioral styles may involve syncretism of traditional styles with those exhibited by members of the superordinant culture.

If a revitalization movement is successful in overwhelming the traditional culture or converting large segments of the population, members often try to erase vestiges of the previous system, especially those things most directly in conflict with the new codes, or associated with unpleasant features of the superordinant culture. Therefore rampant iconoclasm, and razing of portions of public architecture and other symbols of the old order are common features of a stage in the evolution of successful revitalization movements. Large scale public architecture involving heavy labor investment may be modified to meet the new code's requirements rather than being completely destroyed.

The historical record indicates that revitalization movements are not just the recent outcome of contact between simpler societies and complex industrialized states, but occur at many levels of cultural complexity (Harris 1980). Why, then, have archaeologists not considered revitalization processes as responsible for some of the most dramatic examples of large scale sociocultural change? Certainly one plausible reason is that until recently, archaeologists have not been comfortable with exploring the dynamics of cultural change accomplished in relatively short time intervals. Successful revitalization movements usually accomplish their goals in time spans that in many cases would be archaeologically invisible. Acculturative change may be gradual or disruptive, but given the common archaeological problem of time control, most archaeologists are content to document change rather than study the dynamics of change. Another major difficulty is in assessing the archaeological signatures of revitalization movements. Such movements are highly variable in their makeup: some are primarily political, others more ideologically oriented. Some emphasize major changes in lifeways with little interest in changing the political and economic superstructure, while others are exactly the reverse. Finally, it is difficult to generate unique archaeological signatures for revitalization movements, because many of the signatures can be the result of other processes.

In deciding whether or not a revitalization movement is responsible for certain aspects of the archaeological record, a critical initial step is an assessment of the preexisting state of the sociocultural system in question. Revitalization movements are likely to arise under conditions of stress generated by the sudden appearance of a more complex society in some sort of dominant relationship to the local society. This relationship may have an exploitative nature, which is an additional factor likely to result in the beginnings of a revitalization movement. Any sudden increase in stress under these conditions, such as catastrophic natural events, epidemic diseases, or the addition of added burdens by the dominating society, all add fuel to the potential fire.

Archaeologists should be sensitive to the conditions which generate revitalization movements. This could be signaled by the appearance of alien artifacts in large numbers, especially in elite contexts in ranked or stratified societies. If these items, with or without direct evidence of new populations, appear in important or central political and economic locations, additional evidence of unequal cultural penetration is indicated. In stratified societies, the evidence for drastic increases in stratification would include suddenly greater disparities in house sizes and complexity of decoration or energy expenditure, and/or greater disparities in richness of artifact assemblages. Declines in stature of the lower classes or evidence of malnutrition or more serious diseases would provide additional confirmatory evidence. Marginalization would be indicated by a lesser degree of local specialization and a lower overall diversity of functions than might be expected given the regional population size.

It would be unusual to be able to document the earliest stages of a revitalization movement. In the early stages such movements are usually quite small and often try to keep their distinctive rituals hidden from public view. Only the chance discovery of a household with a significantly different lifestyle, or a remnant of a unique ritual, would be sufficient to indicate a possible early stage of a revitalization movement.

Only when a movement becomes strong enough to "go public" or becomes relatively successful should archaeological evidence become more prevalent. A significant number of households should show differing lifestyles, and there should be more evidence of different types of public rituals. If successful, there would be razing, mutilation, or drastic alteration of many of the public buildings and/ or construction of drastically altered buildings. If there is a significant renewal aspect of the revitalization process, there may be attempts to refurbish or re—erect monuments of previous periods, even to the extent of uncovering them from buried or hidden locations. Archaic styles of architecture and other items of material culture may be reemphasized, and older ritual structures reconstituted at least in part. This pattern is often confused or syncretized with items and styles associated with the superordinant culture. The changes in lifestyles and social units previously confined to a minority now become the dominant, if not the only, pattern demonstrated. Even basic aspects of subsistence economics and settlement pattern may become transformed during this period. Wallace shows that as a part of the revitalization of the Seneca, for example, males became heavily involved in agricultural activity for the first time, and there were major changes in village structure and domestic architecture (A. F. C. Wallace 1969).

Revitalization among the Postclassic Lowland Maya: The Lobil Phase

The Yucatan peninsula is an ideal place to search for archaeological evidence for revitalization movements. Mayanists are familiar with the "Caste War" of the mid– to late nineteenth century, an archetypical revitalization movement spawned by economic and political oppression during the tumultuous Early Independence years (Reed 1964). Similar movements, though less politically successful, had occurred throughout the Colonial period. Political and economic conditions conducive to the generation of nativistic movements predominated during this period. Political and economic control was in the hands of a relatively small elite class, which was ethnically distinct. The situation was often exploitative or perceived by the Maya to be so. Also, expansions and contractions in the world economy can cause unpredictable fluctuations of demands made on the local populations and sometimes dramatic restructuring of interregional economic relationships (Cline 1950; Strickton 1965). When these factors are combined with a population with a strong sense of its own cultural distinctiveness and an almost fierce independence, such as the Maya, the occurrence of numerous local revolts is completely predictable.

The pattern we have discussed for the Colonial and Early Independence periods can be extended backwards well into the Postclassic, if not earlier. During the Late Postclassic much of Yucatan was under the political and economic domination of an elite class with strong historic ties to polities and groups in the central highlands and in the southern Veracruz–Tabasco lowlands. Using the criteria of both political integration and economic structure, Yucatan can best be described as an underdeveloped area during the later Postclassic period. This pattern may well extend back into the earlier Postclassic and Terminal Classic periods.

Within the large geographic area of the Yucatan peninsula, certain areas seem to have been subjected to more stress than others: regions where there were great disparities between population size and political and economic power; regions which were always marginal to major economic or political decision–making. One of these

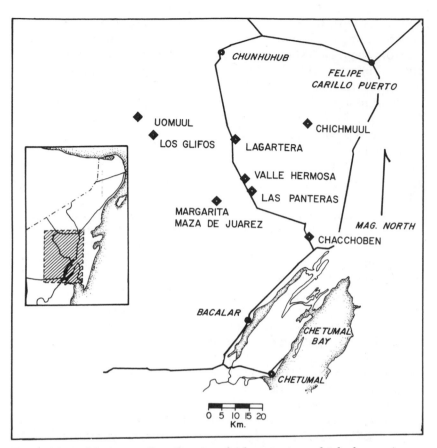

Fig. 1. Map of Quintana Roo showing the largest sites which show evidence of Lobil phase architecture.

was an extensive area in southern and south-central Quintana Roo, the location of the contact period province of Uaymil. Of all the contact period provinces, this is the most poorly known (Roys 1957). The province seems to have been a frontier zone in the Postclassic, as its peoples are described as "the guardians of the sands, the guardians of the sea" (Roys 1933). The zone was poorly known archaeologically due to its relative inaccessibility, and the lack of both well–preserved stelae and substantial standing architecture (Gann 1935; Lizardi Ramos 1939; Escalona Ramos 1946; Muller 1959).

This situation was rectified by the work undertaken by the Uaymil Survey Project (fig. 1; Harrison 1972, 1974, 1978, 1979; Fry 1973, 1974). The survey disclosed population densities comparable to other lowland Maya regions, and a significant number of medium to fairly large sites with temple and palace construction, though there were no sites comparable in scale to a regional capital. Analysis of ceramics from the region showed a strong localized tradition in utilitarian pottery, but a weakly developed tradition in polychromes and serving wares. Instead, much of the regional styles were imitations of and/or imported items from adjacent regions. During the earlier Late Classic period, for example, imported and localized copies of Peten gloss wares predominated while in the later Late and Terminal Classic periods, the northern Yucatecan slateware tradition grew in significance. This seems to indicate that the frontier character of the region noted for the contact period may have extended well into the Classic period.

One of the most puzzling aspects of the region was the apparent scarcity of standing architecture. Only sites near the southern boundary of the region, such as Tzibanche, Kinichna, and Mario Ancona, had well preserved architecture (Harrison 1972). It was not until the last field season of the project that the cause of this scarcity was discovered. There had been a tradition of construction of masonry buildings often elaborately decorated with stucco; however, at some point in time most of these constructions had been heavily modified and buried by a unique form of architecture. The few buildings which could be investigated by small scale excavation and the examination of looter's pits turned out to belong to the widespread central Yucatecan architectural tradition (Potter 1977) dating to the Late Classic and possibly into the beginning of the Terminal Classic. At some time afterwards, these masonry constructions were buried and often differentially razed to create broad, flat-topped summits lacking buildings or stone faced facades. The summits of these platforms were reached by broad slab steps. Harrison (1979: 200) graphically describes the process as involving "the ruthless modification of the Classic buildings and deliberate covering of any decorative facades." Often this remodelling was accompanied by the alteration of the building orientation and, at times, even the reversal of the major axis of the structure. Again, "the form of a Classic structure had little influence on the form of the platform constructed above it" (Harrison 1979: 191). At the same time, round altars of similar crude construction were placed in the plazas of Classic period sites. Harrison refers to this architectural tradition as the "Lobil Phase."

PROBLEMS OF DATING THE LOBIL PHASE

There are several plausible alternative explanations for this pattern of razing and reconstruction. While allowing for the possibility that this pattern is a result of "religious outrage or revolution" (Harrison 1979: 200), Harrison prefers simple cultural changes over a long period of time. Thus, the changes are due to reuse or reoccupation of abandoned sites during the Late Postclassic. Harrison bases this late date for the remodelling activity on the following points:

1. The crudeness of the Lobil architecture represents a significant deterioration in Maya architectural skill presupposing a long period of time to account for such decadence. The definite discontinuity in technical skills as well as breaks in tradition strongly indicate a *long* time gap between the Classic constructions and the Lobil overlay (Harrison 1979: 200; emphasis in original).

2. The relatively good preservation of the crude Lobil architecture indicates a relatively shorter time span since construction.

3. Definite Late Postclassic Chen Mul Modeled effigy incense burner fragments were found on the tops and sides of many of the Lobil phase high platforms. Harrison argues that these are contemporaneous with the construction and use of these platforms.

Another line of evidence used to support a Late Postclassic date comes from comparative data from adjacent regions. Gann (1900) found crude architecture at the Late Postclassic site of Santa Rita postdating the late beam–and–mortar architecture and Mixtec style murals; more recent work has also uncovered similar architecture (D. Chase 1981). Abundant Late Postclassic and Early Colonial ceramics, burials, and architecture have also been discovered in recent excavations at Lamanai in northern Belize. Here crude architecture is associated with the late ceramics (Pendergast 1981a).

An equally strong case can be made, however, that the major architectural changes date to the Terminal Classic or Early Postclassic periods, and thus may be the result of revitalization activities (although a later dating would not preclude such an explanation). This proposed earlier dating is supported by the following evidence:

1. Ceramics have been recovered from controlled excavations and looters' pits from a number of the remodelled structures. The central Yucatecan style of architectural fills contained sherds of Muna and Ticul Thin Slate, indicating a Late Classic through Terminal Classic and/or Florescent date for construction (Andrews V 1981). Fills piled onto the standing architecture in the remodelling process also contain Muna and Ticul Thin Slate wares, although slightly different in shape and color. No Late Postclassic redwares, such as Tulum Red, were found in these fills or in the vicinity of the remodelled structures. Chen Mul Modeled effigy censer sherds were found on top of the structures, but not incorporated into the fills.

2. In areas outside the sphere of most intensive Lobil phase activity at the sites of Tzibanche and Mario Ancona, Late Postclassic

Chen Mul Modeled and/or Cehac Hunacti Composite incense burners have been found on top of *both* modified and unmodified structures. Thus, these censers may have no direct temporal correlation with the architecture with which they are associated.

3. Limited excavations at a number of the sites showing Lobil phase activity revealed no traces of Late Postclassic occupation at the sites. Project settlement sampling programs produced only a few definite Late or Middle Postclassic sherds, and these were from much smaller sites far distant from major public architecture.

4. Although crude construction is found postdating well–dated Late Postclassic architecture at a number of sites in adjacent regions, there is no evidence that this construction represents the same architectural tradition as the distinctive Lobil phase.

5. The argument that dramatic discontinuities in both architectural style and technical skill necessarily implies a long intervening period of time reflects a gradualist position of cultural change. Yet dramatic changes in short time spans have been documented within a single cultural tradition, including revitalization–induced transformations. Great differences do not *necessarily* imply strong temporal differences, but must be proven using other lines of evidence.

KINDS AND CAUSES OF CHANGE

If we accept an Early to Middle Postclassic dating for the Lobil phase architectural tradition, then the nature of the changes in architecture argues for an explanation rooted in the idea of a revitalization movement. A number of the changes indicate "deep structure" changes in both the structure of rituals and their larger symbolic import. For example, during the Classic period, rituals were increasingly isolated from large scale public viewing; plazas which were previously quite open became cut off from most of the populace, and rites in temples were conducted in small rooms out of sight of the bulk of the viewers. In the Lobil phase architecture, the emphasis was on broad open areas on top of the pyramidal substructures, unless impermanent temple structures were used. Both imply a more open access and a greater possibility for visual participation in rituals, harking back to an earlier Preclassic and possibly Early Classic pattern.

In addition, rejection of the previous system of iconography and underlying "deep structure" involving orientation to certain directions is quite obvious. Facades were battered and elaborate polychrome surface decoration in stucco and plaster shattered, and replaced by a simple architectural style with minimal ornamentation and an absence of masonry veneering. One can compare the changes in church architecture during the Protestant Reformation with its icon smashing and "purification" and simplification of detail, or the major transformations in ritual architecture caused by the rapid spread of Islam as parallels to this pattern. Changes in axes of some of the buildings and even outright reversals can also be seen as deliberate attempts to establish a new code.

One major question which must remain unanswered for the present concerns the long term success of the revitalization movement or movements. Certainly, some degree of success is indicated by the changes in a significant amount of ritual architecture in our survey area, but what was the longevity of that success? The final stages of Wallace's revitalization pattern, involving cultural transformation, routinization, and the evolution of a new steady state, may or may not have been achieved in Postclassic Quintana Roo. In order to achieve routinization, "the movement must be able to maintain its boundaries from outside invasion, must be able to obtain internal social conformity without destructive coercion, and must have a successful economic system" (A.F.C. Wallace 1970: 195). Whatever short term stability was achieved, in the long run the movement must not have been successful. Only detailed large scale excavation might reveal whether or not there are a succession of building phases involved in Lobil phase architectural constructs.

There is evidence that populations did not persist in great density near the older sites into the Middle and Late Postclassic periods. Instead, populations seem to have been concentrated along lakes and especially in the coastal zones which became the major focus for occupation and development of political and economic centers in the Middle and Late Postclassic (Miller 1977b).

There is some tantalizing evidence that this shift may not have been completely voluntary, or may have been part of a deliberately planned change. Although the *katun* prophecies as recorded in the Colonial period cannot be heavily relied on for historical information, due to the confusion as to which period of time is being referred to, there is one reference relevant to our argument. In the *katun* prophecy from the Book of *Chilam Balam of Chumayel* for the *Katun 1 Ahau*, there is a description of a period of turbulence especially affecting "the center of the land" (Roys 1933: 156). The turmoil involves political upheavals and a judgment of harsh rulers, followed by plague and drought (a common motif of most *katun* prophecies). This is followed by the passage:

> The remainder of the guardians of the sands, the guardians of the sea, shall be detained together such as the people of

Uaymil, such as the people of Emal. The rest of them shall be assembled in great numbers by the sea at the end of the Katun. (Roys 1933: 156)

Although this prophecy may involve the reduction policy of the missionaries and priests in the Early Colonial period, it is also true that by the Late Postclassic period the bulk of the population in south-central Quintana Roo was already concentrated in the coastal strip north of the mouth of the Rio Hondo and around adjacent Lake Bacalar. Therefore, this prophecy may refer to a much earlier historical event.

The causal factors of one or more nativistic movements in the Uaymil region will remain obscure until we have much more detailed archaeological knowledge. I have alluded, however, to a set of important factors which often generate revitalization movements. One is political marginality. Although the area is one which should have had a distinctive political history and a strong local economy (suggested by potential productivity and what we can infer about population size), the major centers in the region are smaller than would be expected. Major centers such as Tzibanche in the south and Uomuul in the north are at the peripheries of the region rather than centrally located. Tzibanche seems to be oriented toward the Peten and the southern lowlands, while Uomuul is strongly articulated with the northern Yucatecan Florescent traditions.

The marginality of the Uaymil region is partially based on its ecological heterogeneity and partially on its physical location. The southern part of the region is closer to the landforms and even the biota of the southern lowlands, with large areas of bajo, some of which were used for extensive raised field systems (Turner 1974; Harrison 1978). In the north, the drier gently rolling landscape has extensive areas of seasonally inundated savannas without evidence of raised field agriculture. This region straddles the boundary between the more humid southern and the drier northern lowlands. Traditionally, this zone was a gateway of communication and a transportation corridor for northern Yucatan and the Bay of Honduras trade. The southern reaches were also influenced by the northeast Peten "corridor" along the Rio Hondo marking the mouth of the Hondo—Lake Bacalar and Chetumal Bay area, a vital entrepot.

Competition for control of this important region must have always had a strong impact on political and economic developments in the Uaymil region. This is documented in the shifts in time from a more Peten—based orientation in the Early Classic and earlier Late Classic periods, with its replacement by a central Yucatecan and eventually a northern Yucatecan orientation in the Late and Terminal Classic, at least as documented by imported serving ware ceramics. Political and regional marginality is one of the factors critical to the development of repeated revitalization movements in a region, whether as in much of the historic period in ancient Palestine or more recently in the "burning ground" of upstate New York (Harris 1973). It is likely that more surplus was extracted from the Uaymil region through trade and tribute than from most other regions. Much more thorough sampling of residential contexts will be required, however, to document this assertion.

Revitalization Movements and Termination Rituals

While I have used the available evidence from Quintana Roo to argue that the observable events in the region during the Postclassic can be explained by a revitalization movement or movements, alternative explanations must also be considered. In addition to the temporal discontinuity argument outlined above, another possible explanation centers on the pan–Mesoamerican class of termination rituals. These involve the ceremonial deactivation and desecration of structures and monuments redolent with suffused supernatural power. Such rituals may have been part of long term calendrically determined historical cycles, or defined by deaths of important personages. They involve deliberate destruction or mutilation of structures or monuments in a ritualistic manner, often accompanied by special offerings. This pattern is of great antiquity in Mesoamerica going back at least as far as the Middle Preclassic period (Grove 1981). The pattern is well known in the Maya area dating as early as the Late Preclassic, if not earlier.

In most cases the destruction is accompanied by special offerings. If activity is to continue at a locus, the whole assemblage is buried and new construction is begun within a short period of time. If, on the other hand, this activity precedes a change in the locus of ritual activity, the remains are simply left "as is" with no attempt to tidy them up. For example, at the site of Mirador, Chiapas, major construction at several important ritual loci apparently terminated with a series of unique burials (Agrinier 1970, 1975). These have been interpreted as examples of the "god–impersonator" sacrificial ritual known from the contact period in the central highlands (Fry 1980). At the same time, there was a shift in ritual activity to the nearby site of Miramar (Agrinier 1978). The burials were intruded into the main staircases of the temples, but no attempt was made to modify further these now–abandoned ceremonial loci.

The continuation of ritual activity and the use of temple structures after the razing of previous construction thus argues against the role of a series of termination rituals causing the Lobil phase remodelling phenomena. Given the short period of use of the remodelled structures, it is possible that there is a "terminal" aspect to their use, however. Following Wallace's model to its logical conclusion, it is possible that the reconstructive effort was a component part of a transfer culture, with the final goal culture involving the movement of population to the coastal zone.

Revitalization Movements in the Terminal Classic

Revitalization movements have been a regular structural component of Mesoamerican history. I have already indicated that this applies to the Postclassic period, but it also can be extended as a generalization into the Classic. To justify this extension, I will briefly summarize the relevant data from the Terminal Classic period in the area of Tikal, Guatemala.

The Terminal Classic was a period of obvious great stress in the northeast Peten. There is evidence of drastic decreases in population in many zones just before or during this period, especially in Classic period central places (D. Rice and Puleston 1981). This is accompanied by political fragmentation (Marcus 1976) and a marked decrease in occupational specialization at some sites (Fry 1982). At the same time, there is evidence of intrusion in the area by non-culturally Maya groups (Sabloff and Willey 1967; Adams 1973). Such a situation is again ripe for the spawning of revitalization movements. Is there evidence for any such movements in the archaeological record?

Perhaps the most substantial evidence comes from the site of Tikal, Guatemala. Here, stelae were retrieved from their original contexts and re−erected in the Main Plaza, often in incorrect positions. Burials and tombs were reentered and bones of the interred individuals removed, sometimes with ritual refilling of the burial chambers and offerings (W.R. Coe 1965b: 54−55). Although looting of precious jades and other valued items may have been one reason for this activity, other explanations are possible. The local populace may have been attempting to revitalize their decaying political and economic position through reuse of sacred artifacts and even bones of important Classic period persons. One new ritual pattern involved the deliberate smashing of effigy incense burners and portions of utilitarian pottery vessels inside rooms of temples, and on small masonry platforms in the Great Plaza and the North Terrace. Similar activities are documented for the lone standing Early Classic temple at Uolantun, at least one of the temples at the predominantly Late Classic site of Jimbal (Fry 1969), and at Uaxactun. The material remains are strikingly similar to the renewal ceremonies described by Landa for the Postclassic period in Yucatan, where household items as well as old ritual paraphernalia were ceremoniously disposed of at the "year–renewal" ceremonies (Tozzer 1941).

Major changes in rituals can be documented in a number of ways in the Terminal Classic. Incense burners, especially effigy types, were increasingly used in rituals, and in contexts which were new (Ferree 1970). In some cases this involved activities at ground level in front of temples and range style structures. In peripheral locations, activities included deposition of broken whole censers and partial utilitarian vessels inside temple rooms, along with the burning of copal incense. Examples include deposits at Uolantun, Jimbal, and probably Uaxactun. While earlier rituals in these temples may have used incense burners, the late ritual pattern with its utilitarian pottery suggests participation by a broader cross–section of society. Later Postclassic year–renewal ceremonies were performed by not only the priests and lords, but all males in the community:

> . . . the lords and priests and the men of the town assembled
> together and having cleaned and adorned with arches and
> green the road leading to the place of heaps of stones where
> the statue was, they went all together to it with great devotion.
> (Tozzer 1941: 140)

The rituals involved may have included the earliest known examples of the *uayeb* rituals known from the contact period (see also D. Chase, this volume). At the conclusion of each year's *uayeb* rite the idol used was simply tossed aside, never to be used again. The pottery and incense burners found at the Peten sites thus may be discarded remains of one or a series of *uayeb* rituals.

Other new rituals involved the dumping of broken pottery around older civic buildings. This may relate to the known dumping of pottery and other household items after the year–renewal "new fire" ceremonies recorded in contact period Yucatan. Some of the new ritual patterns may reflect borrowing of concepts from other cultural groups including the "Mexicanized" Putun Maya (Thompson 1970). This may include the use of effigy censers, and especially the ladle censers so diagnostic of the Terminal Classic and Early Postclassic periods. Other aspects bespeak a syncretism, combining new and revised Maya themes. Terminal Classic stelae may include Mexican glyphs as in the stela from Jimbal (W.R. Coe 1967); however, a newly reemergent theme is the down–gazing ancestral head, a motif most frequently used during the Cycle 8 and early Cycle 9 period (Marcus 1976: 190). Interestingly, many of the new rituals seem to center on structures showing no major renovation since the Early Classic, such as the temple at Uolantun. This may reflect attempts to revitalize or reinstitute structural forms dominant during the Early Classic, when population density was much lower and populations not as concentrated in major capitals and central places.

The overall pattern suggests that one or more revitalization movements were active in the northeast Peten during the Terminal Classic period. This period shows not only drastic reduction in population, but major population movements. Within the Tikal region, there was a concentration of the new reduced population in and near major public buildings and small nucleated sites in the peripheral zones (Culbert 1973; Fry 1969; Puleston 1973). There are indications of differences in residential patterns and refuse disposal which may indicate shifts in lifestyle during this turbulent period. As in the Quintana Roo case, these movements did not result in a successful steady state. Instead, populations continued to decline and the major centers were abandoned, probably within 100 to 150 years after the onset of the Terminal Classic period.

Conclusions

I have argued that revitalization movements are an important factor in explaining sociocultural change, and that archaeological recognition of such movements is feasible. The two cases that I have presented document the importance of considering revitalization phenomena as a valid explanation. In both cases, the possibility of alternative explanations remains. Only much more detailed and problem oriented research can provide a more satisfactory test of the explanations proposed. Knowledge of the nature of revitalization processes can direct our attention to linkages among seemingly isolated events or cultural changes previously viewed as isolated phenomena.

If the cultural changes outlined above were the result of revitalization movements, this opens up a whole avenue of research for students of the Postclassic in the Maya lowlands, as well as elsewhere in Mesoamerica. The revitalization hypothesis may help explain the reasons for the paucity of data on such territories as Uaymil during the Postclassic period and on many groups resident in the interior zones both before and after the Conquest. It may be possible to trace differing groups or movements and isolate unique patterns of material culture and ritual activity which can distinguish among the groups through time. The kinds of changes discussed here may also be used to explain the weaknesses of Postclassic polities constantly plagued by alternative cultural styles and the possibility of major revolt.

Acknowledgments

The Uaymil Survey Project was supported and sponsored by the Royal Ontario Museum, with additional support from the Canada Council. Assistance from the Purdue Research Foundation and the Penrose Fund of the American Philosophical society was instrumental in the completion of the ceramic analysis program. I am most indebted to Peter D. Harrison, Project Director, for his assistance and stimulating discussions on the possible meaning of the Lobil phase architecture.

 # THE SOUTHERN LOWLANDS

The Southern Maya lowlands, heartland of Classic Maya culture, is centered on the modern Department of Peten in northern Guatemala and extends into parts of adjacent Belize. In this region the Postclassic period has been virtually ignored by archaeologists, who have focused their efforts on the area's spectacular Preclassic and Classic period remains. The core of Classic developments in architecture, iconography, and ceremonialism, the Southern lowlands thrived up to about A.D. 900. Then, sometime around A.D. 900 the Classic Maya cultural trajectory was irrevocably altered, an event or series of events referred to as the "Classic Maya collapse." This so-called "collapse" has been greatly magnified in the imagination of the lay public and scholars alike, with visions of annihilating warfare, epidemic diseases, and other apocalyptic disasters given relatively free rein. It was not until the past decade or two that a more balanced view of this cultural transition has come about (Culbert 1973). And a transition, not a complete cultural collapse, it is. True, there are striking changes or even cessations of previous patterns, such as settlement and ceramic styles, but by no means was there total abandonment of the Southern lowlands, as was previously hypothesized.

Many of the misconceptions surrounding the collapse and subsequent lack of populations in the Southern lowlands can be traced to the prevailing "big site" orientation in Peten archaeology. For example, Harvard University Projects focused on two large sites, Altar de Sacrificios (Willey 1972, 1973; A. L. Smith 1972) and Seibal (Willey et al. 1975), on the Usumacinta drainage on the western periphery of Peten. In this area, evidence was recovered that has been used to support invasion or warfare theories of the collapse (Sabloff and Willey 1967); Fine Orange pottery (R. E. Smith 1958) and Mexican motifs on stelae (J. Graham 1973) also suggested strong influences

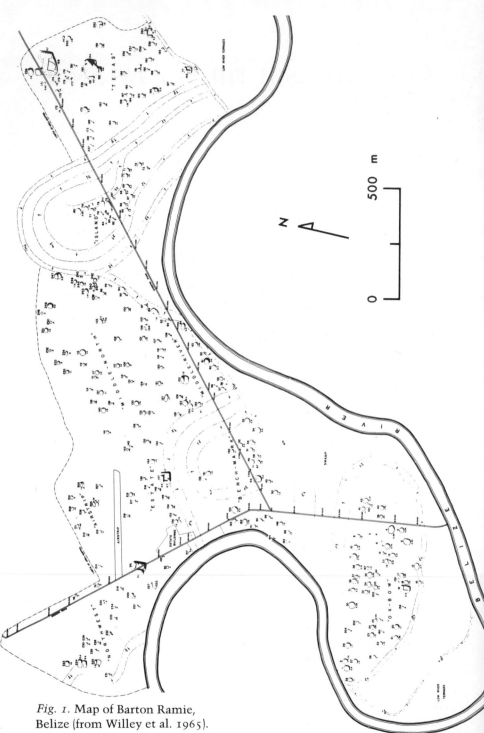

Fig. 1. Map of Barton Ramie,
Belize (from Willey et al. 1965).

from western coastal Yucatan and/or the Tabasco lowlands, and perhaps actual takeover. Similar pottery has been found at other sites in Peten, either as trade pieces or imitations, but in nowhere near the quantities of the Pasion sites. The two other major architectural centers in Peten that have been foci of large archaeological projects, Uaxactun by the Carnegie Institution of Washington (Ricketson and Ricketson 1937; A.L. Smith 1950) and Tikal by the University of Pennsylvania (W. R. Coe 1965a, 1965b, 1967), yielded some Fine Orange pottery but only small quantities of other Postclassic materials, thus fueling the argument of wholesale Postclassic depopulation of Peten. It was at Tikal, however, that one of the major ceramic groups of the Peten Postclassic, the Paxcaman ceramic group, was first identified (Adams and Trik 1961).

It was only through work at smaller sites or in regional approaches to settlement that the nature of the Southern lowlands Postclassic began to be revealed. Two early seminal studies are those by Willey, Bullard, Glass, and Gifford (1965; Gifford 1976) of Barton Ramie in the Belize Valley (fig. 1), and by Cowgill (1963) of the region of Lakes Peten–Itza and Sacpuy. These studies provided a foundation for later work: by Bullard at Topoxte (fig. 2) and Macanche (1970; 1973); by the University of Pennsylvania at Tayasal and Cenote within the Tayasal–Paxcaman Zone of the Lake Peten area (A. Chase 1979, 1983, 1984, 1985a, 1985b, n.d., this volume); by the Central Peten Historical Ecology Project at lakes Yaxha, Sacnab, Macanche, Salpeten, Quexil, and Petenxil (D. Rice and P. Rice 1980a, 1980b, 1982, 1984a; P. Rice and D. Rice, this volume; D. Rice n.d.; P. Rice n.d.a); and by the Macal–Tipu Project at the mission site of Negroman–Tipu in Western Belize (G. Jones 1982, 1983; G. Jones and Kautz 1981a; E. Graham, Jones, and Kautz this volume).

Many of these studies have taken advantage of the extraordinary opportunity to bring together data from both archaeology and ethnohistory in the investigation of research questions of common interest. Such joint efforts are not out of the ordinary in the Northern lowlands, where greater continuity of settlement, more intensive Spanish occupation and concordant documentation, and the Maya's own documents have permitted such close interchanges. In the Southern lowlands, less heavily occupied and long hostile to Spanish overtures, this collaboration has been more difficult to establish successfully. Archaeological verification of the location of individual Itza settlements mentioned in the ethnohistoric documents, beginning with Cortes' A.D. 1525 march across Peten, has been a continuing objective. The location of the Itza capital, Taitza or Taya-

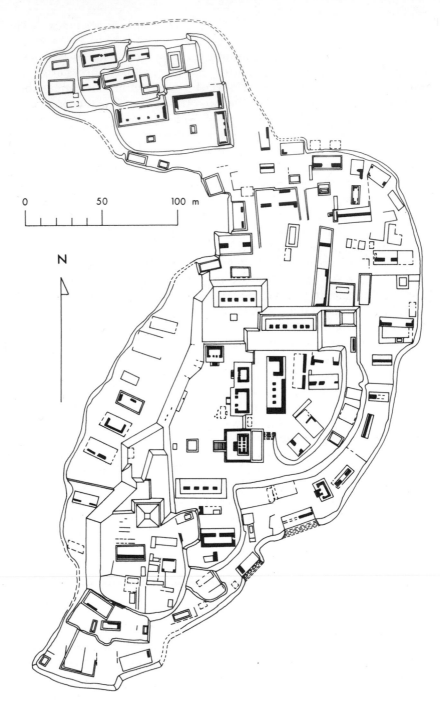

N

0   50   100 m

Fig. 2. Map of Topoxte Island, Guatemala (redrafted by D. Z. Chase from a map made by Nicholas Hellmuth, Foundation for Latin American Anthropological Research, Los Angeles).

sal, has been the source of some debate, suggestions being Topoxte (A. Chase 1976, 1982) versus Flores (G. Jones, Rice, and Rice 1981). Tentative identifications of other settlements, the Tipu mission site at Negroman, Belize (G. Jones and Kautz 1981a; G. Jones 1982), and Yalain at Macanche and Salpeten (Jones, Rice, and Rice 1981), have not yet engendered much controversy (but see A. Chase this volume).

In another sense there has been archaeological confirmation of ethnohistoric statements concerning the general location of Post-classic settlements, i.e., the focus on lacustrine environments. Archaeological research has supported this orientation, suggesting that it may in fact be of considerable duration. Many of these riverine and lacustrine areas, such as Barton Ramie, Tayasal, Lakes Macanche and Salpeten, the Pasion sites, and coastal south-central Belize (see E. Graham this volume), show transitional occupation from the Terminal Classic to the Postclassic. The settlement focus of this time period may have parallels with that of the Preclassic in terms of gradual exchange of riverine for lacustrine habitats. The reasons for this orientation are not yet clear. It may be that simple proximity to water (for drinking, ease of transport, or as a source of edible aquatic fauna) in this water–deficient core area of Peten's tropical forest made it attractive. On the other hand, it may be the moist swampy soils, particularly on the southern shores of the lakes, that enhanced the region's appeal because of the growing requirements of two important Postclassic crops, cacao and cotton. Or, it may be the defensive advantage of island settlements.

Conflict seems to have been a major preoccupation of the inhabitants of the Peten in the sixteenth century. When Cortes passed through the central Peten on his way from Acalan to Naco, Honduras, he mentioned that the Itza were frequently at war with their neighbors and that raiding parties and burned villages were common on his route. Settlement often exhibited defensive constructions in the form of palisades or walls. The antiquity of this phenomenon is unknown, but it may extend well back from the point of initial contact into the Early Postclassic period.

Part of the reason for longstanding conflict in this area may be its equally longstanding role as a frontier, continuously receiving intrusions (sometimes by aggressive groups, sometimes by peoples in flight) from the north, at least as far back as the Classic period. Several papers in this volume (e.g., Andrews and Robles; Ball) discuss the "Putun" movements on the western edge of the Yucatan peninsula, including their thrust up the Usumacinta in the eighth century. Evidence from northern Belize suggests a simultaneous eastern Yucatec intrusion on the eastern border of the Southern lowlands that may have had demographic and political repercussions in the interior (D. Chase and A. Chase 1982; D. Chase 1982a). The most famous of the migrations is the one following the overthrow of Mayapan, whereupon the Itza moved south from central Yucatan to settle on a large lake. This large lake to the south has traditionally been identified as Lake Peten–Itza in the Central Peten. According to the Maya's own legends, this event occurred on a date of *Katun 8 Ahau*, which serves to highlight the problems of correlating Maya and Christian calendars. It has been a matter of some disagreement whether this date of *8 Ahau*, when placed in an 11.16.0.0.0. correlation, fell in the year A.D. 1201 or in A.D. 1458, and this in turn has made it difficult to date ceramic assemblages by their putative links to this Yucatecan migration. Additional migrations occurred later following Spanish contact and missionizing efforts in the north, especially after the brutal conquest of the Chetumal–Bacalar region in A.D. 1544. The Maya response to these events was a series of rebellions against the Spaniards, and continuous population movements into the remote tropical forests of the Southern lowlands. These movements probably continued in varying intensity up through the period of the Caste Wars and beyond (G. Jones 1982).

The continuing archaeological and ethnohistoric research into the Postclassic of the Southern lowlands has demonstrated that there were areas of high population density, complex social systems, and well–organized economic systems involving extensive long–distance trade networks in this area during the Postclassic period. These trade links, through which products such as cacao, cotton cloth, obsidian, jade, and marine shell circulated in abundance, probably acted as a stabilizing force for political interrelations in this zone. Another force promoting stability, and particularly the long resistance of the area to Spanish conquest (the Itza did not fall until 1697) is likely to have been intermarriage. The Maya of Tipu in western Belize were intermarrying with Itza elites in the seventeenth century (G. Jones 1979, 1982), and similar patterns of intermarriage are likely to have aided Itza expansion and/or alliances with completing polities around them in earlier centuries. Intermarriage and assimilation may also account for the broad ceramic homogeneities of Postclassic pottery in the Southern lowlands, as well as the more tenuous resemblances to pottery, particularly censer complexes, in the north.

The papers in this section illuminate many of the points above, using data on pottery and architecture to discuss trade and social interactions. The existence of far more complex architectural variability than known before for the Postclassic is described in the paper by Johnson. His work at Topoxte has documented the presence of an architectural pattern, the "temple assemblage," that appears to be a variant of one that occurs in Yucatan. The paper by P. Rice and D. Rice discusses the existence of this same complex at Macanche and outlines a Postclassic ceramic series spanning the Terminal Classic through the Late Postclassic at Macanche and Topoxte. Architectural as well as ceramic variability is also a theme of the paper by A. Chase, who uses these data as a basis for defining spheres of Postclassic interaction in the central Peten. The paper by Graham, Jones, and Kautz presents a summary of recent work at Negroman–Tipu, Belize, a Spanish and Maya trading center in western Belize that was closely allied with the Itza in central Peten. Finally, Graham's paper discusses Postclassic continuities on the coast of south-central Belize, presenting data which evince ties to both the Northern and Southern lowlands as well as to indigenous traditions of Northern Belize.

Postclassic Maya Site Structure at Topoxte, El Peten, Guatemala

JAY K. JOHNSON

The Topoxte Islands represent one of the major Postclassic settlements in the Southern Maya lowlands. Located on the south side of Lake Yaxha in northeastern Peten, Guatemala, these islands have been visited by many of the major figures in the history of Maya research (Bullard 1970: 251). It was not, however, until Bullard's work in the late 1950s that their major occupation was dated.

Since that time, two research projects have investigated these ruins. In 1973–1974, Don and Prudence Rice excavated several test pits on what Bullard designated as the Third Island as part of a regional survey conducted by the Central Peten Historical Ecology Project (D. Rice 1976; P. Rice 1979). Although a small amount of earlier material was recovered, all 19 of the Rices' excavations contained Postclassic ceramics (D. Rice 1976: 195–197). This lends support to a basic assumption of the following analysis: all the structures on the Topoxte Islands appear to be Postclassic constructions.

During the same period that the Rices were working in the Lake Yaxha region, the Foundation for Latin American Anthropological Research, under the direction of Nicholas Hellmuth, mapped the three main islands. Hellmuth designated Bullard's Second Island as Paxte and the Third Island as Cante. A fourth "island" discussed by Bullard is located to the south of the others and contains only very sparse evidence of occupation. Throughout this paper, Topoxte or Topoxte Island will refer only to Bullard's First Island. Topoxte Islands will be used when it is necessary to designate the islands as a group.

During the summer of 1974, supported by the Foundation for Latin American Archaeological Research (F.L.A.A.R.), I mapped Paxte and Cante Islands using a transit–stadia intercept technique. At that time, the islands were covered with mature tropical forest and structure visibility was excellent. Additionally, preservation was generally very good. This is likely the result of the relatively young age of the structures in combination with the lack of vaulted architecture. At Classic period sites in the same region, vault collapse often obscures structural features. As a result of these factors, an unusual amount of architectural detail is recorded on the two island maps.

These maps form a data base for the following analysis. All observations and measurements were made from the 1:500 scale field maps. Input data for each structure included the orthogonal grid coordinates of each corner of the top of the platform, elevation, distance between contours, slope direction, and the presence or absence of features such as benches, stairs, and columns. Encoding errors were eliminated by producing machine–generated plots of each island showing platform outlines, and overlaying these on the base maps. All other variables used in this paper were derived from the above data by means of a set of FORTRAN IV data transformation routines. Except where otherwise noted, statistics were calculated using the SPSS software (Nie et al. 1975).

Intra–Island Comparisons

STRUCTURE ALIGNMENT

A total of 142 structures were mapped on Cante (fig. 1), as compared to only 68 structures on Paxte. Because of the greater number on Cante, the search for pattern in the placements and configuration of structures will concentrate on the Cante Island subsample.

Although Bullard (1970: fig. 12) mapped the major ceremonial group on Cante with a well–defined plaza and carefully aligned structures, the actual alignments (fig. 1: Structures 1, 2, 3, and 4) are not even close to being at right angles to each other. This apparent disregard for the orientation of adjacent structures is one of the major differences between the organization of Classic and Postclassic sites in the Peten. In order to quantify structural alignment, the orientation of each structure was computed from corner coordinates. This orientation was compared with that of adjacent structures and the differences were measured to the nearest 90 degrees. That is, maximum disorientation would be 45 degrees for, after that angle, the structures begin to approach alignment again.

The average structural alignment between each structure and its first nearest neighbor is 11.8 degrees. There is a gradual increase in the difference in alignment until the eighth nearest neighbor, where the mean divergence from 90 degrees is 17.7 degrees. This

LAKE YAXHA

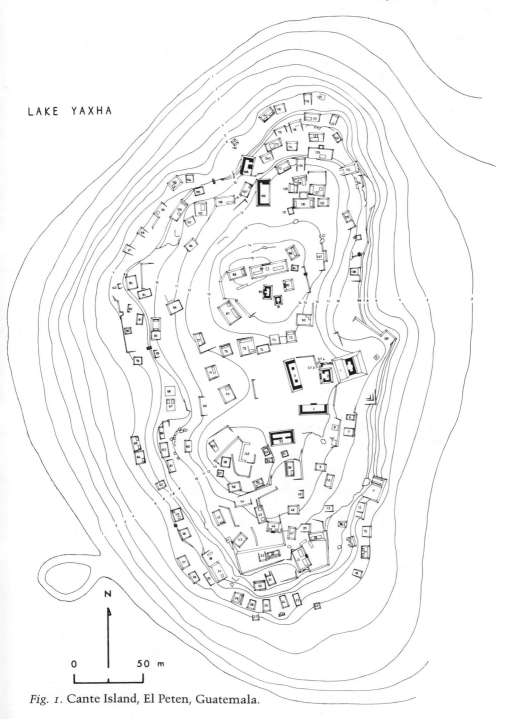

Fig. 1. Cante Island, El Peten, Guatemala.

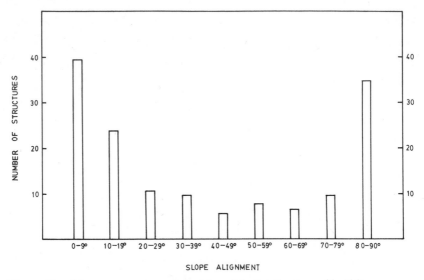

Fig. 2. Graphic presentation of the bimodal distribution of buildings on Cante Island based on a comparison between slope alignment and number of structures.

marks the beginning of a plateau in the distribution. Alignment with more distant structures generally varies between 16 and 18 degrees. The mean of the means of all 142 nearest neighbor comparisons is 17.4 degrees. If structural alignment was completely random, this figure would be 22.5 degrees. The alignment of nearby structures does not appear to be a major factor in the orientation of platforms on Cante Island.

Inspection of the site map (fig. 1) suggests a more critical determinant of structure orientation: direction of slope. When structure orientation and slope orientation are compared (fig. 2), it becomes evident that the distribution is bimodal. One group of structures has a short axis nearly perpendicular to the direction of slope, while a larger group has its short axis and slope in alignment. Therefore, slope alignment was also measured to the nearest 90 degrees.

The average of the difference between structure orientation and direction of slope for the 142 structures on Cante is 13.3 degrees, somewhat greater than the 11.8 degrees of mean divergence from alignment with first nearest neighbor. Two factors must be considered in comparing these measures. First, the average slope alignment includes structures located on the nearly level terrain near the crest of the island. In fact, there is a general trend for the alignment

Table 1. Alignment of Structures with Terrain Slope on Cante Island

Terrain Slope	Number of Structures	Mean Slope Alignment to Nearest 90°
0.0–0.9%	9	15.44°
1.0–1.9%	32	16.72°
2.0–2.9%	37	12.06°
3.0–3.9%	33	12.21°
4.0–4.9%	13	10.46°
5.0–5.9%	11	11.64°
6.0–6.9%	3	13.00°
7.0–7.9%	2	19.50°
8.0–8.9%	0	—
9.0–9.9%	1	10.00°
10.0% or more	1	8.00°

between structures and slope to improve as the slope increases. If the slope distribution is dichotomized using a breakpoint of 4%, the relatively flat areas (slope < 4.0%) have a mean slope alignment of 13.7 degrees, while the steeper areas (slope > 4.0%) have an alignment of 11.6 degrees, slightly better than the average alignment with first nearest neighbor.

The second point to be kept in mind is that structures in the same vicinity are situated on terrain which slopes in roughly the same direction. If structure orientation was determined primarily by direction of slope, then adjacent structures, aligned with similar slopes, should align with one another. Therefore, alignment with first nearest neighbor should improve as slope increases. This is the case: in areas where the slope is less than 4%, the mean structure alignment is 12.0%, while in the steeper areas it is 11.0%.

These data demonstrate a general disregard for inter–structure alignment on Cante Island. This is one expression of the rarity of both plazas among the ceremonial structures and plazuela groupings among the housemounds. Slope alignment seems to be an important factor in structure orientation.

STRUCTURE TYPES

Bullard (1970: 255, 267) already identified the major structure types at Topoxte by means of comparison with structure types at other Postclassic sites. What follows is an attempt to objectify this classification. Structures are first grouped on the basis of the two major continuous variables, length and width. The distribution of

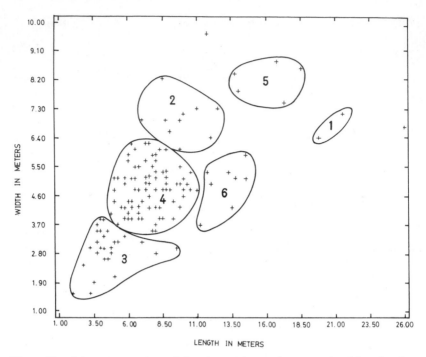

Fig. 3. Graphic presentation of the six resultant clusters gained by plotting the width and length of the structures on Cante Island.

discrete variables across these groups can then be examined in order to suggest correspondences between the derived classes and those of Bullard and others.

Figure 3 is a bivariate plot using length and width to characterize the structures on Cante. The six groupings indicated are the result of a cluster analysis based on these two variables. The BMDP2M subroutine which was used is a Q–mode sequential agglomerative technique (Dixon 1975). The similarity matrix was based on the average Euclidean distance statistic. As the threshold of group inclusion is relaxed, clusters become larger and inter–cluster distances become greater. Inter–cluster distance increases gradually until an order of amalgamation of 134 is reached. The 135th combination brings together clusters which were separated by an average Euclidean distance nearly one third again as large as the distance of the previous amalgamation. This break provides an objective criterion for locating a maximum level of group inclusion yielding six groups which classify all but two structures.
The four major architectural features found in these structures

Table 2. Results of Cluster Analysis of Cante Island Structures

Group	Mean Dimensions in Meters	Structure Numbers
Unclassified	—	75, 89
I	13.05 × 4.96	1, 44, 69, 100, 106, 130, 133, 142
2	9.72 × 6.97	34, 38, 68, 70, 71, 85, 86, 93, 102, 108, 127, 128
3	4.53 × 2.96	5, 6, 8, 14, 22, 25, 26, 35, 41, 49, 51, 53, 54, 57, 59, 66, 78, 80, 82, 94, 110, 120, 124, 131, 135, 136, 140, 141
4	7.53 × 2.96	2, 7, 9, 10, 11, 12, 13, 15, 16, 17, 18, 19, 20, 23, 24, 26, 28, 29, 30, 31, 32, 33, 36, 37, 39, 40, 42, 43, 45, 46, 47, 48, 50, 55, 56, 58, 60, 61, 62, 63, 64, 65, 67, 72, 73, 74, 76, 77, 79, 81, 83, 84, 88, 90, 91, 92, 95, 96, 97, 98, 99, 101, 103, 104, 105, 107, 111, 112, 113, 114, 115, 116, 117, 118, 119, 121, 122, 123, 126, 129, 132, 134, 137, 138, 139
5	16.06 × 8.19	21, 52, 87, 109, 125
6	20.54 × 6.75	3, 4

Table 3. Architectural Features in Cante Island Structure Groups

Group	Total Structures	Stairs	Columns	Walls	Benches
1	8	o	+	o	o
2	12	o	o	o	+
3	28	o	o	o	−
4	85	o	o	o	o
5	5	o	o	+	o
6	2	+	+	+	o

(benches, columns, stairs, and walls) can then be tabulated across these six groups. Although individual cell frequencies are too small to allow a meaningful evaluation by means of the chi-square statistic, it is possible to designate those groups which have more or fewer examples of each feature than would be expected by chance alone. These relationships are expressed in Table 3 by a "+" when the observed value is greater than expected, a "−" when it is less, and "o" when there is no significant difference. This amounts to a componential characterization of each cluster.

Groups 1 and 6 are similar in terms of architectural features, having the largest number of examples of stairs, columns, and walls of any of the groups. These features, in combination with the long, narrow dimensions of these structures, suggest a ceremonial function. In fact, the group includes examples of both open halls and temples as defined by Bullard (1970: 255). These two types could undoubtedly be distinguished if height of platform could be considered. Unfortunately, however, these data were not recorded in all cases, a serious oversight on my part.

Bullard (1970: 275) has already noted the strong resemblance between open halls at Topoxte and colonnaded halls at Mayapan. He observed also that at Topoxte and Mayapan these architectural types are independent buildings, whereas at Chichen Itza they form attached galleries. While Bullard (1970: 266) thought it "probable" that most open halls had steps along the entire length of the open side, it is now evident that most of them, on Paxte and Cante islands, at least, had central stairways. In this feature they resemble colonnaded halls at Mayapan. The structures from the two areas are also alike in floor plan, the only significant differences being the absence of a front row of columns and lack of evidence for interior shrines on the three islands. The halls at both Mayapan and Topoxte have a row of columns on the mid–line of the long axis, while at Chichen Itza most colonnaded halls have several rows of columns.

The structures of Group 5 are the widest on Cante and are second only to Group 6 in total platform area. Two of the five structures in this group show evidence of low walls, while three have benches and one has stairs. Given the common occurrence of the latter two features in other clusters, their appearance in Group 5 is not significantly non-random, and hence the zeros in Table 3. A zero, however, does not mean that the features are completely absent in the group.

Group 2 is similar to Group 5 in overall proportions, but structures in this cluster are generally smaller and contain a larger number of benches. It is difficult to assign function to Groups 2 and 5 on the basis of surface expression alone. The presence of interior benches and the shape of these structures indicate the possibility that they were residential. They are, however, sizeable and display some of the architectural features associated with ceremonial structures. Groups 2 and 5 may represent elite residential structures.

Group 3 structures are small, featureless platforms, many of which are nearly square. Some of the members of this group are similar to structures at Topoxte which Bullard (1970: 267) labeled "shrines" or dance platforms. Others may have supported domestic outbuildings, perhaps kitchens.

The majority of the structures fall into Group 4. These are medium-sized, rectangular platforms, and most have no observed architectural features. Thirty-three of the 85, however, support one or more small, low platforms which are interpreted to have been benches. These benches are located near the edge of the platform. The most common location is on the upslope side toward the ends leaving the center of the side open. From the size and number of these structures, and the presence of benches, it may be argued that Group 4 structures were housemounds.

DISTRIBUTION OF STRUCTURES

A tacit assumption underlying many of the discussions of Maya site plans is that the status differential expressed in other aspects of material culture will be reflected in the layout of the ceremonial center (Arnold and Ford 1980). Recently this assumption has been tested using Classic period data from Lubaantun (Hammond 1975a) and Tikal (Arnold and Ford 1980).

In its simplest form, the model assumes that elite residences will be larger and located nearer the ceremonial precincts. There should, therefore, be a negative correlation between structure size and distance from ceremonial zones. Three clusters of ceremonial structures were observed on Cante, and a central point was selected for each (near Structures 2, 51, and 90). The distance between each structure and the nearest of these points is compared to three measures of structure size (length, width, and area) in Table 4a by means of Pearson's coefficient. All three correlations are negative as predicted, but the correlations, while significant at generally acceptable levels, are not strong. Moreover, these analyses were based on the entire Cante sample including those structures which appear to have been nonresidential. If the presumably ceremonial structures of Groups 1 and 6 are removed from these calculations, all three correlations drop considerably and none are significant (Table 4b).

This does not mean that the distribution of structures on Cante Island is random in relationship to the location of ceremonial architecture. The distances of structures from the nearest ceremonial zone can be divided into three concentric segments (<45 meters; $45-90$ meters; and >90 meters) for purposes of cross-tabulation with the structure groups derived from the cluster analysis. This procedure indicates that the distribution is non-random in a one-tailed test, with a chi-square statistic of 15.34 and an alpha level of 0.0599. The structure groups are located within the three concentric zones in a way that is consistent with the functional characterizations based on architectural features. Group 4 structures, which

Table 4. Correlations between Distance from Concentrations of Ceremonial Structures and Measures of Structure Size on Cante Island

	Length	Width	Area
a. *Total sample*			
Pearson's *r*	−0.2027	−0.1187	−0.2169
Significance	0.008	0.080	0.005
b. *Nonceremonial subsample*			
Pearson's *r*	−0.0195	−0.0702	−0.0740
Significance	0.413	0.213	0.200

seem to be primarily housemounds, occur most frequently in the outer zone (>90 meters), while Group 2 structures, the smaller "elite residences," are found in the mid-range zone. Group 5 buildings, the large "elite residences," are most common in the innermost zone closest to the ceremonial architecture. The two primarily ceremonial clusters are positive in the central zone (Group 6) or the central and middle zones (Group 1). Group 3 structures have a slightly bimodal distribution, with positive loadings in the central and outer zones. This supports the suggestion made earlier that these small platforms may represent shrines or domestic outbuildings.

Inter–Island Comparisons

The majority of the analyses presented in this section will contrast Cante and Paxte. Bullard's map of the central zone at Topoxte (1970: fig. 3) in combination with field sketches and notes resulting from Hellmuth's work on that island allow a limited number of generalizations which cover all three islands.

STRUCTURE TYPES

As a first step in comparing Paxte and Cante Islands, a cluster analysis was performed for the Paxte structures using the measurements of platform length and width as derived from the site map (fig. 4). The procedures were the same as those used in the analysis of structures on Cante Island. All but three of the 68 structures were classified into 5 groups. There is a nearly one–to–one correspondence between the cluster groups of Paxte and Cante Islands as based on mean dimensions and architectural features. The exception is that Groups 2 and 5, the "elite domestic" structures on Cante, are subsumed by a single cluster, Group 2, on Paxte.

Table 5. Results of Cluster Analysis of Paxte Island Structures

Group	Mean Dimensions in Meters	Structure Numbers
Unclassified	—	2, 18, 41
1	17.99 × 9.02	10, 11, 14, 43, 44, 53
2	11.63 × 7.37	13, 17, 19, 20, 21, 22, 25, 28, 29, 31, 35, 39, 40, 45, 46, 55, 59, 61, 63, 66, 67, 68
3	2.66 × 2.15	3, 4, 5, 8, 9, 33, 58
4	7.60 × 4.46	7, 12, 15, 16, 23, 24, 26, 27, 30, 32, 34, 36, 37, 38, 42, 47, 48, 49, 50, 51, 52, 54, 56, 57, 60, 62, 64, 65
6	29.44 × 7.15	1, 6

Table 6. Architectural Features in Paxte Island Structure Groups

Group	Total Structures	Stairs	Columns	Walls	Benches
1	6	+	o	+	o
2	22	o	o	o	o
3	7	o	o	o	—
4	28	—	o	—	o
6	2	+	+	+	o

Table 7. Percentage of Residential Structures on Paxte and Cante Islands

Island	Housemounds (Structure Group 4)	"Elite Residential" (Structure Groups 2 and 5)
Cante	60.71	12.14
Paxte	43.06	33.84

Table 8. Mean Structure Alignments for Paxte and Cante Islands

	Paxte	Cante
Slope alignment	18.17°	13.26°
Nearest neighbor alignment	11.04°	11.70°

Comparable structure groups are not represented equally, however, on the two islands. A cross-tabulation of the Cante structure types and equivalent Paxte groups shows that major differences occur (chi-square statistic of 17.13 and a significance level of 0.0018). There are considerably fewer housemound structures on Paxte, and considerably more "elite residential" structures.

STRUCTURE ALIGNMENT

Both slope alignment and first nearest neighbor alignment were computed for each structure on Paxte Island using the conventions developed in the Cante analysis. The mean values for these statistics among the 68 Paxte structures were compared to corresponding values for Cante in Table 8. There is considerably less agreement between structure alignment and slope alignment on Paxte as compared to Cante, which would suggest that alignment with adjacent structures might be better on Paxte. As Table 8 demonstrates, this is not the case when the Paxte structures are considered as a group. If Paxte is divided into three concentric zones (<30 meters, 30–60 meters, and >60 meters), however, on the basis of distance from nearest ceremonial area (three points located near Structures 1, 2, and 3; Structures 7, 8, and 10; and Structures 53, 58, and 59), the inner two zones have considerably better mean nearest neighbor alignment than does the outer zone (Table 9). Moreover, there is no corresponding pattern across the zones on Cante.

The greater emphasis on inter-structure alignment within the ceremonial precinct on Paxte corroborates the results of the structure types analysis in the preceding section. That is, features commonly associated with elite architecture are more prevalent on Paxte. Bullard's map and Hellmuth's notes on Topoxte indicate that ceremonial architecture is even more common on that island. The three islands appear to form a continuum ranging from predominantly domestic architecture at Cante to primarily ceremonial structures on Topoxte.

BROADER COMPARISONS

Similarities between the structures of Topoxte Island and those of other Postclassic Maya sites, based on architectural features and dimensions, have already been noted. Within Maya studies, there has been a recent interest in comparisons at the next higher scale: types of structural arrangements. At Tikal, these types are called "plaza plans," calling attention to the fact that formal groupings of Maya buildings commonly focus on a plaza (C. Jones 1969; Becker

Table 9. Nearest Neighbor Alignments within Zones Based on Distance from Concentrations of Ceremonial Structures, Paxte and Cante Islands

	Paxte Island		Cante Island	
Zone	Number of Structures	Mean Alignment	Number of Structures	Mean Alignment
1	21	9.36°	30	11.19°
2	37	9.78°	56	12.71°
3	7	21.63°	54	11.14°

1971; Ashmore 1981). George Andrews (1975: 53–71), without reference to the Tikal work, defines a series of "basic building groupings" which have primary relevance to Classic period site organization.

Preceding the above studies and dealing with data of direct relevance to the Topoxte Islands, Proskouriakoff (1962a: 91) set the standard in structure group typology in her Mayapan analysis: "In the typical *temple assemblage*, a pyramid temple . . . stands at right angles to the colonnaded hall, and the shrine, which remains roughly centered on the hall, is turned to face the temple." There are three Topoxte Islands structure groups which are analogous to the Mayapan temple assemblage. One, located on Topoxte, consists of Bullard's (1970: fig. 3) Structures C (temple), B (open hall), J (shrine), and K (shrine). There are two examples on Paxte (fig. 4), the most easily recognizable centering on the plaza defined by Structures 10 (temple), 6 (open hall), 8 (shrine), and 9 (shrine). The other, just to the north, is formed by Structures 2 (temple), 1 (open hall), 3 (shrine), and 4 (shrine).

These groups conform to Proskouriakoff's temple assemblage typology by having a plaza defined by an open hall and temple situated at right angles to one another. There are small, square platforms near the middle of the plaza located on the main axis of the temple and only approximately centered on the open halls. The Topoxte Islands' groups depart from the Mayapan model most radically in the absence of any structure which could be classified as an oratory on Topoxte, Paxte, or Cante. Oratories are a regular feature of the temple assemblage at Mayapan. Also, the center court platforms at Mayapan are usually "raised shrines" supporting single room structures. Furthermore, in all three plazas on the islands there is a second, smaller platform located behind the first platform.

While the majority of the open halls on the Topoxte Islands do not form part of an assemblage which conforms to this plaza type,

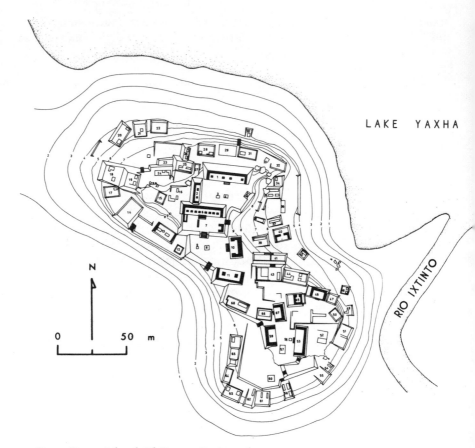

Fig. 4. Paxte Island, El Peten, Guatemala.

the fact that three do fill positions analogous to those of colonnaded halls at Mayapan strengthens the comparison between colonnaded and open halls.

Conclusions

The Topoxte plaza type, defined on the basis of a temple located at approximate right angles to an open hall with two small platforms lined up on the main axis of the temple, has recently been identified elsewhere in Peten (D. Rice and P. Rice 1981; P. Rice and D. Rice, this volume) and should form a basis of comparison for further analysis of Postclassic settlement patterns. This plaza type was not identified on Cante, a fact in keeping with other indicators of dissimilarity between Cante and the other Topoxte Islands. These differences are best expressed in the relative importance of ceremonial architecture on the islands. The distinctions between Cante, Paxte, and Topoxte may be the result of temporal differences; however, ceramic evidence seems to indicate that occupation of the islands was contemporaneous (P. Rice 1979). If so, there appears to be an inter–island settlement hierarchy with Cante being primarily residential, Paxte elite residential and ceremonial, and Topoxte mainly ceremonial.

This hierarchy, coupled with the distribution of structure types relative to centers of ceremonial architecture on Cante, suggests that Postclassic Maya society was stratified rather than ranked. That is, there is no gradual increase in structure size which correlates with greater centralization and more access to ceremonial and administrative structures. Rather, there is a series of structure types, each containing buildings similar in both architectural features and dimensions, reflecting what may have been discrete steps in the distribution of status on the Topoxte Islands. If this was the case, the search for status indicators in settlement studies and other types of analyses should utilize statistics based on hierarchical and paradigmatic models, rather than those based on linear regression.

Acknowledgments

I would like to thank Nicholas Hellmuth and the Foundation for Latin American Anthropological Research for the fieldwork which produced the island maps. For the analyses of these data, I am indebted to the University of Mississippi for its generous support. Specifically, the Center for Archaeological Research provided drafting and secretarial services as well as travel money for me to attend the 1979 AAA symposium in Cincinnati. The Department of Sociology and Anthropology supplied computer time.

Topoxte, Macanche, and the Central Peten Postclassic

PRUDENCE M. RICE AND DON S. RICE

The six centuries of central Peten prehistory from the Classic collapse to the time of Spanish contact in A.D. 1525 are not well understood archaeologically. The depopulation and cessation of construction associated with the collapse ca. A.D. 900 were probably not absolute, but the size and location of remnant populations and their rate of increase through succeeding generations are unknown. Ethnohistoric records provide a brief glimpse into the Postclassic; they tell of numerous groups in the Peten in the sixteenth century. These groups farmed, traded with areas as distant as Honduras, and engaged in more or less chronic conflict with their neighbors. At the time of these Spanish writings, the Peten occupation was focused on lacustrine environments, particularly on the islands, or *petenes*, in the lakes of central Peten (fig. 1).

Archaeological research has supported these sixteenth and seventeenth century observations as to settlement location, and suggested that the lacustrine focus may be of some duration. Much of what is currently known about the Peten Postclassic occupational sequence has come from excavations at three island sites: Flores Island in Lake Peten–Itza (Cowgill 1963), Topoxte Island in Lake Yaxha (Bullard 1970), and Macanche Island in Lake Macanche (Bullard 1973). These investigations have answered some questions, but they have raised new ones as well. The most troublesome of these questions have been chronological, because Peten Postclassic sites have notoriously poor stratigraphy and localized ceramic traditions. Consequently, it has been difficult to factor existing variability into components that are clearly identifiable as temporal, functional, or ethnic in significance.

For example, until recently a clear continuity from Late Classic through Terminal Classic to Postclassic had not been demonstrated archaeologically in the Peten core area proper, as it had at the site of

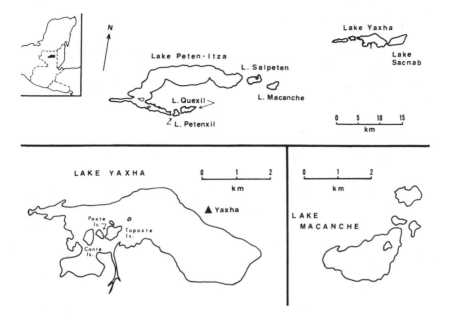

Fig. 1. The central Peten lakes area, showing islands in Lakes Yaxha and Macanche.

Barton Ramie, in Belize. Vaughan's (1979) analysis of pollen from Lake Yaxha suggested continued disturbance, and therefore occupation, by some minimal population in that area, but this had not been confirmed archaeologically. Thus, a hiatus of unknown duration between the Classic collapse and the start of the Postclassic occupation was possible in some areas of Peten.

Ceramic and architectural variability are additional areas of interpretational difficulty, particularly with respect to regional and interregional interaction. Cowgill's (1963) excavations on Flores Island formed the basis for definition of the indigenous Peten Postclassic ceramic traditions, comprised of the red-slipped Augustine and Paxcaman ceramic groups. Bullard's (1970) later investigations on Topoxte Island, however, indicated strong ties to Mayapan, and hence a late date for that occupation, by virtue of distinctive ceramic (effigy censers; red-on-cream Topoxte ceramic group decoration) and architectural traits. Subsequent work at Macanche (Bullard 1973) was carried out in the hope of obtaining data from the Classic through the Late Postclassic periods of occupation in order to integrate these two bodies of information. The resultant synthesis included the chronological ordering of the three red-slipped Postclassic ceramic groups known in Peten into the "Peten Postclassic Tradition" (Bullard 1973).

This sequence, which was interpreted as spanning the years from the collapse to just prior to the conquest (no Spanish artifacts were recovered from Macanche or Topoxte) placed the Augustine group earliest, followed by the Paxcaman group, with the Topoxte group overlapping the end of the Paxcaman pottery, contemporaneous with the Tases late occupation of Mayapan.

Historical Ecology Project Excavations

Recent excavations at two of these Postclassic island sites, Topoxte in 1974 and Macanche in 1979, have led to some reinterpretations of this sequence, and identification of areas of Classic–to–Postclassic settlement continuity. These excavations were carried out as part of an ongoing historical ecology project surveying Maya population growth and impact on tropical lacustrine environments (Deevey et al. 1979; D. Rice and P. Rice 1980a, 1984a). The foci of this project in 1973–1974 were in the basins of lakes Yaxha and Sacnab in the northeast Peten; in 1979–1980, Lake Macanche, 25 kilometers to the southwest of Lakes Yaxha–Sacnab (D. Rice and P. Rice 1980b), and its sister, Lake Salpeten (D. Rice and P. Rice 1984b), were investigated. Also surveyed in 1980 were the basins of lakes Quexil and Petenxil, small lakes south of the main body of Lake Peten–Itza.

LAKE YAXHA AND THE TOPOXTE ISLANDS

Postclassic occupation in the basins of Lakes Yaxha and Sacnab is almost entirely confined to the Topoxte Islands, a group of three islands and a landlocked peninsula in the southwestern portion of Lake Yaxha. The largest of the islands is referred to as Topoxte Island (Hellmuth 1974), and was the site of Bullard's testing in 1959. The material recovered from his excavations into ceremonial architecture on this island was incorporated into his preliminary definition of the Postclassic Isla phase of occupation of the islands. No clearly identifiable Postclassic settlement is known from the mainland around the lakes (Bullard 1970: 252; but see A. Chase 1976: 155–156), although scattered Postclassic sherds have been recovered from surface contexts on the north shore of Lake Yaxha. No Postclassic artifacts were noted around Lake Sacnab (D. Rice and P. Rice 1980a).

In 1974, a non-probabilistically selected transect was placed over another of the islands in the Topoxte group, Cante Island. One hundred twelve structures were mapped (cf. Johnson, this volume) in close–packed arrangement on the island, and test pits were placed into nineteen structures and/or associated collapse. Six of these tested areas yielded remains of construction activity in the Preclassic or Classic periods, while all 19 yielded Postclassic evidence.

The ceramics of the Postclassic Isla complex have two characteristic components of interest to this discussion (see P. Rice 1979): an assortment of red-slipped tripod dishes, jars, bowls, and miscellaneous forms of a distinctive cream–colored marly paste (Clemencia Cream paste ware), and a censer subcomplex, consisting of elaborately modeled human effigy censers as well as simpler impressed–fillet vase type censers.

Marked differences were noted in comparing the distribution of these ceramic forms and types from Bullard's excavations into ceremonial architecture on the largest island with those from historical ecology project excavations into primarily residential contexts on Cante Island. Bullard's excavations had yielded quantities of the censers, as well as large amounts of red-slipped pottery, principally sherds exhibiting elaborate interlocking scroll–like and rectilinear decorations in dark red paint on the cream background. The dissimilarity of these materials to known indigenous Paxcaman Postclassic ceramics from Peten, the ties of the effigy censers to Yucatan, plus the architectural context which suggests affinities to Mayapan, led Bullard (1970) to hypothesize close links between the Postclassic occupation at Topoxte and that late Yucatecan Postclassic site.

The materials recovered from the 1974 historical ecology project excavations on the smaller island suggested greater ties of the Topoxte Islands ceramics to the indigenous Postclassic tradition of central Peten, exemplified by the well–known Paxcaman group. In terms of forms, the Topoxte group shares the range of shapes exhibited by Paxcaman, including tripod basal break dishes, collared bowls, wide– and narrow–necked jars, *tecomates*, and round–sided bowls. The vessel sizes or proportions differ, however (P. Rice 1979).

Relationships are particularly evident in the decorative treatments of the red-slipped vessels. Typological parallels to the defined units of the Paxcaman and Trapeche groups from central Peten could be named in the Topoxte collections from Cante Island on the basis of decorative technique (Table 1).

Decorative motifs in the painted types of the Topoxte group also have parallels in the Paxcaman group. Sherds of the Akalche Variety of Chompoxte Red-on-Cream, as well as sherds of Pastel and Cante Polychromes, have patterns of design structure, motifs, and arrangement that are similar to those of Ixpop and Saca Polychromes. A simple design band, which encircles the interior vessel wall of tripod dishes, the exterior of jar bodies, and the interior collar of collared

Table 1. Major Decorative Types within Central Peten Postclassic Ceramic Groups

Diagnostic Decoration	Ceramic Group		
	Paxcaman	Trapeche	Topoxte
Black-on-Cream polychrome	Ixpop Polychrome	Mul Polychrome	Pastel Polychrome
Red-and-Black on-Cream polychrome	Saca Polychrome	Dolorido Polychrome	Cante Polychrome
Postfire incising	Picu Incised	Xuluc Incised	Dulces Incised
Red-on-Cream polychrome	Macanche Red-on-Paste	Picte Red-on-Cream	Chompoxte Red-on-Cream

bowls, bears single or paired vertical and diagonal lines, hooks, plume–like elements, and curls, often arranged in panels. Areas exterior to the design band, including the interior floors of tripod dishes, are red-slipped.

These points of decorative similarity between the Cante Island material and Paxcaman pottery must be contrasted with the very distinctive attributes noted in the sherds recovered by Bullard on Topoxte Island. Most of the ceramic materials from Bullard's excavations have been subsumed within a separate variety of Chompoxte Red-on-Cream type, the Chompoxte Variety (P. Rice 1979), that is very different from the Akalche Variety described above. These Chompoxte Variety vessels show a complex pattern of scrolls, dots, tics, mat motifs, combs, plume–like elements, nested rectangles, etc., executed in dark red paint on a cream background, and occasionally appearing by "negative painting." These designs on tripod dishes cover the entire interior of the vessel, rather than occurring in bands around the wall.

The variability within the Topoxte ceramic group may be interpreted on several different levels. The first concerns differences with respect to depositional context and function, that is, the distribution of Topoxte group pottery over the Topoxte Islands. Bullard's excavations into ceremonial contexts on the largest island yielded quantities of the unusual Chompoxte Red-on-Cream: Chompoxte Variety pottery and effigy censers, the latter of which have parallels with Mayapan and the northern peninsula, while excavations into residential contexts on Cante Island provided fewer censers but a broader range of slipped wares showing ties to indigenous central Peten decorative styles. Johnson's (this volume) analysis of architectural variation between the islands supports this hypothesis of the islands having different functions with respect to the relative importance of residential versus ceremonial activity.

A second interpretation is that of temporal variability. If the earlier ceramic chronology is accepted, materials from Bullard's excavations into ceremonial contexts on Topoxte Island suggest closer ties to Mayapan and, thus, late temporal placement, while on Cante Island the pottery more similar to indigenous Paxcaman styles would be dated somewhat earlier. Given the sharing of architectural (Johnson, this volume) and ceramic styles among the islands, however, we think it is unlikely that there is substantial temporal difference in occupation of Cante versus Topoxte Island.

A recent review of the ceramic collection from Cante Island has resulted in identification of three separate "patterns" or clusters of types (P. Rice n.d.a), which have a bearing on questions of dating and function. The "Group B" pattern consisted principally of the types most closely related to types of the Paxcaman group in decoration; censers were rare. The "Group A" pattern consisted primarily of red-on-cream decorated Chompoxte type (the category into which Bullard's material was classified), and in general was rather heterogeneous in its typological makeup. The "Group C" pattern was mixed in terms of having both the red-on-cream and Paxcaman–like types, but in general is characterized by relatively small quantities of decorated pottery as opposed to unslipped and censer forms. These patterns were found in stratigraphic association in some of the mounds, with Group C being associated always with late surface and/or midden debris on the island. In four excavations Group C overlay Group B, while in two excavations Group C overlay Group A; in no case, however, were Groups A and B found in association. Thus while Group C is clearly later than A and B, it is not known if A and B are coeval or if one is later than the other.

In the absence of clear temporal differences between the two very different decorative schemes represented by Groups A and B pottery, other sources of variability, such as status and/or function, are logical suggestions. One means of investigating this possibility is by looking at the distribution of these "patterns" in the structure/function groups suggested by Johnson (this volume) for Cante Island. Our excavation program resulted in test pits being placed in or near at least one structure in all six of his functional categories, and the largest number of pits (9) was in his largest category, the housemounds of category 4. The only tentative association that could be postulated from this comparison is that the Group A (Chompoxte) pattern occurred only in Johnson's category 4 housemounds, and in no other group. Category 4 housemounds also included Group B and

Group C, while Group B was also noted in excavations into small and large elite residences (Johnson's categories 2 and 5), and the domestic outbuilding/shrine category (category 3). Our excavations into the ceremonial contexts on the island were in midden rather than construction, and yielded only the mixed late Group C ceramic pattern.

In sum, although there seems to be a stratigraphic basis for differentiating earlier (A and B) from later (C) ceramic material at Cante Island, there is no readily apparent explanation for the significant decorative differences between A and B that can tie them to particular statuses or functions, at least as these correlate with architecture on Cante Island. It is probably significant that virtually the only examples of Topoxte group pottery found outside of the Topoxte Islands themselves are sherds of the red-on-cream Chompoxte type that was characteristic of Group A.

Whatever the functional, status, or other significance of this distinctive decorated pottery within the Topoxte settlement or as part of the larger Peten sphere, the source of inspiration for the style cannot be securely determined. Initially, at least, the source was thought to be northern Yucatan. Ethnohistoric reports tell of legends of migrations into Peten in a *Katun 8 Ahau*, believed to fall either in A.D. 1458 or A.D. 1201, when the Itza fled Mayapan. The ceramic evidence from Mayapan and other sites in Yucatan (R. E. Smith 1971; Sanders 1960) does reveal some parallels, having some superficially similar red-on-buff and polychrome painted vessels in addition to the distinctive effigy censers that accompanied the red-on-cream pottery at Topoxte. No clear precedents, however, have been identified for these Yucatecan materials.

The Chompoxte Red-on-Cream pottery seems to be a local expression of a broader generalized Postclassic style of decoration that has distinctive variants throughout Mesoamerica and beyond. Red-on-cream or -buff decoration featuring scrolls, spirals, dots, plumes, and so forth can be found in highland Maya Postclassic ceramics (Wauchope 1970), as well as all along the Gulf coast. Some of the Chompoxte materials are similar to decorative patterns occurring in the Late Postclassic Veracruz area, for example (see also Ball's discussion of Campeche, this volume), which are continued in some twentieth century manufactures in the vicinity (S.J.K. Wilkerson, personal communication). The more restrained or simple paneled band designs suggest resemblances with Late Aztec black-on-orange decoration on tripod dishes. Participation of the lowlands in wider spheres of interaction with the Gulf coast and highland Mexico, for example, may be responsible for some of these similarities.

Regardless of the specific external affinities of this small but distinctive subset of the Topoxte pottery, the bulk of it is considered to be a localized technological and decorative variant of the already known and described Paxcaman group. As such, it shares typological analogues as well as a basic repertoire of forms and decorative styles with Paxcaman, but is executed in a distinctive paste, and is probably largely temporally equivalent. This view contrasts with earlier interpretations of the Topoxte ceramic group as belonging to a post–Paxcaman complex distinguished by largely intrusive stylistic and formal elements. We suggest that occupation of the Topoxte Islands and production of Topoxte group pottery were not exclusively late phenomena in the Peten Postclassic sequence.

LAKE MACANCHE: ISLAND AND MAINLAND

Excavations at Lake Macanche, the focus of the 1979 field season of Proyecto Lacustre, allowed supplementation of Postclassic materials from Bullard's 1968 testing of Macanche Island. One of the principal accomplishments of these excavations was to allow phasing and faceting of the Postclassic period, suggesting the possibility that this area might be one of Classic–to–Postclassic continuities. Further evidence for such continuity comes from Macanche's sister lake, Salpeten, lying to the west (D. Rice and P. Rice 1984b), but is outside the scope of this report. Additional discoveries in the Macanche lake basin relevant to an understanding of the Peten Postclassic included the identification of a considerable amount of Postclassic construction on the mainland around the lake and Postclassic structures within a substantial defensive wall located on elevated terrain northeast of the lake (D. Rice and P. Rice 1981).

Macanche Island is a small, roughly triangular island in the northeast corner of Lake Macanche. On its northern apex is a low trapezoidal platform, approximately 55 meters long by 28–40 meters wide, 3.0 meters high, and oriented northwest-southeast. This platform has been badly disturbed by modern activity, but a few lines of stone suggest the existence of at least two structures atop the mound (fig. 2). Five of eight test pits on the island yielded stratigraphic information on the Postclassic occupation and mound construction. They provided the basis for dividing the Postclassic sequence into two phases, Early and Late, with the Early phase being further subdivided into early and late facets (P. Rice 1980).

The early facet of the Early Postclassic phase at Macanche is characterized by the presence of Paxcaman and Trapeche slipped ceramic groups, plus Pozo Unslipped type. In addition, three unslipped types characteristic of the Late Classic continued to be used in the

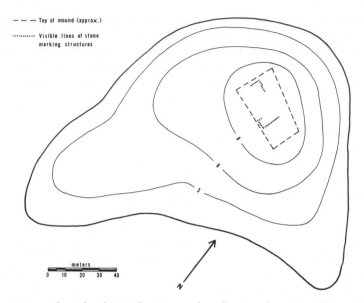

– – – Top of mound (approx.)

·········· Visible lines of stone
            marking structures

meters
0   10   20   30   40

Fig. 2. Macanche Island in Lake Macanche, showing location of Postclassic platform and approximate positioning of structures; contours are in meters.

early facet of the Early Postclassic. A diversity of pastes in the slipped groups suggests multiple manufacturers or manufacturing loci, while the heavy fireclouding and apparent low level of firing skills register a lack of craft specialists in ceramic production and/or a lack of familiarity with the working properties of locally available resources (P. Rice 1980). In terms of trying to determine the nature of the initial post–collapse occupation of Peten, this ceramic evidence might be interpreted to suggest the coexistence of both new and old inhabitants in this area. An "old" or remnant group still in the region after the "collapse" may have continued to make and use the Late Classic unslipped vessels while new or "pioneering" occupants attempted to make red and cream slipped vessels using clays and firing materials with which they were unfamiliar. In this sense it is plausible that any such "pioneering" aspect refers not necessarily to new people moving into the area, but also to economic pioneering: individuals who had not made pottery before were starting to adopt this unfamiliar craft.

In any case, the early facet Early Postclassic occupants of Macanche Island had few intra– or extra–regional economic ties. Lithic materials recovered from the early facet Early Postclassic deposits on the island were of generally poor quality, suggesting lack of knowledge of or access to cherts of better quality (M. Aldenderfer, personal communication). Only one piece of obsidian was recovered and one fragment of marine shell, and a few sherds of a trade ceramic, Fine Orange. To the extent that the occupation of Macanche Island represents the Early Postclassic in the central Peten area, this period appears to be one of small populations, economically unspecialized and relatively isolated.

The late facet of the Early Postclassic represents a considerably altered and more developed socioeconomic situation. Paxcaman and Trapeche ceramic groups continued with increasing frequencies of decorated types in these groups. The heavy fireclouding noted in the early facet sherds is absent and the potters appear to have much better control of the firing process. Variability in pastes declines, likewise suggesting more standardized resource use and manufacturing behavior. The three unslipped Late Classic wares ceased to be utilized in the late facet of the Early Postclassic, with Pozo Unslipped taking over as the most common undecorated type. Small quantities of sherds of the Augustine group, a ceramic group occurring in abundance at Barton Ramie in the Early Postclassic and also present in considerable quantities around Lake Peten–Itza (A. Chase 1979, this volume), appear at Macanche in the late facet of the Early Postclassic. The presence of this group at Macanche may indicate newly opened avenues of communication with some group or region previously outside such contacts, but because the area or areas of manufacture of Augustine pottery are unknown, little more can be said.

Chipped stone artifacts reflect access to both a greater variety of cherts and to higher quality materials (M. Aldenderfer, personal communication). Larger numbers of obsidian fragments were found in late facet deposits, as well as some fragments of basalt and quartzite manos and metates, suggesting trade with the highlands. Thus, a wider variety of exterior contacts and greater economic organization (as evidenced by production and trade) appears to be indicated for the late facet, as compared to the early facet, of the Early Postclassic.

The Late Postclassic phase at Macanche Island is represented by the building of the structure on the northwest end of the platform on the island, plus a 30–50–centimeter–thick midden all over the mound's upper surface and south and western sides. Ceramically, the Late Postclassic is characterized by the presence of three slipped types (Paxcaman, Trapeche, and Topoxte), two unslipped types (Pozo and Chilo), and a censer subcomplex. In exchange relationships, there appears to be little change from the preceding late facet of the Early Postclassic period at Macanche Island. Access to nonceramic resources (chert, obsidian, and basalt) continues the earlier patterns, and one greenstone votive axe fragment was also found. Indications of ceramic trade are still virtually nil, except for the presence of quantities of Topoxte pottery and effigy censers. The censers were made of at least three pastes, one being the marly Clemencia Cream paste characteristic of the Topoxte group (red slipped) and Idolos group (censers) of the Isla Late Postclassic sphere at Topoxte (P. Rice 1979), while a second was the gray snail–inclusion paste characteristic of Paxcaman group pottery. Full participation in the Isla sphere, and therefore contemporaneity with occupation of the Topoxte Islands, is indicated for Macanche Island.

One of the unexpected discoveries of the 1979 season of work in the Lake Macanche basin was the existence of numerous Postclassic structures on the mainland around Lake Macanche. Such mainland Postclassic habitation had not been encountered at Lake Yaxha, where the Postclassic occupation appeared to have been confined to the islands. Postclassic pottery was recovered in excavations at 10 locations on Operations 1 and 3 and in the "intertransect" area between these operations on the south shore of Lake Macanche, and at 8 locations in Operation 4 on the north shore. Postclassic materials were also found in Operation 2, Muralla de Leon, a large walled–in area northeast of Lake Macanche. The wall is of dry limestone construction and is situated at the edge of a sloping mesa–like surface 42 meters above lake level, with a steep drop–off on three sides down to bodies of water. Although the wall itself appears to be a Terminal Preclassic (or "Protoclassic") construction (D. Rice and P. Rice 1981), five excavations into structure or plaza areas within the wall enclosure suggested the area was utilized in the Postclassic as well.

Thus Postclassic materials were recovered in 23 mainland locations around Lake Macanche. Of these, 16 represented construction, 2 were middens, and 5 suggested usage but were not clearly constructional. Eight appear to have been Late Postclassic episodes, judging from the presence of Topoxte group sherds and/or censers, while the remainder can only be classed as "general" Postclassic in date.

A variety of structure forms was noted in these Postclassic excavations (fig. 3); these give some suggestion as to architectural and functional variability within settlements. One structure type consists of large rectangular or squarish platforms, ca. one meter or more in height. These typically bear no stone outlines indicating superstructures; any structures that may have existed atop these platforms were presumably of perishable materials. A second Postclassic structure type consists of open rectangular lines or arrangements of

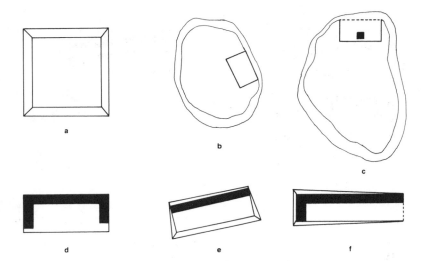

Fig. 3. Postclassic platform and structure types in the Lake Macanche basin: (a) large platform; (b and c) open rectangle marked by foundation stone outline; (d) "C-shaped open hall" structure; (e) general "open hall" structure; (f) "L-shaped open hall" structure.

foundation stones, one course in height. Generally, these are simply open rectangles, but in at least one case there appeared to be a small squarish low stone platform in the center of the rectangle. The two Late Postclassic structures atop the mound on the island were of this open rectangle form. Johnson (this volume) suggests shrine or kitchen functions for structures similar to these on Topoxte Island in Lake Yaxha (his "Group 3").

The third and most distinctive of these forms is somewhat difficult to label succinctly, but is probably best described as an "open hall" (Proskouriakoff 1962a). It consists of an elevated rectangular substructure, with the superstructure represented by a back "wall" and one side "wall" (i.e., L–shaped), or a back and both side "walls" (i.e., C–shaped). In no case is there a front "wall" present. These structures are reminiscent of open halls or colonnaded halls at Mayapan and Topoxte (Bullard 1970), but the front pillars characteristic of these structures at those two sites are absent in the Macanche area. The "walls" that are visible are variable in width, and may actually be benches, benches and wall foundations (for upper portions of perishable materials), or simply wall footings. Similar structures occur elsewhere in the Maya lowlands as well as in the highlands (A. L. Smith 1955, 1962; Fox 1978, 1980; D. Chase 1981; D. Rice n.d.).

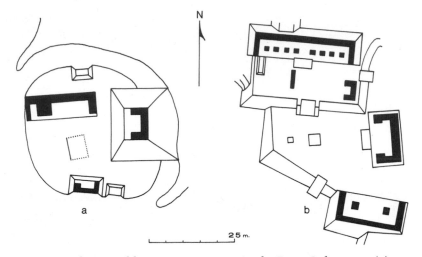

Fig. 4. "Temple assemblage" arrangements in the Peten Lakes area: (a) temple assemblage at the Muralla de Leon walled site in the Lake Macanche basin; (b) Paxte Island, Lake Yaxha (redrawn from map by Johnson, this volume, fig. 4).

Three unexcavated open hall structures occurred within Muralla de Leon in the Peten variant of the "temple assemblage" arrangement noted at Mayapan (Proskouriakoff 1962a; Johnson, this volume). This arrangement within the wall at Macanche consists of three "C–shaped" open hall structures with benches, one atop a pyramidal "temple," arranged at right angles to each other, forming a plaza (fig. 4). In this open plaza is a low structure (a "shrine"): at Muralla de Leon it appeared to be an open rectangular alignment of foundation stones. Excavations into this central structure as well as into a nearby midden yielded Late Postclassic materials, including Topoxte group sherds and censer fragments. A fourth open hall structure was noted within the wall, a solitary construction that consisted of a Postclassic bench superstructure atop a sizeable Terminal Preclassic ("Protoclassic") platform.

Fourteen of the test–excavated structures on the mainland and island that revealed Postclassic activity were of these three forms (six open halls, three large platforms, and five open rectangles). The remaining seven structures (excluding the two middens) were of no distinctive form or size as to provide surface indications of Postclassic activity. When the phasing of the excavated material is compared to structure form, it is interesting to note that the three forms

Table 2. Temporal Distribution of Postclassic Structure Forms

Structure Form	Late Postclassic	General Postclassic	Total
Hall, platform, lines	10	4	14
Miscellaneous	3	8	11
Total	13	12	25

described above seem to be associated with the Late Postclassic (Table 2).

Besides the mapped and tested structures on the mainland operations, an open hall structure was also located in Cerro Ortiz. Cerro Ortiz is a small center on the southeast shore of Lake Macanche, between Operations 1 and 3, that has much of its construction dating to the Middle and Late Preclassic periods. The presence of a characteristic Postclassic architectural form in this center suggests that parts of this site functioned in this late occupation of the basin as well. Thus, a total of 34 structures of the three predictable Postclassic types were mapped in the Lake Macanche mainland and island areas surveyed. In addition, Postclassic utilization or construction of eleven other structures of variable form on the south shore of the lake was revealed through test excavation (Table 3).

One additional feature remains to be mentioned in the context of the Postclassic occupation of the Macanche mainland. This is the discovery of the interment of twelve crania in the fill of an otherwise unprepossessing platform in the intra–transect area between Operations 1 and 3. At a depth of ca. 40 centimeters below surface in Mound 70, these skulls were placed in two rows, one containing five skulls and, behind it, a second row of seven, all upright and facing west. Largely on the basis of dental criteria and mandibular robusticity, all the skulls were adjudged to be probably males with all but one appearing to be young adults, the exception being a mature adult (M. Aldenderfer, personal communication). Postclassic pottery was found in the fill above and below this interment to a depth of 70 centimeters, at which level there is a floor, and below this was Late Classic construction. No distinctive ceramic or nonceramic artifacts were recovered in the area of this putative offering or cache to suggest anything about the status or roles of the individuals so interred.

Sacrificial decapitation was apparently an important symbolic and ritual practice all over Mesoamerica in the Postclassic as well as earlier in the Classic period (Wilkerson 1979). In Peten, besides this burial at Macanche, Postclassic skull burials without associated

Table 3. Distribution of Postclassic Structure Forms, Lake Macanche Basin

Structure Form	Operation/Location							
	Op. 1	Op. 3	Inter-Trans.	Op. 2	Op. 4	Cerro Ortiz	Island	Total
Open hall								
C-shape (d)[a]		1*		3	4**	1		9
L-shape (f)				1*	2**			3
General (e)			3		7			10
Open rectangle (b, c)	2**		1	1*	1		2**	7
Large platform (a)	1		2**		2*			5
Other Postclassic structures (no distinctive form)		1*	3***	3***	4****			11
Total	3	2	9	8	20	1	2	45

*Location of a test-pit excavation in 1979 or 1980 season. No excavations were undertaken into structures in Cerro Ortiz.
[a]Letters refer to structure forms illustrated in figure 3.

offerings have been found at Topoxte (D. Rice 1976), where the skull was inverted rather than upright, and at Flores, where two crania facing each other slightly over a meter apart were hypothesized to have possibly been part of "some larger cluster" (Cowgill 1963: 20–22). This treatment of skulls calls to mind the Toltec or Aztec *tzompantli*, or skull rack, as well as recalling the seventeenth century Itza practice of displaying skulls of enemies on stakes (Thompson 1951: 394). Also worthy of mention is the present–day practice in San Jose, on the northern shore of Lake Peten–Itza, in which skulls are venerated in the church and removed for particular annual ceremonies (Reina 1961).

Summary and Conclusions

Some of the most important archaeological problems of the central Peten Postclassic period are focused on chronology and on interaction, both regional and interregional. Currently available inforformation from two lacustrine areas of Peten having Postclassic occupation, Macanche and Topoxte (Yaxha), has shed some light on these issues, but much work remains before the Peten Postclassic can be fully understood.

It is evident that the ceramic chronology of the Peten Postclassic is not adequately summarized by a simple sequential model of occurrence of three ceramic groups, Augustine, Paxcaman, and Topoxte. Instead, there appears to be considerable temporal overlap of these groups. In addition, at least in the Early Postclassic, there seems to be a great deal of regionalism of ceramic types or groups, which doubtless have their own distinctive micro–temporal interrelationships. Paxcaman appears to be the most geographically widespread and temporally enduring of the Peten Postclassic ceramic groups. But in the Early Postclassic, it is preceded or accompanied by varying types, some restricted within particular areas, suggesting localized production and the possibility of remnant groups from the Classic period collapse.

Topoxte group pottery is widely distributed in Peten only in the Late Postclassic period, and is associated with the production and use of effigy censers in the style of those found all over Yucatan after A.D. 1300. However late the Topoxte group, though, it does not postdate production and use of Paxcaman group pottery, for the two are found together in construction fill and midden refuse on Macanche Island as well as elsewhere on the Macanche mainland. The Paxcaman, Augustine, Trapeche, and most of the Topoxte group vessels draw from a common pool of elements of form and decoration, suggesting intercommunication among multiple producing units. Localized differences in pastes, firing conditions, and vessel sizes and proportions support a reconstruction of unspecialized local or regional production, especially in the Early Postclassic, but do not obscure the essential contemporaneity of many of these groups.

Despite this temporal and ceramic "overlap" of Postclassic manifestations at Macanche and Topoxte, the two regions are dissimilar in some aspects of their late occupation. Lake Macanche had considerable mainland settlement, while Lake Yaxha did not; Macanche Island had an appreciable quantity of non-local pottery (small amounts of Augustine and sizeable amounts of Topoxte group), while excavations at Cante Island yielded Postclassic slipped sherds that were almost exclusively of the local Topoxte group, with only 30 or so sherds of Paxcaman.

The Topoxte Islands appear to have been an elite and/or functional "special place" in the Postclassic, judging from the existence of the ceramic ritual subcomplex and the volume of stone construction on the islands. The area of Muralla de Leon at the northeast end of Lake Macanche, with its "temple assemblage," may have had an identical function. The significance of these two areas in the Peten Postclassic may lie in their effective location for defense. The island focus of Peten Postclassic settlement has often been noted, together with the good defensive position of island occupation in time of warfare, and ethnohistoric reports clearly indicate widespread hostilities in sixteenth century Peten (Pagden 1971). Lakes Yaxha and Peten–Itza had a number of islands in their waters that afforded the desirable defensive location for sizeable settlements, but Lake Macanche had only a single small island. The high terrain to the northeast of Lake Macanche, however, having a defensive wall since the Terminal Preclassic period, might have been regarded as effectively constituting another "island" by virtue of its being partially surrounded by water and already fortified. As Webster (1976: 370) has noted in consideration of Maya warfare in general, "what was protected was not the bulk of the population but rather the organizational apparatus around which the population could rally and which could formulate effective military countermeasures." The ceremonial ceramic materials and architectural complexes noted on Postclassic island sites (e.g., Topoxte) and within Muralla de Leon at Macanche represent such nodes of ritual and sociopolitical organization in the Postclassic period.

At or just prior to the time of Spanish contact, there appear to have been five, possibly six, distinct and competing ethnic, kin, or sociopolitical subgroups in the northern Peten: the Cehach in northwestern Peten; the Lacandon in the Usumacinta area; the Coboh to the north of Lake Peten–Itza; the Itza on the islands in Lakes Peten–Itza, Seipuy, and Eckixil, as well as in the territory to the south of the lakes; the settlement of Yalain to the east of Lake Peten–Itza, which includes communities of Maconche and Zacpeten; and the site of Topoxte (although settlement in the Yaxha area is not mentioned in ethnohistoric accounts). These communities apparently shared ritual practices, as seen by the distribution of effigy censers over a wide area of Peten, but they seem to have existed in active competition and warfare during the sixteenth century.

Given the ethnic distinctions and hostilities indicated in the ethnohistoric material, it is likely that archaeologists working with the central Peten Postclassic will find highly varied assemblages from site–region to site–region, and these may eventually be correlated with ethnic or sociopolitical variation. It is already apparent, for example, that the strong ceramic differences that exist between Macanche on the one hand and Tayasal on the other (A. Chase 1979, 1982) may be partially explainable by the fact that Tayasal, at least in the sixteenth century, was Itza, while Macanche may have been part of the settlement of Yalain (G. Jones, Rice, and Rice 1981), said to have been at war with the Itza. The similarities of some of the Topoxte pottery to Paxcaman pottery from Macanche, but not to that of Barton Ramie or the Lake Peten–Itza area, and the presence of Topoxte group pottery at Macanche as compared to its rarity in the Tayasal region, may indicate some level of socioeconomic ties between Topoxte and Yalain in part of the Postclassic period. The antiquity of these "ethnic" differences, particularly in light of a tradition of migrations into Peten from Yucatan, will be difficult to ascertain, but will have to be taken into consideration in attempts to explain cultural process in the Peten Postclassic.

Postclassic Peten Interaction Spheres: The View from Tayasal

ARLEN F. CHASE

The purpose of this essay is twofold, first to provide information on the Tayasal Project as it relates to the Postclassic period in the Maya area, and second to point out several problems in attempting to define a uniform archaeological situation for the central Peten of Guatemala. In reviewing the Maya Postclassic from the standpoint of Lake Peten (or Lake Peten-Itza) archaeological data, questions concerning ethnohistoric interpretation of the central Peten are also raised.

Tayasal Project Survey and Excavations

The University Museum–University of Pennsylvania Tayasal Project began in 1970 with its express purpose being the delineation of a Postclassic sequence for the central Peten of Guatemala. During May through August of 1971, a series of excavations was carried out in the Tayasal-Paxcaman Zone (fig. 1). These investigations resulted in the intensive excavation of 34 structures throughout the zone. An extensive sampling strategy, devised to test the large area called Tayasal (fig. 2), resulted in the overall sampling of 99 loci at that site (largely for dating purposes); most often, these tests were placed into the summits of structures. During the 1971 season, other excavations were also carried out at the sites of Cenote and Punta Nima. Reconnaissance undertaken in 1977 as a continuation of the project supplemented the original work in the zone and produced archaeological data from the islands in Lakes Peten and Quexil.

As a result of the 1971 and 1977 investigations, a general understanding has been gained of the extensive variability evident within the Tayasal-Paxcaman Zone (A. Chase 1979, 1983, 1984, 1985a, 1985b). Cenote proved to have a Preclassic to Late Classic occupation with a widespread Terminal Classic domestic overlay. Punta

Nima proved to have Preclassic to Postclassic occupation as did Tayasal. The majority of the mapped structures on the high ground forming the Tayasal Peninsula, however, were found to be Classic Period or earlier in date. Postclassic occupation was found at: (1) Punta Nima in both of the structures excavated, (2) Chaja to the northwest of Lake Quexil, (3) Tres Naciones, (4) the islands in Lakes Peten and Quexil, and (5) at Tayasal in widespread deposits, specifically bordering the shores of Lake Peten.

Postclassic Archaeology within the Tayasal-Paxcaman Zone

In order to provide a background to the archaeology of the Tayasal-Paxcaman Zone, the Postclassic occupation uncovered in its various parts will be reviewed with regard to matters of chronology and spatial variation. The Tayasal investigations are of primary concern here as Postclassic architectural remains were encountered along with occupational debris both in the site core and, more commonly, along the shores of Lake Peten–Itza. Special attention will be given to two of the excavated structures, Structure T100, located within the heart of the primarily Classic period Main Group at Tayasal, and Structure T19, one of a number of structures located near the edge of Lake Peten. These are important not only as indications of two distinct structure and construction types, but also for their associated features and relationships to other nearby constructions. A sketch of the Lake Peten area sequence is provided following a review of the extant archaeology. The review of the sequence, in light of the Postclassic archaeological data from the zone, leads to a larger discussion of spatial patterning within the central Peten.

POSTCLASSIC ARCHAEOLOGY AT TAYASAL: MAIN GROUP

The site of Tayasal (fig. 2) may be tentatively subdivided into 11 sectors (fig. 3). The majority of these sectors provided Postclassic archaeological remains, but a very evident dichotomy presents itself in the topography, for very few Postclassic period remains are found in the inland areas; in fact, only three loci within the upland terrain (fig. 3: Sectors 1, 2, and 11) produced Postclassic remains upon testing. While little Postclassic settlement was found on this higher ground, a plethora of platforms, structures, and other constructions dating to earlier time periods were encountered on the elevated peninsular spine; these comprise the bulk of the site known as "Tayasal" (fig. 2). The lakeside situation is somewhat different from the inland area; extensive remains, probably representing a Middle Postclassic village, were found in excavations at Ensenada Tayasal (fig. 3:

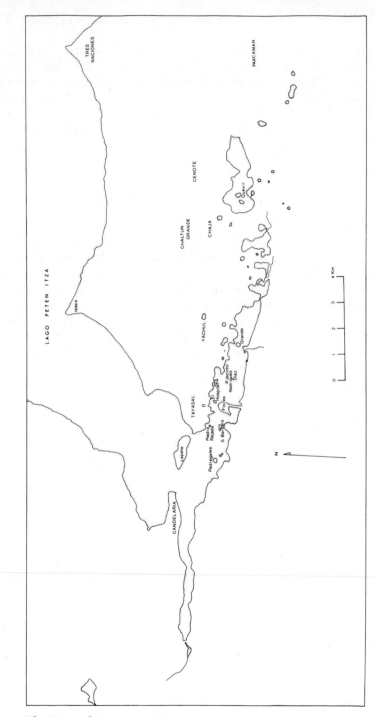

Fig. 1. The Tayasal-Paxcaman Zone.

Fig. 2. The site of Tayasal, Peten, Guatemala; the majority of the structures and platforms on this map date to the Classic Period.

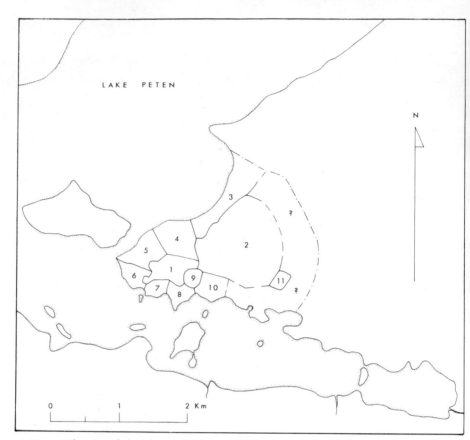

Fig. 3. The tip of the Tayasal Peninsula illustrating the different sectors of the site of Tayasal:

(1) Tayasal Main Group   (6) Southwest Tayasal
(2) North-Central Tayasal   (7) Punta Trapeche
(3) Ensenada Tayasal   (8) West San Miguel
(4) North Tayasal   (9) San Miguel Aguada
(5) Northwest Tayasal   (10) East San Miguel
                          (11) El Joboito

Sector 3) and all other lakeside sectors produced Postclassic materials in some abundance. While the areal extant of some of these Postclassic constructions is often considerable, most do not exhibit the height commonly found in structures or platforms of earlier periods.

The first construction to be excavated at Tayasal was located in the western portion of the site (fig. 3: Sector 1) and was a low mound approximately 1.5 meters in height, subsequently labeled Structure T100 (figs. 4 and 5). Its excavation revealed two significant facts: (1) it was an entirely Postclassic period building within the other-

Fig. 4. Photograph of Tayasal Structure 100, a Middle Postclassic ceremonial building from the western part of the Tayasal Main Group.

wise Classic period Tayasal Main Group; and (2) the recovered stratigraphy at the Structure T100 locus indicated that construction of plaza floors in this portion of the site spanned the Classic to Postclassic periods. Structure T100 was a two-phase construction. Its latest phase, or Structure T100–1st–A, was too decomposed to determine absolute building shape, but was most likely a heightened version of Structure T100–1st–B. In the hearting of the fill of Structure T100–1st–A was found a composite stone cist which, although empty, is reminiscent of similar cists found in the Postclassic construction of Piedras Negras Structure O–7 (Satterthwaite 1954, Part VI (4)). In fact, the stone cist–small rounded stone altar assemblage noted for Structure O–7 at Piedras Negras is also present at Structure T100. On the basis of the presence of similar miniature monuments in front of Structure D at Topoxte, it is posited that stone cists, similar to those at Tayasal and Piedras Negras, will be

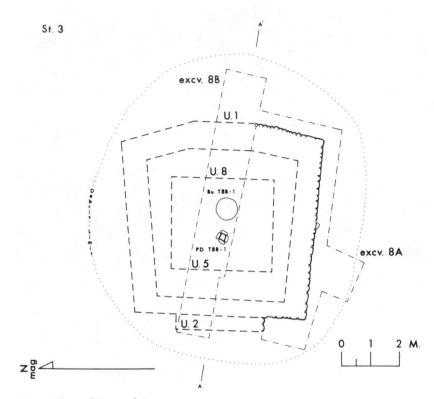

Fig. 5. Plan of Tayasal Structure 100.

encountered in excavation either in or in front of that building. Similar miniature round altars were found at Santa Rita (D. Chase 1981: 30, this volume), but the existence of stone cists in combination with them was not ascertained. Although the cist at Tayasal was apparently devoid of nonperishable remains, two of those at Piedras Negras were noted as probably having contained "cremated human remains" (Satterthwaite 1954, Part VI (4): 28). It may be hypothesized, on the basis of comments made by Landa (Tozzer 1941: 98, 130), that a recurring association of small altars with cists in Postclassic contexts could represent the veneration of important Postclassic individuals after their death, quite possibly by their own descendants.

Structure T100–1st–B had a protruding eastern side (rear) which gave it a hexagonal shape. A stairway was located on its west side. Excavation in Structure T100–1st–B revealed a centrally placed flexed burial intruded into the underlying plaza floors at the time of construction. This burial dates to either late facet Chilcob phase or, more likely, the Middle Postclassic Cocahmut phase based on Paxcaman ceramics found in the core fill. Structure T100–1st–B was built over a well preserved plaza floor. This flooring contained only Augustine sherd material in its fill, implying a Chilcob phase, or Early Postclassic dating. An earlier construction, Structure T100–2nd, also surmounted this flooring and was buried under Structure T100–1st–B.

The placement of Structure T100 in a bounded plaza area is important for it implies that the western part of the Tayasal Main Group was utilized into the Postclassic period. Other surface indications from this part of the site would suggest that Structure T100 was not an isolated phenomenon, but may have been associated with the Postclassic use of this part of the site core, immediately following, or perhaps interdigitating with, the Terminal Classic. Other Postclassic use of this part of Tayasal is indicated by the repositioning of a Classic period stela, Tayasal Stela 3, northeast of Structure T100. This activity echoes that noted for Tikal (Satterthwaite 1958). The repositioning of a fragment of a Classic period monument in presumed association with a Postclassic structure in a central portion of Tayasal could be considered as evidence for a continuity in belief systems, if not population of the site, between the Classic and Postclassic periods.

POSTCLASSIC ARCHAEOLOGY AT TAYASAL: LAKESHORE OCCUPATION

Whereas Structure T100 is a mounded Postclassic structure on the higher bluff upon which the site core of Tayasal was built, the majority of the Postclassic material found in the western area of Tayasal came from lower lakeshore platforms or "vacant terrain" excavations. Stratigraphic information was recovered from the testing of approximately 42 Postclassic "lakeshore" buildings or activity loci at Tayasal and Punta Nima. Three Postclassic refuse deposits were located and partially excavated in the western portion of Tayasal. Analysis of the recovered stratigraphy and deposits associated with the excavated and tested platforms has allowed the definition of a temporal frame which spans from the Terminal Classic–Early Postclassic to historic times.

Investigations along the western lakeshore of Tayasal provided evidence for a sizeable Postclassic population strung out along the lake much like modern San Miguel is today. While testing operations revealed the remains of a Middle Postclassic village north of the peninsular spine (fig. 3: Sector 3), only three lakeside Postclassic

Str. T19

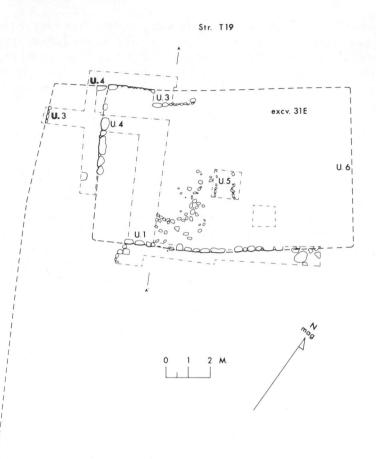

Fig. 6. Plan of Tayasal Structure 19, a Late Postclassic line-of-stone house platform from the lakeshore area, southwest of the Tayasal Main Group.

structures were areally exposed for their ground plans: Structure T112 in West Tayasal (fig. 3: Sector 5) and Structures T15 and T19 in Southwest Tayasal (fig. 3: Sector 6). As with most other known Postclassic buildings within the zone, all three of these structures consisted of lines of stone in rectangular form; these platforms had once been surmounted by perishable superstructures. The Tayasal substructure platforms exhibit a general similarity in form and construction technique to other known Postclassic house platforms from the lowlands (see D. Chase 1981, 1982a, n.d.; Johnson, this volume; P. Rice and D. Rice, this volume). Structure T19 (fig. 6), which

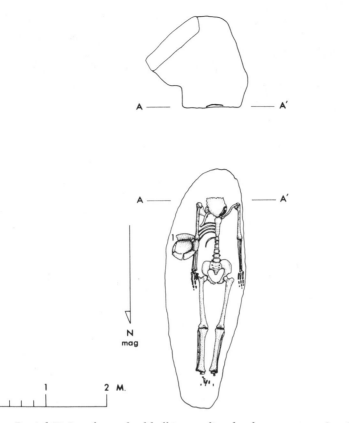

Fig. 7. Burial T9I–2 from the bluff immediately above eastern San Miguel.

is fairly representative of the Postclassic Tayasal platforms, was about 0.6 meter in height, 11 meters in length, and 7 meters in width.

An additional result of excavations in the lakeshore area in the northwestern portion of Tayasal was the definition of a burial pattern using Late Classic bowls in what appear to be Postclassic contexts. The body was intruded into or included in a low Postclassic construction with the killed vessel, of "Late Classic" form, being placed near the individual's head. This pattern also occurs in the area around the San Miguel Aguada.

Excavations in the San Miguel area of Tayasal to the east of the site core produced the same type of occupation dichotomy evident in the western part of Tayasal (fig. 3: Sector 10). A large platform on the bluff above the lake proved to be entirely of Postclassic construction. This platform, which supports Structures T205 and T206, measures 82 by 87 meters at its base. It is reminiscent of the large low

Postclassic platforms found at the site of Santa Rita, Belize (D. Chase 1981, 1982a). Structure T206, located on this platform, was investigated. From surface inspection and on the basis of its small size, it was believed to have functioned as a low shrine for the larger Structure T205 to its north. Excavation first showed the existence of a continuous plaster floor underneath which was found an earlier surface. Sealed beneath this earlier surface was a pit containing two individuals, cut into construction core. Upon excavation of this core, a nonintrusive burial crypt was found which contained an extended body, with an Augustine Red plate with effigy supports placed near the head of the individual (fig. 7). Structure T205 was also tested in 1971 and revealed an extended burial with a single Nohpek Unslipped vessel of unusual form. This burial had been burned following its deposition, a pattern also noted in other burials recovered in this portion of the site and ascribable to the early to middle part of the Postclassic period at Tayasal.

Investigations near the lake area in the modern town of San Miguel (fig. 3: Sectors 8 and 10) produced other living platforms and interments of Postclassic date. Two burials in this area were each accompanied by a single Postclassic vessel; one of these was a small tripod Plumbate jar. Recent historic period interments were also uncovered in the San Miguel excavations (fig. 3: Sector 8). These were identified as such by the presence of square coffin nails and were immediately reburied. One other Plumbate vessel was recovered in 1971. This was located in the core of Structure T120 which is on the lake bluff west of the San Miguel Aguada (fig. 3: Sector 1). This Tohil Plumbate vessel was seemingly intentionally cached in the latest phase of construction of Structure T120. If such is the case, it was apparently Terminal Classic in date based on contextual associations, and provides evidence for the overlap of the Terminal Classic and Early Postclassic pottery complexes in the Tayasal-Paxcaman Zone.

OTHER POSTCLASSIC ACTIVITIES WITHIN THE ZONE

Investigations at Punta Nima (see fig. 1) resulted in excavation of two Postclassic structures showing multiple rebuilding during the Postclassic. Although no special deposits were found at Punta Nima, the stratigraphy for both structures clearly demonstrates that Augustine ceramics preceded Paxcaman ceramics at this site. Widespread surface collections of material largely uprooted by modern sand diggings located at Nima showed the former site to have had a heavy Postclassic occupation. Although Chen Mul Modeled–style incensarios are reported to have been collected from this site (Cow-

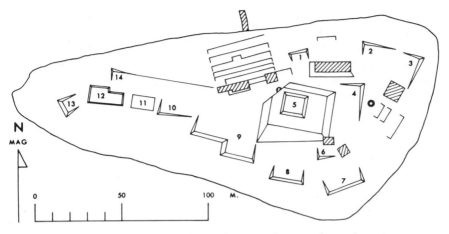

Fig. 8. Map of Islote Santa Barbara, showing the Postclassic (numbered platforms) and Modern (diagonal hatching) settlement distribution.

gill 1963: 51; M. Orrego, personal communication, 1979), no ceramics ascribable to this type were collected in either 1971 or 1977.

Other areas which evinced Postclassic activities were documented during the 1977 season (see fig. 1). Middle Postclassic remains were identified at Tres Naciones on the northern side of the Tayasal Peninsula. Other Postclassic remains were recovered from the surface of a single structure at Chaja and from the lakeshore of the north side of the Candelaria Peninsula in the western part of Lake Peten–Itza. Although the large site of Cenote was extensively excavated and surface collected (A. Chase 1983, 1985a), only one pottery support and one netsinker ascribable to the Postclassic period were recovered from that site. Further investigation at the site of Yachul may yield Postclassic activity in its northwestern portion where, on the basis of mapped surface features, it is likely that a stela may have been reset.

ISLANDS

An island survey was also undertaken in Lakes Peten–Itza and Quexil to augment the already sizeable Postclassic collection excavated from the adjacent Tayasal Peninsula in 1971. As Postclassic peoples appear to have had an affinity for inhabiting islands (Bullard 1970, 1973), one objective of this island survey was the identification of archaeological remains assignable to the Postclassic period. A second objective of this survey was to garner information which would aid in the temporal and geographical placement of the ethno-historically known Itza peoples (Avendano y Loyola 1696; Means 1917; Thompson 1951; Cowgill 1963; Hellmuth 1977). Although the 1977 survey was superficial in that, with the exception of Flores, it consisted primarily of mapping and surface collections, it is possible to make several statements relevant to the Itza problem based on these data. All the islands in Lake Peten were visited. All were mapped save for Lepet and Flores for which topographical maps existed. The island of Santa Barbara (fig. 8) and Flores both showed evidence of Postclassic settlement. The other islands in Lake Peten either showed no evidence of occupation or only a slight amount of ceramic material conjoined with a few mounds or platforms. Sizeable sherd collections were obtained from various constructional activities on Flores; many of these may be related to recorded stratigraphy.

In general, it would seem that only Flores and Santa Barbara had any sizeable Postclassic populations. The material collected from Flores, consisting of about 5,000 sherds, suggests that this occupation occurred largely in the early and middle parts of the Postclassic period. Whereas the Santa Barbara ceramic material is largely Paxcaman, both Paxcaman and Augustine ceramics and Terminal Classic finewares (see A. Chase 1979) are in evidence on Flores. Effigy censers of the Chen Mul style also occur in small amounts, but from unknown contexts; a Mixtec incensario, similar to ones illustrated by Ball (1980: 79–81) for Chinkultic, was also recorded (A. Chase 1983: fig. 4–13). Building construction in the vicinity of the Flores church uncovered an hourglass incensario covered with blue painted stucco as well as a stela (fig. 9) portraying a diving individual and Chichen-style glyphs; the last glyph in the text (D2) occurs frequently on the jades of Chichen Itza (see Proskouriakoff 1974: 206, figs. 3, 4, 11, 14, 16). A tentative reading of the short count date on this monument places it at 9.19.5.0.0. (S. Houston, personal communication, 1983).

The stela was found within a buried structure which was sealed by various "plaza" floorings which run under the modern Flores church (M. Orrego, personal communication, 1979). When considered in combination with (1) Terminal Classic–Early Postclassic finewares on Flores as well as Yucatec Trickle ware, (2) the Plumbate finewares from the San Miguel mainland, (3) form and stylistic affinities between Pek Polychrome (Augustine Red ceramic group) and Yalton Black-on-Orange (Silho Fine Orange), and (4) the distribution of Dolorido Cream Polychrome (Trapeche Pink group) as a tradeware in the Northern lowlands (see A. Chase 1979), this Chichen-style stela may indicate Terminal Classic–Early Postclassic Yucatec

Fig. 9. Flores stela of a diving god associated with Chichen style glyphs, recovered during excavations in the vicinity of the modern church (redrawn from an original drawing by Ian Graham and from photographs).

influence in the central Peten Tayasal area, perhaps having a bearing on the Classic Maya collapse. Such an interpretation would find support in recent archaeological evidence from Nohmul, Belize where a direct intrusion of Chichen-related peoples is suspected to have taken place on this same temporal horizon (D. Chase 1982a, 1982b; D. Chase and A. Chase 1982).

Some interpretations (see A. Chase 1976, 1982; as well as G. Jones, Rice, and Rice 1981) locate the Itza on the island of Flores and on the islands of Sacpuy and Quexil. Villagutierre (1701: 519) indicated that there were two islands in a lake called "Equexil" with much population and a house of idolatry. This lake called "Equexil" has been equated with the modern day "Quexil"; the two islands in Lake Quexil were assumed, therefore, to have a heavy Late Postclassic—early historic occupation. These two islands were visited and mapped in 1977 and revealed a heavy occupation which had transformed the islands through extensive terracing. These settlement remains are not as dense as those on Topoxte (D. Rice and P. Rice 1979, 1980a). Sherds were collected from the surface and from looters' trenches on each island; although the collections are fairly large, nothing later than Early Postclassic equivalent material could be discerned; no Augustine or Paxcaman sherds were found in 1977. The major occupation of Quexil islands appeared to be earlier, therefore, than the population ascribed to them. The Rices (1980b: fig. 12; 1982), however, reported that they recovered Postclassic material in all seven of their excavations; the material in at least two of these excavations was dated by them to the Late Postclassic period.

Tayasal Chronological Sequence

The Tayasal sequence was established largely on internal stratigraphy and contextual associations; to a smaller extent, cross—datings to other sites were employed. Although the major class of data used to establish the sequence was pottery, architecture and artifacts were also used whenever possible (A. Chase 1983, 1984). Of the 99 datable excavation loci at Tayasal, 44% revealed Late Classic (Hobo) occupation and 18% of these loci evinced Early Postclassic (Chilcob) occupation. In general, there appears to be continuity between the Classic and Postclassic periods; it is in fact possible that the early facet of Chilcob (Early Postclassic) overlaps temporally, and spatially interdigitates, with the late facet of Hobo (Terminal Classic; see A. Chase 1983, n.d.).

The early facet of the Chilcob phase in the Tayasal area appears to be denoted primarily by Augustine effigy support pieces and may possibly include the introduction of Trapeche Pink (A. Chase 1979). There is apparently a continuity of plainware forms, such as the incurving bowl, from Terminal Classic into this Early Postclassic time period. If there was a population movement into the Lake Peten area, it occurred during this phase and presumably amalgamated with the resident population. It is hypothesized that Trapeche Pink is transitory through to true Paxcaman Red and probably represents an "experimental" ceramic type. Following the early facet of the Early Postclassic, there is heavier use of Augustine Red in jar and plate forms with the rare introduction of Paxcaman group Ixpop Polychrome plates and possibly decorated censers (?) of a probable hourglass form. A later variety of Trapeche Pink may exist during the end of this phase. If Augustine ever existed by itself, it would have been very early in the Postclassic, possibly prior to the use of Trapeche.

During the later facet of the Early Postclassic period, Augustine forms became more elaborate and resembled some of the flanged forms found at Lamanai which are dated to the Middle Postclassic period. Chalice–form incensarios and plates, both unslipped, also occurred along with low-necked plainware jars (Nohpek Unslipped) in this late facet of Chilcob. Toward the end of the Early Postclassic, Paxcaman Red appeared in the Tayasal sequence and burgeoned in frequency of use with the onset of the Middle Postclassic period. Paxcaman jar forms became popular along with the typical flat-bottomed redware plate and collared bowl forms which had first appeared in the Early Postclassic (but with slightly different modes). Augustine Red and Paxcaman Red seem to have coexisted in the Lake Peten area for some time with a gradual replacement of assemblage forms. Gradually, Paxcaman group ceramics appear to have become dominant. Hourglass and effigy incensarios are present in the sequence by the onset of the Late Postclassic and may have been introduced early during the Middle Postclassic Cocahmut phase; these latter forms, however, are extremely rare at Tayasal. Forty-one percent of the excavated loci at Tayasal evinced Middle Postclassic activity.

By the end of the Cocahmut phase, red line-work on the interior of plates (Macanche Red-on-Paste) appeared within the zone; this may have been due to possible Topoxte influence on a post–A.D. 1350 date. New plainware forms of oval incurved bowls and jars with strap handles, which are oval in section, occurred at Tayasal in the Late Postclassic Kauil phase. Paxcaman forms became cruder and a sandy paste began to replace the former dominant gray snail paste. Topoxte group pottery is also introduced into the Lake Peten area, but only in small amounts. There appears to have been a marked decrease in population in the Lake Peten area after the Middle Postclassic period peak; only 9% of the excavated loci at Tayasal revealed securely dated Late Postclassic–early historic occupation.

The Tayasal–Paxcaman Zone shows no close resemblances to Mayapan–style civic architecture or ceramics. On the whole, the Lake Peten region does exemplify typological and stylistic overlap with the Barton Ramie Postclassic material through the middle part of its sequence. It is interesting to note the complete lack of red-line decoration in the Barton Ramie ceramics. This red-line tradition is prevalent at Topoxte and present as well at Macanche; it occurs late in the Tayasal sequence, implying that the Barton Ramie sequence may end earlier than Tayasal's sequence (A. Chase 1982). While P. Rice (1979: 80–81) had earlier suggested that Barton Ramie's sequence did not continue through the Middle or Late Postclassic periods, this conclusion had been premised upon the lack of effigy censerware at that site; as this material is also largely absent in the Tayasal collections, which continue through historic times, the suggestion may be made that the indigenous Postclassic peoples of the southern lowlands did not participate in the religious networks common in the northern lowlands during the Late Postclassic period.

In summary, the Lake Peten pottery exhibits close ties between Paxcaman and Augustine forms and with the Barton Ramie sample at least through the Middle Postclassic period. In the Late Postclassic, the Lake Peten Paxcaman tradition continued in only a slightly modified form, but saw the greater occurrence of red-line decoration. There is general continuity in the Tayasal–Paxcaman Zone from the Terminal Classic through the Late Postclassic.

Postclassic Peten Archaeological Comparisons

The recovered archaeological data pertaining to the Postclassic period in the Lake Peten area contrasts with that from the eastern Peten lakes. In the Macanche–Topoxte area, the pastes, especially in the Late Postclassic, are divergent from the more typically gray Paxcaman pastes which occur to either side of this area (P. Rice 1979, 1980; Sharer and Chase 1976; A. Chase 1982, personal observation). This eastern lakes region, centered on Topoxte, also witnessed an extensive use of red-line decoration which was often applied to different design areas on vessels (see P. Rice 1979: 31–42; Bullard 1970) than is found in the Tayasal–Paxcaman Zone. The red-on-cream and cream wares that appear on a later horizon in the eastern lakes (Bullard 1970; P. Rice 1979, n.d.b) seem to have had no counterparts in the Lake Peten area. Pottery form differences are also evident within the various Peten lake basins. As compared to Paxcaman and Augustine group redware supports from the Lake Peten area, those in the Topoxte group are of a much smaller size; there also appears to be a predominance of the sag-bottom bowl form in this latter group as compared to the Augustine and Paxcaman groups of Lake Peten and Barton Ramie. At Macanche, intermediate between the Tayasal and Topoxte, the pottery bowls are the same size as those and Topoxte and are intermediate between being "sag" and "flat" bottomed (P. Rice, personal communication). It is probable that there are significant form differences in other members of the true Topoxte assemblage from Paxcaman forms. While the seemingly intrusive Topoxte pottery (A. Chase 1982) influences Late Postclassic Paxcaman pottery in the Tayasal–Paxcaman Zone, it does not appear to dominate it; although the sag-bottomed bowl is introduced into the Tayasal area in the Kauil phase, the typical flat-bottomed plate forms continue.

The eastern Peten lakes evince more affinities to the Northern lowlands in their Late Postclassic material remains than do the recovered archaeological remains from the Lake Peten area. Effigy censers, with overt Late Postclassic Northern Yucatec links, were seemingly found in abundance at Topoxte (Bullard 1970), but are not at all common in the Tayasal–Paxcaman Zone. The eastern Peten lakes also appear to be associated with Yucatecan–style architecture and Mayapan–type structural groupings (D. Rice and P. Rice 1981; Johnson, this volume) which do not occur in the Lake Peten area.

Interaction Spheres of the Postclassic Peten

On the basis of the data obtained through archaeological research in the central Peten by the Rices (P. Rice 1979, 1980; D. Rice and P. Rice 1979, 1980b, 1981, 1982) and Bullard (1970, 1973) at Topoxte, Macanche, and Salpeten, and by Cowgill (1963) and myself (A. Chase 1976, 1979, 1982, 1983, 1984, 1985a) in the Lake Peten–Itza area, and Sharer and myself (1976) on the ceramics of Barton Ramie, two major regions may be defined for central Peten Postclassic archaeology. It is believed that these distributions are not merely of temporal significance, but may reflect regionalism among the populations of the central Peten, at least for the Late Postclassic (see A. Chase 1982). These two areas are geographically bounded and may be defined as the following: (1) the area including Lakes Salpeten, Macanche, and Yaxha, and possibly Lake Yalloch; and (2) the Lake Peten–Itza area and, peripherally, the Belize Valley area. While the artifactual complexes have not yet been fully defined for these two regions and thus cannot be compared, it is evident that these two areas differ from each other ceramically and architecturally.

The archaeological differences evident between the two Late Postclassic areas may find ethnohistoric confirmation. Tozzer provides tantalizing bits of information when he (1913: 499) describes the Barrios Leal expedition of 1695 which "made vain attempts to reach Peten from Los Dolores, both by the river and by land, and came to the conclusion that there must be two places called Itza or Aitza." This notion, rejected off-hand by G. Jones, Rice, and Rice (1981: 531−532), may well be the solution to the problem of the geographical location of the "Itza." That two separate Itza locales existed can also be garnered from the account of a certain Martin Can.

Martin Can was a nephew of "Kin Canek" who had been sent to Merida, Yucatan, to offer Canek's submission in 1697. Upon his return to the Peten, Can was unable to return to his own village "eight leagues away" (Means 1917: 181; reported as 4 leagues by Cowgill 1963: 439) because it was under the rule of Cintanek or Quincanek (?), who was at war with Canek and who had already attacked the islands of Canek on account of Canek's friendly attitude toward the Spaniards. Martin Can's village was among those subject to Cintanek, a day away from Canek's area of rule (Villagutierre 1933: 336). According to Villagutierre (1933: 336), Quincanek was in control of the following areas: "Chaltuna, Sacpeten, Maconche, Saca, and Coba" while Canek was in control of "Oraptun, Zacui, Chee, Chacha, Sacsinil, Linil, Oboncox, Chulul, and Eckixil, which were all located on the same lake." This distribution of locales would bolster the interpretation of there being two locations called "Itza" and possibly two "Tayasal"s. Avendano y Loyola (1696: 41b) makes it clear that Chaltuna contains Tayasal; therefore, according to this distribution, Canek does not control Tayasal, but it is outside his region and to the east. While Sacpeten has often been equated with the Lake "Salpeten" in the modern Peten of Guatemala, the Fancourt map of 1854 locates a "Zacpeten" in the vicinity of Lake Yalloch, northeast of Lake Yaxha (fig. 10); this may, in fact, be the "Sacpeten" referred to above, especially if there was any conservative trend in place names. If "Maconche" is equated with Lake Macanche and "Sacpeten" with Lake Yalloch, Chaltuna, Saca, and Coba may be hypothesized to lie between these two extremes and may be equated with Lakes Yaxha and Sacnab and perhaps Chompoxte. Recent work by the Rices (1980b, 1982) would also indicate that Lake Salpeten fits into this sphere. Such an interpretation would accord well with the distribution of the archaeological remains, both ceramically and architecturally (A. Chase 1982). Only by assuming the nonexistence of ceramics in protohistoric Peten can one state that the archaeologi-

Fig. 10. Fancourt map of 1854 showing a Lake "Zacpeten" north of Lake "Yaxhaa."

cal pattern does not exist in historic times. On the basis of documented trade routes for the Itza and known protohistoric and historic pottery elsewhere, this is doubtful.

One other piece of ethnohistoric information is of interest to this discussion. Avendano y Loyola (1696: 38a–38b) presented a list of the various districts within the Itza domain. One of the listed subdivisions within the province was that of a *halach uinic*, who was not "King" Canek. The presence of a *halach uinic* within the Peten is suggestive of a Yucatec form of social organization; such a person would generally be the head of the entire province (Roys 1957; D. Chase n.d.). As the *halach uinic* was not in residence in Canek's place of domicile and was listed as belonging elsewhere, it is possible that the *halach uinic* was in charge of Chaltuna (and concomitantly, Tayasal). This organizational division would also accord with Can's reported Itza civil war.

The presence of a *halach uinic* within the Peten has other implications as well for it indicates that other Yucatec affinities should be expected within the Southern lowlands. It further suggests that Avendano y Loyola's Canek was probably not the head of the Itza province, assuming conformity with the Yucatec organizational systems; that he was referred to by the Spaniards as "Rey" or "King" (while a *halach uinic* was also present) is probably indicative of their confusion over the local political system. Canek may have been referred to as a king due to a false belief on the part of the Spaniards that they were dealing with the head of the Itza territory or perhaps for political reasons. The division within the Itza province that appears to have been encountered by the Spaniards may have mirrored a deeply rooted organizational split within the south-central lowlands. This areal segmentation may ultimately be traceable to differences and tensions between indigenous Peten and intrusive Itza Postclassic populations; the temporal and spatial distributions of Postclassic archaeological remains within the Peten suggest that this may be the case.

Summary

The archaeology of the central Peten shows definite variation in material culture remains. This variation, however, is not just site by site, but appears to form regional patterns which must correspond to important cultural, political, and/or territorial divisions among the protohistoric Maya. While identification of the archaeological sites representing the legendary Itza occupation in the central Peten continues to lead to traditional settings and locations (G. Jones, Rice, and Rice 1981), archaeological information from the Peten suggests alternative interpretations (A. Chase 1976, 1982, 1983). The true Itza, following their southern migration, most likely located themselves at Topoxte (A. Chase 1976, 1982); this is reflected both in architecture and in ceramics, both of which show resemblance to Postclassic Yucatec material culture (see also Johnson, this volume; P. Rice and D. Rice, this volume). It is hypothesized that the Itza gained control of a sizeable part of the eastern Peten, including Macanche and Salpeten. Peripheral control may have been gained over the indigenous populations of the Lake Peten region. In time, however, the term "Itza" was extended to refer to groups which were assimilated by the original Itza from Yucatan. This situation led to terminological problems, as documented by Means' (1917: Appendix I) list of 21 variants of the term, which have further obfuscated ethnohistoric interpretation. The archaeological evidence, however, clearly defines at least two distinct, although overlapping spheres of influence, only one of which derives its inspiration from Late Postclassic Yucatan.

Archaeology and Ethnohistory on a Spanish Colonial Frontier: An Interim Report on the Macal-Tipu Project in Western Belize

ELIZABETH A. GRAHAM, GRANT D. JONES, AND ROBERT R. KAUTZ

The discovery of the Classic through Spanish Colonial period site at Negroman in western Belize has provided, through its Spanish Colonial component, Tipu, an opportunity to combine ethno-historical and archaeological approaches in order to explore the inter-action of Spanish and Maya spheres of influence in a colonial frontier context. The identification of the Late Postclassic–Spanish Colonial period component at Negroman as Tipu itself is based on the con-junction of ethnohistorical and archaeological data. Ethnohistorical documents (e.g., Lopez de Cogolludo 1971; Avendano y Loyola 1696) scrutinized by Thompson (1977; Scholes and Thompson 1977) and Jones contain accounts of journeys to Tipu made by Spanish friars on their way to proselytize, unsuccessfully, the Itza in Peten. On the basis of these accounts, Jones in 1978 located the prospective site of Tipu at Negroman, in the open pastures of a ranch owned by Mr. J. S. Espat. In 1980, during the first season of excavations at Negroman under Kautz's direction, a structure of probable Spanish Colonial pe-riod style was encountered, and in 1981 excavation showed it to be a Spanish church (fig. 1: S1E1; fig. 2), thus confirming that the site is the Tipu of the Spanish sources.

Tipu is ethnohistorically documented as having had a promi-nent position in sixteenth and seventeenth century plans for the conquest of Peten, then largely controlled militarily and economi-cally from the Itza capital of Tayasal (A. Chase 1976, 1982, this vol-ume; G. Jones, Rice, and Rice 1981). Part of the Spanish plan was to effect the gradual erosion of Itza influence in communities along the eastern boundary of the Itza polity in Belize, a step that would effec-tively eliminate riverine and coastal trade and communication be-tween the Itza and Yucatan (G. Jones 1982, 1983). This strategy was later abandoned in favor of a direct attack upon Tayasal from the north, but there were other factors that continued to focus the Spaniards' gaze on Tipu. The community's location, midway between the Spaniards of the Yucatan peninsula and the Itza of Peten, was instrumental in attracting refugees fleeing the harsh effects of Spanish policies in the north. Partly as a result of an influx of apparently resourceful, nominally assimilated Maya, Tipu's trading influence spread, inflating the importance of the community in the eyes of all those who were vying for political and economic domination of the Southern Maya lowlands.

The Spanish interest in Tipu and other Maya settlements in Belize was a reflection of colonial efforts to maintain a corridor through which the conquest of the Itza and other hostile Maya could be pursued from Yucatan. We know, on the basis of information from documents studied by Jones at the Archivo General de las Indias in Seville, that a Spanish mission at Tipu had been established before A.D. 1567 and that the town was occupied continuously until the forced removal of its population to the shores of Lake Peten-Itza in A.D. 1707. The mission at Tipu may have been established as early as A.D. 1544. While further study of the documents may or may not confirm such early contact, it is already within the bounds of reason to suggest that continuity existed between the Late Postclassic populations of the Belize River tributaries and those in the area at the time of contact. This possibility remains to be fully tested archaeologically.

At the present time, the archaeological evidence provides only indirect support for the hypothesis of Postclassic–contact period continuity. Some of the relevant data come from an elaborate Late Postclassic civic–ceremonial architectural complex situated not far southeast of the apparent center of the Spanish Colonial period community (fig. 1: S2E2). Had this complex been active at the time of contact, the Spaniards would most likely have insisted on its destruction and the construction of the church nearby, where they could watch to see that the complex was not reused. On the other hand, it is also possible that the Spaniards found Tipu near an already abandoned Late Postclassic civic and ceremonial complex, in which case such proximity was the result of Maya patterns of residential continuity.

Archaeological evidence from the excavation of the complex in the form of ceramics, censer fragments, *Spondylus* shell, jade, and copper, suggests that construction and use of the structures date predominantly to the fourteenth and early fifteenth centuries. By the time Tipu was established as a Spanish mission community in the sixteenth century, full scale maintenance of the complex seems to have ceased. Spanish olive-jar fragments were found in association

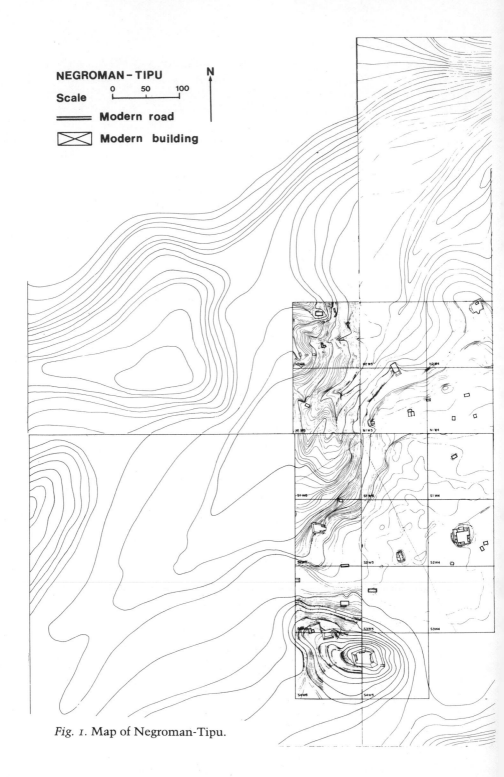

Fig. 1. Map of Negroman-Tipu.

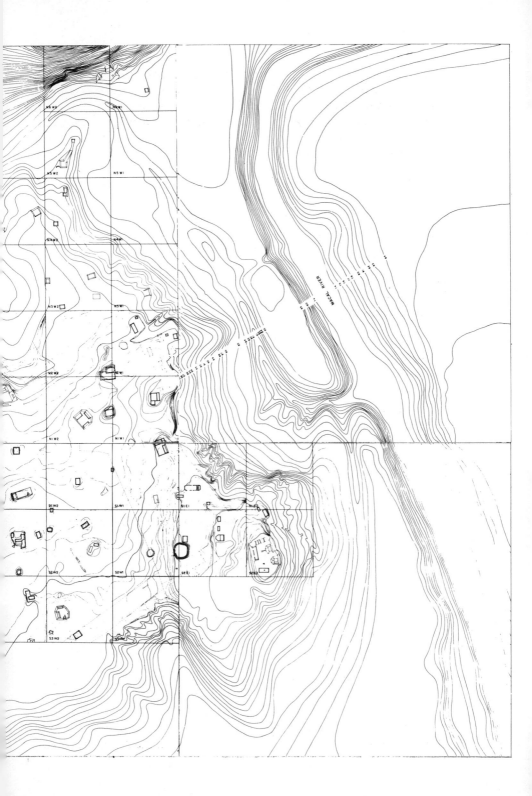

with the complex, but in soil accumulation above the latest plaster floor of one of the principal structures. The same context yielded reconstructable fragments of a Lacandon–type censer. Though the evidence so far tells us little about population continuity from Late Postclassic into Spanish Colonial times, the presence of the Lacandon–type censer does indicate that Maya deities were not neglected in spite of an apparent acceptance of Christianity. Further ethnohistorical study of whether such acceptance was only nominal, or more integral (see Miller and Farriss 1979), obviously will have a major effect on our understanding of the contexts in which the various material cultural remains are found.

Until evidence for or against population continuity from the Late Postclassic to the historic period is more firmly within our grasp, we think it preferable to refer only to the Spanish Colonial or historic period component at Negroman as Tipu, and reserve the name "Negroman" for the Late Postclassic and earlier settlements about which less is known.

On the basis of evidence to date, the history of the Tipu settlement can be roughly broken down into the following periods:

1. Between A.D. 1544 and 1567: Spanish mission established at Tipu.

2. Before A.D. 1608: Spanish control apparently weak; religious practices include both Maya and Christian manifestations.

3. A.D. 1608–1622: Tipu region reduced again by the Spaniards; Tipu assigned to a new *encomendero* from Bacalar. Stronger Spanish presence; heightened activities associated with Christian practices, and extraction of tribute, including cacao.

4. A.D. 1622–1637: Increased disaffection with Spaniards. Continued influx of refugees from Spanish–controlled towns in northern Belize and Yucatan.

5. A.D. 1637–1695: Rebellion centered at Tipu, and expulsion of Spanish civil and ecclesiastical authorities from all Belize missions until A.D. 1695.

6. A.D. 1695–1707: Tipuans recontact colonial authorities in Merida and cooperate with Spaniards in conquest of Itza in A.D. 1697; intensive Spanish activity; 11 missionaries baptize several hundred individuals in Tipu region. Spaniards force removal of Tipu community to Peten.

While more than one church may have been constructed at Tipu, only one has been confirmed by archaeological excavation (fig. 2). It is situated less than 300 meters from the Macal River, near the eastern edge of the river terrace (on which most of the ruins lie) and above the modern floodplain. It is 23 meters long and 8 meters wide, with apsidal east and west ends. Many of the stones that formed the foundation of the church walls remained in situ, which permitted us to reconstruct in simplified form the plan, shown in figure 2. The 80 centimeter thick walls stood to full height at the east end of the church, around the altar and chancel, but probably stood only to a height of 1.5 meters around the nave, where poles were set into the walls to support a roof that was very likely of thatch. This reconstruction is based not on the presence of postholes, but rather on the volume of collapse debris. The wall core of clay and river stones was faced with limestone blocks. Single lines of limestone blocks formed the steps that led up to the altar, which itself was constructed of clay and river cobble core faced with limestone. Interior and exterior walls of the church were plastered, as indicated by remains of plaster on the interior walls of the chancel and the plaster collapse found around the church's perimeter. Around the church, portions of stone pavements were encountered just outside the doorways to the nave on the north and south sides. Some modification of the church structure seems to have taken place through time; for example, the exterior door of the chancel was at one time sealed. Further excavation of the church is planned, but the construction sequence is essentially in hand and it is clear that the building is largely a single phase structure.

A total of 180 burials have been excavated thus far from beneath the church floor and from the western periphery of the church outside the nave. The skeletal material is presently being analyzed by Mark Cohen, with the assistance of Sharon Bennett, at the State University College of New York at Plattsburgh. Like the burials in the earlier of the two churches at Lamanai (D.M. Pendergast, personal communication), individuals were interred in fully extended dorsal position with the head to the west. The only burial accompaniment was a small, unslipped jar interred with a subadult. The manner in which the jar is perforated suggests that it was used as a censer. Copper pins were recovered from within the chest cavities of some individuals; their presence suggests the use of burial shrouds.

Though Cohen's analysis is still in the early stages, it is apparent that the sample is skewed because there is almost no one under two years of age, and no one over age 40. Until the relative health of the population can be more firmly established (that is, compared to the church period population at Lamanai and to an earlier population sample at Negroman), little can be inferred from the presence or absence of evidence of diseases or trauma. The age skew is especially puzzling. Because only the portion of the nave south of the central east-west axis and a small portion of the area outside the nave have

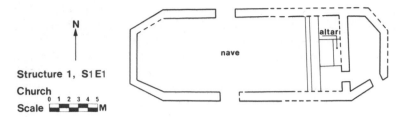

N

Structure 1, S1 E1
Church
Scale 0 1 2 3 4 5 M

Fig. 2. Plan of the excavated church at Negroman-Tipu.

been excavated, further testing may demonstrate that those individuals over 40 years of age and the very young were buried elsewhere in the church area. The less likely possibility remains that during the period of church use the older members of the community refused church burial, and the newborn were not baptized.

The date of construction of the church has not yet been determined. The architectural style suggests an early date, perhaps mid–sixteenth century with minor modifications after A.D. 1608. The style, however, does not exclude the possibility that the church was built in the first half of the seventeenth century, with the establishment of an *encomienda* in the region during the time of the intensive missionary activities of Fuensalida and Orbita. Excavation strategy for future seasons includes testing for the presence of another church, as well as excavation of historic period residential structures. The approximate whereabouts of a number of probable historic residences are known as a result of archaeological testing; in addition, the specific locations of several of these, given in reference to the church, are noted in the ethnohistoric documents. The identification and excavation of these structures, which are also dated by the documents, will give us the archaeological associations we need to provide finer chronological bracketing for the excavated church.

In past seasons, 50 random (one meter by one meter) units have been excavated in a 100 meter quadrat just south of the church (fig. 1: S2E1). Several units revealed primary middens and stone features, either terrace faces or walls; on the basis of the ceramic sample, it is quite likely that both the features and the middens are associated with historic period structures. Future plans include the extension of excavations within the quadrat south of the church in an attempt to determine the plans of the indicated structures, and to define relationships between the buildings and the church, as well as associations between structures and middens. Portions of what appear to be the low stone faces of the church-centered plaza were also encountered through testing; in 1984 Graham plans to extend the excavations in an attempt to delineate the plaza itself.

The data on the location of the houses of wealthy Tipuans derived from ethnohistoric documents and the features encountered through archaeological sampling in the area of the church have combined to give us some idea of the plan of the historic community center, and suggest where we might expect to recover material remains from elite households. The ethnohistoric documents have also provided us with information on what constituted the economic base of the elite: wealth derived from the production and distribution of cacao. The post-conquest disruption by the Spaniards of native trade networks throughout Yucatan (G. Jones 1982) left gaps that were understandably not entirely filled by the new trade links forged by the Spaniards to meet their needs and the demands of distant Spain. As a result of the disruption, some areas of Yucatan and all of Peten became more dependent, because of the native market for cacao, on cacao production in Belize and its distribution via Tipu (G. Jones 1982).

Other than the preservation of pollen or pods, it is difficult to predict how cacao production might be manifested in the archaeological record. Extensive cacao–drying floors like those used today in Central America (see Ekholm 1969: fig. 3) might be detectable, and test excavations will be carried out on the historic community periphery in an attempt to locate possible floor areas. Indirect evidence for cacao production should, however, be manifested in the greater material wealth of elite households. Because, according to ethnohistorical sources, these households were headed in large part by refugees from the northern Maya lowlands, we anticipate elite material culture parallels with sites such as Santa Rita (D. Chase 1982a) and Lamanai (Pendergast 1981a) in northern Belize. If we are able to recover an appreciable quantity of data from lower status households, we might expect to see stronger local parallels with sites downriver along the Belize valley, and with the Stann Creek District to the east. Nearest coastal access is through the Hummingbird Gap to the Stann Creek valley, where there is archaeological evidence of Late Postclassic activity both inland, at the site of Mayflower on Silk Grass Creek, and along the coast at the Colson Point sites (E. Graham, this volume). The Stann Creek valley evidence makes it appear very likely that the Hummingbird–Stann Creek corridor served as an access route to the coast in Late Postclassic and historic times, as it did in the Protoclassic–Early Classic period (E. Graham 1983). This route was apparently unknown to the Acalan traders of Tabasco at the time of the Conquest (see Thompson 1970: 131–132);

perhaps because of this, it never seems to have figured importantly in Spanish designs. Therefore it may have been an ideal corridor to the sea and to coastal trade in times when native exchange networks were in jeopardy elsewhere.

Of further interest is the fact that the Stann Creek District's acid soils are well suited to the growing of cacao. All of the free-draining acid soils of Belize occur only in the foothills and valleys of rivers draining the eastern flank of the Maya Mountains, and cacao is a crop ". . . which will grow really *well* only in this region" (Wright et al. 1959: 156−157, emphasis theirs). This does not constitute proof that cacao was grown in the area of Belize to the east of Tipu in historic times, but it makes it a strong possibility, especially considering that the communities on the eastern side of the Maya Mountains had never been brought within the sphere of Spanish control (Thompson 1977; Scholes and Thompson 1977). In addition, the region to the east of the Maya Mountains in the Stann Creek District has virtually no limestone and hence no sources of chert. Communities were therefore compelled throughout prehistory to look outside the region for sources of raw materials for chipped stone tools.

The historic scenario provided here leaves much to be resolved. Nonetheless, we are progressing in the acquisition of knowledge about Tipu, its inhabitants, its material culture and networks of exchange, and its place within the post-contact regional framework. In addition to augmenting the body of data on historic period developments and material culture, it is our hope that a pattern of integration will emerge from the conjunction of archaeological and ethnohistorical approaches, and that this pattern will form the basis of models that can be applied toward elucidating the contact period experience at other sites.

Facets of Terminal to Postclassic Activity in the Stann Creek District, Belize

ELIZABETH A. GRAHAM

Excavations carried out at sites along the rivers, creeks, and coast of the Stann Creek District have revealed minimal but unmistakable evidence of Postclassic activity. The evidence is minimal not necessarily because occupation was sparse, but rather because pottery is so poorly preserved. Acid ground−water conditions erode slips and dissolve calcite temper, leaving little for the archaeologist to recover or classify. These conditions of preservation have particular import with regard to inferences about the Postclassic, for in few cases in the Stann Creek District are ceramics preserved without the protection of overlying construction. This means that once massive architectural undertakings ceased (as they seem to have done throughout most of the lowlands by Postclassic times) we cannot expect pottery to be preserved even in circumstances of heavy settlement.

Fortunately, construction continued in some areas of the district in Terminal Classic−Early Postclassic times, so that we have some fragmentary pottery from this time period to guide us, and we were also fortunate to encounter the remains of two later Postclassic offerings.

Most of the evidence for Terminal Classic−Early Postclassic activity comes from the Mayflower group of sites along the upper reaches of a small creek that drains the foothills of the Maya Mountains about seven kilometers south of Pomona (fig. 1). Silk Grass Creek and its tributaries form the next drainage system south of the North Stann Creek River. Unlike the North Stann Creek valley, however, which supports intensive cultivation of citrus on an expanse of fertile soils, only a ribbon of moderately fertile soil borders Silk Grass Creek from the foothills to the sea, and it is cultivated only along the middle reaches, by Creole and Maya milperos from the village of Silk Grass.

The three sites of the Mayflower group, Maintzunun, May-

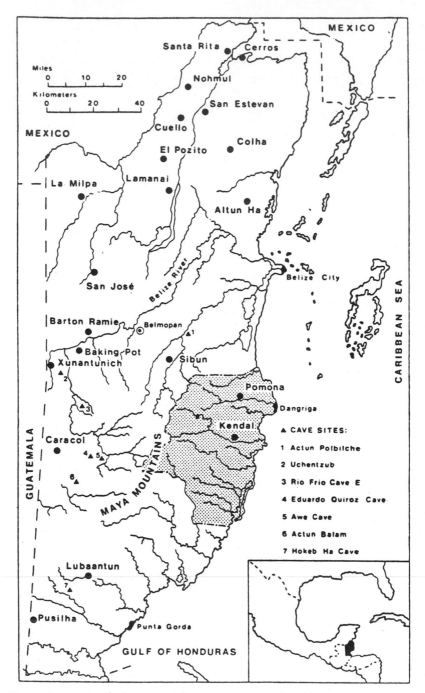

Fig. 1. Stann Creek District and major sites in Belize (drawing by Rita Granda).

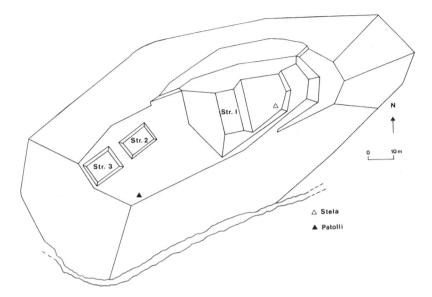

Fig. 2. Map of Maintzunun.

flower, and T'au Witz, were all part of fairly intensive Terminal Classic to Early Postclassic occupation. Maintzunun, on the north side of Silk Grass Creek, is a massive, acropolis–like terraced plat- form that supports three basal building platforms, and probably sup- ported other perishable buildings (fig. 2). A fallen needle–like granite stela lies on the uppermost, eastward–facing terrace top, and proba- bly once stood there on the south side. Mayflower (fig. 3), on the south side of the creek, is a more typical arrangement of structures around a plaza. T'au Witz, also south of the creek and only one kilo- meter southeast of Mayflower, is a broad terrace of artificial con- struction buttressed against the eastern slope of a spur of the Maya Mountain foothills (fig. 4). A granite stela and altar stand on the ter- race near the eastern edge; the only constructed mound is located on the north edge of the terrace.

Radiocarbon data anchor the construction and major occupa- tion of Structure 1 at Maintzunun, the focal point of the site by vir- tue of height and centrality, to the eighth century A.D.[1] We do not know whether or not the entire complex was built then, but the magnitude of construction suggests that there may be greater time depth for use of the site than that represented by the eighth century dates for Structure 1a and Structure 1b. In any case, a short gap in

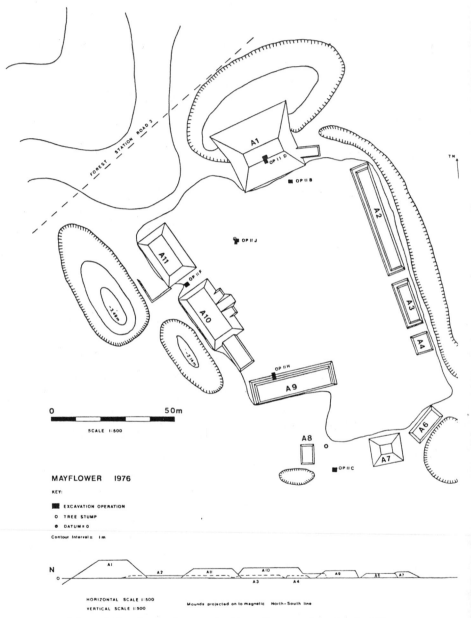

Fig. 3. Map of Mayflower (survey by Peter Barron; drawing by Rita Granda).

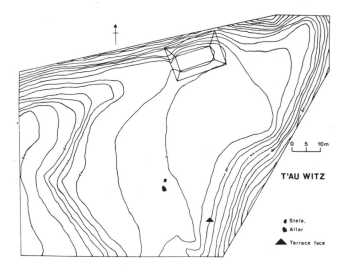

Fig. 4. Map of T'au Witz.

occupation followed the burning of the perishable portion of Structure 1b in the latter part of the eighth century; subsequent use is dated to the ninth century, and probably continued into the tenth century.

The dating for ninth-century reuse is based largely on a modeled-carved vase cached in eighth-century collapse debris (E. Graham et al. 1980: 166). A solid censer handle from surface soil accumulation and a large patolli board fragment from the surface (fig. 5a) suggest that occupation continued into Early Postclassic times.

A stone artifact of note from Terminal Classic–Early Postclassic habitation debris is a complete stemmed macroblade. Its presence indicates that this type of implement continued in use in the district from Protoclassic times, thus providing evidence of continuity in an important area of technology. The obsidian recovered is almost entirely from El Chayal, with only one of eleven blades or blade fragments from San Martin Jilotepeque. Dependence on El Chayal as the primary source for obsidian parallels the Protoclassic pattern at Stann Creek District coastal sites.

As at Seibal (A. L. Smith 1977), it is not clear whether the patolli dates to as early as the ninth century or appeared on the scene slightly later. The fact that the game boards occur on or very near the surface at Maintzunun, Mayflower, and Kendal leads me to believe that they are, at the earliest, from the last part of the Terminal Classic–Early Postclasssic occupation continuum.

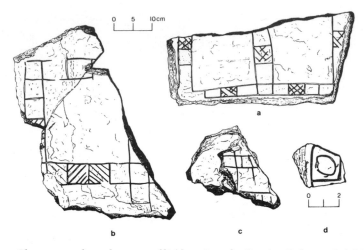

Fig. 5. Slate game boards or patolli (drawings by Louise Belanger): (a) Maintzunun; (b and c) Kendal; (d) game piece (?), Kendal.

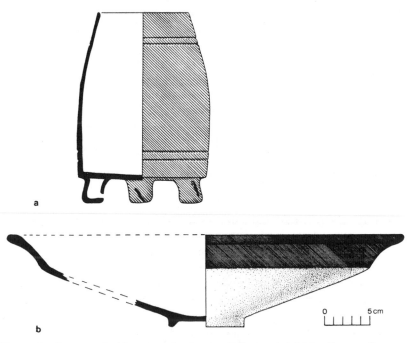

Fig. 6. Cache vessels (drawings by Louise Belanger): (a) Mayflower, Structure A–1 construction; (b) T'au Witz, stela cache.

What few sherds we have from Terminal Classic—Early Post-classic occupation refuse show some continuity with late eighth-century ceramics, such as the ash-tempered sherds from the Belize ceramic group and those from San Jose V—type pedestal base bowls with sharp medial angle (fig. 6b; Thompson 1939: fig. 93). Evidence from the artifacts and architecture taken together, however, strongly suggests that there was a change in the inhabitants' view of Maintzunun as a focus of constructional, and perhaps also ritual, activity. The ninth-century occupants undertook no major architectural endeavors, and the presence of uncleared collapse debris around Structure 1 at this time indicates that either the site had diminished in importance, or the labor could not be mustered to maintain the structures as they had been maintained in the past. Evidence for substantial construction activity at Mayflower in the ninth-century suggests that diminished importance for Maintzunun is the more likely explanation. The focus of ceremonial activity, at least, seems to have shifted to Mayflower, on the south side of Silk Grass Creek.

Test excavations were carried out on two structures at Mayflower: Structure A—1, the presumed major ceremonial building that stands just over seven meters high, and Structure A—9, a range—type platform 35 meters long and 10 meters wide, that faced Structure A—1 by intruding into and hence dividing the larger plaza on which Structure A—1 faced (fig. 3).

Most of the Structure A—1 construction is dated to the Terminal Classic period, probably to the ninth century. Only 4.5 meters of Structure A—1 was penetrated by excavation, however, and two meters remain to be excavated above plaza level; initial construction may, therefore, be Late Classic in date. Chronological anchoring derives mainly from the presence of two vessels presumably deposited as an offering on the structure's primary axis. The construction stage with which the offering is associated is the earliest of four distinguished. The fragmented vessels are two orange-red slipped, tripod, barrel—shaped vases with double—line, preslip groove—incised lines around the bases and below the rims (fig. 6a). The lower vase contained a light green perforated stone bead.

The three construction stages that postdated cache deposition involved, either wholly or in part, the amassing of sand and/or clay as core, the construction of retaining faces of granite with some sandstone and slate, the laying down of a clay, sand, or gravel floor, and the construction of wattle and daub superstructures. The few worn sherds present in construction core and occupation refuse are like those described from Maintzunun, though fragments of hollow oven—shaped supports were also recovered from surface soil accumulation over collapse debris. The assignment of a very Late to Terminal Classic date for the earliest construction is, therefore, on reasonably secure ground, and the fact that three stages of fairly massive construction followed suggests that intensive occupation continued throughout Terminal Classic times and possibly into the early part of the Postclassic.

Although no modification of Structure A–1 was ever again carried out, the ruined structure was visited in Middle or Late Postclassic times. Sherds from a censer were recovered from soil accumulation above Terminal Classic–Early Postclassic collapse debris. The censer type is so far known only from the site of Lamanai, where it was in use from the mid–twelfth to the fourteenth century A.D. (Pendergast 1981a: 44–46, Fig. 20) and from Altun Ha, where a vessel was deposited in circumstances closely similar to those at Mayflower (Pendergast 1982a: 140).

Structure A–1 was already a well developed entity when construction of the range–type Structure A–9 began in the late eighth or ninth century. A fragment of a vase similar to the Structure A–1 cache vessels, and sherds from ash-tempered vessels, were recovered from the old land surface beneath the core of the initial platform. Structure A–9 underwent three stages of modification before it was abandoned, probably in the tenth century. The layer of refuse that accumulated on portions of the platform terraces suggests that A–9 was a residence, though it is curious to find refuse on the structure's presumed front side. Extensive refuse accumulation around buildings is a phenomenon that is documented, however, for an elite residence at Altun Ha in Late Classic times (Pendergast 1979: 127–128, 195, 197) and at Yaxha in the Terminal Classic period (P. Rice n.d.a).

A fragment of a slate patolli board was recovered from soil accumulation over collapse debris, a context that suggests an Early Postclassic or tenth-century date for the artifact. The chert inventory demonstrates that stemmed bifaces were in use; obsidian blades were recovered, but they have not been provenienced. Fragments of manos, metates, and other ground stone tools were more common than chert, an expectable reflection of the proximity of granite sources.

Collapse debris of Structure A–9 lay undisturbed until Late Postclassic times, when two granite stelae were erected on the north or front side of the platform. Presumably the stones had been moved from somewhere else in the plaza. Two vessels were buried on the north side of the larger stela in fill that was deposited to support the stone. Four greenstone beads, two of them jade, were buried on the east side; a unifacially worked, triangular point or knife (fig. 8a)

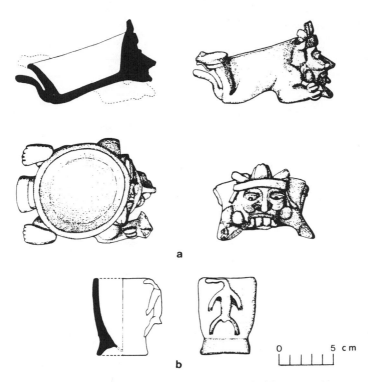

0   5 cm

Fig. 7. Mayflower, Structure A–9 stela cache vessels (drawings by Louise Belanger): (a) effigy censer; (b) mortar–cup.

manufactured from a thin, translucent light brown chert blade, as well as one complete and two broken obsidian blades, were buried on the west side. One of the vessels is an unslipped effigy censer bowl (fig. 7a) that is typical of small incensarios made in Quintana Roo and Belize in the Late Postclassic period (Andrews IV and Andrews 1975: 73). The other vessel is a small cup or mortar with an animal applique on one side, possibly a lizard, positioned as if it were crawling down the side of the cup toward the base (fig. 7b). The head of the creatures is missing. A small hole, ca. 10 millimeters in diameter, was worn through the base of the cup from the inside. The effigy bowl had been placed on a flat stone, together with a piece of slate decorated with a single incised line. Some burnt sherds were found just north of the mortar–cup, and shell fragments were recovered from the earth around the vessels.

One other area of Mayflower yielded data on the Terminal Classic–Early Postclasic period; this is a group of fallen stone monuments

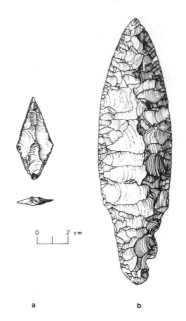

a   b

Fig. 8. Chipped stone from Mayflower (drawings by Louise Belanger):
(a) unifacially worked chert blade from stela cache, Structure A–9;
(b) stemmed, notched biface from stela-altar group.

in the northwest part of the plaza. All stones are in fragments or are
cracked, and they may have been tampered with, if not shifted, in
recent times. All of the seven monuments identified are stelae or
stela–like stones except for one round altar, ca. one meter in diameter and 15 centimeters thick. The material of six of these is granite,
while the seventh is of slate. An incised slate fragment from another
stela–like stone was also recovered. Although dating of the group is
open to question, artifact associations suggest that erection of the
monuments took place in the Terminal Classic.

   A limestone (?) pendant carved in a Late Classic jade–working
style was found near the monuments in loose surface soil. More securely associated with the stones are five stemmed chert bifaces and
one hoe–like implement, all of which were recovered from various
places around the monuments, and are assumed to have been buried
at the stela bases. The most interesting of these is a biface with
double–notched stem (fig. 8b). Notching of stems does not seem to
be a part of Classic Maya chipped stone technology in the Southern
lowlands, though it does appear at the end of the Classic period at
some sites such as Altar de Sacrificios (Willey 1972: 161–163). The

bifaces are usually notched on both sides at the shoulder, however, and tend to have shorter stems. The notched biface from the Mayflower stela–altar group may typify a technology in transition from Late Classic to Terminal Classic times. This instance suggests that we may learn more about the pace of changes that characterized the Terminal Classic by focusing not on ceramics, but on chipped stone technology.

Analysis of another class of artifact that is usually considered to be less productive of information, daub, has revealed a phenomenon that may be significant in the interpretation of culture change in the Terminal Classic period. The evidence from Maintzunun demonstrates that the eighth-century Structure 1a and Structure 1b, presumed to have been ceremonial buildings, were constructed of pole and probably thatch, and were coated first with red clay and then with a thin coat of white clay mixed with sand. The remains of the ninth-century Structure 1c were only a few centimeters below the surface, and though daub chunks coated with white clay were recovered from surface accumulation, there is some uncertainty as to whether this daub is from Structure 1c or earlier buildings.

The notable comparison is with daub from the remains of Structure A–1 and Structure A–9 at Mayflower. At this site, where most of the evidence comes from the buildings of Structure A–1, the daub (usually red or orange but sometimes yellow) was mixed with fiber, and no white clay coating was applied. Because both Structure 1 at Maintzunun and Structure A–1 at Mayflower seem to have been ceremonial in nature, the change in construction technique suggests more than a shift in ceremonial focus from Maintzunun to Mayflower, and may reflect changes in societal priorities and practices.

The third site of the Mayflower group, T'au Witz, yielded evidence of Terminal Classic–Early Postclassic use in the form of a datable vessel whose fragments were buried around the four sides of the base of a granite stela (fig. 9). The vessel is a San Jose V–type bowl with pedestal base and sharp medial angle or "shoulder" (fig. 6b). The pedestal in this case had been ground down and carved to form tabs. The slip that remains is red, and is most similar to Roaring Creek Red from the Belize valley (Gifford 1976: 240–243). The presence of this vessel indicates that erection of the stela, and probably placement of the altar, date at the earliest to Terminal Classic times. Whether or not the stela was originally a Classic product is impossible to determine. Its needle-like shape is unusual, though similar to the stela at Mayflower and to stones reported from Kendal (Price 1899). Because only 56 centimeters of the stela was buried beneath the ground surface, it appeared possible that it was a broken

Fig. 9. Photograph of the stela and altar at T'au Witz.

portion of a larger stone, and that originally the "needle" end was the stela butt. No matching portion was located, however, and it may be that the coarse-grained nature of the granite limited the options for the form of the final product. That monument shapes more typical of the Classic could be achieved in granite at Mayflower is seen in the round altarstone from the stela–altar complex and in the stela associated with Structure A–9. The needle–like shape may therefore be a characteristic form of Terminal Classic or Early Postclassic times.

Other evidence of Postclassic activity in the district is even more fragmentary than that from Silk Grass Creek, though a picture of widespread Postclassic presence is slowly emerging. The surface near Middlesex in the upper North Stann Creek valley has yielded the hollow handle of a Postclassic ladle censer. Through the Hummingbird Gap west of Middlesex lies the Sibun valley, where Mayapan–like effigy censer fragments were found on the surface before large scale agricultural clearing was begun in the 1960s. In the North Stann Creek valley at Pomona, one structure was excavated at Mamey Hill (MacKie n.d.) in which a patolli fragment was reused as a facing stone in platform construction. Along the coast at Colson Point, ca. 12 kilometers north of the mouth of the Stann Creek River, Tulum Red ware and notched ovoid ("date seed") pottery net sinkers were found at the swamp sites of Kakalche and Watson's Island.

On the Sittee River at Kendal, there is fragmentary evidence of Terminal Classic–Early Postclassic occupation in the form of hollow oven–shaped supports, a hollow ovoid foot (probably later than the Early Postclassic), and fragments of patolli boards from the surface (fig. 5b, c). Early excavations at Kendal (Price 1899) recovered the fragments of an effigy censer at the base of "slate needles" atop a high mound. The vessel was likened to those found throughout the Yucatan with ". . . human figures in high relief on the outside" (Price 1899: 344). The occurrence of the censer at the base of a stela– like stone is paralleled ritually, and perhaps chronologically, in the Structure A–9 stela cache at Mayflower.

The next major river south of the Sittee, South Stann Creek, is not known to flow past any standing mounds, at least along its middle reaches. A set of stone artifacts has been assembled by a resident citrus grower, however, who collected the specimens from the surface in his groves on the north bank of the river, west of the Southern Highway. Two of the implements are stemmed, straight base, side–notched bifaces (Sheets 1978: fig. 2c1), also known as expanded stem type (Willey 1972: 161–163). As noted above, this chipping style is not typical of the Classic Maya in the Southern lowlands, and the evidence indicates that stemmed, side–notched bifaces are Terminal Classic or Early Postclassic in date (Willey 1972: 161–163; Sheets 1978: 24, 73; Hester et al. 1981: fig. 3). A broken, apparently asymmetrical bipointed biface in the South Stann Creek collection may also be Postclassic in execution (see Proskouriakoff 1962: 356).

The foregoing review of extant Terminal Classic and Postclassic data from the Stann Creek District demonstrates that the information, though scanty, permits us to bring southern Belize within the sphere of Postclassic activity. Extension of understanding of the last centuries of pre–Columbian life in the district will obviously have to depend on further archaeological investigation. We are, however, at a stage in such investigations that allows the drawing of some inferences regarding the Stann Creek District Postclassic.

The apparent disruption in the ceremonial pattern, and the shift in activity from Maintzunun to Mayflower in the Silk Grass Creek area, parallel the Tenth Cycle florescence at Seibal and are probably related phenomena. The Maintzunun cache vessel is not Fine Orange ware, but is characterized by modeled-carved decorative treatment similar to that of the Pabellon type. It has been argued elsewhere (E. Graham et al. 1980: 166) that the modeled-carved pottery vessels which are widespread in Belize (see R. E. Smith 1955: 43–44; E. Graham et al. 1980: 165–166) should not be characterized as imitations of Fine Orange, though this is a valid viewpoint if the intended implication is that the makers of Fine Orange ware pulled the strings of political and economic power in the Terminal Classic–Early Postclassic period. If, however, we agree that this has not been established, then we would be on safer ground if we were to view all the makers of modeled-carved vessels as members of communities which, throughout the lowlands, were adjusting to changes in the seats of political and economic authority.

The Terminal Classic period is a time of contradiction. On the one hand, it is closely tied culturally to the Classic; for example, the production of modeled-carved vessels is an expression of the same phenomena that we see manifested in Late Classic polychromes. That is, ritual vessels were designed to depict realistic human or god–like figures acting out a ceremony that in some cases had become standardized and presumably widely understood. From this we might infer that Terminal Classic rulers expected the same responses from the ruled as in Classic times.

On the other hand, the observation by D. Rice and P. Rice (1982: 67) that Terminal Classic pottery is notable for a variety in pastes that reflects great regionalization in ceramic manufacture suggests that other forces were at work reordering ceramic priorities; this would presumably have counteracted Classic traditions and practices. It seems probable that the Terminal Classic saw some loosening of intercommunity ties, and that a formerly well–knit communications network based on exchange was in the process of unravelling. We might speculate that a breakdown occurred in the widespread distribution of slip clays and paints that were crucial to the decoration of polychromes; such an event would have left polychrome production to continue, in altered form, only in its area of production. Terminal Classic ceramics, wherever found, suggest that communities may have had to depend more on their own resources than on a complex exchange network for ceramic production and expression.

The crosscurrents of continuity and change that characterized the Terminal Classic period may have been set in motion by forces that were acting over a longer period than has usually been reckoned where the "collapse" is concerned. This may help explain why sites such as Lamanai could adjust and weather the tenth-century turmoil. An alternative possibility is that the forces which effected change in the structuring of ceramic and lithic manufacturing priorities in the Terminal Classic did not actually disrupt community ties that had existed in Classic times. There can be no doubt, however, that the character of such ties and the relative political positions of communities underwent a transformation. Determination of the nature of the transformation and reorientation of lowland communities will not lead us directly to a greater understanding of the breakdown of Classic society, but it will contribute to a clearer perception of the origins of Postclassic society.

The Postclassic data from the Stann Creek District are presently too minimal to contribute substantially to interpretation of Postclassic events. What we can say, however, is that the route from the North Stann Creek valley through the Hummingbird Gap to the Sibun, Caves Branch, and upper Belize River valleys was probably as important a communications link with the Peten in Postclassic times as the Stann Creek District coastal sites suggest it was in the Protoclassic period. Though this may not have earthshaking implications, it does mean that the Peteneros had relatively uncomplicated access to the sea, to its resources, and to whatever items were traded along the Caribbean coast; such access was surely of importance, especially to any groups who may have moved into Peten from Yucatan. Further investigations in the Stann Creek District will probably not bring about any radical alteration of our understanding of major Postclassic trends; a focus on avenues of communication such as the North Stann Creek valley will, however, unquestionably illuminate the significant role played by southern Belize in Postclassic and earlier Southern lowlands prehistory.

Note

1. The following radiocarbon dates pertain to the construction and occupation dates of Structure 1 at Maintzunun:

Structure 1a: 1270 ± 50 radiocarbon years: A.D. 680 (LJ–3680) calibrated to A.D. 730 on the basis of the Suess bristlecone pine tree-ring calibration curve.

Structure 1b: 1250 ± 50 radiocarbon years: A.D. 700 (LJ–3678) calibrating to A.D. 750.

Structure 1b: 1230 ± 40 radiocarbon years: A.D. 720 (LJ–3679) calibrating to A.D. 770 (E. Graham et al. 1980: 166).

# THE PERIPHERIES

The lowland Maya Postclassic peoples did not exist in a vacuum. They interacted with other groups to the west, south, and southeast. Except for the highland Maya to the south, little information exists concerning their other neighbors. To the west, the only work that really has been done in this area is by Ruz (1969), Andrews IV (1943), and Berlin (1956). Ball attempts to place this area into perspective in his paper.

Ethnohistoric accounts note that the Maya carried on an active trade with their southeastern neighbors through the communities of Nito and Naco (Strong, Kidder, and Paul 1938). Little is known, however, concerning the Postclassic archaeology of this region. Sharer's paper relates some of the University of Pennsylvania findings at Quirigua to the crucial transition from Terminal Classic to Postclassic. It is interesting to note the existence of human effigy censers in Late Classic Quirigua and to speculate on their relationship to the later widespread effigy cult (Chen Mul Modeled; Idolos Modeled; Kol Modeled) of the Northern lowlands. The important site of Naco and the Sula Plain of Honduras are the focus of Wonderley's paper; the information he provides does much to fill in the previous archaeological void for the Middle to Late Postclassic period in this ethnohistorically important southeastern area.

Extensive archaeological research on the Postclassic period has been carried out in the highlands of Guatemala; perhaps the best-known Postclassic archaeological data come from this region. Wauchope defined a Postclassic presence at Zacualpa (1947, 1975) and further defined a Protohistoric ceramic presence (1970) for different sites within the highland area. Woodbury and Trik (1953) reported on the spectacular Postclassic-Protohistoric Mam capital of Zaculeu. Guillemin (1977) worked on the Cakchiquel Postclassic city of Iximche, while Lehmann (1968) published on the Postclassic capital of

Fig. 1. Map of Guatemalan highland site of Utatlan, capital of the Quiche Maya (after Carmack and Weeks 1981).

the Pokomam, Mixco Viejo. Carmack (1968, 1973, 1977) and Fox (1977, 1978, 1980) have provided a significant body of detail on the Quiche area and its Postclassic capital of Utatlan (fig. 1). The central Quiche region has been cited frequently as receiving Mexican (Tol-tec) or "Toltecized-Maya" influences from the Gulf Coast to the north. Recent work by Brown, summarized in his paper, suggests that this interpretation is incorrect and that a far more complex cycle of political and economic interactions obtained between high-lands and lowlands in the Postclassic period.

What must be stressed here is that the lowland Postclassic Maya were fully aware of their neighbors and actively interacted with them. Fortunately, many of these interactions leave their mark in the archaeological record as items that were clearly traded back and forth. Metal objects (Bray 1977) for ornamentation, for example, must have been obtained either from central Mexico or from Central

America. Long-distance trade even involved South America, as evidenced by a vessel, probably of highland Peruvian origin, which was cached by the Maya at Santa Rita, Belize (D. Chase 1982a: 258–259, 299). Nicoya Polychrome from Central America occurs as an Early Postclassic trade item at Chichen Itza and in the central Peten (at Punta Nima—A. Chase 1983: 1100). Highland tradewares, such as Plumbate (Shepard 1948) and "Mixtec" incensarios (Brainerd 1958; Ball 1980; A. Chase 1983: 1078, fig. 4–13), also occur in the Northern and Southern lowlands in the Early Postclassic period. The Mixteca-Puebla style (Nicholson 1960, 1961; Robertson 1970), most noted in central Mexico, additionally appears in the Southern lowlands, especially in murals and in Postclassic decorative modes on pottery where it achieved a synthesis of its own.

Militarism may be suggested as one means by which many of the foreign goods and ideas were brought into the lowlands. The Aztec *pochteca* definitely knew the area: Aztec warriors went to Mayapan in the Late Postclassic as part of an alliance with the ruling Maya lord. While the amount and type of influence may be argued *ad infinitum*, the simple existence of the objects, art styles, and few ethnohistorically recorded data relate that the lowland Maya were in a symbiotic relationship with their neighbors on their peripheries.

The Postclassic Archaeology of the Western Gulf Coast: Some Initial Observations

JOSEPH W. BALL

Oddly, given its ethnohistorically documented pivotal role in the events of Postclassic Maya culture history, the Postclassic archaeology of western Campeche remains poorly known and under–investigated.[1] In part, this can be attributed to the uncomfortable environment and, until recently, the relative inaccessibility of much of the region. Its paucity of impressive monumental remains and the inevitably distracting magnetism for those who have penetrated it of the enigmatic Olmec sites on its western extreme have doubtless further hampered the progress of research. Exploratory and extractive operations by PEMEX are now rapidly destroying the region's pre–Republican era cultural resources, and while it is to be fervently hoped that concurrent conservation activities will preserve the existing remains and add new information to our store, experience suggests that the now available data may well be all that we ever possess. This essay is intended essentially as a synthesizing review of those data.

Probably the fullest archaeological record currently available to us for the Postclassic period of the western peninsula is that of the Campeche–Tabasco Gulf coastal plain. Reconnaissance, survey, and excavation programs by a number of institutions and individuals have resulted in a comparatively impressive bibliography for this zone, of which a number of sources deal wholly or in part with Postclassic materials. To these, of course, it is hoped will be added substantially more as cultural resource conservation efforts are increased in conjunction with the mushrooming destructive exploitation of the zone by PEMEX.

For the Campeche–Tabasco coastal plain lying west of the Laguna de Terminos at the southwestern extreme of the zone, Berlin (1956) has defined a tentative Postclassic pottery sequence consisting of two apparently discontinuous "horizons" or, more properly, phases. The earlier of these, Jonuta, appears to have origins coeval with the late Late Classic period, perhaps sometime during the eighth-century A.D. Its duration remains a very open question; however, assuming the validity of a correlation of the Christian and Maya calendars at 11.16.0.0.0, a terminal date falling sometime between approximately A.D. 950 and 1150 seems most probable.

Compositionally, the Jonuta phase ceramic assemblage is dominated by Fine Orange paste ware of the Balancan and Altar groups. Also important, although less abundant, are Chablekal–Tres Naciones group Fine Gray paste wares, a polished, black-slipped glossware group, and an unslipped coarse ware. Minority elements include Tohil group Plumbate, Silho group Fine Orange, and an assortment of late Tepeu 2–3 horizon decorated types possibly obtained from communities farther inland or northward.

The vessel form repertoire is extensive and complex, including a wide range of necked jars, basins, vases, bowls, dishes, plates, drums, and flutes. Solid and hollow tripod supports occur, as do ringstand, pedestal, and rattle–chamber bases. Decoration is primarily by means of surface manipulation (incising, gouge-incising, punctating, fluting, and modeling), although instances of multicolored slipping and/or painting also occur.

Of the contemporary architecture, little can be said other than that it is characterized by earth–cored platform mounds faced with shell–derived lime plaster.

Probably the most widely familiar Jonuta phase artifacts are the moldmade anthropomorphic and zoomorphic figurines named for its type–site. Berlin (1956: 125) provides a succinct treatment of these, and Corson (1976) discusses them and their significance at considerable length. Apart from Jonuta itself, examples are known from Isla Jaina, where a Terminal Classic dating for their occurrence seems most likely. Iconographic and stylistic affinities with the figurine traditions of south-central Veracruz, on the one hand, and north coastal Campeche, on the other, are strongly evident (Corson 1976). Other Jonuta phase artifacts are too poorly known to merit treatment.

Berlin's second phase, named Cintla, is dominated by Fine Orange paste ware of the Matillas ("V") and Cunduacan ("U") groups. Together with an unslipped coarse ware, confined in its form repertoire to ladle and spiked hourglass censers, and a tempered orange to gray paste ware group, appearing only in the form of modeled effigies and miniature temples, these two groups comprise the entire known Cintla phase ceramic assemblage.

Both Berlin (1956: 135–141) and R. E. Smith (1971: 20) assign sequential temporal positions to the Matillas and Cunduacan groups, distinguishing them on grounds of formal and decorative differences. In general, Matillas group vessels are more regularly and elaborately decorated by means of color – differential slipping, polychrome painting, incising, gouge-incising, and modeling in various combinations. Cunduacan group pieces are contrastingly plain, with the exception of a modeled human effigy censer component. The form repertoires of the two are set apart by the restriction of miniature vases with pedestal bases, ladle censers, modeled human effigy censers, and thin, solid slab supports as well as a series of architectural, human, and animal "models" to the Cunduacan group. Hollow mold-made human and animal effigy feet, on the other hand, appear only on Matillas group vessels.

Again little is known of the contemporary architecture, although Berlin (1956: 106) notes the use of fired clay bricks as well as earth fill, mortar, and plaster in some platform construction. A small miscellanea of shell tinklers, jade beads, green obsidian blades, copper bells, and a copper arrowhead round out the portable artifact assemblage.

In discussing the probable chronology of the Cintla phase, Berlin (1956: 140–141) points out the potential temporal significance of the Matillas group effigy supports as indicators of a Postclassic horizon placement for the group. Applying a unilinear, sequential replacement approach to his materials, and believing that his "V" Fine Orange postdated the time of Tohil Plumbate, he concluded that the group, as well as the Cintla phase, appeared about A.D. 1200, an opinion with which R. E. Smith (1971: 20–21) later concurred. Berlin simply placed the Cunduacan, or "U," group later in the phase, suggesting termination during the early sixteenth century. Smith is more specific on this subject, basing his interpretations on the work at Mayapan; he assigns the group an A.D. 1450–1550 position, immediately succeeding and replacing the earlier Matillas (A.D. 1250–1450).

It should be noted at this point that although Berlin (1956: 135–136) cites some evidence in support of a sequential relationship between Matillas and Cunduacan group Fine Orange from his excavations at El Coco, Tabasco, on the whole this has not been demonstrated conclusively and in fact may not be the case. Excavations at Aguacatal (Matheny 1970: 93) and Atasta (Berlin 1956: 136) in Campeche, for example, yielded a general admixture of the two, while at other sites in Tabasco, such as Juarez and Tamulte, the Cunduacan group occurs exclusively. At Mayapan, Coba, and several sites along the coasts of Quintana Roo and Campeche, on the other hand, only the Matillas cluster is found.

I have previously stated my belief (Ball 1978: 91–92) that the two were at least in part contemporary rather than strictly sequential, and that they represent distinct geographical zones rather than temporal phases of production. This is not to deny the possible primacy of Matillas over Cunduacan Orange with respect to time of initial appearance; the Mayapan evidence *would seem* to suggest the absence of the latter during the occupational life of that center, an interval during which the former was contrastingly of considerable importance. On the other hand, it should be remembered that the presence/absence situations with respect to these two exotic tradewares at Mayapan could reflect interaction/distribution sphere dichotomies as well as temporal factors. Whatever the case, it is my belief that the Matillas group did not suddenly vanish with the mid–fifteenth-century collapse of Mayapan but continued on into proto–Colonial and possibly even early Colonial times as well, while coexisting, at least during these eras, with the technologically superior Cunduacan group.

I would also suggest that the temporal span of the latter remains to be determined correctly. Berlin's (1956: 140) observations on the Aztec III–IV (Late Horizon) parallels to the inverted stepped silhouette–form of Cunduacan group solid slab vessel supports suggest the possibility of their appearance at least as early as A.D. 1350 (on the basis of dating in Sanders, Parsons, and Santley 1979: 466–467). This would serve to place modeled human effigy censers (possibly derived from south-central Veracruz traditions) in the western Campeche-Tabasco Gulf coastal plain region somewhat prior to the suggested time of their introduction at Mayapan (ca. A.D. 1400; see Ball 1982), a historically attractive scenario given the reputed introduction of idolatry to the latter center from that area.

On a still more conjectural level, I would call attention to the generally close stylistic similarities linking the Matillas ("V") and Silho ("X") Fine Orange groups (cf. Ruz 1969: figs. XXXVII 1–41, XXXIX 1–4, XLIII 1–3; Brainerd 1958: figs. 76–82a, 83a, 84). These two, at least, may well represent a single continuing tradition of ceramic production on the western Campeche coast. In the generally harder fine paste types of the Cunduacan group, alternatively, we may be seeing the direct successors of Balancan–Altar group pottery. Distributional differences and overlaps between the Matillas and Cunduacan groups could conceivably be of immense importance in working out the culture history and understanding the culture dynamics of Postclassic through early colonial times.

Whether or not a disjunction actually exists between the established Jonuta and Cintla phases remains uncertain, but on the whole I am inclined to agree with Berlin that something is missing. The

Matillas group, as represented in his sample, appears "mature" in form and design elaboration, and I would not care to place its age at greater than A.D. 1150–1200. Given the validity of an 11.16.0.0.0 correlation, on the other hand, it is difficult to argue a persistence much beyond A.D. 1000–1050 for many of the types and forms comprising Jonuta (see Ball 1979a and 1979b for an extended discussion of this problem). Further, I have elsewhere suggested and remain inclined to believe that the Plumbate and Silho group Fine Orange recovered at Tecolpan are of tenth-century rather than later vintage (Ball 1978: 139–140). Obviously, I could be quite wrong, but if so the effect would be to add considerable support to what I have termed the "total overlap model" (Ball 1979a: 33–34, fig. 17) of northern Maya chronology and culture history, and to extend the lifespan of Balancan–Altar Fine Orange paste ware well into the eleventh or possibly even the twelfth century. As things currently stand, a vacuum–like cultural gap of between one and two or more centuries appears to separate the Jonuta and Cintla phases.

Similar problems of chronology plague any coherent treatment of Postclassic period culture history in the Laguna de Terminos subregion. Again, either the interval extending from roughly A.D. 950–1050 to A.D. 1200+ must be regarded as a void, or the temporal ranges assigned to many Terminal Classic and/or Middle Postclassic ceramic types, forms, and modes are seriously out of alignment.

At this time, I am most inclined to extend the upward limits of the Terminal Classic ceramic set into the eleventh century *at the least*, but this should not be regarded by others as a new "final solution" to the problem. It is at best a stopgap measure intended to bring the known archaeological record into better concordance with probable historical reality. Like any such initial corrective maneuver, however, it may well err.

On the basis of materials collected at Guarixes, Isla del Carmen, by Ruz Lhuillier (1969) and Eaton (1978), I have tentatively defined a ceramic assemblage for the zone that probably emerged as a distinctive entity during the eighth century A.D. and persisted, with minor modifications, additions, and subtractions, into the eleventh century or later (see Ball 1978). Key elements of its composition include a predominance of Balancan–Altar group Fine Orange paste ware and undesignated unslipped coarse ware types, followed in quantitative importance by Chablekal–Tres Naciones Fine Gray paste ware and an undesignated polished, black-slipped glossware group. Smaller quantities of Thin Slate, Puuc Slate, and Puuc Red types also occur.

In essence, this is nothing other than a local variant of Berlin's

Jonuta "horizon," and I am inclined to link the Guarixes complex to the latter in a provisional "Jonuta ceramic sphere" (see also Ball 1978: figs. 12–14, 19). The eventual dissolution of this sphere represents a major reflection of Postclassic transformations in the western Campeche zone but remains undated and undatable at this time. Its origins, unfortunately, remain equally ambiguous.

The Guarixes complex clearly was intrusive to Isla del Carmen, its presence documenting the existence of a Tabasco–derived settlement on the island sometime between the late eighth and the eleventh or twelfth centuries A.D. Elsewhere on the Laguna de Terminos, the Ruz and Eaton surveys and Matheny's Aguacatal study have documented the apparent persistence of communities possessing fine paste ware pottery traditions or "importing" fine paste ware ceramics into the tenth century or later. Just when or even whether any of these were abandoned during the Postclassic cannot presently be determined with certainty.

As in the case of the Tabasco coastal plain, there exists an apparent "gap" between the Terminal Classic (ca. A.D. 770–950) and putative Middle Postclassic (ca. A.D. 1200–1450) assemblages, but whether or not this really is so remains to be seen. Matheny (1970: 88–93) attempted to remedy this gap through the creation of an artificial Early Postclassic "Mangle complex," but his supporting stratigraphic data are unconvincing and, if anything, belie the existence of such an entity (pp. 101–109). The Middle through Late Postclassic (ca. A.D. 1200–1550) situation is equally unclear.

At Tixchel on the Rio Sabancuy, for example, Ruz (1969: 65–66, 112–115) found evidence of two occupations. The earlier of these pertained to the late Middle or early Late Preclassic (see Ball 1978: 122). The second was characterized by a Matillas ("U"–"V" Fine Orange) group–dominated ceramic assemblage closely related to another from Champoton discussed below. Ethnohistoric sources place Putun Maya settlements at Tixchel during the fifteenth century and again during the late sixteenth through early seventeenth centuries (see Scholes and Roys 1968: 10–12, 81–82 passim). While it is not unreasonable to assume that Ruz' Postclassic materials pertain to the ethnohistorically indicated fifteenth-century occupation, such is not a necessary conclusion, and I find it somewhat bothersome that there exist no apparent reflections of the substantially better–documented and lengthier settlement at Tixchel of the A.D. 1550s through 1630s. I suspect that something is wrong here, most probably the traditional assignment of the Matillas group and its ceramic associations to the Middle Postclassic period exclusively.

In contrast to the Rio Sabancuy situation, Isla del Carmen is known to have been uninhabited by the time of the A.D. 1517–1518 Cordoba and Grijalva exploratory voyages, although it possibly may not long have been so, and Maya traders plying the waters of the Laguna de Terminos and the Gulf of Campeche were still visiting shrines along its shores (Scholes and Roys 1968: 88–90). Just when abandonment of the island took place cannot be stated accurately on either ethnohistoric or archaeological grounds. Scholes and Roys' reconstruction (1968: 80–81) of the preconquest history of the Acalan–Tixchel Putun does suggest, however, that traces of a four-teenth- and/or fifteenth-century occupation by this people might well be expected to occur, especially at locations commanding passage between the lagoon and the gulf. A tiny collection made by Eaton at Punta Estuardo on the extreme northeastern tip of the island, which consisted of red Mama (Mayapan Red) and unslipped Panabchen (Mayapan Unslipped) group sherds, very possibly reflects just such an occupation. No other Postclassic ceramics were recovered on the island.

Farther north along the coast at Champoton, excavations by Ruz (1969: 117–141) and Eaton (1978: 25–27) produced large collections of Postclassic materials isolated from anything earlier. In both cases, the overwhelming majority of the sherds recovered pertained to a Matillas group–rich ceramic assemblage which tradition would assign to the Middle Postclassic Mayapan horizon of ca. A.D. 1200–1450. Also present were a number of what appear to be either "late" Silho ("X") or "early" Matillas ("U"–"V") group Fine Orange paste ware transitional varieties (see Ruz 1969: figs. XXXVII–XXXIX), as well as the Xcanchakan Black-on-Cream (Peto Cream ware) type, which spans the Early to Middle Postclassic periods as traditionally defined.

On the available evidence, it seems probable that the Champoton settlement was established near the close of the twelfth or the start of the thirteenth century, with continuity of occupation through the thirteenth and into the fourteenth centuries as well. Not a single sherd relatable to the Late Postclassic or Protohistoric period occupations of the site was recorded, however, despite areally dispersed sampling, the large size of the combined Ruz–Eaton samples, and the known size, importance, and continuity of contemporaneous settlement at this site. Thus, we are led to consider the implausible alternatives that chance alone resulted in the exclusion of any post–Mayapan horizon remains from the samples collected or that the production, importation, and use of pottery vessels by the inhabitants of this location ceased with the collapse of Mayapan.

There is a third and to my mind more likely possibility, however, which is that the Middle Postclassic pottery configuration continued into and through the Late Postclassic and into the full Protohistoric period as well. Several rather specific form correspondences suggest this, and I believe it a possibility seriously warranting consideration and field investigation. Should it prove correct, not only would entirely new light be shed on the culture history of the Protohistoric period in the Maya lowlands, but a whole new realm of possibilities would be opened up with regard to associating specific historically identified ethnic groups and ceramic clusters and directly tracing both back through time.

Farther up the coast, from approximately the vicinity of present-day Ciudad Campeche northward, a separate and highly complex scenario characterizes the Terminal Classic–Postclassic interval. I have treated this to the extent now possible elsewhere (Ball 1977, 1978) and will not do so again here other than to note that in this zone the roots of a fully and archaeologically "acceptable" Silho group ("X") Fine Orange–associated Postclassic manifestation can be traced without interruption back to early Late Classic (ca. A.D. 550–700) predecessors. For this reason alone, the area deserves considerable archaeological attention in the future.

Summary

In this essay, I have intentionally avoided drawing interpretive inferences in favor of systematically reviewing a portion of the rich but disparate data currently available pertaining to the Postclassic archaeology of the Campeche-Tabasco Gulf coastal plain. Several potentially fruitful directions for future research were highlighted by this approach.

First, there is the obvious dual problem of an inadequately documented archaeological chronology coupled with the ready acceptance of traditional but unsubstantiated temporal values for "key" ceramic markers, such as the Matillas, Silho, and Balancan-Altar groups of Fine Orange paste ware. Linked to this as well is the question of the ca. A.D. 1000–1200 "gap." Does the latter exist, or not? If so, why, and what is its significance in cultural historical terms? If not, then just what are the proper alignments and relationships of the various pottery wares, types, and modes currently assigned to the pre–eleventh-century Terminal Classic or the post–twelfth-century Middle Postclassic? What would be the chronological and historical ramifications of the hypothetical gap's nonexistence? Should currently defined "Terminal Classic" culture complexes be prolonged in duration, or should "Middle" Postclassic ones be extended backward, or both?[2] Alternatively, is the "gap" but a product of an incorrect correlation of the Christian and Maya calendars at 11.16.0.0.0 in the latter? Arlen Chase (n.d.) has dealt with this last possibility at some length.

Finally, there is the persisting question of the southwestern Campeche–eastern Tabasco Postclassic cultures' historical roots. Adequate, convincing stratigraphic documentation of a Classic–Postclassic developmental continuum has yet to be presented for any portion of the area, and south of present-day Ciudad Campeche even typological data for such are lacking. Matheny's Aguacatal sequence (1970) plainly pertains to a localized circum–Laguna de Terminos system which, while viable in its own right, lay outside the sphere of groups producing and circulating the major Fine Orange and Fine Gray paste wares of the Terminal Classic through Late Postclassic.

All in all, the Postclassic archaeology of western Campeche comprises an important and fertile field for future research efforts. A regionally informed program of problem-oriented studies in the zone could contribute an almost inconceivable amount of new data toward our understanding of cultural history and process in the lowland Maya area from the preconquest Late Classic period into and through Spanish Colonial times. Let us hope one is undertaken before present-day industrial and urban processes forever obliterate the possibility.

Notes

1. For the purposes of this essay, the "Postclassic" has been regarded as a strictly chronological interval rather than as a developmental or cultural stage. Its beginning, duration, and end consequently have been fixed by arbitrarily chosen temporal (historical) points rather than on the basis of cultural content and changes therein. My reason for adopting this approach lies largely in the uneven nature, quality, and quantity of available relevant data, factors which render coherent organization on the basis of anything other than broad geographical region and general temporal interval little short of impossible. By outlining the archaeological record for an arbitrarily demarcated block of time throughout the area of interest, I hope that any patterning of regularities or variations that might be present therein will be highlighted. These, in turn, might form the basis for more productive formulations at a future date or at least suggest questions and problems meriting attention by future researchers.

The specific chronological framework employed throughout this chapter is as follows:

Terminal Classic A.D. 770–950
Early Postclassic A.D. 950–1200

Middle Postclassic A.D. 1200–1450
Late Postclassic A.D. 1450–1550
Protohistoric A.D. 1550–1700

At least two historical reference points suggest themselves as convenient demarcators of pre–Postclassic (Classic) from Postclassic times in the northern Maya area overall. One of these, linked directly to the finale of elite–level Classic Maya culture in the central Yucatan peninsula, consists of the latest–known glyph–bearing manifestation of the stela–altar cult. It is here assumed (perhaps presumed would be more accurate) that the erection of this monument at San Lorenzo, southeastern Campeche, indicates the continued existence of at least some semblance of the high culture which characterized the Classic period in the Rio Bec–Chenes regions and that a Postclassic period cannot properly be said to have started prior to its carving and emplacement in A.D. 928 (10.5.0.0.0.; Thompson 1953).

A second "watershed" date of historical significance is one cited frequently as formally opening the Postclassic, that being A.D. 987, the traditional advent of Kukulcan and his hordes at Chichen Itza. To better comprehend this event as a result as well as a cause of others, however, and to truly examine its effects on regional conditions and processes, it would seem necessary to include it within the period of study rather than simply to set it at the start. Consequently, for the purposes of this review, I have chosen the convenient but arbitrary date of A.D. 950 at which to begin the Postclassic period along the western edge of the Yucatan Peninsula. The materials which I consider thus fully postdate the era of Classic Maya civilization but encompass those immediately preceding as well as following the establishment at Chichen Itza of Postclassic Maya civilization as traditionally defined.

Given the all but total inadequacy of our current grasp on either the upward chronological limits of non-hispanicized Maya culture in western Yucatan or the material manifestations of its existence, I have adopted the rounded–off, conquest–linked convenience date of A.D. 1550 at which to end the Postclassic period for this treatment. Similarly, in view of persisting uncertainties concerning the real occupational spans or even the relative temporal positions of such influential centers as Tulum, Mayapan, and Chichen Itza, any internal subdivision of the period must be regarded as extremely tentative.

2. A similar opinion has been expressed by L. Ochoa and L. Casasola (1978: 38–39), on the basis of fieldwork carried out by them during 1974 and 1975.

Terminal Events in the Southeastern Lowlands: A View from Quirigua

ROBERT J. SHARER

The southeast Maya lowlands, dominated during the Classic period by the centers of Copan and Quirigua, were an important zone of economic and political interaction between the Maya and peoples on the northwest periphery of Central America. Evidence recently recovered at Quirigua, including a new stela (Monument 26, with a 9.2.18.0.0 Initial Series date) indicates that this center in the lower Motagua valley was founded during the Early Classic period (ca. A.D. 250–600) as a colony from the central lowlands, most probably Tikal (Sharer 1979; Ashmore, Schortman, and Sharer 1983).[1] I believe the same may be said of Copan. One important motive for the founding of Classic Maya colonies in the southeast lowlands would certainly have been to secure important local resources such as cacao, as well as to control the Motagua jade route and trade connections to and from Central America.

Elsewhere my colleagues and I have reported the results of our research showing that Quirigua rose to an independent political and economic power during the Late Classic period (Ashmore 1977; Ashmore and Sharer 1978; C. Jones 1977; Sharer 1978, 1979). Here I will address the issue of terminal events at Quirigua and the general question of the Classic–Postclassic transition in the Maya southeast. This paper presents only a trial formulation of thoughts regarding this transitional period because, while the archaeological data gathering at Quirigua is completed, the evaluation and analyses of these data are still underway. For the purposes of this paper I shall follow the generally accepted chronological divisions in the Maya area and define the Terminal Classic, the period of Classic-to-Postclassic transition, as corresponding to ca. A.D. 800–900.

As at many Classic period lowland Maya sites, the archaeological evidences of terminal occupation are scant at Quirigua (fig. 1). Later disturbance or destruction of such remains at Quirigua was

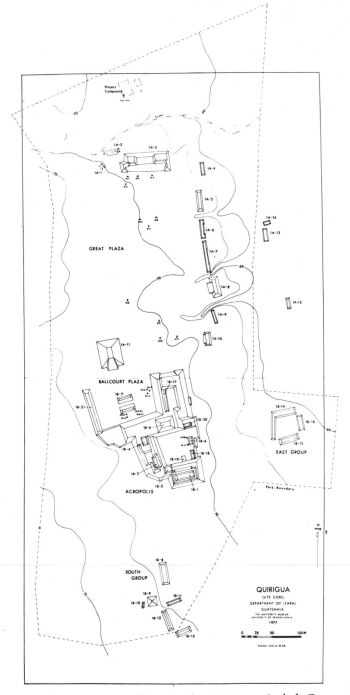

Fig. 1. Map of the Main Group (Site Core) at Quirigua, Izabal, Guatemala (originally published in Quirigua Report I, 1979).

compounded by two factors: scouring by Motagua flood waters that appear to have removed occupation debris that may have remained associated with domestic structural platforms, and previous archaeological work that just as effectively removed most terminal debris from the more conspicuous elevated buildings and platforms, such as the elite residential complex in the site–core, the Acropolis.

Nonetheless, some traces of terminal activity at Quirigua were recovered by our investigations. The chronological placement of this evidence is, however, often less than secure. Some remains in the site–core can be linked to construction that in turn is dated as Terminal Classic by association with the latest calendrical inscriptions (C. Jones 1977). Other remains, especially those on the site–peripheries, can only be assigned to the Terminal Classic or later periods by links to traditional Mesoamerican horizon markers, such as Plumbate pottery, metal artifacts, and projectile points.

In the site–core, the last known calendrical date corresponds to the early years of the Terminal Classic, 9.19.0.0.0 (A.D. 810), from the frieze of Structure 1B–1 (Morley 1935: 123). This building, together with the slightly later and much larger "palace" of Structure 1B–5, is associated with the reign of the last identified ruler at Quirigua, "Jade Sky" (Kelley 1962; Sharer 1978). This individual appears to be the final member of the Classic Maya Sky dynasty, probably descended from or allied to the great Sky dynasty of Tikal (Sharer 1979; see also Kelley 1976: 223). Jade Sky's fate is unknown, but it is doubtful that his heir ever ruled at Quirigua.

Soon after Jade Sky appears to have taken power (about A.D. 800), a series of changes occurs at Quirigua. There are conspicuous shifts in the artifactual record. Some of these arrive at Quirigua from new trade contacts. Tohil Plumbate pottery was excavated from the construction fill of a large, ninth-century A.D. platform built between two eighth-century Late Classic structures (1B–3 and 1B–4) (W. R. Coe and Sharer 1979). In a modest masonry house platform (Structure 2C–3) about a kilometer northeast of the Acropolis, an individual was buried with copper artifacts, small disks that probably once decorated a funeral shroud (fig.2; Sharer, Jones, Ashmore, and Schortman 1979: 59). It has been suggested that copper metallurgy was established at Quirigua during the Terminal Classic or Early Postclassic era. An earlier discovery of copper bells near Quirigua included one specimen that had exploded when cast, indicating that the bells were locally produced (fig.3; Lothrop 1952: 25).

A more sweeping change occurs at this time in the Quirigua pottery inventory. The dominant local fine ware, the Tipon group, is drastically diminished in frequency. Two new fine wares appear.

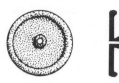 

Fig. 2. Perforated copper disk from a human burial in Structure 2C–3 at Quirigua (drawing by Diane Z. Chase).

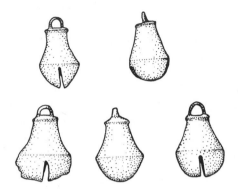

Fig. 3. Copper bells found near Quirigua (drawing by Diane Z. Chase after Kidder 1954: fig. 10a). The specimen at lower left burst during casting (see Lothrop 1952: fig. 8).

One, a slipped specular hematite red, is apparently of local manufacture, but its shape and decorative modes are typical of the Early Postclassic. One vessel fragment of this type, found on the surface of Structure 1B–8 (South Group), had moldmade animal effigy supports. The other new fine ware is a calcite-tempered, bright orange-slipped pottery, certainly imported; its closest affinities are to Early Postclassic types from the central portion of the Southern Lowlands (e.g., the Augustine group at Barton Ramie; Sharer and Chase 1976: 291–294).

Excavations in the site–core provide most of the examples of Terminal Classic activity that exemplify other changes during this period. At several locations evidence of incomplete construction was encountered, often involving ambitious expansions of Late Classic buildings that were halted in the midst of their renovations. For instance, the broad frontal staircase of Structure 1A–3 was removed, presumably to be replaced by a new stairway at the same time that the platform was nearly doubled in size. While the fill for this expansion was put in place, neither the new stairs nor the facing of the expansion were begun (W. R. Coe and Sharer 1979). Similar expansions were left incomplete on the flanks of the Acropolis.

In other cases, several buildings outside of the Acropolis appear to have been robbed of their masonry facings. Structure 1A−11, the only free−standing pyramidal platform at Quirigua, probably the funerary shrine of the dominant Late Classic ruler, Cauac Sky, appears to have lost its masonry facing (Sharer et al. 1983). In at least one case, it can be shown that this robbing activity occurred at least several years after the cessation of construction. The stripped staircase of Structure 1A−3 eroded for a period of time, depositing a layer of outwash on the plaza at its base, before the sandstone blocks of the adjacent stela platform, for Monument 4, were removed (one block, displaced several meters but not carried away, was found resting upon this outwash; W. R. Coe and Sharer 1979).

Immediately west of Structure 1A−11, excavation revealed the edge of a paved plaza platform that served as the eastern bank of a deep, water−filled depression or basin. Because geomorphic evidence gathered by the Project's Periphery Program indicates that the Motagua River probably flowed adjacent to the west side of the site−core in Classic times (Ashmore, Schortman, and Sharer 1983), it is likely that this basin was an embayment connected to the river. As such, it may have provided a docking or landing facility for riverine traffic.

On the surface of this possible landing area were found two large sandstone monoliths. Judging from their shape and size, these monoliths must have been intended to serve either as supports for a very large monument, or perhaps as small stelae themselves. Circumstances indicate that they may have been unloaded from their transport by river from the quarry, but were never moved to their intended location. Scattered over the plaza and around these monoliths was broken Terminal Classic and Postclassic pottery (Ashmore, Schortman, and Sharer 1983).

On the east side of the Acropolis, a low platform between Structure 1B−1 and 1B−6 supported a building constructed of adobe blocks. Its function seems to have been domestic, for when it collapsed (presumably during an earthquake), it crushed an assemblage of Terminal Classic storage jars and a small infant. The debris was never cleared, and no evidence of subsequent activity was discovered on this platform (C. Jones, Ashmore, and Sharer 1983).

These and other bits of evidence, taken together, indicate an important change occurred at Quirigua during the Terminal Classic. From the cessation of erecting monuments and sculpting hiero-

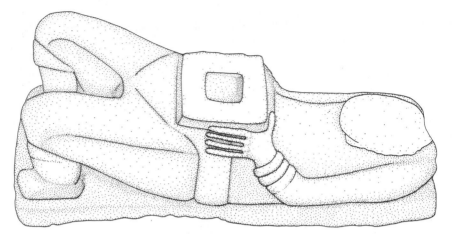

Fig. 4. Carved stone *chacmool* reportedly from Quirigua (drawing by Diane Z. Chase).

glyphic inscriptions, it can be inferred that this change profoundly affected the traditional dynastic political order at Quirigua, as at other lowland sites. Yet the former elite residential complex in the Acropolis did not cease. Terminal Classic activities were reoriented, however, from those typical of the Late Classic period. Former construction projects were abandoned, often abruptly. In the case mentioned previously, the transport of two new monumental sandstone blocks was seemingly halted before their final destination was reached. Subsequently, outlying buildings and even stela platforms were robbed to furnish ready–cut masonry to be used, presumably, for construction in the Acropolis. These late constructions included the aforementioned platform containing Plumbate pottery and a new monumental staircase around the Acropolis court. While the latter project was perhaps the largest single construction ever undertaken at Quirigua, overall building activity is reduced and confined to the Acropolis during this terminal period.

It is postulated that this terminal activity was directed by a new elite group at Quirigua, residing in the Acropolis. These new rulers at Quirigua were obviously interested in embellishing their own residential compound, but totally ignored the ceremonial and dynastic priorities so important to the old Classic elite.

Although they appear to have replaced the traditional Sky dynasty, the newcomers maintained Quirigua's trade contacts to several areas, including Central America or Mexico (metallurgy), the

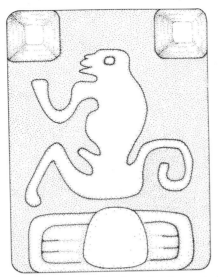

Fig. 5. Carved motif on the underside of a tripod metate (lower leg absent) reportedly found at Quirigua (drawing by Diane Z. Chase).

Pacific coast (Plumbate pottery), and the eastern part of the Southern Lowlands (Augustine–like pottery). The new rulers also brought with them a material culture that included a new pottery inventory and chipped–stone projectile points.

Who were these newcomers? Our excavations revealed no direct evidence as to their identity. Several earlier investigators, however, discovered some important clues at a time when Quirigua was still relatively undisturbed. The first of these suggests a Central Mexican affinity. This is the report by Saville (1892; Richardson 1940: fig. 35) of a small stone *chacmool* from Quirigua, now in the Museum of the American Indian, Heye Foundation (fig. 4). The same institution possesses a tripod metate found at Quirigua, with a lizard sculpted on the underside, its head forming one leg. This object, together with a similarly sculpted Quirigua metate now in the Peabody Museum, Harvard University (fig.5), was linked by Thompson (1970: 131) to a type of metate from the Gulf Coast (see Strebel 1885–89 [2]: Pl. 14).

On the basis of ethnohistoric and archaeological evidence, several scholars have suggested that "Mexicanized" Maya from the Gulf coastal region of Acalan (see Scholes and Roys 1948) developed and dominated seacoast trade around the Yucatan peninsula during the Postclassic era, with an initial founding and colonization of trade centers beginning by the Terminal Classic (Thompson 1970: 3–47;

Sabloff and Rathje 1975a; see also Chapman 1957). Although the ethnic identity is debated (they have been variously referred to as Chontal Maya, Putun Maya, and the Putun-Itza), there seems to be no doubt that the sea-traders of Acalan possessed a fusion of Maya and Central Mexican culture, represented in their language, sociopolitical organization, and religion (Scholes and Roys 1948).

Both Thompson (1970) and Ball (1974) propose that the initial expansion of the Chontal included forays inland via rivers to control several former Classic period centers, such as Seibal (see Sabloff and Willey 1967). I would suggest that in order to control the Motagua River trade route, as well as local cacao production, a similar colony was established in the Terminal Classic at Quirigua. This would be consistent with the evidence of Central Mexican and northern elements appearing at Quirigua during this interval. It is also in line with previous suggestions that the Motagua River provided an avenue for Gulf Coast (Chontal) mercantile settlement (Fox 1978: 272–273; see also Seler 1902: 575). Parenthetically, it is interesting to note that the earliest recorded place name (1536; U.S. Department of State 1919–1920) from the Quirigua region is Chapulco, a word of probable Nahua origin, and possibly the name associated with the postulated Chontal colonization of Quirigua.

Regardless, the archaeological evidence strongly suggests that Quirigua remained the primary trading center in the lower Motagua valley during the Terminal Classic period, although under the control of a new ruling elite. It is proposed here that this occurred under the aegis of a new elite, probably a Chontal Maya group representing an expanding sea-trade orientation, which usurped the established lowland Maya dynasty during the Terminal Classic. Sometime before the end of the Early Postclassic, however, Quirigua was abandoned by its new rulers. Its apparent successor was Nito, some 80 kilometers to the northeast on the Rio Dulce, where a colony of merchants from Acalan was reported by Cortes (1908). Nito's location nearer the Caribbean was undoubtedly advantageous with the further growth of sea trade (Sharer 1979).

The thesis advanced in this paper may be seen as a corollary to the hypothesis that the emergence of sea-trade networks bypassed the traditional centers of Maya power, such as those in the central lowlands (C. Jones 1979), and greatly contributed to the phenomena conveniently labelled as the "Classic Maya collapse" (Sabloff and Rathje 1975a, 1975b; Sharer 1982). In a larger sense, therefore, the Terminal Classic developments at Quirigua reflect profound changes in Maya economic and political power that led to the emergence of what we now define as Postclassic society.

Note

1. The Quirigua Project was formed in 1973 under terms of a contract between the University Museum, University of Pennsylvania, and the Government of Guatemala (under the auspices of IDAEH, the Instituto de Antropologia e Historia) to investigate and conserve the Classic Maya site of Quirigua (see Sharer and W. R. Coe 1979). Archaeological research was conducted for six seasons (1974–1979) under three interrelated programs: the Site-core Program (Quirigua proper), the Site-periphery Program (within an area of 95 square kilometers surrounding the site-core), and the Valley Program (outside the periphery, but within the lower Motagua valley, a region of some 2,125 square kilometers). IDAEH is currently continuing their program of conservation within the site core.

Research funding for the Quirigua Project was provided by the University Museum (especially the Francis Boyer Fund), the National Science Foundation (Grants BNS–7602185, BNS–7603283, and BNS–7624189), the National Geographic Society, the Ford Foundation, the Tikal Association of Guatemala, the Ministry of Defense of Guatemala, and several private benefactors. Our appreciation for this support is extended to all these institutions and individuals. The conservation program at Quirigua is funded by the Ministry of Education, Government of Guatemala, and is being directed by Arqueologo Marcelino Gonzalez C. of IDAEH.

The Land of Ulua: Postclassic Research in the Naco and Sula Valleys, Honduras

ANTHONY W. WONDERLEY

To the Maya of the Yucatan peninsula in late prehistoric times, the neighboring Naco and Sula valleys of northwestern Honduras were known as the land of Ulua, a nearly fabulous place famed for its "gold, feathers, and cacao" (Roys 1972: 55). From a more prosaic archaeological perspective, the same region is characterized by relatively unimposing remains that seem to be concentrated along the waterways. Following a brief overview of conquest period documentation, I will review the archaeological data from the Postclassic time segment of this region (ca. A.D. 950–1536). The presentation will suggest more questions than it can possibly answer, but a more definitive treatment is not possible because the requisite archaeological and documentary researches are still in progress.

Much of what is known about the prehistory of northwestern Honduras is the result of recent archaeological programs sponsored by Cornell University in the Naco valley (1975–1979; J. S. Henderson, Director) and the Instituto Hondureno de Antropologia e Historia in the Sula plain (1979–present; Ricardo Agurcia F. and J. S. Henderson, Codirectors). Information about the Postclassic of the Naco valley is derived from Urban's (1980) survey and testing project and my work at the site of Naco (Wonderley 1981). For the Sula plain, I draw primarily on the preliminary reports of the Smithsonian-Harvard Expedition (Strong, Kidder, and Paul 1938) and Sheehy (1977), as well as my own brief examination of a portion of the Chamelcon River in early 1982. The Naco valley will receive attention disproportionate to its size in this account because we have not yet achieved an areal and temporal coverage of the Sula plain comparable to that of the much smaller Naco area.

Setting and Ethnohistoric Summary

The Sula plain (or valley), an extensive alluvial fan formed by the Chamelcon and Ulua Rivers, is the largest contiguous trace of cultivable land in Honduras (figs. 1 and 2). It is about 100 kilometers long north to south, and generally 20 to 35 kilometers wide. Physiographically part of the Caribbean lowlands, this area presumably was characterized by tropical forest cover in aboriginal times. The Spaniards were impressed both by the size of the population and the scale of cacao production here. Alonso Davila, speaking of either the Ulua or Chamelcon valleys in 1533, described how "from one extreme to the other of 30 leagues on both banks [the valley] is all covered with groves of cacao trees, and is very rich, and peopled with innumerable Indians who are established close to each other, [especially] near the mouth of the river" (in Chamberlain 1948: 125). The foundation document of San Pedro Sula (1536) lists nearly 100 Indian settlements in the vicinity (Veliz R. 1977: 3–5) and there can be little doubt that several were major towns. Cortes wrote of at least two pueblos in the Sula plain, Zula and Cholome, with a minimum of two thousand houses each (Pagden 1971: 407).

The Naco valley, located 13 kilometers upstream from (southwest of) the Sula plain on the Chamelcon River, is a relatively small area, 10 kilometers in length, with a maximum width of 8 kilometers. Its elevation is higher than that of the Sula plain but the climates of the two valleys do not differ greatly. Writing in A.D. 1544, Cristobal de Pedraza believed the Naco valley was "the finest thing discovered anywhere in the Indies, densely populated and wellordered in its manner and [with] roads as broad as those characteristic of Valencia" (Documentos Ineditos 1898, 11 [I]: 411). Naco, its largest pueblo, was situated on a small river of the same name at the base of a mountain range seven kilometers from the main channel of the Chamelcon River. Spanish "order of magnitude" population estimates consistently placed Naco in the 10,000-person range, and the town is generally thought to have been the principal commercial center of the Ulua region (Pagden 1971: 407; Scholes and Roys 1948: 320; Sherman 1978: 49; Strong, Kidder, and Paul 1938: 27; Thompson 1970: 130).

It is unclear if the Naco and Sula valleys were unified in any organizational sense. Some sources seem to indicate the existence of four to six major *caciques* in the region (Documentos Ineditos 1870, 14: 236–264). Others imply a measure of political integration. Ciudad Real, for example, referred to the Sula plain as the "great province of Naco" (in Henderson 1979: 371) and Montejo described a

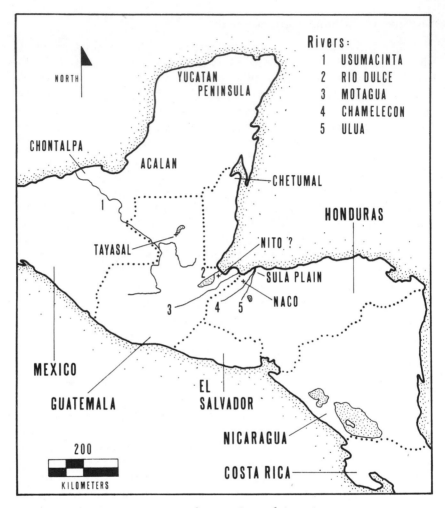

Fig. 1. Eastern Mesoamerica and upper Central America.

province containing "27 or 28 towns" that he called "Zula and Naco" (Bancroft 1886 [2]: 161).

By at least the early sixteenth century, the linguistic character of the area was extremely variegated. Languages associated with Central American peoples to the east and south (Jicaque, and possibly Lenca and Paya) were spoken here as was Maya (recent linguistic summaries are provided by Henderson 1979: 367–370 and Thompson 1970: 84–102). The latter tongue is perhaps the best documented in the Naco-Sula region. In a series of judicial proceedings between

A.D. 1530 and 1533, Montejo successfully established a case that the area extending from the Chontalpa to the Ulua River was "all one language" (Scholes and Roys 1948: 130; cf. Thompson 1970: 91), that language undoubtedly being one of the Maya Cholan group, which includes the Chol, Chorti, and Chontal dialects (Kaufman 1976). It is also possible that a central Mexican language was spoken in this land (Strong, Kidder, and Paul 1938: 21).

Montejo emphasized that the economies of Ulua and the Yucatan peninsula were linked through a vigorous long-distance trading system, a point abundantly confirmed in early colonial accounts of the Yucatecan Maya. "The occupation to which they had the greatest inclination," according to Bishop Landa, "was trade, carrying salt and cloth and slaves to the lands of Ulua and Tabasco, exchanging all they had for cacao and stone beads" (Tozzer 1941: 94–96). Oviedo described "an extensive trade in said fruit cacao . . . [in which] canoes go from Yucatan loaded with clothing and other goods, to Ulua, and from there they return loaded with cacao" (in Strong 1935: 17). The Ulua-Yucatan commerce was a highly organized enterprise administered by the lords of various principalities throughout the peninsula (Chapman 1957; Pollock et al. 1962: 34; Tozzer 1941: 39). Maya nobles from the Chontalpa, Chetumal, and other provinces probably maintained emissaries in northwestern Honduras to monitor their commercial interests (Chamberlain 1966: 53–57; Roys 1957: 162; Scholes and Roys 1948: 3, 34, 130).

Early Postclassic and Transitional Late Postclassic Material

The most archaeologically visible time span in the Naco–Sula region is the Classic period, which is characterized by several extensive centers with large public architecture, numerous minor centers, small mound groups of apparently residential character in virtually every part of the area, and the development of the stylistically complex Ulua Polychrome tradition. While it is clear that this cultural pattern was transformed during the Early Postclassic period (ca. A.D. 950–1200), the nature of the alteration is very poorly known.

The Early Postclassic architecture of the Naco valley appears to be a modest continuation of local Late Classic patterns. La Sierra, a massive Classic center, was evidently inhabited during at least the initial portion of the Early Postclassic although no construction activity is dated to that time. Nonresidential architecture is perceptible at two other sites including Naco, where several cobble–faced mounds three meters high were erected toward the close of the Early Postclassic. By and large, however, there seems to be a reduction in the volume of ceremonial architecture and a possible simplification of settlement hierarchy.

Urban located a number of loosely arranged residential mound groups consisting of low, earthen platforms with rather crudely constructed cobble retaining walls along at least one side. Such mound groups tend to be concentrated on the high ground of the northwestern part of the valley but this apparent shift in settlement distribution is not accompanied by any material evidence of subsistence reorientation. Site numbers and sizes do suggest some diminution in population (Urban 1980: 13).

Ceramically, the Early Postclassic phase of the Naco valley is recognizable as an essentially simplified assemblage of Classic phase domestic types with paste that becomes progressively more coarse and micaceous. Polychromes are rare. There is little plastic or painted embellishment although rough, vertically punctated slashes commonly occur on strap handles of both this and the previous time period. The censer form, a lid or plate scored on one side, also was present during the Late Classic.

At the beginning of the Early Postclassic, influences in Naco valley ceramics come from the Ulua Polychrome tradition, the lower Motagua valley, and the "Peten Postclassic Tradition" (Augustine group). It may be that such connections decrease over time, because it becomes increasingly difficult to identify evidence for outside contact at the close of the Early Postclassic (Urban, personal communication). Obsidian, probably from the southeastern Guatemalan highlands, is present in limited quantity.

Even less is known about the Early Postclassic of the Sula plain. The Smithsonian–Harvard Expedition may have encountered traces of this phase in 1936 excavations at Santa Rita, Honduras (fig. 2). Their riverbank cut yielded a stratified sequence of primarily Classic phase material described as being comprised of four levels in the preliminary report. Of interest here is the highest unit, 55 centimeters thick and 2.3 meters beneath the bank summit, which was designated as stratigraphic level A. This level produced a few polychromes but no censer fragments:

> Level A contained a large amount of plain cooking ware of a red brown to blackish gray color. The vessels were fairly large, including direct bowls and pots with flaring necks and vertical handles. These handles are either round or flat in cross–section and, in a few cases, have a monkey head lug on the bend. Rounded, flat, and dimpled bases and a few conical and round hollow feet occur. There are also some highly polished

thin sherds tan or buff in color. The upper portion of level B
contained the same types but in the lower portions crudely
painted ware superseded the plain cooking ware. In C and D
plain cooking ware was very scarce except for a few very thick
gray and brown sherds and some vertical strap handles.
(Strong, Kidder, and Paul 1938: 55)

When Glass restudied the Santa Rita material, he concluded
that the upper portion of the Smithsonian–Harvard level A constituted "a distinct chronological deposit" characterized by the virtual
absence of Ulua Polychrome and the presence of 57 "thin buff to
cream to orange–colored sherds" (1966: 174). These latter he defined as Sula Fine Orange, a type possessing brittle, untempered
paste and thinly slipped surfaces. Glass (1966: 174) perceived a similarity between Sula Fine Orange and Silho (X) Fine Orange, a relationship suggesting an Early Postclassic placement for the latest material at Santa Rita, Honduras.

In 1976, Sheehy encountered the same type of ceramic in a
trench at Travesia, a large center of the Classic phase bordering the
Ulua River (fig. 2). Sheehy (1977: 11) favored a Terminal Classic
placement for the fine paste pottery on the basis of "the close similarity in vessel shape with Altar group ceramics at Altar de Sacrificios and Seibal."

It seems, therefore, that fine paste ceramics overlie Late Classic
material at various places in the Sula plain. Whether the dating is
Terminal Classic, Early Postclassic, or both, the local fine paste tradition is absent or very weakly developed in the Naco valley. This
suggests that the Naco valley, unlike the Sula plain, was relatively
isolated from events of the Early Postclassic occurring around the
Gulf Coast and Yucatan peninsula.

The upper levels excavated at Santa Rita imply, on the other
hand, that the Sula plain, like the Naco valley, experienced a reduction in polychromes and an increase in simple utilitarian vessels
with coarse paste after the Late Classic phase. Major Late Classic
centers may have been occupied to an unknown extent in both valleys during the Early Postclassic, but little evidence for large scale
construction activity after the Classic has been encountered. Consequently, the Early Postclassic of the Naco and Sula valleys currently
seems nearly bereft of such familiar manifestations of elite supervi-
sion as probable craft specialization (Ulua Polychrome production)
and monumental architecture, a situation broadly analogous to that
observed elsewhere in the southern Maya lowlands.

In the Naco area, Urban (1980: 16) found "no striking 'collapse'

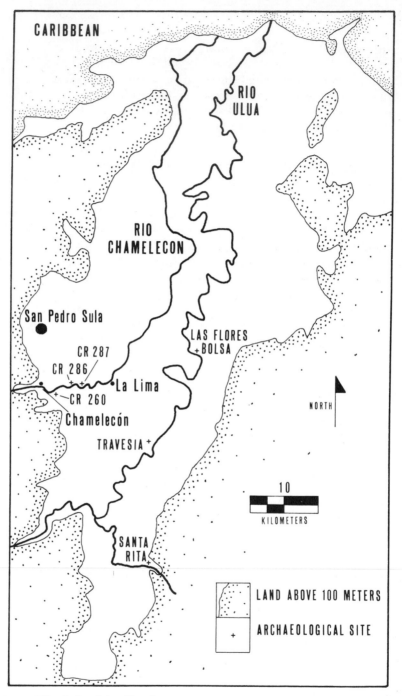

Fig. 2. The Sula plain, Honduras.

or disjunction in the valley's development until the middle of the Postclassic." At Naco itself, a population nadir may have occurred during a problematic early facet of the Late Postclassic phase, estimated at A.D. 1200 to 1250. A low earthen platform with a rock–strewn summit and several unmodified obsidian blades are the only nonceramic cultural traits attributable to this time. Most pottery derives from jars with low, flaring necks and simple bowl forms. The sherds are composed of a fairly micaceous paste characteristic of the entire Late Postclassic phase but initially present toward the end of the Early Postclassic. Similarly, Cofradia Unslipped, a category consisting chiefly of large jars with beige paste, occurs both at this time and in the Early Postclassic. Cofradia, in fact, is a direct descendant of a type characteristic of the Classic phase and provides an especially clear instance of local continuity.

The early facet of the Late Postclassic is distinguished from the latter portion of the Early Postclassic by the addition of red-on-white surface treatment and new censer forms. The design motifs of the painted type, Nolasco Bichrome, are badly eroded in the existing sample but it is at least clear that the type occurs in two forms: a tripod bowl with hollow, tubular legs sometimes possessing on the interior base a grater surface composed of a raised applique design; and a ladle censer with a hollow, tubular handle. The ladle form and an unslipped bowl with spiked applique completely displace the plate censers of the previous phase.

Two observations can be made about this material. First, the ceramics are typologically intermediate between those of the Early Postclassic and the later facets of the Late Postclassic. Second, this congeries of traits appears to be rare at Naco and is currently unknown in the Sula plain. I believe the assemblage may reflect a dwindling population at a point transitional between the less ambiguously defined Early and fully Late Postclassic phases. This certainly is not the only possible explanation, but it is congruent with apparent reduction of contemporary populations at other sites in Honduras and the southern lowlands (e.g., Lake Yojoa, Honduras, and Barton Ramie, Belize; see Bullard 1973: 227–230; P. Rice 1979: 81; Willey 1973: 101; and Baudez and Becquelin 1973: 407).

Late Postclassic Material

Whether or not remains of the transitional early facet have been correctly interpreted, it appears that Naco experiences a massive and archaeologically abrupt transformation at the beginning of the middle facet, about A.D. 1250. The community balloons into a town

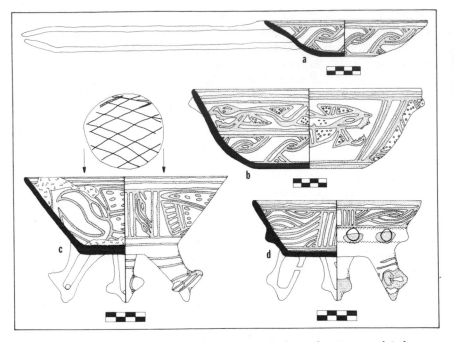

Fig. 3. Red-on-White Nolasco Bichrome vessels from the Naco and Sula valleys: (a) ladle censer with tubular handle from Naco; (b) hemispherical bowl with opposed side lugs from Naco; (c) tripod bowl with scored grater surface on interior base from site CR 260 on the Sula plain; (d) tripod bowl with reed-stamped flange from the Sula plain (No. 18 over 3209 in the Museum of the American Indian, Heye Foundation). Scales are 4 centimeters long.

sprawled over 160 hectares. Accompanying the quantum leap in site area is an astronomical increase in obsidian. Middens contain an average of 20 grams of obsidian per cubic meter of soil, one of the highest obsidian consumption ratios of any period in the lowland Maya area. Other innovations occur in ceramic forms (e.g., jars with high vertical necks, small tripod cups, spindle whorls), pottery decorative modes (e.g., stamp–impressed rather than appliqued grater surfaces; reed–stamped bowl flanges shown in fig. 3d; hollow, pseudo–effigy legs with three lateral projections shown in fig. 3c, 3d), and lithic characteristics (small, side–notched projectile points; a high percentage of retouched blade tools). A new architectural style emphasizes plaster elements as well as residential and public building without substructural platforms. A subsistence reorientation toward riverine resources is indicated by substantial quantities of mollusks (particularly river snails of the genus *Pachychilus*) and grooved spheroids of fired clay probably used as net weights.

Some traits previously present at Naco (e.g., the red-on-white painted surface treatment of Nolasco Bichrome; also Cofradia Unslipped) are found in conjunction with the host of elements lacking local antecedents. The totality of these characteristics, defined as the Nolasco subcomplex, presents the difficulty of accounting for both a perceptible continuity in material culture and a substantial, rapid transmutation of the site. I think the Nolasco subcomplex is best interpreted as the result of site–unit intrusion (possibly from the southern portion of the Maya lowlands) with a subsequent fusion of intrusive and autochthonous elements. In this view, the Nolasco subcomplex is thought to be another example of the migration and cultural reformulation occurring in eastern Mesoamerica after the eclipse of Toltec Chichen Itza (cf. Fox 1978: 274–275).

There are indications that a privileged group resided around a centrally located precinct containing the only public architecture discernible at Naco. The use of plaster in residential structures is known only from this central area and it appears that faunal remains (primarily deer and dog bones) may be more numerous and diverse in the same zone. Beyond hints of architectural and dietary perquisites, those who were centrally located evinced distinctive preferences in food preparation (the comal vessel form occurs chiefly in this portion of the site), stone tool manufacture (ground, as opposed to striated, core platforms cluster in the central zone), and cultic–iconographic emphasis (depictions of the feathered creatures shown in fig. 3b are known only from the central area, whereas nearly all tripod bowls with pseudo–effigy legs are associated with more peripheral locations). It is possible that the latter characteristics reflect the existence of a Putun (Chontal) or Putun–derived elite segment similar to the Mexicanized Maya nobilities ruling at Acalan, Chetumal, Tayasal, and Nito in late precolumbian times (Thompson 1970: 73–79, 1977: 36; Feldman 1975).

Clearly some group at Naco, presumably the ruling stratum, possessed whatever managerial expertise may have been required to obtain large quantities of obsidian from the Guatemalan highlands, but there is virtually no indication that a hierarchical chain of command was exercised within the community. Certainly there were no major public works projects necessitating an administrative apparatus and large labor pool. There is no evidence for differential access to the potentially valuable obsidian. There is no indication that pottery manufacture and stone tool production were specialized or localized except in the sense indicated above. And, excluding the traits associated with the centrally located group, forms and proportions of artifacts are distributed in a uniform fashion over the entire site.

Thus, the social formation associated with at least a partial commitment to riverine resources seems, at Naco, to have involved a large, settled community recognizing some form of social privilege but generally homogeneous, unspecialized, and, in several respects, egalitarian in its inventory of material culture. Naco may have been capable of expending considerable organizational effort in its inter-regional relationships, but if superordinate means of social control were applied within the community, they left scant trace in the ar-chaeological record.

Only two other sites in the Ulua area are known from test ex-cavations to be at least roughly coeval with middle facet develop-ments at Naco. One site of undetermined dimensions was located by Urban in the course of her Naco valley survey less than a kilometer downstream from Naco on a bank of the Naco River. Test pits dis-closed a primary deposit at a modest depth containing the basic con-stituents of middens at Naco: quantities of mollusks (mostly *Pachy-chilus*), sherds, obsidian, and bone. In comparison to Naco middens of the middle facet, however, this riverbank site yielded little painted pottery (Nolasco Bichrome constituted 7%, versus 16% for Naco middens) or obsidian (8 grams per cubic meter of excavated soil, ver-sus 83 grams for Naco middens).

A second site, located on a bank of the Chamelcon River in the Sula plain, extends about five hundred meters along the river (fig. 2, site CR 260). The extent of its inland width is unknown. Agurcia recently encountered a burial associated with two apparently identi-cal tripod bowls of Nolasco Bichrome here (fig. 3c). Subsequent test-ing demonstrated the presence of late prehistoric debris including a midden deposit a little more than a meter beneath the bank summit. The ceramics of CR 260 seem technically and typologically very similar to those of Naco, and the midden lens of the Sula plain site is composed of the same classes of material noted in the Naco valley. As is the case with the site immediately southeast of Naco, the CR 260 midden contains, relative to Naco, little obsidian (17 grams per cubic meter of excavated soil) or Nolasco Bichrome (2%).

There are, however, differences between CR 260 and the sites of the Naco valley that may be significant. CR 260 lacks the type Co-fradia Unslipped although it contains a vessel form (unslipped cylin-der with complex lip) unknown at Naco. Several sherds from CR 260 are thickly coated with lime on the interior surface, a characteristic rare or absent at Naco. *Pachychilus* shells from CR 260 retain the reddish brown exterior rind or periosteum, while the Naco valley specimens do not, a contrast that implies the shells were boiled at the latter location but not at the former. Additional work is needed to establish whether these apparent contrasts are due simply to sampling error or effects of differential soil conditions. If the differences are not a result of these causes, the cylinder vessel form, the lime encrustations, the snail shell rinds, and, possibly the scored rather than stamp—impressed grater surfaces (fig. 3c) collectively would indicate a set of food preparation procedures in the Sula plain distinct from those of the Naco valley.

A number of changes in the Naco community are apparent near the close of its precolumbian existence. This late facet is tentatively bracketed between A.D. 1450 and 1536, the year Naco probably was destroyed by Alvarado's forces. The site area remains about the same and, in most of Naco, the late facet is marked primarily by deviations from modes and frequencies characteristic of the middle facet. Many utilitarian sherds of this time have combed or incompletely smoothed surfaces. The amount of obsidian available to the community probably increases, while the frequency of Nolasco Bichrome declines.

Changes associated with the late facet are far more dramatic in the central architectural zone, where new pottery and building styles appear. Two ceramic subcomplexes are known chiefly from architectural fill. In overall counts, the sherds of both subcomplexes are numerically minor. Both are functionally incomplete vessel inventories composed almost entirely of painted tripod bowls and ladle censers. The subcomplexes are stylistically distinct from Nolasco Bichrome and from one another.

The Forastero subcomplex, represented by a black-on-white type of the same name in which an undulating and usually slanting dark line is enclosed within borders of straight lines, cannot be associated with either artifacts or architecture. Its origin and significance are unclear. The Vagando subcomplex is represented by red-and-black-on-white painted sherds about four times as plentiful as those of the Forastero type. Vagando Polychrome features a serrated serpent in conjunction with geometric elements such as step—frets, butterflies, balls, vertical zigzags, and S—hooks. Its stylistic affinities lie with a series of ceramics distributed along the Pacific slopes of Central America such as Nimbalari Trichrome in Chiapas and the so-called "Dull Paint Style" of the western Guatemalan highlands (Navarrete 1966: 53—56; Wauchope 1970: 108—110). Of all of these very late derivatives of the Mixteca–Puebla style, Vagando Polychrome is most closely related to Managua Polychrome: Nindiri Variety in Nicaragua (Haberland 1975).

In attempting to assess the social significance of the Vagando subcomplex, it is necessary to consider two factors. First, Vagando Polychrome seems to have been prestigious because some of its design elements are incorporated into painted ceramics of the Nolasco subcomplex. The process is not reciprocal, nor is stylistic crossover from Forastero to the other subcomplexes perceptible. Second, the central precinct is extensively refurbished at about this time in the course of a construction program emphasizing new materials and new techniques. Stained and molded plaster surfaces of the middle facet are largely supplanted by thick, unstained plaster caps and facings composed of roughly shaped schistose slabs. The most striking additions are a circular temple in juxtaposition with an I–shaped ball court, a pattern I believe to have been derived ultimately from Toltec central Mexico. The approximately coeval appearance in the central precinct of an influential pottery style and distinctive canons of architecture suggest the influence of a new ruling elite, a Late Postclassic version, perhaps, of earlier Pipil migrations.

Knowledge of the late facet outside Naco is virtually nonexistent. Combed or incompletely smoothed sherds do occur above the midden layer thought to be of middle facet date at the Sula plain site CR 260. In addition, a black-on-white tripod bowl (presumably Forastero Bichrome), housed in the Middle American Research Institute and attributed to the southeastern portion of the Sula plain, may date to this time (J.S. Henderson, personal communication).

Discussion

At present, archaeological coverage of the Postclassic throughout the Naco–Sula region is extremely uneven. Urban's survey and testing program provides a broad outline of the Early Postclassic in the Naco valley but no comparable information is available from the Sula plain. Overall, the Early Postclassic of northwestern Honduras appears to be a somewhat parochial simplification of a Late Classic base of material culture, perhaps accompanied by reduction of population and elite control. Yet, this generalization may be extremely misleading should future work demonstrate the vigorous development of a fine paste ceramic tradition during the Early Postclassic of the Sula plain.

The regional Late Postclassic is known primarily from Naco and most of that information is skewed toward the middle facet. When I compare the archaeological manifestations of this phase to early Spanish descriptions of the region, I am struck by the disparity between the paucity of remains and the putative scale of occupation. If the region was densely inhabited, where are the sites? Urban located only one certain Late Postclassic site during her examination of the Naco valley. A stratified and systematic survey program in the Sula plain has located hundreds of sites, none attributable to the last precolumbian phase.

A large part of the answer must be that the remains characteristic of the Late Postclassic generally are not detectable by the usual survey methods that rely heavily on surface indications. The only standing architecture associated with this time (at Naco) is extremely modest in scale and many, possibly most, of the structures were built on ground level of perishable material. Additionally, all of the Late Postclassic material known from this region derives from riverbank locations. This is true of Naco, the site downstream from Naco, and CR 260 in the Sula plain. It seems to hold true for sites in which a late prehistoric presence can only be suspected, such as the "bundle burials" encountered by the Smithsonian–Harvard Expedition on the Ulua River at Las Flores Bolsa (fig. 2). Those interments included artifacts of possible Late Postclassic date, such as ceramic spindle whorls and a copper fishhook (Strong, Kidder, and Paul 1938: 41, 44) and may be similar to the burial excavated by Agurcia at CR 260. Two other sites of probable Late Postclassic placement in the Sula plain have been found by examining the riverbanks between the present–day towns of Chamelcon and La Lima (fig. 2: CR 286 and CR 287). All of this suggests a good correlation between river loci and late material. In this region of extensive alluvium, the Late Postclassic sites probably are buried under a meter or more of sediment.

When the apparent disposition of late sites along waterways is considered in conjunction with the quantities of freshwater mollusks at all tested locations, and with the probable net weights at Naco, it seems reasonable to conclude that Late Postclassic life literally centered about the perennial streams of the region. I do not mean to imply that farming and harvesting of terrestrial resources were unimportant but rather that the commitment to rivers as settlement focus, food source, and possibly transportation medium was far stronger than it was in preceding periods. Although the material culture of the last prehispanic phase is unprepossessing, there is no reason to assume that the social formation associated with a riverine adaptation was correspondingly simple.

This society appears to have been capable of supporting large population aggregations as well as obtaining and distributing impressive amounts of foreign obsidian. The region's political economy probably was pervaded by complex social relations, to judge by the origin and development of the Nolasco subcomplex, the apparent differences in cultic emphasis and food preparation behavior within and between sites, and the stylistic and contextual contrasts among three contemporaneous ceramic subcomplexes at Naco. Finally, I want to emphasize a perspective present in the early documents but barely perceptible in the archaeological record: the land of Ulua was considered to be, by the standard of the times, a wealthy, cosmopolitan district.

Attempting to assess the implications of these data, I have elsewhere (Wonderley n.d.) drawn upon Terray's (1974, 1975) analysis of the West African kingdom of Gyaman to speculate that an archaeological record of this sort may have resulted from the operation of two essentially separate production strategies. The first, a village–level mode of production, probably consisting of milpa farming supplemented by hunting and gathering, would have been a more or less self–sustaining subsistence regime. Politically dominant over the agricultural sector, an elite of foreign origin pursued an alternate strategy of predatory production presumably based upon slaving, fighting, and long–distance trading.

Grandiose public works projects were not a feature of the society largely because the lords sought to satisfy their own requirements for subsistence and prestige by siphoning off the products of more distant territories instead of directly appropriating the labor, land, and goods of their own vassals. Noble–commoner relationships were undoubtedly complex but a fragile symbiosis may have rested ultimately on lower class fulfillment of military obligations and upper class distribution of obsidian and other utilitarian goods. Large population aggregations such as at Naco would have facilitated these interchanges and offered security benefits to all concerned. The same trend toward nucleation may also have required a broadening of the subsistence base. If so, the riverine (or maritime, or lacustrine) focus could represent an attempt to increase food production without resorting to the managerial hierarchies and hydraulic works frequently associated with agricultural intensification.

A scheme of dual modes of production seems to me to be generally congruent with the ethnohistoric picture throughout the late period Maya lowlands, providing one takes into account local variations. In the case of Ulua, for example, the nobles may have undertaken comparatively few foreign adventures, concentrating instead on developing wealth based on cacao estates manned, perhaps, by slaves or serfs. Regardless of the extent to which the specific interpretation is justified, however, this form of analysis possesses the advantage of forcing us to consider basic productive impulses and possible interests of distinct social segments in the light of archaeological, documentary, and ethnographic evidence. The approach does not require us to assume a set of cultural relationships that would be either simple or degenerate in comparison to those of the Late Classic.

Whether or not the material culture and issues we are encountering in the land of Ulua are directly applicable to regions more traditionally considered to be Maya is problematic, because there is an archaeological void for the Late Postclassic period in a vast region of the southern Maya lowlands adjacent to the Naco and Sula valleys. This is a tropical riverine setting drained by the lower Motagua, Rio Dulce, and much of the greater Usumacinta system (fig. 1). Writings from the conquest period of the area describe a way of life capable of producing remains comparable to those of Ulua (Hellmuth 1977; Thompson 1938; Wonderley 1981: 311–317), so it is possible that the riverine mode of adaptation under study in northwestern Honduras will prove to be widely distributed in late prehistoric times along the major drainages at the base of the Yucatan peninsula.

Postclassic Relationships between the Highland and Lowland Maya

KENNETH L. BROWN

> . . . it is obvious that there are a large number of similarities
> in culture history between Mayapan and the Late Postclassic
> in highland Guatemala. There are, of course, differences . . .
> The striking parallels between the two areas may be explained
> in terms of the similar direction, duration, and nature of
> the Toltec influence reaching these areas. (Carmack 1968: 86)

This quotation represents a fair summary for many Mesoamerican archaeologists concerned with the Postclassic period in the Maya area, both the highlands and lowlands alike (Thompson 1966; M. Coe 1966; A. L. Smith 1955, 1961; Carmack 1968, 1973, 1977; Fox 1978, 1980; Weaver 1972; Adams 1977). The cultural patterning of the final 600 years of prehistoric occupation in the Maya area is often considered to be the result of the intrusion of central Mexican (i.e., Toltec) cultural patterns, if not people, into the region. This is not unlike the version of prehistory related by some archaeologists concerned with the rise of the Classic period in the Maya area as well.

Some of the debate has focused upon what group actually entered the area with the "Mexican" traits. Thompson (1945, 1966) has argued for actual Toltec peoples entering the northern Maya lowlands and establishing Chichen Itza. Roys (1962), on the other hand, argued for more indirect influence: Toltec traits seen and modified through Mayan eyes. Possibly Chontal Maya speakers from the Gulf coastal lowland area were responsible for the "Toltec" changes introduced into the region (Tozzer 1941; Roys 1943; Thompson 1945; Carmack 1968). In any case while this initial contact was earlier in the lowlands, both the lowlands and the highlands were apparently greatly affected by these Toltecs or "Toltecized"—Maya. Both regions experienced major cultural changes: in architecture, in political organization, in religious organization, belief, and practice, and possibly in social organization. Also in both regions, though occurring later in the highlands, foreign groups employed their superior organizational abilities to consolidate major empires. Thus, one of the major similarities between the Maya lowlands and highlands during the Postclassic has been hypothesized to be this experience of foreign contact and possible control.

Unfortunately, there is little evidence to support the reconstruction outlined above, at least for the central Quiche area of the Maya highlands. No evidence of the Toltecs or the Toltecized-Maya has been located during major archaeological research conducted over the past three years. This represents a significant problem to the traditional interpretations of the Maya Postclassic, because the Quiche are considered to have been the major highland group dominated by the Gulf coastal Toltecized-Maya (Carmack 1968, 1973, 1977; Fox 1978, 1980). This paper represents a summary of recent archaeological research on the Postclassic materials in and around the central Quiche area, and a reinterpretation of the Postclassic culture of the region. Given these data, the ethnohistoric accounts of foreign intrusions, and the data from several other areas of Mesoamerica, an alternative version of the "Mexicanization" process within the entire Maya area will be presented.

The Central Quiche Sequence

Major excavations have been undertaken at several of the Late Postclassic political centers located in the highlands, including Zaculeu (Woodbury and Trik 1953), Mixco Viejo (Lehmann 1968), Iximche (Guillemin 1965), and Utatlan (Wauchope 1949, 1970; Carmack, Fox, and Stewart 1975; Weeks 1977; D. Wallace 1977; Babcock 1980; Brown 1978, 1979a, 1979b; Brown and Majewski 1979). A number of minor centers have also been excavated, in units varying from test pits to nearly complete stripping. This group of smaller centers includes Zacualpa (Wauchope 1948, 1975), Pueblo Viejo Chichaj (Ichon 1975, 1977), Cauinal (Ichon 1979), Chinautla (Feldman 1969), Tajumulco (Dutton and Hobbs 1943), and Chitinamit (Brown 1979a; Brown and Majewski 1979; Majewski 1980). Other valuable data on the Postclassic occupants of the highlands have come from several surface reconnaissance projects (Smith 1955; Carmack, Fox, and Stewart 1965; Fox 1978, 1980; Stewart 1977; Brown 1979a, 1979b; Brown and Majewski 1979). Despite statements such as the opening quotation citing similarities of mound organization at many of these sites with that of Mayapan, however, none of these areas has demonstrated clear contacts with lowland Maya groups. This is particularly

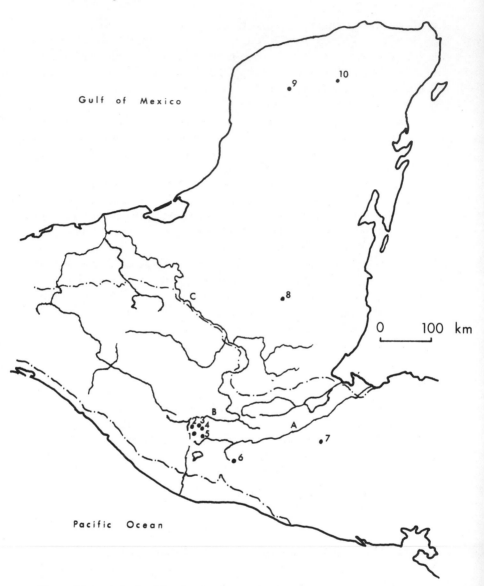

Fig. 1. Map of the highlands of Guatemala showing sites mentioned in the text. Dot-dash line indicates the limits of the highlands. Other place-names are as follows:

(1) Utatlan	(6) Kaminaljuyu	(A) Rio Motagua
(2) Jocopilas	(7) Copan	(B) Rio Chixoy o Negro
(3) Chitinamit	(8) Tikal	(C) Rio Usumacinta
(4) Chujuyub	(9) Mayapan	
(5) Chiche	(10) Chichen Itza	

true of the southern band of the highlands adjacent to the Pacific piedmont. Those populations on the Yucatan peninsula side of the highlands appear to have maintained a low level of contact with at least the Gulf coast groups, if not the populations in the northern portion of the Yucatan peninsula.

Much of the data from the central Quiche area were collected in order to test the degree and extent of foreign impact on local populations of the area during the Classic and Postclassic periods. Material from extensive excavations at three major political centers, Chujuyub, Chitinamit, and Utatlan, exists, as well as surface survey data on some 625 sites within the central Quiche area. The latter material includes collections from all but two of the Late Classic–Early Postclassic political centers in the area. Excavations were conducted in both the mound complexes and their surrounding "residence" zones, in order to test the various locations at which this foreign material might be found. The following represents a summary of our findings by time period, highlighting the settlement patterns and the foreign goods recovered. (It should be pointed out that the phase designations are tentative, as we have not yet received the results of our radiocarbon determinations. The dates are based upon ceramic cross–ties with other areas of Mesoamerica.)

CHICHE PHASE (A.D. 500–800)

During this phase, the central Quiche area appears to have been controlled by two political groups, Chiche on the south and east, and Jocopilas on the north. The site of Chujuyub appears to have been founded at this time; either by the nucleation of three small political units originally located in the Chujuyub area and ordered together by the Chiche elite, or through a local elite response to the use of the area for long-distance, elite item commerce by foreign traders. It is likely that the latter alternative is a more accurate reflection of what happened, because the actual settlement pattern within the Chujuyub area remained very stable with the exception of the construction of this site (Brown 1980; Majewski 1980). Excavation revealed no apparent nucleation of population, elite or otherwise, at the site (Majewski 1980). A large number of foreign imports were recovered from the site area itself, however, including green obsidian blades, stuccoed black ware sherds, imported white paste sherds, Peten polychrome sherds, imported flint (from Peten?), and non-local highland Maya ceramics. Elsewhere in the area, more green obsidian and several pieces of jade were recovered from sites dating to this period. Near the site of Chiche a small mound complex with a large quantity of Teotihuacan–like sherds on the surface may represent a small Teotihuacan compound associated with Chiche (Stewart, personal communication, 1976).

This material indicates some type of strong foreign contact within the central Quiche area. The Chujuyub site may have been a major node in the conduct of long-distance, elite item trade through the western highlands of Guatemala, controlled by the Chiche elite. The timing of this contact is still in question (awaiting radiocarbon determinations), but it would appear to postdate the Teotihuacan and lowland Maya contact which has been noted within the Valley of Guatemala (Brown 1977a, 1977b). The proposed route would have connected the upper Motagua River region with the upper Chixoy River and, ultimately, with the Maya lowlands through the Chixoy–Usumacinta drainage. Thus, during the Middle Classic and the early Late Classic, the central Quiche area was engaging in some form of communication with the lowlands as well as with Teotihuacan. There is no significant evidence, however, to suggest widespread influence of either foreign group on the local material culture, as represented by the artifacts or architecture of the indigenous populations.

WUKAMAK PHASE (A.D. 800–1300)

At some point around A.D. 800, the political/economic system in the central Quiche area changed radically. While we are still attempting to determine how rapidly the changes occurred, we can make some comment on their extent. The large sites of Chiche and Chujuyub were all but completely abandoned, and each was replaced by several smaller centers. In the place of Chiche at least four, and possibly five, political centers emerged. It is actually more accurate to say that these centers reemerged, because they are all within approximately two kilometers of the location of the early Classic centers which existed prior to Chiche domination. Jocopilas continued to be occupied, although some shift of the major focus of activities at the site did occur. The Chujuyub site was abandoned as a political/economic center in favor of three emerging centers. One of these sites, Chitinamit, was clearly dominant, if overall size, architectural complexity, and activity area complexity are any indication of a site's status vis-a-vis other nearby sites. The other two smaller centers were located close to small Early Classic sites, suggesting a "return" to earlier patterns as was occurring in the rest of the central Quiche area. Unlike the earlier sites in the Chujuyub valley area, however, in this time period one of the sites may have assumed some dominance over the other groups.

One of the most interesting and surprising features of the archaeological record of this time period, as currently defined, is the drastic reduction in non-local items reaching the area. While foreign elite items were both abundant and variable at Chujuyub, they are almost totally lacking at Chitinamit. This observation does not extend to obsidian, one sure sign of external contact in the central Quiche area. The only elite import recovered in even small quantities in extensive excavations at Chitinamit was Plumbate pottery. None of the other hallmarks of Early Postclassic trade were recovered at this site. A complete Plumbate vessel was recovered from an Early Postclassic cache in one of the mounds of the largest complex at Chujuyub, and it had apparently been placed sometime after the abandonment of the site (Majewski 1980).

Elsewhere in the central Quiche area, no other obviously imported materials were located. A small amount of Fine Orange pottery came from the apparent religious shrine site of Tojil (Fox 1978), and a sizeable fragment of a seemingly local imitation of a modeled-carved Maya vessel was recovered from a secondary mound complex in the main basin floor area. These data suggest that, except for trade of small amounts of non-elite items (i.e., obsidian), the populations of the central Quiche area became rather isolated from the other developments within Early Postclassic Mesoamerica.

This distribution is highly significant, because it is during the latter portion of this period that the Toltecized-Maya are thought to have entered the area and established their capital at Chitinamit. While the imported ceramics may suggest that long-distance trade was still being undertaken by the local elite, this trade was at an extremely low level. In fact, it may be that many of the items came from trade with surrounding populations (i.e., Zacualpa, Sacapulas, and/or the Lake Atitlan area), and as an important sidelight to subsistence-oriented trade. To date, the only objects with a definite Gulf Coast origin are the Fine Orange ceramics located by Fox. The architecture of these sites also appears to be typical of highland Maya architecture in general. Although both Fox (1978, 1980) and Carmack (personal communication, 1979) have stressed the foreign style of architecture at Chitinamit, our excavations failed to support any of their impressions from their surface surveys. We were not able to find any definite indications of foreign architecture at the site, despite excavation into all but one of the structures. Rather, there was evidence of a continuity in the architecture from the Chujuyub site, at least in the overall construction techniques (Majewski 1980).

Thus the data from the central Quiche area suggest that elite item trade in the highlands was primarily carried out with Pacific coastal populations. Communication with lowland populations both to the north and south seems to have been at a low level, as indicated by the lack of impact the foreign contact had on the traditional highland material culture. The data absolutely fail to demonstrate the extensive contact with Gulf Coast Toltecized-Maya postulated by ethnohistorians (Carmack 1968, 1973, 1977, personal communication, 1979; Edmonson 1971) and some archaeologists (Fox 1978, 1980). In fact, to judge from our archaeological evidence, no such contact appears likely at any point in the prehistoric sequence, but it is notably absent during this Late Classic and Early Postclassic occupation of the area.

QUICHE PHASE (A.D. 1300–1524)

This phase may be characterized by the rise of the Quiche to a level of political dominance within the central Quiche area and, ultimately, over much of the surrounding highlands. It is this rise which ethnohistorians and archaeologists have associated with the intrusion of Toltecs into the highland Maya area. This event is similar to the conquest initiated from Chichen Itza within Yucatan after the "Toltec" intrusion at that site, though of course the highland empire of the Quiche was on a much smaller scale, both in terms of area and populations controlled.

The problem with the data from Gumarcaaj (the Quichean name for Utatlan and the name for the site in the ethnohistoric documents) and other major Late Postclassic capitals in the highlands, is the timing of the introduction of foreign items and the location of the source of these items. In a recent paper, Navarrete (1976) demonstrated that elite item imports into the highlands during the Late Postclassic came from central Mexico and/or were highly influenced by the Mixteca-Puebla art style. While a number of authors have also noted this (Carmack 1968, 1973; Weeks 1977; Fox 1978; Weaver 1971), Navarrete has further shown that in many cases these items were additions to local elite goods that continued in use on the basis of traditional patterns of behavior, rather than being replacements of them. Architectural features normally linked with Toltec expansion began to appear at this time also, rather than earlier during the period of actual Toltec expansion. This makes a certain amount of sense, because features such as the defensive placement of sites (actually more common early in the Postclassic), long structures with colonnaded halls, structure arrangements on sites, and twin–temple pyramids do not occur together in central Mexico until post–Toltec times. All in all, the impression given by these general highland data is that sometime after A.D. 1400, extensive foreign contact was opened (or reopened) with central Mexican or central "Mexicanized"

Maya groups. The question then becomes one of specifically where these elements were originating.

Despite linguistic evidence of Gulf Coastal contacts (L. Campbell, personal communication, 1979), the archaeological evidence from Gumarcaaj suggests that the major, if not the only, focus of trade for the Late Postclassic Quiche area was the Pacific coastal region. This is supported on several grounds. First, the shell recovered from the Gumarcaaj excavations came only from the Pacific Ocean (probably from the Oaxaca coastal area), and this is probably true of all the shell currently known from Postclassic sites in the highlands (L. Feldman, personal communication, 1979 and 1980). Second, we recovered a number of vessels which appear to have been imports from the Pacific piedmont/coastal plain area; these were either direct imports or were made to copy foreign originals using non-local clays. All these vessels and sherds come from the higher status areas of Gumarcaaj and its residence zone (Babcock 1980). It should be pointed out that we recovered only a few pieces of Mixteca-Puebla style material from one complex, so that the Pacific coast goods may have had a slightly lower status definition rating.

Third, we recovered no items which obviously originated in the Gulf Coast region. This is the weakest line of evidence, of course, because it is negative, but nonetheless no material was recovered from the Maya lowland area north of the highlands. All of the imports came from areas located to the west and southwest of the highlands. Given the major Late Postclassic port of trade area of Soconosco (Chapman 1957), heavily utilized and ultimately controlled by the Aztecs, the Mixteca-Puebla material, and the Pacific coast artifacts, the suggestion of a Pacific route for contact rather than the more difficult Gulf Coast route to the north appears to make more sense.

This should not be taken to mean that the Quiche had no trade contacts to the north. In fact, as Fox (1977, 1978) has argued, much of their initial expansion was in that direction. They likely did get a number of items from this area, such as feathers, copper ore, and copal. The point is that major elite items came from the Pacific coast, thus suggesting limited Quiche contact with the lowland Maya groups.

To summarize the data from the central Quiche area, four major points must be highlighted: (1) the heavy central Mexican influence defined during the Classic and Postclassic periods; (2) the heavy Maya lowlands contact only during the Classic, with a falloff in importance afterward; (3) the nearly complete absence of evidence of contact with Gulf Coast lowland groups at any time in the prehistoric sequence in the southern portion of the highlands; and (4) the lack of foreign contact during periods of extreme political fragmentation. While all these points are closely interlinked, the first three relate to the central Quiche area specifically. The fourth point may be important during a consideration of the so-called Toltec or Toltecized-Maya intrusions into the northern Maya lowlands during the latter portion of the Late Classic and the Early Postclassic.

Highland–Lowland Relationships: An Alternative View

The Maya highland region appears to have been a major resource procurement area during much of the prehistory of Mesoamerica after the development of elite roles and the need for status–defining objects arose. These elites "required" objects made from raw materials and animals found within this area of Mesoamerica. Such items as jade, quetzal feathers, hallucinogenic mushrooms, and metal ores occur within the Maya highlands and were exploited at various times for the production of a wide variety of status–defining objects. Other more "basic" resources are also located within at least the southern band of the highlands (e.g., obsidian, basalt, highly fertile agricultural land), which were not all obtainable in the adjacent portions of the Maya area, particularly in the Pacific piedmont zone. Early external trade from the highlands may have begun with these "non-status–defining" objects (at least with the products from the fertile agricultural fields), thus establishing early (i.e., Middle Formative) and important trade ties with the immediately adjacent groups, again particularly with the Pacific piedmont peoples. Finally, the highlands are located between major resources from the Gulf of Mexico/Yucatan peninsula and the Pacific Ocean/Coastal plain. These areas provided a variety of shells, tropical plants (e.g., rubber, cacao), feathers, and animal skins.

Given the distribution of these resources and the presence of the large consuming populations, the Maya highlands represent a strategic position for foreign contact and exchange. Such contact began by the Middle Formative and continued intermittently until the Spanish conquest. The question of the effect of this foreign contact on the somewhat less highly developed highland Maya populations will be a subject of major debate for a long time to come (Cheek 1977; Brown 1977a, 1977b, 1979b).

Over time, the foreign contact underwent several major changes. Most important for this discussion is the shift in the number and point of origin of the foreign groups. Two major groups of foreigners were involved: Teotihuacanos entering from the Pacific piedmont, and lowland Maya entering from the Motagua and the Chixoy valleys. With the fall of Teotihuacan, however, the southern lowland Maya population "collapse," and the shift within the lowlands of major long-distance trading activities to the central Gulf Coast, foreign-"directed" elite item trade slowed in the Maya highlands. Although several routes remained in operation through the highlands at this time, they do not appear to have moved the volume or the variety of materials previously exchanged. This may have been a function of the greater costs of transport through the highlands, the lower consuming population vis-a-vis other areas of Mesoamerica, the lack of specialists in the conduct of long-distance trade among the highland populations, and/or the increasingly peripheral nature of the highland region with the decline in population in the southern Maya lowlands, as well as the fall of Teotihuacan and the shift in the control of long-distance trade. The Maya highland populations were small, relatively simple chiefdom-like societies (Michels 1979). Such societies do not support large numbers of elite within them. Thus, at least for a time, the traders did not attempt major operations within the highlands.

With the beginning of the Quichean expansion, ca. A.D. 1400, the highlands once again became a profitable market for elite item trade. Given the proximity of the Pacific piedmont populations and the long history of trade with these groups, one might predict initially heavy trade with the piedmont area. Central Mexican traders were operating in the Pacific piedmont area procuring a number of items, some of highland origin, at this time and it is also at this point that central Mexican (Mixteca-Puebla) material was brought into the highlands. Maya material from the Gulf of Mexico side of the highlands was not added at this time. Trade seems to have been strictly with the Pacific piedmont Maya and the central Mexican group(s?).

Although the data are meager, it appears that there was little in the way of a relationship between the southern highland groups and any of the lowland Maya groups during the Postclassic. Possibly the single most important event in the Postclassic relationship between the populations of the two areas was the southern lowland "collapse" which began around A.D. 800. This event removed many of the consumers of highland goods, both elite and "non-elite" items, and also radically altered the distribution of population within southern Mesoamerica. This shift made the more sparsely settled highlands somewhat more peripheral to the main consuming populations, for both elite and non-elite items. Given the small size of the consuming groups, the rough terrain, and the high incidence of warfare, trade (particularly from the Gulf side of the highlands) would have been both unprofitable and risky. The larger piedmont populations and the longstanding trade relationship at the elite and subsistence level probably acted as encouragement for adjacent highland populations to turn in that direction for necessary items. Thereafter, the Gulf coast never played a major role except for the populations in the northern band of the highlands, i.e., those groups more or less adjacent to the Gulf Coast lowlands.

Two other points need to be addressed. The first is the whole question of highland–lowland similarities noted at the beginning of this paper. For example, Carmack (1968: 85–86) mentions a series of features, such as settlement patterning, architecture, ceramics, and ritual, which link Mayapan and the Guatemalan highlands. If, as has been argued, direct Toltec or Toltecized-Maya control is not responsible for the Late Postclassic similarities between the cultures of the highlands and the lowlands, what is responsible? In part, this alleged comparability may be the result of a misinterpretation of the archaeological record of the two areas. More recently acquired archaeological evidence reveals that the "similarities" have great time depth in both areas and are almost totally independent of one another, as well as of the so-called Mexican influences.

Another part of this similarity may be the ethnohistoric sources which state that Toltec influence was important within the two areas. Unfortunately, the people who have done the translations of the documents did not have dictionaries which defined precisely what the term "Toltec" meant and how it was used by the writers of the documents. Nor do we have any definite indications as to when this "myth" was added to the documents and, thus, to our "official" history of the Maya. This problem cannot be adequately handled in this paper or with the data which we now have. There are strong indications, however, that at least for the Quiche, the Toltecs may have actually been Teotihuacanos remembered for the wealth their presence helped amass, though not for their impact on any local population (Brown and Majewski 1979). The measurable Teotihuacan impact on culture within the central Quiche area was slight.

The second problem that needs to be raised at this point is closely related to this whole question of testing the documents with archaeologically-derived information. That is, the whole question of Toltec influence and Chichen Itza needs to be reopened and investigated. The Quichean data demonstrate that during periods of extreme political fragmentation, long-distance elite item trade either did not take place through the area or was heavily curtailed. This suggests that both safety and a sufficiently large market were important considerations to the various trading groups. While these are hardly original ideas, they might be usefully applied to organizing research on the whole question of Chichen Itza, its apparent control of the northern Yucatan peninsula populations, and the importation of Toltec items and architecture. Given the political fragmentation of the peninsula's populations and the shift in population from the interior and southern areas, one could predict the shifting of the long-distance elite item trade routes toward the areas with increased consuming populations. If the area was politically fragmented into mutually hostile groups, such trade would be risky, but in a situation in which one of the political groups assumed control over a number of the others, then trade became much less risky and increasingly profitable. If this were the case, then the political group assuming control could have originated within the area as easily as from the outside. The introduction of central Mexican traits may then have been a status symbol of a fairly high order.

Conquest is not necessary for the movement and partial incorporation of foreign traits within and between cultures. Certainly the evidence of Maya influence at Cacaxtla (Lopez de Molina 1976, 1977; Kubler 1980) is fairly solid; the question is just how it got into the Mexican highlands. While a conquest model could be applied, it is interesting that the Maya would then be conquering areas of highland Mexico at the same time that highland Mexicans are "taking over" areas of the Maya lowlands. Maybe the indigenous elites were actually importing foreign craftsmen to produce these status-defining objects and buildings. Any one of a number of scenarios is possible, and the data from the Postclassic in the Guatemalan highlands suggest that it is high time such hypotheses are generated and subjected to rigorous archaeological testing.

CONCLUSION

As it is customary to provide a grand synthesis at the end of a collection of papers on a shared theme, David Freidel offers such for this volume. In his discussion, Freidel views the lowland Postclassic period from the particular vantage point of Cozumel Island. We do not wish to anticipate any of his conclusions, yet we might restate our own observation that the Postclassic is not a uniform period in any of the regions, sites, or classes of archaeological material that have been treated here. Each site discussed in this volume varies from the others, and each survey or excavation provides important new data to illuminate the period as a whole. For example, there appears to be a good deal of regionalization during the Postclassic period; this is particularly evident in pottery forms. While this volume has definitely raised many questions, it has also suggested a few answers as to regional and site–specific variants of Postclassic culture in the Maya lowlands. It should be clear that Postclassic studies have evolved considerably since the early work at Chichen Itza and Mayapan. Future research will undoubtedly add much to this picture, but it can hardly negate the diversity evident in the data provided in the papers assembled here.

New Light on the Dark Age:
A Summary of Major Themes

DAVID A. FREIDEL

This volume of papers on the Maya Postclassic does not lend itself easily to thematic summary, because neither the original symposium nor the subsequent revised papers were solicited with particular methodological or theoretical issues in mind. Rather, the prime objective of the session and of this resulting volume was presentation of new research on the period of some six centuries between the collapse of the Southern lowlands and the Spanish conquest. Thematic discussion hence inevitably imposes the interests of this author on the subject matter. At the same time, I believe that there really are themes pervading the volume which register an emerging consensus of interest on the part of Mayanists specializing in the Postclassic period. The degree to which I have succeeded in capturing such subliminal and tacit consensus must be judged by the reader.

The themes selected here are interrelated and contingent; their isolation is for analytical purposes only. The first issue is that of continuity and disjunction between indigenous developments on the peninsula during the Classic era and the developments following the collapse in the south. In general, these papers tend to seek out continuities in order to place the disjunctions in context. A second theme is the role of external groups in developments on the peninsula during the Postclassic. The general inclination of the papers is to regard external influence in light of a more outward-looking indigenous population, but several of the contributors maintain the stance that the lowland Maya were under severe acculturative pressures of an involuntary nature. Third, there is a trend toward viewing the peninsula during the Postclassic as a heterogeneous mosaic of sociocultural organizations rather than as a relatively homogeneous territorial block undergoing sequential cultural expressions. This position is producing a radical reevaluation of traditional chronological schemes.

These three major themes address the essential cultural historical framework of the Maya Postclassic. Contained within them are the "nuts and bolts" issues of methodology: how do artifacts register change through time and cultural affinity in space in the Maya lowlands? On the theoretical side, there are forays into the issues of local and regional economy, socioreligious organization, demographic fluidity and stability. No real consensus emerges around these issues, which is not surprising in light of the volatile state of the historical framework. Nevertheless, there is promise of important breakthroughs in the near future.

Finally, in the aggregate, these papers mark a step in the direction of a broader evolutionary view of Maya prehistory in which the Southern collapse is a signal event, but by no means is it the last gasp of a civilization, for that civilization persisted thereafter for more than half a millennium.

Continuity and Disjunction

NORTHERN LOWLANDS

Traditionally, interest in the lowland Postclassic has focused on the sector of the peninsula north of the eighteenth parallel. That region is relatively underrepresented in this collection because most recent research has dealt with lesser known parts of the lowlands. Santa Rita and Lamanai, included in the Northern section of this volume, are actually located in the Southern area as traditionally defined for the Classic period.

Andrews and Robles C. illustrate the current controversies surrounding the theme of continuity and disjunction in the north. In their scenario, the collapse period, A.D. 800–900, also called the Terminal Classic, witnessed the indigenous development of a ceramic sphere called Cehpech throughout the north, with significant external technological and stylistic input from neighboring marginal groups in the Gulf Coast lowlands. Continuity with the Classic cultures of the north is highlighted primarily in architecture. This can be seen in regional styles: the Puuc architectural style derived at least partially from earlier styles of the central peninsular region; the Rio Bec and Chenes style (found above the eighteenth parallel and hence included here); and the even stronger architectural continuities at the great community of Coba in the northeast of the peninsula. Indeed, while the pottery from Coba suggests membership in the Cehpech ceramic sphere, the magnitude and design of its architecture remain very much in the Southern lowland tradition.

While the Puuc–dominated western sector and the Coba–dominated eastern sector of the northern lowlands can be distinguished on architectural grounds, both adhere to a traditionally northern lowland settlement organization expressed in the use of inter–site masonry causeways or *sacbeob* (Kurjack and Andrews V 1976). Insofar as there is disjunction in Terminal Classic times in the north, it is expressed through the incorporation of foreign symbols, architectural decoration, and ceramic techniques into an ongoing and flourishing material inventory. These are the products of outward-looking, "internationalizing" Maya, not those of conquered subordinates.

In the view of Andrews and Robles C., the establishment of Chichen Itza between A.D. 900–1200 constitutes a direct intrusion into the peninsula of foreigners, and a disjunctive episode of substantial magnitude. Chichen Itza, and its strategic satellite communities along the coast, exhibit the distinctive Sotuta ceramic sphere. The persistence of Cehpech ceramics at Coba through the ensuing centuries of the Early Postclassic (A.D. 900–1200) leads these authors to envision a stand–off between foreign–dominated Chichen Itza and a basically indigenous polity at Coba. Ultimately, both these territorial giants succumb and, following a hiatus, the Late Postclassic cultures emerge.

For some time there has been a consensus that during the period of collapse in the Southern lowlands, the north enjoys florescence (Andrews IV 1973). What is new here is the notion that Coba, a massive community showing strong cultural ties to the south in the form of a traditional focus on stela monuments celebrating kings and huge pyramids which were likely mortuary monuments, not only survives the collapse but grows in strength. The conjunctive collapse in the south and florescence in the north might be attributed broadly to differences in culture and social organization (Freidel n.d.) and the successful accommodation of northerners to strong external alliances. Yet Coba exhibits a much more insular and conservative culture than the Puuc sphere communities and strong ties to the Southern Classic polities. No doubt Coba differed from the Southern centers in ways which can be discovered only by further research, but its survival of the collapse suggests that factors of geographic locale, environment, and basic production technology figured into the Southern demise.

Although Andrews and Robles C. make the case for the Chichen Itza—based Sotuta ceramic sphere as a direct intrusion of foreigners into the peninsula, others disagree. These scholars (Ball 1979a; D. Chase and A. Chase 1982; A. Chase n.d.; Lincoln n.d.) view this cultural florescence as at least partially contemporary with the Puuc sites and the centers of the Terminal Classic Southern lowlands, and partially derived from indigenous cultures of these regions. Contemporaneity and continuity are judged in light of ceramic deposits containing Sotuta and Cehpech diagnostics along with Terminal Classic sherds. Certainly the architectural techniques of Chichen Itza and its general settlement pattern suggest continuity out of the Puuc style and traditional northern community organization.

Continuities in material symbol systems between the Terminal Classic Southern lowlands and "Toltec" Chichen Itza provide further support for the argument for continuity and contemporaneity. The Cenote of Sacrifice at Chichen Itza yielded a rich assemblage of portable artifacts decorated with elaborate symbols. The jade collection, described by Proskouriakoff (1974), displays a substantial range of Late and Terminal Classic Southern images. Proskouriakoff suggests that these Southern style jades resulted from massive looting of Classic Southern tombs during the Collapse period, presumably by the people of the Sotuta sphere or their trading partners. W. R. Coe (1965a, 1965b) affirms the existence of such looting at the great Southern center of Tikal during Terminal Classic times.

Nevertheless, not all the Cenote materials evidence disjunction. A collection of "battle disks" in gold, a material popular among the Maya only after the collapse, shows clear connections between the "Toltec" iconographic program and those of the Terminal Classic south and Puuc regions. In particular, Disk C (Lothrop 1952: 31) depicts a clear Southern lowland image in the sky band above an interrogation and humiliation scene in typical "Toltec" style, which displays the "Toltecs" in triumph. This sky band image is clearly the cruller-eyed jaguar god, GIII of the Palenque triad (Schele 1976), the Sun and younger brother to Venus. The Sun and Venus are the Classic period hero twin ancestors of all the Southern lowland Maya (and perhaps of the northern Maya as well) and their images are central and pervasive theologically and politically. The other battle disks with sky band personages (Lothrop 1952: fig. 15) are more typically "Toltec," with tight-fitting caps or eagle helmets, knee pads, and bird pectorals.

One might attribute the Southern image to a simple case of archaistic borrowing, because Late Classic polychrome vessels were certainly known, but there are reasons to see this as syncretic merging of contemporary images whose meaning was well understood. First, the GIII image, like the other sky band personages, carries a throwing stick and spear in one hand, the prime weapons of the "Toltecs." Second, the "Toltec" image in the sky band occurs on a Terminal Classic Cycle 10 stela at the site of Ucanal (Stela 4; Proskouriakoff 1950: fig. 76) in the context of an otherwise standard Classic Maya monumental scene. Two types of "Toltec" figures occur on the battle disks, the capped individual and a bird–helmeted individual. Both of these images occur in the sky band of another late stela, Ixlu Stela 1 (Morley 1937: pl. 158), but also floating in the sky band are mannikin figures of GIII of the Palenque Triad, marked with a scroll–topped jaguar helmet, and GI, marked with a shell ear plug. Mannikin portrayal of the ancestral hero twins of the Maya is relatively rare but occurs, for example, in a series of stelae at the site of Xultun (Von Euw 1978). In summary, the syncretism found at Chichen Itza is paralleled by syncretistic images on Late Classic Southern stelae in Peten, Guatemala. It is perhaps more than coincidental that Ixlu and Ucanal both lie on the plausible transportation route running along the base of the peninsula connecting the western and eastern river drainages via the lakes district.

SOUTHERN LOWLANDS

The notion that "Toltec" Chichen Itza might have been contemporary with the Terminal Classic polities of the Southern lowlands inevitably turns the discussion to continuities below the 18th parallel, and to the nature of routes connecting the north and south in the centuries of the collapse and its immediate aftermath. Andrews and Robles C. refer to the possibility that peoples of the Sotuta sphere jumped around the section of northern coastline held by Coba via the island of Cozumel. Substantial deposits of Sotuta ceramics were found on Cozumel both by Robles C. (this volume, and personal communication) and by the Harvard–Arizona Cozumel Project (Sabloff and Rathje 1975a). In addition, I excavated part of what appears to be a "patio–quad" structure (D. Chase and A. Chase 1982) at the site of Chen Cedral on Cozumel and discovered a Sotuta offering containing green obsidian blades as well. The patio–quad structure is peculiar to the site of Chichen Itza and was likely a special form of elite residence there (Freidel 1981). The Chases (1982) have reported the presence of another patio–quad structure at the site of Nohmul in northern Belize, in association with Sotuta, Cehpech, and Terminal Classic Southern lowland ceramics. Nohmul is situated in an advantageous position to control major river routes into the interior, especially the Rio Hondo.

Other sites in northern Belize also show persistence of occupation and monumental construction through the collapse period. Lamanai, at the head of the New River, is discussed by Pendergast and Loten in this volume. Lamanai not only survives the collapse, but appears to flourish while such nearby centers as Altun Ha (Pendergast 1981a) have been abandoned. Major architectural projects are initiated at Lamanai in Terminal Classic times, and other monuments are maintained or refurbished. The preliminary evidence from Lamanai suggests a marked perpetuation of Southern lowland Classic organization and culture with little direct intrusion of "Toltec" materials, a situation analogous to that found at Coba in the north.

Clearly there is no single network of relations linking the flourishing northern polities to communities in the south experiencing survival of the collapse. The multi—roomed "range" or palace masonry structures erected at Lamanai during the Terminal Classic, reflecting a centuries—old indigenous tradition, carry elaborate polychrome facades which strongly resemble in their range of colors the facades of contemporary buildings at the site of Seibal on the far side of the Southern region. In both these cases, there is evidence of foreign influence in the art and portable artifacts, but neither connect directly with Chichen Itza and the Sotuta sphere. And yet, whatever the local factors might be in the persistence of the Lamanai polity through the collapse, participation in some kind of trans—peninsular network across the lakes district, right through the area showing syncretism with Chichen Itza, appears to be an equally telling force. The mechanics of this discontinuous geographical pattern of affinities is a major challenge to scholars working on the Postclassic.

Lamanai not only flourishes through the collapse period, but continues to function as a center through the Postclassic and the collapse of Coba and Chichen Itza. Beginning in the twelfth century, the site witnesses the elaboration of a modeled effigy ceramic complex which provides a link between the effigy censer tradition of the Southern Classic communities and the famous pottery idols of the Late Postclassic period found throughout the peninsula. Whatever accommodations Lamanai was making to foreigners on and off the peninsula, it was perpetuating the Southern Classic Maya culture and organization which enjoys something of a revival in Late Postclassic times. Despite the substantial and pervasive disjunctions of the Postclassic era, Lamanai provides a thread of continuity linking the Classic cultures to the ethnohistorical Maya of the Spanish conquest period.

Several contributors to this volume deal with the chain of lakes across the center of the Department of Peten in Guatemala, and bear on the issue of continuity through the collapse. Arlen Chase hypothesizes the existence of resident populations in the Lake Peten–Itza area through Terminal Classic into Early Postclassic times. For the most part, Chase bases his arguments for continuity on ceramics and particularly the perpetuation of utility ware forms from Terminal Classic into Early Postclassic times. Certain fine wares, however, such as Augustine effigy–footed vessels and possibly Trapeche Pink, appear to span this transition. Although the associations are tentative, it seems that Terminal Classic architecture was continuously modified and occupied into Early Postclassic times in the western sector of Tayasal. Indeed, this area maintains significant populations through the later Postclassic period.

Chase notes the presence of distinctive large, low platforms dating to Early Postclassic times here analogous to platforms found at the Late Postclassic site of Santa Rita in Belize. Such platforms are also a common occurrence in Postclassic communities of the northeastern part of the peninsula and on Cozumel island (Freidel 1976). On Cozumel, such platforms show continuous construction back into Terminal Classic times. Although the evidence is preliminary, there are grounds for Chase's suggestion that the well–documented ethnohistoric populations of the lakes district resulted from a merging of migrants with an established set of communities which survived the collapse, rather than an entirely new group of outsiders. It is a hypothesis which raises again the old question of why some parts of the lowlands, such as the northeastern Peten, experience virtual abandonment while others, such as the lakes district and the river drainages, appear to maintain populations in the same period.

Chase also reports the unanticipated discovery of a "Toltec" style stela and associated Early Postclassic tradewares under the modern Flores Church area. The "diving god" description of the monument suggests that it might fall into the iconographic program discussed previously in regard to Terminal Classic Southern lowland and "Toltec" Chichen Itza syncretism. This is another hint that a network of communities across the Southern lowlands was being maintained through the period of the collapse with affinities to the northern flourishing polities. Such an overland trade route, tying in with the otherwise predominantly coastal networks of the north, is well documented for the ethnohistorical period. A strip of viable polities in the south may have survived the collapse because of their role in long-distance commerce.

Intensive research in the lakes district has also been carried out by Pru and Don Rice, as reported in their contribution to this volume and in related papers (D. Rice and P. Rice 1982; D. Rice 1981, n.d.). In general, their research offers further evidence for the persistence of Classic populations in the lakes district through the collapse which decimated such communities as Tikal to the north in Peten. On the one hand, there is again evidence of continuities in ceramic assemblages spanning Terminal Classic to Early Postclassic times; on the other, there are continuities in the occupation of centers from Terminal Classic into the Postclassic.

Although only alluded to in this report, Don Rice's architecture data suggest to him that while there are local residual populations around the lakes surviving the collapse, new intrusive groups are registered in the form of C–shaped, benched single–room buildings and long, open–sided colonnaded buildings. The C–shaped benched building, presumably a dwelling in most cases, is the typical house form at the site of Seibal during its Terminal Classic florescence. The possible connection between Lamanai and Seibal has already been mentioned, and here is a promising link between these distant sites. It is worth noting that the C–shaped benched structure plan is well represented at several sites on Cozumel Island, dating from Terminal Classic through the Late Postclassic (Freidel 1976; Sabloff and Freidel 1975).

While D. Rice regards the open–sided colonnaded building as intrusive to the lakes area, I suspect that this building form, which becomes pan–peninsular in later Postclassic times, can be viewed as a derivation from the simpler "range" structures found in middle echelon elite residence groups of the Classic period (Haviland 1965). Rice notes that when such buildings occur at Terminal Classic centers, as at Ixlu for example, they are placed without regard for previous group plans (i.e., in the middle of open courtyards). While it is reasonable to suggest on this basis that we are dealing with groups intrusive to such sites, there is no reason to derive such groups from distant areas if local prototypes are to be found in Peten immediately to the north of the lakes. Refugees from the great communities might well be expected to bring with them their traditional house forms. The C–shaped building, on the other hand, lacks any prototype, and is best regarded as intrusive. This kind of amalgam of local and nonlocal is in keeping with what the Chases report elsewhere in the lakes district. The Rices report a gradual diminishing of occupation through the Early Postclassic which ends in an upswing in Late Postclassic times, perhaps registering the temporary denouement in regional networks accompanying the collapse of great northern polities at the end of the Early Postclassic in the north, Chichen Itza and Coba in particular.

PERIPHERIES

Other hints of continuity through the period of the collapse come from the peripheries of the lowlands. Sharer notes that while Classic Maya ritual activity virtually ceases in the center of Quirigua, monumental construction either continues or is restarted soon after this termination. Sharer also notes that a *chacmool*, a throne or sacrificial block typical of Chichen Itza, was found at Quirigua suggesting links with the Sotuta sphere. E. Graham observes that the site of Mayflower in the Stann Creek district of Belize evinces continued central construction through the Terminal Classic/Early Postclassic transition. The Stann Creek district offers yet another avenue into the interior from the eastern coast. Ball suspects ceramic continuity through the collapse period in western Campeche, although the evidence is very circumstantial.

RESPONSES TO THE CRISIS

The importance of the preliminary data favoring survival of the collapse in some parts of the Southern lowlands lies in its context: the most devastating demographic and cultural disjunction prehistoric Mesoamerica ever experienced. The survivors stand out in the midst of ruin and the value of their record is in providing more clues to the causes of the general disaster. The magnitude and nature of the collapse are the subject of several contributions in this volume.

From the perspective of the central peninsular region and the center of Becan, Ball offers evidence that the few survivors in that region might be almost invisible, as a result of an economic collapse so penetrating that the survivors gave up the use of pottery for a time. This is an argument of significant proportions, for it attempts to distinguish the cultural from the demographic dimensions of the collapse. In a region in which pottery has been used for some three thousand years, archaeologists have come to identify occupation in a time period primarily on the basis of diagnostic ceramics. If groups gave up pottery, they would be virtually invisible until other means of detecting them were devised. The prospect of non-pottery using populations in the lowlands is an epistemological nightmare, but even were this the case, it seems likely that vast areas of the lowlands, including the central peninsula, were suffering eventual demographic decline because we witness no ultimate resurgence of culture in these areas later in the Postclassic. It is noteworthy that the central peninsular region lacks the extensive swamps of northeastern Peten and yet also collapsed decisively.

The Uaymil region, to the east of the central peninsular area, also suffers severely in Terminal Classic times. Fry's discussion of this region raises a number of important issues. Monumental architecture of the Late Classic period is partially dismantled and buried by much cruder architecture of the Lobil phase. Fry makes the case that this destruction and replacement is carried out by surviving populations indigenous to the region, populations still producing ceramics diagnostic of the Terminal Classic. Fry suggests that this radical change in central activity might register a revitalization movement. The notion that there might be abrupt changes in culture in the context of indigenous populations is very important theoretically (cf. G. Jones and Kautz 1981a) for archaeology, and for the Maya in particular (Freidel 1981).

There is the problem, however, of whether revitalization is the right word to cover such rapid and radical episodes. As Fry points out, revitalization most generally refers to a case of crisis precipitated by overwhelming acculturative pressure by a dominant society on a simpler one. While there is everywhere evidence of outside influence on the lowland Maya from Terminal Classic times onwards, the kind of domination appropriate to this use of revitalization as a concept is problematic even in the best of cases, such as Chichen Itza. Evidence for such intrusion is generally lacking in the Uaymil region where the Lobil phase occurs. Granting, for the sake of argument, that Fry correctly identifies the Lobil phenomenon as immediately following the Late Classic florescence in the Uaymil region, the result might be a cultural pathology very similar to that found in some documented cases of revitalization, but resulting from internal collapse rather than acculturative pressure. If this is the case, then the Lobil phase provides a useful example in a spectrum of responses to pan–peninsular crisis, a spectrum including such successful resolutions as those taken by Lamanai, Coba, and Chichen Itza at the other end.

The question then becomes, why did the Uaymil communities respond in a fashion that was pathological and led rapidly to abandonment of the region, while other regions and communities survived and flourished? As Harrison (1978) has noted, the Uaymil region contains much swampland which preliminary data suggest was used for intensive, raised field agriculture. As in northeastern Peten, refugee populations appear to move out of the swampland into neighboring areas, in the case at hand, to the east coast of the peninsula. Although regions away from the swamps, such as the central peninsula, clearly suffer collapse as well, the swamplands are emerging as particularly vulnerable. Resolution of this pattern requires reliable means of distinguishing cultural from demographic disjunction.

While such resolution may hold a vital key to the nature of the general crisis, such distinction will be hard to wrest from the record.

The spectrum of responses to the crisis which resulted in survival rather than total collapse and abandonment allows us to investigate disjunction in the context of continuity. The situation described by Sharer at Quirigua suggests a very basic demographic continuity in the community combined with a profound disjunction in elite material culture. Here the principles of hierarchical organization have survived to provide labor to build central structures, but the power is in the hands of people who are not participating in Classic Maya culture. There are hints that these people have relations with the Sotuta sphere, but their relations with the local population, foreign conquerors, or locals eschewing the ways of their dead elite remain a pressing empirical issue.

Disjunction at Lamanai is much more subtle and takes the form of a gradual introduction of new ceramic types, use of a wider range of colors in polychrome architectural decoration than usually favored in earlier Classic times, and the use of colonnaded doorways on public buildings. Here we can envision an essentially Southern lowland Maya Classic community making minor accommodations to the pressures of change from without. A similar situation, on a much grander scale, occurs at Coba. The pan–peninsular crisis, whatever its causes, is definitely permeating the linkages between the vast array of participating communities in the Southern lowland tradition. What local circumstances allowed these centers to survive virtually intact while related centers around them went down? Pendergast suspects that Lamanai forged new alliances with the flourishing Terminal Classic communities of the north, the Puuc region in particular. Ceramics suggest that Coba, too, was tied into these communities. But if minor accommodation to new centers of power was the key to survival, we might expect to find simply a shift in the tides of dominance in elite material culture from north to south, rather than the widespread collapse which occurs. Particularly strong local economy or strategic position on regional networks are the kinds of local conditions which might tip the balance in favor of survival. The pattern implies, however, that we must examine the crisis on a case–by–case basis before arriving at useful generalizations at the regional level.

Disjunction among the surviving centers and populations of the lakes district and the Pasion drainage of Peten takes the form of a substantial influx of new ceramic types, architectural forms, and new images in elite material culture such as monumental stelae. Willey and Sabloff (1976) argued for outright invasion of the Southern lowlands by more vital marginal groups and the weight of evidence supports such intrusion (cf. Sabloff 1973; J. Graham 1973; Willey and Shimkin 1973; D. Rice n.d.). At the same time, these survivors do not experience complete erasure of their elite material culture, as in the case of Quirigua. Rather, there are indications of an attempt to graft new production systems and new leadership onto the Southern Classic sociopolitical order.

The iconographic syncretism of the Terminal Classic Southern lowlands does not display a simple parody of earlier greatness through the manipulation of dead symbols by the ignorant. It is rather a positive and creative, if desperate, attempt by surviving Southern elite to rejuvenate the theological structure of political power at the local level through the adoption of religious concepts from neighbors whose destiny is clearly on the ascendancy. Insofar as these foreign neighbors to the north and west are in a position of dominance, this situation might properly fit the definition of revitalization movement as discussed by Fry. But here the disjunction with the past is by no means so radical as that evidenced in the Lobil phase. Moreover, syncretism clearly characterizes the flourishing communities of the Puuc region as strongly as the failing communities of the south, and this is one likely source for the foreigners operating in the south.

Can this northern florescence be considered as a successful revitalization? Andrews and Robles C. discount the prospect of outright foreign conquest and domination of the Puuc region in favor of international alliance between lowlanders and outsiders, so again this situation does not fit the strict definition of revitalization. Even the more radical disjunctions found at Chichen Itza, which Andrews and Robles C. attribute to outside conquest, incorporate indigenous traditions of architectural technique, ceramic style, settlement plan, and elite symbolism. If the "Itza" are indeed foreigners, then they are as much absorbed by the local traditions as they are perpetuators of a foreign culture. There are no vastly superior states elsewhere in Mesoamerica in this time period which could instigate a true revitalization response in the Maya lowlands. The syncretic disjunctions found in the record point to mutual acculturation between lowlanders and outsiders, the breakdown of cultural insularity on the peninsula and the incorporation of the surviving Maya into a pan–Mesoamerican elite culture.

SPECIFIC CLASSIC–TO–POSTCLASSIC TIES

If mutual acculturation and syncretism characterize the Terminal Classic/Early Postclassic transition in a range from moderate accom-

modation through full–scale transformation, then it should be possible to discern features of Late Postclassic lowland society which
derive ultimately from the Classic period. Diane Chase's contribution bears on this issue. Her preliminary findings at Santa Rita in
Belize suggest that the effigy censers were integral to the circulation
of political power among elite households. As discussed previously
in the context of Lamanai, there is good potential for linking this
effigy censer complex to the Classic modeled censer tradition. In the
Classic period, such censers feature both gods and rulers, and as a
complex they are clearly part of the material paraphernalia of politics. While the Late Postclassic censers evidently focus exclusively
on deities, there is the prospect of general continuity in form and
function from the Classic period.

There are many intriguing possibilities in this linkup. The year–
bearer annual ceremonies and *katun*–ending ceremonies discussed
by Diane Chase are ethnohistorically described as involving a quadripartite cosmic scheme, a quadripartite arrangement of noble families
in neighborhoods or territorial units (cf. Marcus 1973), and a recruitment of representatives from these constituencies into positions of
official power in central governments. The material connection with
the effigy censer complex opens the possibility that such a quadripartite scheme for the regular recruitment of government officials
operated in the Classic period in a way amenable to archaeological
documentation. In lieu of needed contextual investigation, it would
be well worth the effort to analyze the specific changes and continuities in the iconographic programs of the censer complexes.

Johnson's spatial analysis of the Late Postclassic communities
on Topoxte, Cante, and Paxte islands in Peten documents the absence of regular structure and group orientation of the kind typical
at such great Classic centers as Tikal. He views these communities
as growing by accretion rather than by any overall plan. This is in
keeping with other evidence of in–migration into the lakes district
during the Postclassic. As argued previously, however, it is possible
that the central colonnade plan derives from Classic period simple
"range" or place structure types. The central location of a plan found
dispersed in the Classic communities is perhaps significant; the
middle range of hierarchy may be surviving as the leaders, following
the ultimate failure of the Terminal Classic attempts at syncretistic
accommodation by the highest authorities. On these islands, as elsewhere in the Late Postclassic, the modeled effigy censers are the
prominent form of ritual and political paraphernalia. The survival
and florescence of the effigy censer complex, and related full figure
representations of deities on murals and carved monuments, com-

bined with the virtual extinction of the cult of the ruler in the Southern lowlands as displayed on stelae, pyramids, and a panoply of portable objects, suggest to me that the elements of political religion carried from the Classic into the Late Postclassic are those pertaining to councilors, priests, and ritual advisors, the educated but non-royal leaders of communities making up the Classic polity.

One certain legacy from the Classic into the Late Postclassic period is literacy and the distinctive Maya hieroglyphic form of writing. Only a handful of native manuscripts survived the Spanish conquest, but one, the Dresden Codex, is generally regarded as a copy of an earlier Classic period work. This and the other fragments of Maya books show a distinct format and focus on full figure representation of deities, a subject focus which contrasts significantly with the focus on rulers and disembodied head portrayal of deities in the monumental and imperishable mediums (with the notable exception of painted pottery, which seems more closely related to the codices).

Is it possible that books provided a key medium for the survival of Classic theological and political precepts into the Late Postclassic? In his discussion of temporal sequences on the east coast of the peninsula, Arthur Miller provides a potential clue to the nature of this continuity. His earliest mural painting style, which he dates to the time of the collapse, appears to be crude and experimental. This style, however, evidently develops into a more refined one dating to the centuries immediately following the collapse, which he calls the "codex" style because in format and composition it shows strong resemblances to surviving codices. Miller hypothesizes that the inspiration and guide for this style derive from existing codices, and its subject matter follows as full figure deity portrayal. Eventually, this style is succeeded on the east coast by a distinctive one represented most powerfully at the Late Postclassic center of Tulum. This later style differs in many ways, but maintains a focus on full figure deities. Moreover, this later style shows clear iconographic ties to the Late Postclassic effigy censer complex, suggesting an interplay between these media by this time period. Miller is of the opinion that changes in the archaeological record of this region correlate with ethnohistorically documented invasions from without, and no doubt there are data supporting external contact (Miller 1982). Nevertheless, there is the prospect of continuity in his sequence linking the Classic to the Late Postclassic.

Maya literacy was thoroughly suppressed by the Spaniards and with good reason: the sacred lore in the conquest period continued to be a focus of rebellion in the hands of native elite. Jones, Kautz, and Graham have been investigating the Maya–Spanish community

of Tipu in Belize, a frontier between the Spanish—held and independent Maya states situated in Yucatan and Peten. Although the linkage between the Postclassic and the contact period Maya is not securely demonstrated, the evidence again points to persistence of
some particular categories of material culture; specifically, the continued use of Lacandon—type deity censers may be interpreted as indicative of syncretism in ritual activities. On the one hand, there is a
church in the community; on the other, there is a pagan temple
complex which, even if not operational, was clearly remembered.

No doubt Spanish control of Tipu was never very great, and
pagan political—religious forms of the "apostate Maya" enjoyed
regular resurgence here. Nevertheless, similar pagan rituals must
have been carried out on more firmly held Spanish territory to elicit
the brutal suppression of the auto—da—fe and the Inquisition. Tipu
perhaps registers just how weak and transformed the dominant culture of the Spaniards is outside the immediate centers of power in
the centuries following the contact. If a clearly superior invading
force determined to conquer can have such limited impact, how
should we judge the precolumbian intrusions and contacts from the
Gulf Coast and Mexico in Maya lowland country? I suspect that
there was more cooperation and less resistance to produce the syncretism found in the record.

Invasion and Alliance

It has been virtually impossible for me to extricate the theme of
continuity and disjunction from that of invasion versus alliance
with outsiders. Clearly this is because external contact is a major determinant of change when dealing with any regional expression of a
larger "nuclear" civilization such as found in Mesoamerica. Nevertheless, there are two papers in this volume reporting on areas outside the lowlands which provide an appropriate shift in gears from
the first to the second major theme.

Brown's evidence from the Quiche region of highland Guatemala challenges the traditional conception of strong links between
the Maya lowlands and highlands in Early Postclassic times. The essential point of his construct is that much of the evidence for external contact between highland Maya country and Mexico need not go
through lowland Maya territory, but can be viewed as the result of
waxing and waning trade alliances between more or less stable populations in those primary areas, with perhaps the Pacific coastal region as the major intermediary. This is a provocative and stimulating scenario, and one which fits with the general tenor of previous

arguments in this summary favoring more communication and less actual influx of new populations into Maya country. The fact remains, both here and in the lowlands, that native documents of the contact period time and again refer to invasion by conquering foreigners. Indeed, the famous Quiche Popol Vuh or Book of Council (Edmonson 1971) stipulates that the Quiche rulers were foreign conquerors. These ethnohistorical documents have been the mainstay of invasion and conquest scenarios in the Maya Postclassic. While empirical identification for or against such interpretations must be fought out, literally, in the trenches, they provide an historical leitmotif worthy of intrinsic examination. To take Brown's position, if migration and conquest stories actually mask long–distance alliances occurring periodically between Maya and non-Maya, why is this the case?

Brown suggests that the Quiche myths register remembrance of the great international alliances of the Middle Classic period when Teotihuacan had ties with Kaminaljuyu. This is one possibility to be sure, but it seems likely to me that these migration myths are at least partly based in historical fact on the one hand and reflect a general means of legitimizing elite authority on the other. The Mexica prominently display their peregrinations in their political histories, and the myths of wandering Quetzalcoatl are widely distributed in Mesoamerica.

Because migration does not seem to be part of the iconographic interests of the great city of Teotihuacan, it is possible that such mythical support for authority dates from the time of the diaspora from that city and the establishment of new bases of power in such centers as Tula, Cholula, Xochicalco, and Cacaxtla. The migrations might then register attempts to bolster local power by means of establishing historical connections with the "master builders" of the great city. The Mexica focus on their own migrations might then register syncretism between an actual migration and a previously established political means of legitimizing rise to power. Applying such reasoning to the Maya case, both lowland and highland, the same kind of syncretism might involve the actual population movements of the collapse period with an adopted means of legitimizing power through connections with external nobility, a nobility ultimately descended from the great Middle Classic Teotihuacanos.

Such a scenario, in which Terminal Classic populations migrate from the Southern lowlands into the highlands in conjunction with a general period of syncretism to highland Mexican cultural means of legitimizing power, might account for the migration myths of the Quiche and other Maya-speaking groups in the highlands. It would also account for the strong connections between the hero twin genesis myth of the Quiche Popol Vuh and the political-theological charters of the Southern lowland Classic Maya as currently being reconstructed iconographically and epigraphically (Schele 1976).

In this regard, it is perhaps telling that at Yaxchilan several stelae show a conjunction of the hero twins, Sun and Venus, with representations of the father and mother of the ruler displayed as the sun and moon (Schele, personal communication). Conflation of these images could account for the curious fact that in the Popol Vuh the younger brother of the twins is the moon instead of the sun, and the older brother is the sun instead of Venus. Indeed, the younger brother in the Popol Vuh is called Xbalanque, or "Jaguar" with a female affix ("x"). In Classic Maya theology, the sun is called jaguar and is male; here the moon is called jaguar and, as in Classic theology, it is female. Such confusion might well arise among groups attempting to maintain a grasp on the religion of their forebears without fully comprehending its intricacies.

At the very least, the Popol Vuh registers a syncretism of Southern lowland Classic theology with a migration myth concept employed prominently in highland Mexico. From the kind of modest lifestyle evinced by apparent lowland refugee populations in the Peten lakes district and elsewhere, one would not expect migrants from the lowlands into the Maya highlands to bring florescence and international commerce with them. On the other hand, one might well expect the defensive settlement patterns which come into vogue in the Quiche region at this time, analogous to the settlement on islands in Peten. Evidence from the lowlands suggests that inter–regional networks were severely curtailed in the south and that populations were relatively isolated, in keeping with Brown's interpretations of the Quiche region in Terminal Classic/Early Postclassic transition times. Finally, Brown notes the presence of Late Classic and possibly Terminal Classic Southern lowland ceramics in the Quiche region, suggesting at least a connection in the time of the collapse. In sum, the genesis myth of the Quiche suggests that they are cultural heirs of the Southern Classic Maya, a civilization clearly evincing population movement and migration in the collapse period; the migration myth itself shows connections to highland Mexico, but might as well show a mythical means of legitimizing local power as a historical reality. Whether this myth was adopted by Southern lowlanders in the Terminal Classic and brought with them to the highlands, or has deeper time depth in the highlands as argued by Brown, remains to be empirically resolved. The fact remains that this Mexican myth is being used by culturally and linguistically

Maya peoples, and this in itself argues for syncretic adoption rather than actual long–distance migration.

Wonderley's report on research in the Ulua region provides an intriguing defense of the importance of invasion and conquest in the Maya Postclassic. Working from ethnohistorical documents indicating the presence of foreign elite elements and a mosaic of ethnic enclaves in the area, Wonderley offers archaeological data and methods for identifying such ethnic diversity in prehistoric contexts. Wonderley posits foreign elites which are small, relatively mobile, and relatively detached from their subservient populations, bearing a parasitic economic relationship to them without fundamentally impinging on their lifestyle. The notion of small, mobile, and predatory elite groups is generally corroborated ethnohistorically in the documents of the Acalan–Tixchel groups (Scholes and Roys 1948). Those elite groups are, however, at most Mexicanized or "internationalized" Maya rather than newcomers to the peninsula. J.E.S. Thompson hypothesized that the elites of the Postclassic peninsula could be generally derived from such mobile groups of marginal Maya, the Putun (Thompson 1970), with a homeland in Tabasco and southwestern Campeche. Drawing on analogy from Africa, Wonderley suggests a "dual mode of production" for the Postclassic lowlands, in which elite foreigners are maintaining commerce and locals are interested primarily in subsistence.

Although Wonderley's model seems to fit the particular case of the Ulua region well, there are difficulties in extending it to cover the lowlands. The kind of ethnic diversity found in the Ulua region historically is not found on the peninsula, where instead there are large blocks of single dialect speakers and virtually all of the inhabitants speak Mayan languages. To be sure, there are complicated and partially disjunctive patterns in the distribution of artifact types, pottery styles, architectural plans, tool shapes, and so forth, but it is difficult to assign these patterns to distinctive ethnic groups because they do not factor out as coherent assemblages. Rather, they overlap in a variety of ways. We have seen, for example, that while Cehpech ceramics are found over most of the northern peninsula in Terminal Classic times, the architecture of the Puuc hills region and Coba are discernibly distinctive. Not only is this true of geographic patterns; it is also the case with putative elite versus commoner segments within communities and regions. The traditional model of cultural homogeneity on the peninsula, for any period, fails in the face of such diversity. At the same time, we are far from certain how to qualify this diversity socially and culturally. I shall return to this theme again shortly.

Ethnohistorically, the Late Postclassic Maya did indeed espouse a foreign heritage and did try to assert that they were ethnically different from commoners. In actuality, they shared their names with commoners, their daily material culture differed little in kind, and they worshipped the same Maya gods, although they made an exclusive cult of Kukulcan/Quetzalcoatl. In brief, the Maya nobility shared a "cult of foreignness" rather than a foreign culture. It is quite reasonable to suppose that the origins of such a cult lie at least partially in actual incursions onto the peninsula by successfully dominant foreign groups. The broad assimilation of such groups into Maya culture, basically indigenous, however much syncretized and transformed, suggests that the groups were small, representative of profitable connections of an economic nature to societies off the peninsula, and allied with indigenous Maya nobility. The "cult of foreignness" may well have been a significant ideological schism between noble and commoner, with implications for the relatively dispersed and architecturally diminished political and religious buildings of the Late Postclassic era (Freidel and Cliff 1978), but it seems unlikely to have been a real ethnic division. At the same time, alliance with foreigners must have been a driving force in Postclassic Maya society for such a cult to have flourished.

Perhaps the strongest argument for direct invasion and military conquest can be made for Chichen Itza, as discussed by Andrews and Robles C. They point to the strategic deployment of Sotuta–related sites along the coast, commanding both the salt trade and, more generally, canoe traffic vital to inter–regional commerce. There can be no question of the military tenor of this site displayed in warriors and battle scenes. The elite material culture of Chichen Itza shows definite ties to the Gulf Coast region and to highland Mexico, and it is reasonable to suppose that such foreigners involved in the rise of this military state came from these areas.

While it seems undeniable that foreign participation was vital to the consolidation of the Chichen Itza polity, it is very difficult to defend the notion that these foreigners were either emissaries from vastly superior states or that they imposed their will upon a totally resistant native population. In the first place, Chichen is as substantial and cosmopolitan a city as can be found in the Mesoamerica of its era; it cannot realistically be viewed as a satellite to any contemporary foreign state. Second, architectural and ceramic techniques, many political and religious symbols, hieroglyphic writing, and settlement patterns all show substantial derivation from local antecedents on the peninsula: Chichen Itza is as much a Maya city as it is a foreign one. The syncretism at Chichen Itza, the assimilation of foreign concepts and materials into a Maya framework, suggests that the success of the polity was due as much to active collaboration between Maya and foreigner as to coercive imposition of a new order. Whether we are dealing with a successful conquest by a relatively small and rapidly assimilated group of foreigners or with an alliance of foreigners and Maya bent on forging a new kind of military state in the lowlands may not be resolvable archaeologically. Questions of invasion or alliance aside, Chichen Itza was a new kind of international Maya state based upon military conquest and principles of warfare quite different from those of the Classic Maya. The success of this state no doubt inspired much of the "cult of foreignness" found in Late Postclassic society.

In general, external influence in Maya lowland civilization registers strongly and pervasively from Terminal Classic times to the Spanish conquest. In light of the collapse, this might be regarded as the product of a weakened and more vulnerable group of societies. But the florescence of the Puuc region, Chichen Itza, and other polities following the collapse suggest that internalization was as much a new instrument of power as a sign of decay. Moreover, the same kind of eclecticism and syncretism was occurring all over civilized Mesoamerica, not just among the lowland Maya: if the Maya were subject to external influence, they were also a source of it. This interplay will continue to challenge specialists on the Postclassic for some time to come.

Cultural Mosaics and Kaleidoscopes

The geography of the Maya lowlands provides few natural frontiers. This environment, combined with evidence of broadly shared material culture in the region from Preclassic times onwards, has made it easy to consider the peninsula as a Maya culture area. On the other hand, it has always been difficult to delineate societies within the lowlands and to isolate inter–polity from intra–polity relationships. In light of the varied regional and community responses to the crisis of the Terminal Classic, students of the Postclassic are particularly pressed to address this issue.

There is a general trend, summarized by Ball (1979a, 1979b), toward envisioning a set of distinctive subregional cultural expressions operating contemporaneously on the peninsula: Terminal Classic Southern polities, Puuc polities, the state of Chichen Itza, the polity of Coba, and the central peninsular Rio Bec polities. The actual degree of overlap between these subregional cultures is a matter of considerable debate, and most specialists still regard the set as time transgressive, moving from Terminal Classic Southern polities contemporary with the central peninsular group of communities, overlapping with the Puuc communities, which in turn overlap with the Chichen Itza state, with Coba persisting through this whole sequence. Some evidence favoring contemporaneity between Chichen Itza in its "Toltec" phase and the Terminal Classic Southern lowland polities has already been discussed in previous sections of this essay. This kind of "total overlap" would throw existing chronological frameworks for the last six centuries of lowland prehistory into chaos.

The principle of "overlap" or geographic coexistence of distinctive subregional lowland societies depends upon the establishment of cross–ties in certain ubiquitous artifact categories, such as pottery and architecture, which show that stratigraphic phases are contemporary at given sites. If the overall assemblages are significantly different but contain such cross–ties, then we are dealing with a cultural mosaic.

Andrews and Robles C. show this principle in operation. Coba and the Puuc region generally share the Cehpech ceramic sphere, but their monumental art and architecture are quite different. Sotuta sphere ceramics of the Chichen Itza polity are not found within the Coba sphere of influence as this can be detected through inter–site masonry causeways, a traditional means of demarcating political alliance in northern Yucatan (Kurjack and Andrews V 1976), but are found around its borders. Evidence from Coba suggests that Cehpech ceramics are still in use and construction at the site is continuing through the time period traditionally assigned to the Sotuta ceramics. Moreover, Sotuta and Cehpech ceramics have been found together in some deposits elsewhere (D. Chase and A. Chase 1982). In essence, the Cehpech ceramics of Coba and the Sotuta ceramics of Chichen Itza show a complementary geographic pattern with intermixture at the border areas.

Ball, in his two contributions to this volume, addresses some of the current problems in the epistemology of ceramic chronologies brought out by such arguments. It can no longer be assumed that the absence of detectable change in ceramic inventory, as found in some cases from southwestern Campeche, represents a hiatus in occupation: it might represent a developmental plateau in ceramic style and technique. Nor can it be assumed that distinctive ceramic assemblages are not contemporary: the distribution of styles and techniques might well register hostile and contending socioeconomic networks. Alternatively, persistence of ceramic assemblages into periods characterized by later ones might register relative isolation of the first from primary trade networks.

The reevaluation of the space–time dynamics of ceramics will inevitably compromise tacit assumptions of constant change and automatic geographic distribution so useful to Mayanists in their chronological framework. The trade–off for losing pottery as an independent time–marker is that it can now be used to detect actual social, economic, and political relationships between communities, as a gauge for conscious and deliberate interaction. Arlen Chase pursues this prospect in his discussion of contemporary Late Postclassic interaction spheres in the lakes district of Peten; Elizabeth Graham discusses the implications of such interpretation for Postclassic fine wares from the perspective of south coastal Belize. The Rices investigate changing economic networks through time in Peten from the vantage of ceramics. Finally, Ball suggests that occupation around Becan may have persisted after a complete collapse of ceramic production, the most extreme demonstration of the contingent and dependent position of pottery–using behavior in the larger scheme of Maya life. There is a veritable revolution underway in the interpretation and analysis of lowland ceramics, one that promises a richer and more realistic culture history. At the same time, future arguments of contemporaneity between sites are going to have to be based upon a much broader range of artifact categories and dating techniques.

Wonderley uses a cross–correlation of multiple artifact categories to suggest the existence of a fine–grained mosaic of ethnic groups in the Ulua region, and of a dual mode of production incorporating elite and commoner groups. The strength of the ethnic diversity model here lies primarily in the historical descriptions of the area at the time of the Spanish conquest, for the same pattern might as well register multiple overlapping networks of production–distribution–consumption among groups speaking the same language and sharing the same culture. While the ethnic mosaic model generally works well for the historically documented Maya groups of the southern highland region, the linguistic and cultural patterns of the lowlands generally emerge as large blocks of language speakers broadly sharing material culture. There are regional variations, to be sure. For example, the standard house type for Late Postclassic Cozumel is a single–roomed rectangular plan often with benches (Freidel 1976; Sabloff and Freidel 1975). In contrast, the northwestern Yucatan region favors the apsidal form in the same period (Kurjack 1974), and Mayapan displays the two–roomed rectangular plan.

This kind of variation might well have implications for ethnicity, but if there is a cultural mosaic on the peninsula, it is coarse grained and largely confined to the commoner class.

Barrera, like Wonderley, believes that careful cross–correlation of artifact categories will reveal socioeconomic class divisions. Reporting on the artifacts of Tulum on the east coast of the peninsula, Barrera notes that there are some artifact forms which occur both in exotic and local materials, for example, stone and shell axes. He suggests that such multiple media for tool types might reflect status–determined differential access to exotics. This is a sensible and promising avenue of inquiry. Unfortunately, Barrera's sample is drawn from contexts within the walled settlement of Tulum, a sector that might well be generally regarded as elite. With a broader sample of contexts, including architecturally modest households, this kind of analysis might allow useful qualification of elite–commoner distinctions. His preliminary findings tend to support Wonderley's dual mode of production scheme, but confident appraisal of the degree of integration or segregation of elite and commoner economic activities will require more contextual analysis of artifacts.

Overall, there is a clear trend toward viewing the lowlands as occupied by contemporaneous and distinctive cultural groups in the centuries following the collapse. Such subregional interaction spheres are being traced by a number of means, but an essential measure is the degree and quality of connections to other regions in Mesoamerica. It must thus be presumed that the heterogeneity displayed in post–collapse times is a result of changing external influence on lowland developments. Actually, the methods of measuring similarity and difference between subregions and sites are not contingent upon material content introduced from outside the lowlands. When such methods are applied to pre–collapse times, significant diversity is also found. Indeed, Mayanists have long recognized that the gross characterization of the lowlands as culturally homogeneous masks diversity (Andrews IV 1965a, 1973). The view of homogeneity results from weighting certain artifact categories which do show extensive networks of interaction and downplaying others. Copan and Palenque, for example, are both definitely participating in the lowland Classic theological and political order, but the ceramic assemblages from these sites are very different. When multiple artifact categories are used to map out interaction between sites and subregions, a very complicated set of overlapping networks emerges.

The practice of weighting certain artifact categories, such as monumental art and architecture, is no doubt warranted because they relate to political alliance of primary interest to the Maya themselves, but it would be misleading to break the lowlands down into a set of cultural subregions on this basis alone. It is significant, for example, that while Coba shows many ties in monumental art and architecture to the Southern lowland Classic polities, it participates in a ceramic interaction sphere connecting it to the Puuc sites, where monumental architecture and art are quite distinctive. These styles of the Puuc region, in turn, show strong ties to the Rio Bec central peninsular region (Potter 1977), where ceramics suggest links to the Peten early in the Late Classic period followed by a shift to northern ties later in that period. Each major artifact category can thus provide a different cultural geography when mapped out across the lowlands.

To be sure, some material features show general concentration in broadly defined subareas such as north versus south: for example, the use of carved stone stelae is a Southern trait. Nevertheless, any given subregion in the lowlands exhibits less a coherent and distinctive assemblage than a complicated layering of affinities to other subregions. While it is probable that sites and even subregions experienced isolation, on the whole the pre–collapse Maya polities were constantly adapting to neighbors on the peninsula. Perhaps it is better to view the lowlands as a cultural kaleidoscope rather than as a mosaic: shifting patterns of shared diagnostic material forms rather than spatially juxtaposed stable sets of them. No doubt there were ethnic divisions among the lowlanders and local perceptions of "we–they," but they appear to have been dynamic and changing through time. I suspect that as our patterns gain resolution, they will reveal extensive networks of alliances linking polities on strategic communication–transportation routes rather than territorial blocks.

The processes outlined for pre–collapse times make sense to me for the post–collapse period as well, harking back to the spectrum of responses to the crisis of Terminal Classic times. What has clearly changed is that during and following the collapse, lowland Maya are adapting as much to non-Maya societies as they are to each other. The lowland Maya always interacted with other civilized peoples in Mesoamerica, but on terms which left their regional culture generally intact. The Postclassic witnesses the dismantling of the "great wall" of cultural distinctiveness and the attempted incorporation of the lowlands into a Mesoamerican international culture.

The Dark Age

The ongoing research reported in this volume reveals an increasingly complicated Maya world in the second millennium A.D. The great collapse in the south is neither as complete nor as decisive as once thought; moreover, it is now part of an array of responses to crisis in the wider lowlands which includes florescence and persistence as well as decline. Whatever the environmental parameters of this crisis prove to be, and I have no doubt that they are instrumental in some fashion, the heart of the problem appears to be cultural identity. The general evolutionary trend in Mesoamerica, from the Middle Classic domination of the great city of Teotihuacan onward, was toward cultural unification following networks of political and economic alliance. There is every evidence that the Maya elite understood this trend and attempted to participate in it as the Classic period continued after the fall of Teotihuacan. In some instances they were successful, as in the case of the Puuc sites and Chichen Itza; in some instances they successfully resisted the trend, as at Coba.

In the last analysis, however, the elite carried neither the force of arms nor the persuasion to change the world view of their people from Maya to Mesoamerican. The general decline in the central control and deployment of social energy after Chichen Itza truly marks a dark age for a people no longer celebrating their own vision of the world and unable to accept a foreign one.

Bibliography

ADAMS, R. E. W.

1971   *The Ceramics of Altar de Sacrificios, Guatemala*, Papers of the Peabody Museum of Archaeology and Ethnology, No. 63(1), Harvard University, Cambridge.

1973   Maya Collapse: Transformation and Termination in the Ceramic Sequence at Altar de Sacrificios, in T.P. Culbert, Ed., *The Classic Maya Collapse*, pp. 133–163, University of New Mexico Press, Albuquerque.

1977   *Prehistoric Mesoamerica*, Little, Brown, and Co., Boston.

ADAMS, R. E. W. AND A. TRIK

1961   Temple I (Str. 5–1): Post Constructional Activities, *Tikal Reports* No. 7, Museum Monographs, University Museum, Philadelphia.

ADAMS, R. E. W. AND F. VALDEZ JR.

1980   The Ceramic Sequence of Colha, Belize: 1979 and 1980 Seasons, in T. Hester, J. Eaton, and H. Shafer, Eds., *The Colha Project Second Season, 1980 Interim Report*, pp. 15–40, Center for Archaeological Research, The University of Texas at San Antonio and Centro Studi e Ricerche Ligabue, Venezia.

AGRINIER, P.

1970   *Mound 20, Mirador, Chiapas, Mexico*, Papers of the New World Archaeological Foundation, No. 28, Provo.

1975   *Mounds 9 and 10 at Mirador, Chiapas, Mexico*, Papers of the New World Archaeological Foundation, No. 39, Provo.

1978   *A Sacrificial Mass Burial at Miramar*, Chiapas, Mexico, Papers of the New World Archaeological Foundation, No. 42, Provo.

ANDREWS, A. P.

1977a   Archaeological Mollusca from Tancah, Quintana Roo: A Brief Report, unpublished manuscript.

1977b   Reconocimiento Arqueologico de la Costa Norte del Estado de Campeche, *Boletin de la Escuela de Ciencias Antropologicas de la Universidad de Yucatan* 4(24): 64–77, Merida.

1978a   La Fauna Arqueologica de El Meco, Quintana Roo, unpublished manuscript.

1978b   Puertos Costeros del Postclasico Temprano en el norte de Yucatan, *Estudios de Cultura Maya* 11: 75–93.
1980   The Salt Trade of the Ancient Maya, *Archaeology* 33(4): 22–33.
1983   *Maya Salt Production and Trade*, The University of Arizona Press, Tucson.

ANDREWS, A. P. AND F. ROBLES CASTELLANOS
n.d.   Eds., *Excavaciones Arqueologicas en el Meco, Quintana Roo*, Instituto Nacional de Antropologia e Historia, Mexico.

ANDREWS IV, E. W.
1943   The Archaeology of Southwestern Campeche, *Contributions to American Anthropology and History* 8(40), Carnegie Institution of Washington, Publication 546, Washington, D.C.
1965a   Archaeology and Prehistory in the Northern Maya Lowlands, *Handbook of Middle American Indians* 2: 288–330, University of Texas Press, Austin.
1965b   Dzibalchaltun Program, *Middle American Research Records* 4: 23–67, Middle American Research Institute, Tulane University, Publication 40, New Orleans.
1969   *The Archaeological Use and Distribution of Mollusca in the Maya Lowlands*, Middle American Research Institute, Tulane University, Publication 34, New Orleans.
1973   The Development of Maya Civilization after the Abandonment of the Southern Cities, in T.P. Culbert, Ed., *The Classic Maya Collapse*, pp. 243–265, University of New Mexico Press, Albuquerque.

ANDREWS IV, E. W. AND A. P. ANDREWS
1975   *A Preliminary Study of the Ruins of Xcaret, Quintana Roo, Mexico*, Middle American Research Institute, Tulane University, Publication 31, New Orleans.

ANDREWS IV, E. W. AND E. W. ANDREWS V
1980   *Excavations at Dzibilchaltun, Yucatan, Mexico*, Middle American Research Institute, Publication 48, Tulane University, New Orleans.

ANDREWS IV, E. W., M. P. SIMMONS, E. S. WING, E. W. ANDREWS V, AND J. M. ANDREWS
1974   *Excavation of an Early Shell Midden on Isla Cancun, Quintana Roo, Mexico*, Middle American Research Institute, Tulane University, Publication 31, pp. 147–197, New Orleans.

ANDREWS V, E. W.
1979   Some Comments on Puuc Architecture of the Northern Yucatan Peninsula, in L. Mills, Ed., *The Puuc: New Perspectives*, pp. 1–17, Central College Press, Pella, Iowa.
1981   Dzibilchaltun, in J. A. Sabloff, Ed., *Supplement to the Handbook of Middle American Indians* 1: 313–341, University of Texas Press, Austin.

ANDREWS, G. F.
1975   *Maya Cities: Placemaking and Urbanization*, University of Oklahoma Press, Norman.

ARNOLD, J. E. AND A. FORD
1980   Statistical Examination of Settlement Patterns at Tikal, Guatemala, *American Antiquity* 45: 713–726.

ASHMORE, W.
1977   Research at Quirigua, Guatemala: Thé Site-Periphery Program, Paper Presented at the 42nd Annual Meeting of the Society for American Archaeology, New Orleans.
1981   Ed., *Lowland Maya Settlement Patterns*, University of New Mexico Press, Albuquerque.

ASHMORE, W. AND R. J. SHARER
1975   A Revitalization Movement at Late Classic Tikal, Paper presented at the Area Seminar in Ongoing Research, West Chester State College, Pennsylvania.
1978   Excavations at Quirigua, Guatemala: The Ascent of an Elite Maya Center, *Archaeology* 31(6): 10–19.

ASHMORE, W., E. M. SHORTMAN, AND R. J. SHARER
1983   The Quirigua Project: 1979 Season, *Quirigua Reports II*, pp. 55–68, Museum Monographs, University Museum, Philadelphia.

AVENDANO Y LOYOLA, A. DE
1696   Relacion de las Dos Entradas Que Hize a La Conversion de Los Gentiles Ytzaex y Cehaches, original ms. in Newberry Library, Chicago.

BABCOCK, T. F.
1980   Protohistoric Community Organization of a Quiche Center: Investigations into the Utatlan Residence Zone, Ph.D. Dissertation, Tulane University, New Orleans.

BALL, J. W.
1974   A Coordinate Approach to Northern Maya Prehistory: A.D. 700–1200, *American Antiquity* 39: 85–93.
1977a   *The Archaeological Ceramics of Becan, Campeche, Mexico*, Middle American Research Institute, Publication 43, Tulane University, New Orleans.
1977b   An Hypothetical Outline of Coastal Maya Prehistory: 300 B.C.– A.D. 1200, in N. Hammond, Ed., *Social Process in Maya Prehistory*, pp. 167–196, Academic Press, London.
1978   Archaeological Pottery of the Yucatan-Campeche Coast, *Middle American Research Institute*, Publication 46, pp. 69–146, Tulane University, New Orleans.
1979a   Ceramics, Culture History, and the Puuc Tradition: Some Alternative Possibilities, in L. Mills, Ed., *The Puuc: New Perspectives*, pp. 18–35, Central College Press, Pella, Iowa.
1979b   The 1977 Central College Symposium on Puuc Archaeology: A Summary View, in L. Mills, Ed., *The Puuc: New Perspectives*, pp. 46–51, Central College Press, Pella, Iowa.
1980   *The Archaeological Ceramics of Chinkultic, Chiapas, Mexico*, Papers of the New World Archaeological Foundation, No. 43, Provo.

1982   The Tancah Ceramic Situation: Cultural and Historical Insights from an Alternative Material Classic, Appendix I, in A. Miller, *On the Edge of the Sea: Mural Painting at Tancah-Tulum*, pp. 105–113, Dumbarton Oaks, Washington, D.C.

1983   Notes on the Distribution of Established Types in the Corozal District, Belize, in R. Sidrys, *Archaeological Excavations in Northern Belize, Central America*, UCLA Institute of Archaeology Monograph 17, pp. 203–220, University of California Press, Los Angeles.

BALL, J. W. AND J. D. EATON

1972   Marine Resources and the Prehistoric Lowland Maya: A Comment, *American Anthropologist* 74: 772–776.

BANCROFT, H. H.

1886   *The Works of Hubert Howe Bancroft, Vol. III, History of Central America, Vol. II, 1530–1800*, Reprinted McGraw-Hill, New York.

BARRERA RUBIO, A.

1977   Exploraciones Arqueologicas en Tulum, Quintana Roo, *Boletin de la Escuela de Ciencias Antropologicas de la Universidad de Yucatan*, Ano 4, no. 24: 23–63.

1980   Patron de Asentamiento en el Area de Uxmal, Yucatan, *XVI Mesa Redonda de la Sociedad Mexicana de Antropologia* (Saltillo, 1979) II: 389–398, Mexico.

BARRERA VASQUEZ, A.

1957   *Codice de Calkini*, Biblioteca Campechana No. 4, Campeche.

BAUDEZ, C. F. AND P. BECQUELIN

1973   *Archeologie de Los Naranjos, Honduras*, Mission Archeologique et Ethnologique Francaise au Mexique, Mexico.

BECKER, M.

1971   The Identification of a Second Plaza Plan at Tikal, Guatemala and Its Implications for Ancient Maya Social Complexity, Ph.D. Dissertation, Department of Anthropology, University of Pennsylvania.

BENAVIDES CASTILLO, A.

1976   El Sistema Prehispanico de Comunicaciones Terrestres en la Region de Coba, Quintana Roo, y sus Implicaciones Sociales, Universidad Nacional Autonoma de Mexico, Escuela Nacional de Antropologia e Historia, professional thesis.

1977   Los Caminos Prehispanicos de Coba, *XV Mesa Redonda de la Sociedad Mexicana de Antropologia* (Guanajuato 1977) II: 215–225, Mexico.

BENAVIDES CASTILLO, A. AND F. ROBLES C.

1975   Coba: Sus Sacbeob y Dzib Mul, *I.N.A.H. Boletin*, Ep. 2, No. 15: 55–61, Mexico.

BERGMANN, J. F.

1969   The Distribution of Cacao Cultivation in Pre-Columbian America, *Annals of the American Association of Geographers* 59: 85–96.

BERLIN, H.

1953   *Archaeological Reconnaissance in Tabasco*, Carnegie Institution of Washington, Current Reports 1(7), Washington, D.C.

1956   *Late Pottery Horizons of Tabasco, Mexico,* Contributions to American Anthropology and History 12(59), Carnegie Institution of Washington, Publication 606, Washington, D.C.

BLAKESLEE, D. J.
1981   The Origin and Spread of the Calumet Ceremony, *American Antiquity* 46: 759–768.

BOLLES, J. S.
1977   *Las Monjas: A Major Pre-Mexican Architectural Complex at Chichen Itza,* University of Oklahoma Press, Norman.

BRAINERD, G. W.
1958   *The Archaeological Ceramics of Yucatan,* University of California Anthropological Records Vol. 19, Berkeley and Los Angeles.

BRAY, W.
1977   Maya Metalwork and Its External Connections, in N. Hammond, Ed., *Social Process in Maya Prehistory,* pp. 365–403, Academic Press, New York.

BRINTON, D. G.
1881   Notes on the Codex Troano and Maya Chronology, *American Naturalist,* Sept., pp. 719–24.
1882   *The Maya Chronicles,* Brinton's Library of Aboriginal American Literature Number 1, Philadelphia.

BROWN, K. L.
1977a   The Valley of Guatemala: A Highland Port of Trade, in J. Michels and W. Sanders, Eds., *Teotihuacan and Kaminaljuyu: A Study in Prehistoric Culture Contact,* The Pennsylvania State University Press Monograph Series on Kaminaljuyu, No. 2, pp. 411–440, The Pennsylvania State University Press, University Park.
1977b   Toward a Systematic Explanation of Culture Change within the Middle Classic Period of the Valley of Guatemala, in J. Michels and W. Sanders, Eds., *Teotihuacan and Kaminaljuyu: A Study in Prehistoric Culture Contact,* The Pennsylvania State University Press Monograph Series on Kaminaljuyu, No. 2, pp. 411–440, The Pennsylvania State University Press, University Park.
1978   The Ethnohistory and Archaeology of the Development of the Quiche State, Paper Presented at the Annual Meeting of the American Society for Ethnohistory, Austin.
1979a   Ecology and Settlement Systems in the Guatemalan Highlands, Paper Presented at the 44th Annual Meeting of the Society for American Archaeology, Vancouver.
1979b   Trade and a Model of Central Mexican Influences in the Guatemalan Highlands, Paper Presented at the XVI Reunion y Mesa Redonda de la Sociedad Mexicana de Antropologia, Saltillo, Mexico.
1980   A History of Settlement Systems in the Central Quiche Area, Guatemala, in K. Brown, Ed., *Quiche Basin Archaeology: A Report on the Field Investigations and Artifact Studies,* The Institute for Mesoamerican Studies, Albany.

BROWN, K. L. AND T. MAJEWSKI
1979   Culture History of the Central Quiche Area, Paper Presented at the Conference on the Popol Vuh, Santa Cruz del Quiche, Guatemala.

BULLARD, W. R., JR.
1970   Topoxte: A Postclassic Maya Site in Peten, Guatemala, in W. Bullard, Ed., *Monographs and Papers in Maya Archaeology*, Papers of the Peabody Museum of Archaeology and Ethnology, No. 61, pp. 245–308, Harvard University, Cambridge.
1973   Postclassic Culture in Central Peten and Adjacent British Honduras, in T.P. Culbert, Ed., *The Classic Maya Collapse*, pp. 225–242, University of New Mexico Press, Albuquerque.

CARMACK, R. M.
1968   Toltec Influences on the Postclassic Culture History of Highland Guatemala, *Middle American Research Institute*, Publication 26, pp. 49–92, New Orleans.
1973   *Quichean Civilization*, University of California Press, Berkeley.
1977   Ethnohistory of the Central Quiche: The Community of Utatlan, in D. Wallace and R. Carmack, Eds., *Archaeology and Ethnohistory of the Central Quiche*, pp. 1–19, Institute for Mesoamerican Studies, Albany.

CARMACK, R. M., J. W. FOX, AND R. STEWART
1975   *La Formacion del Reino Quiche*, Instituto de Antropologia e Historia de Guatemala, Publication Especial No. 7, Guatemala.

CARMACK, R. M. AND J. M. WEEKS
1981   The Archaeology and Ethnohistory of Utatlan: A Conjunctive Approach, *American Antiquity* 46: 323–341.

CHAMBERLAIN, R. S.
1948   *The Conquest and Colonization of Yucatan, 1517–1550*, Carnegie Institution of Washington, Publication 582, Washington, D.C.
1966   *The Conquest and Colonization of Honduras, 1502–1550*, Octagon Books, New York.
1974   *Conquista y Colonizacion de Yucatan, 1517–1550*, translated by Alvaro Dominguez Peon, Biblioteca Porrua No. 57, Editorial Porrua, Mexico.

CHAPMAN, A. M.
1957   Port of Trade Enclaves in Aztec and Maya Civilizations, in K. Polanyi et al., Eds., *Trade and Market in the Early Empires*, pp. 114–153, Free Press, Glencoe.

CHASE, A. F.
1976   Topoxte and Tayasal: Ethnohistory in Archaeology, *American Antiquity* 41: 154–167.
1979   Regional Development in the Tayasal-Paxcaman Zone, El Peten, Guatemala: A Preliminary Statement, *Ceramica de Cultura Maya* 11: 86–119.
1982   Con Manos Arriba: Tayasal and Archaeology, *American Antiquity* 47(1): 167–171.
1983   A Contextual Consideration of the Tayasal-Paxcaman Zone, El

Peten, Guatemala, Ph.D. Dissertation, Department of Anthropology, University of Pennsylvania.

1984   The Ceramic Complexes of the Tayasal-Paxcaman Zone, Lake Peten, Guatemala, *Ceramica de Cultura Maya*, Vol. 13.

1985a Archaeology in the Maya Heartland: The Tayasal-Paxcaman Zone, Lake Peten, Guatemala, *Archaeology*, Vol. 37(5).

1985b Contextual Implications of Pictorial Vases from Tayasal, Peten, in E. Benson, Ed., *Cuarto Mesa Redonda de Palenque*, Vol. 5, University of Texas Press.

n.d.   Time Depth or Vacuum: The 11.3.0.0.0. Correlation, The Books of Chilam Balam, and Maya Lowland Archaeology, in J. Sabloff and E. W. Andrews V., Eds., *Late Lowland Maya Civilization: Classic to Postclassic*, University of New Mexico Press, Albuquerque.

CHASE, A. F. AND D. Z. CHASE

1981   Archaeological Investigations at Nohmul and Santa Rita, Belize: 1979–1980, *Mexicon* 3(3): 42–44.

CHASE, D. Z.

1981   The Maya Postclassic at Santa Rita Corozal, *Archaeology* 34(1): 25–33.

1982a Spatial and Temporal Variability in Postclassic Northern Belize, Ph.D. Dissertation, Department of Anthropology, University of Pennsylvania.

1982b The Ikilik Ceramic Complex at Nohmul, Northern Belize, *Ceramica de Cultura Maya* 12: 71–81.

1984   The Late Postclassic Pottery of Santa Rita Corozal, Belize: The Xabalxab Ceramic Complex, *Ceramica de Cultura Maya*, Vol. 13.

n.d.   Social and Political Organization in the Land of Cacao and Honey: Correlating the Archaeology and Ethnohistory of the Postclassic Lowland Maya, in J. Sabloff and E.W. Andrews V., Eds., *Late Lowland Maya Civilization: Classic to Postclassic*, University of New Mexico Press, Albuquerque.

CHASE, D. Z. AND A. F. CHASE

1982   Yucatec Influence in Terminal Classic Northern Belize, *American Antiquity* 47: 596–614.

CHEEK, C. D.

1977   Excavations at the Palangana and the Acropolis, Kaminaljuyu, in J. Michels and W. Sanders, Eds., *Teotihuacan and Kaminaljuyu: A Study in Prehistoric Culture Contact*, The Pennsylvania State University Press Monograph Series on Kaminaljuyu, No. 2, pp. 1–204, The Pennsylvania State University Press, University Park.

CIUDAD REAL, A. DE

1932   Fray Alonso Ponce in Yucatan, 1588, E. Noyes, Ed. and Translator, *Middle American Research Institute*, Publication 4, pp. 297–372, Tulane University, New Orleans.

CLINE, H. F.

1950   *War of the Castes and the Independent States of Yucatan*, Related Studies in Early Nineteenth Century Yucatecan Social History, Part

1, Nos. 1 and 2, Microfilm Collection of Manuscripts on Middle American Cultural Anthropology, No. 32, University of Chicago Library.

COE, M. D.

1965   A Model of Ancient Community Structure in the Maya Lowlands, *Southwestern Journal of Anthropology* 21(2): 97–114.

1966   *The Maya*, Praeger, New York.

COE, W. R.

1965a Tikal, Guatemala, and Emergent Maya Civilization, *Science* 147: 1401–1419.

1965b Tikal: Ten Years of Study of a Maya Ruin in the Lowlands of Guatemala, *Expedition* 8(1): 5–56.

1967   *Tikal: A Handbook of the Ancient Maya Ruins*, University Museum, Philadelphia.

COE, W. R. AND R. J. SHARER

1979   The Quirigua Project: 1975 Season, *Quirigua Reports I*, pp. 13–32, Museum Monographs, No. 37, University Museum, Philadelphia.

CONNOR, J. G.

1975   Ceramics and Artifacts, in J. Sabloff and W. Rathje, Eds., *A Study of Changing Pre-Columbian Commercial Systems*, Monographs of the Peabody Museum of Archaeology and Ethnology, No. 3, pp. 114–135, Harvard University, Cambridge.

CORSON, C.

1976   *Maya Anthropomorphic Figurines from Jaina Island, Campeche*, Ballena Press Studies in Mesoamerican Art, Archaeology, and Ethnohistory, No. 1, Ramona.

CORTES, H.

1908   *Hernando Cortes: His Five Letters of Relation to the Emperor Charles V*, Trans. by F. A. MacNutt, New York.

COWGILL, G. L.

1963   Postclassic Period Culture in the Vicinity of Flores, Peten, Guatemala, Ph.D. Dissertation, Harvard University.

1964   The End of Classic Maya Culture: A Review of Recent Evidence, *Southwestern Journal of Anthropology* 20: 145–159.

CULBERT, T. P.

1973a Ed., *The Classic Maya Collapse*, University of New Mexico Press, Albuquerque.

1973b The Maya Downfall at Tikal, in T. P. Culbert, Ed., *The Classic Maya Collapse*, pp. 63–92, University of New Mexico Press, Albuquerque.

DAHLIN, B.

1976   An Anthropologist Looks at the Pyramids: A Late Classic Revitalization Movement at Tikal, Guatemala, Ph.D. Dissertation, Department of Anthropology, Temple University.

DEEVEY, E. S., L. J. GRALENSKI, AND V. HOFFREN

1959   Yale Natural Radiocarbon Measurements IV, *American Journal of Science Radiocarbon Supplement* 1: 144–72.

DEEVEY, E. S., D. S. RICE, P. M. RICE, H. H. VAUGHAN, M. BRENNER, AND M. S. FLANNERY

1979   Maya Urbanism: Impact on a Tropical Karst Environment, *Science* 206: 298–306.

DIAZ DEL CASTILLO, B.

1933   *Verdadera y Notable Relacion del Descubrimiento y Conquista de la Nueva Espana y Guatemala*, Sociedad de Geografia e Historia de Guatemala.

DIXON, W. J.

1975   Ed., *BMDP: Biomedical Computer Programs*, University of California Press, Berkeley.

DOCUMENTOS INEDITOS

1870   *Coleccion de Documentos Ineditos, Relativos al Descubrimiento, Conquista y Organizacion de las Antiguas Posesiones Espanolas de America y Oceania*, Jose Maria Perez, Madrid.

1898   *Coleccion de Documentos Ineditos Relativos al Descubrimiento, Conquista y Organizacion de las Antiguas Posesiones Espanolas de Ultramar*, Establecimiento Tipografico, Madrid.

DRUCKER, P. AND R. F. HEIZER

1960   A Study of the Milpa System of LaVenta Island and Its Archaeological Implications, *Southwestern Journal of Anthropology* 16: 36–45.

DUTTON, B. P. AND H. R. HOBBS

1943   *Excavations at Tajumulco, Guatemala*, Monographs of the School for American Research, No. 9, The University of New Mexico Press, Albuquerque.

EATON, J. D.

1974   Shell Celts from Coastal Yucatan, Mexico, *Bulletin of the Texas Archaeological Society* 45: 197–208, Austin.

1975   Ancient Agricultural Farmsteads in the Rio Bec Region of Yucatan, *Contributions of the University of California Archaeological Research Facility*, No. 27, pp. 56–82, Berkeley.

1976   Ancient Fishing Technology on the Gulf Coast of Yucatan, Mexico, *Bulletin of the Texas Archaeological Society* 47: 231–43, Austin.

1978   Archaeological Survey of the Yucatan-Campeche Coast, *Middle American Research Institute*, Publication 46(1), pp. 1–67, Tulane University, New Orleans.

EDMONDSON, M. S.

1971   *The Book of Counsel: The Popol Vuh of the Quiche Maya of Guatemala*, Middle American Research Institute, Publication 35, New Orleans.

1982   *The Ancient Future of the Itza: The Book of Chilam Balam of Tizimin*, University of Texas Press, Austin.

EKHOLM, S. M.

1969   *Mound 30a and the Early Preclassic Ceramic Sequence of Izapa, Chiapas, Mexico*, New World Archaeological Foundation Papers, No. 25, Provo.

ERASMUS, C. J.
1968   Thoughts on Upward Collapse: An Essay on Explanation in Archaeology, *Southwestern Journal of Anthropology* 24(2): 170–194.

ESCALONA RAMOS, A.
1940   *Cronologia y Astronomia Maya-Mexica (con un Anexo de Historias Indigenas)*, Mexico.
1946   Algunas Ruinas Prehispanicas en Quintana Roo, *Boletin de la Sociedad Mexicana de Geografia y Estadistica* 61(3): 513–628.

FANCOURT, C.
1854   *The History of Yucatan from Its Discovery to the Close of the Seventeenth Century*, John Murray, Albemarle Street, London.

FARRISS, N.
1978   Nucleation vs. Dispersal: The Dynamics of Population Movement in Colonial Yucatan, *Hispanic American Historical Review* 58: 187–216.

FARRISS, N., A. G. MILLER, AND A. F. CHASE
1975   Late Maya Mural Paintings from Quintana Roo, Mexico, *Journal of Field Archaeology* 2: 5–10.

FELDMAN, L. W.
1975   *Riverine Maya—the Torquegua and Other Chols of the Lower Motagua Valley*, Museum Brief 15, Columbia Museum, University of Missouri.

FERREE, L.
1970   The Pottery Censers of Tikal, Guatemala, Ph.D. Dissertation, Southern Illinois University, University Microfilms, Ann Arbor.

FOX, J. W.
1977   Quiche Expansion Processes: Differential Ecological Growth Bases within an Archaic State, in D. Wallace and R. Carmack, Eds., *Archaeology and Ethnohistory of the Central Quiche*, pp. 82–97, Institute for Mesoamerican Studies, Albany.
1978   *Quiche Conquest*, University of New Mexico Press, Albuquerque.
1980   Lowland to Highland Mexicanization Processes in Southern Mesoamerica, *American Antiquity* 45(1): 43–54.

FREIDEL, D. A.
1976   Late Postclassic Settlement Patterns on Cozumel Island, Quintana Roo, Mexico, Ph.D. Dissertation, Department of Anthropology, Harvard University.
1978   Maritime Adaptation and the Rise of Maya Civilization: The View from Cerros, Belize, in B. Voorhies and B. Stark, Eds., *Prehistoric Coastal Adaptations*, pp. 239–265, Academic Press, New York.
1979   Culture Areas and Interaction Spheres: Contrasting Approaches to the Emergence of Civilization in the Maya Lowlands, *American Antiquity* 44(1): 36–54.
1981   Continuity and Disjunction: Late Postclassic Settlement Patterns in Northern Yucatan, in Ashmore, Ed., *Lowland Maya Settlement Patterns*, pp. 311–332, University of New Mexico Press, Albuquerque.

n.d.   Terminal Classic Lowland Maya: Successes, Failures, and After-maths, in J. Sabloff and E. W. Andrews V., Eds., *Late Lowland Maya Civilization: Classic to Postclassic*, University of New Mexico, Albuquerque.

FREIDEL, D. A. AND M. B. CLIFF

1978   Energy Investment in Late Postclassic Maya Masonry Religious Structures, in R. Sidrys, Ed., *Papers on the Economy and Architecture of the Ancient Maya*, pp. 184–208, Institute of Archaeology Monograph 8, University of California, Los Angeles.

FRY, R. E.

1969   Ceramics and Settlement in the Periphery of Tikal, Guatemala, Ph.D. Dissertation, Department of Anthropology, University of Arizona.

1973   The Archeology of Southern Quintana Roo: Ceramics, *40th International Congress of Americanists* 1: 487–493.

1974   Settlement Systems in Southern Quintana Roo, Mexico, Paper Presented at the XLI Congreso Internacional de Americanistas, Mexico.

1980   A Possible Toxcatl Ritual at Mirador, Chiapas, Mexico, Paper presented at the Annual Meeting of Midwestern Mesoamericanists, Iowa City.

1982   Occupation Specialization in Peripheral Tikal, Guatemala, Paper presented at the Annual Meeting of the American Anthropological Association, Washington, D.C.

GADACZ, R. R.

1979   *Pre-Spanish Commerce in the Gulf Coast Lowlands of Mexico*, Western Publishers, Calgary.

GANN, T.

1900   Mounds in Northern Honduras, *Nineteenth Annual Report, 1897–1898, Bureau of American Ethnology*, Smithsonian Institution, Part 2, pp. 661–692, Washington, D.C.

1918   The Maya Indians of Southern Yucatan and Northern British Honduras, *Bureau of American Ethnology Bulletin No. 64*, Washington, D.C.

1935   Tzibanche, Quintana Roo, Mexico, *Maya Research* 2(2): 155–166.

GARZA T. DE GONZALEZ, S. AND E. B. KURJACK

1980   *Atlas Arqueologico del Estado de Yucatan*, Instituto Nacional de Antropologia e Historia, Mexico.

GIFFORD, J. C.

1965   Ceramics, in G.R. Willey et al., *Prehistoric Maya Settlements in the Belize Valley*, Papers of the Peabody Museum of Archaeology and Ethnology, No. 54, pp. 319–390, Harvard University, Cambridge.

1976   *Prehistoric Pottery Analysis and the Ceramics of Barton Ramie in the Belize Valley*, Memoirs of the Peabody Museum of Archaeology and Ethnology, Vol. 18, Harvard University, Cambridge.

GLASS, J. B.

1966   Archaeological Survey of Western Honduras, in R. Wauchope, Ed., *Handbook of Middle American Indians*, Vol. 4, pp. 157–179, University of Texas Press, Austin.

GRAHAM, E. A.

1983   The Highlands of the Lowlands: Environment and Archaeology in the Stann Creek District, Belize, Central America, Ph.D. Dissertation, Newnham College, Cambridge University.

GRAHAM, E. A., L. MCNATT, AND M. A. GUTCHEN

1980   Excavations in Footprint Cave, Caves Branch, Belize, *Journal of Field Archaeology* 7: 153–172.

GRAHAM, J. A.

1973   Aspects of Non-Classic Presences in the Inscriptions and Sculptural Art of Seibal, in T.P. Culbert, Ed., *The Classic Maya Collapse*, pp. 207–217, University of New Mexico Press, Albuquerque.

GREEN, E. L.

1973   Location Analysis of Prehistoric Maya Sites in Northern British Honduras, *American Antiquity* 38(3): 279–293.

GROVE, D. C.

1981   Olmec Monuments: Mutilation as a Clue to Meaning, in E. P. Benson, Ed., *The Olmec and Their Neighbors*, Dumbarton Oaks Research Library and Collections, Washington, D.C.

GRUHN, R. AND A. L. BRYAN

1976   An Archaeological Survey of the Chichicastenango Area of Highland Guatemala, *Ceramica de Cultura Maya* 9: 75–119.

GUILLEMIN, J. F.

1965   *Iximche: Capital del Antiguo Reino Cakchiquel*, Instituto de Antropologia e Historia de Guatemala, Guatemala.

1977   Urbanism and Hierarchy at Iximche, in N. Hammond, Ed., *Social Process in Maya Prehistory*, pp. 228–264, Academic Press, London.

GUTHE, C. E.

1921   Report of Dr. Carl E. Guthe, *Carnegie Institution of Washington Yearbook* 20: 364–368, Washington, D.C.

1927   Report on the Excavations at Tayasal, *Carnegie Institution of Washington Yearbook* 21: 318–319, Washington, D.C.

HABERLAND, W.

1975   Further Archaeological Evidence for the Nicarao and Pipil Migrations in Central America, *Actas del XLI Congreso Internacional de Americanistas* 1: 551–559, Mexico (1974).

HAMMOND, N.

1973   Ed., *British Museum–Cambridge University Corozal Project 1973 Interim Report*, Centre of Latin American Studies, Cambridge University.

1974   Preclassic to Postclassic in Northern Belize, *Antiquity* 48: 177–189.

1975a   *Lubaantun: A Classic Maya Realm*, Monographs of the Peabody

Museum of Archaeology and Ethnology, No. 2, Harvard University, Cambridge.

1975b   Ed., *Corozal Project 1974–1975 Interim Report*, Centre of Latin American Studies, Cambridge University.

1976   Maya Obsidian Trade in Southern Belize, in T. Hester and N. Hammond, Eds., *Maya Lithic Studies: Papers from the 1976 Belize Field Symposium*, pp. 71–81, Special Report No. 4, Center for Archaeological Research, the University of Texas at San Antonio.

1977a   Ex Oriente Lux: A View from Belize, in R. E. W. Adams, Ed., *The Origins of Maya Civilization*, pp. 45–76, University of New Mexico Press, Albuquerque.

1977b   The Early Formative in the Maya Lowlands, in N. Hammond, Ed., *Social Process in Maya Prehistory*, pp. 82–101, Academic Press, London.

1977c   The Earliest Maya, *Scientific American* 236(3): 116–133.

1978   Ed., *Cuello Project 1978 Interim Report*, Archaeological Research Program, Douglass College, Rutgers University, New Brunswick.

1980   Early Maya Ceremonial at Cuello, Belize, *Antiquity* 54: 176–190.

HAMMOND, N., D. PRING, R. WILK, S. DONAGHEY, F. SAUL, E. WING, A. MILLER, AND L. FELDMAN

1979   The Earliest Maya? Definition of the Swasey Phase, *American Antiquity* 44: 92–110.

HARRIS, M.

1973   *Cows, Pigs, Wars, and Witches: The Riddles of Culture*, Vantage Books, New York.

1980   *Culture, People, Nature*, 3rd edition, Harper and Row, New York.

HARRISON, P. D.

1972   Precolumbian Settlement Distribution and External Relationships in Southern Quintana Roo, Part 1: Architecture, *Atti del XL Congresso Internazionale degli Americanisti*, pp. 379–386, Rome.

1974   Archaeology in Southwestern Quintana Roo: Interim Report of the Uaymil Survey Project, Paper Presented at the XLI Congreso Internacional de Americanistas, Mexico City.

1978   Bajos Revisited: Visual Evidence for One System of Agriculture, in P. D. Harrison and B. L. Turner, Eds., *Prehispanic Maya Agriculture*, pp. 247–254, University of New Mexico Press, Albuquerque.

1979   The Lobil Postclassic Phase in the Southern Interior of the Yucatan Peninsula, in N. Hammond and G.R. Willey, Eds., *Maya Archaeology and Ethnohistory*, pp. 189–207, University of Texas Press, Austin.

1982   Subsistence and Society in Eastern Yucatan, in K.V. Flannery, Ed., *Maya Subsistence*, pp. 119–130, Academic Press, New York.

HAVILAND, W. R.

1965   Prehistoric Settlement at Tikal, Guatemala, *Expedition* 7(3): 14–23.

HELLMUTH, N.

1974   Maps of the Topoxte Islands, Unpublished Data, FLAAR, Guatemala City.

1977   Cholti-Lacandon (Chiapas) and Peten-Ytza Agriculture, Settlement Pattern, and Population, in N. Hammond, Ed., *Social Process in Maya Prehistory*, pp. 421–448, Academic Press, London.

HENDERSON, J. S.

1979   The Valle de Naco: Ethnohistory and Archaeology in Northwestern Honduras, *Ethnohistory* 24: 363–77.

HESTER, T. R.

1979   Ed., *The Colha Project, 1979: A Collection of Interim Papers*, Prepared by the Center for Archaeological Research, The University of Texas at San Antonio.

HESTER, T. R., J. D. EATON, AND H. J. SHAFER

1980   *The Colha Project, Second Season, 1980 Interim Report*, Center for Archaeological Research, The University of Texas at San Antonio and Centro Studi e Ricerche Ligabue, Venezia.

HESTER, T. R., G. LIGABUE, J. D. EATON, H. J. SHAFER, AND R. E. W. ADAMS

1981   The 1980 Season at Colha, *Belizean Studies* 9: 12–26.

ICHON, A.

1975   *Organizacion de un Centro Quiche Protohistorico: Pueblo Viejo Chichaj*, Instituto de Antropologia e Historia de Guatemala, Publicacion Especial No. 9, Guatemala.

1977   A Late Postclassic Sweathouse in the Highlands of Guatemala, *American Antiquity* 42(2): 203–209.

JONES, C.

1969   The Twin-Pyramid Group Pattern: A Classic Maya Architectural Assemblage at Tikal, Guatemala, Ph.D. Dissertation, The University of Pennsylvania, University Microfilms, Ann Arbor.

1977   Research at Quirigua: The Site-Core Program, Paper Presented at the 42nd Annual Meeting of the Society for American Archaeology, New Orleans.

1979   Tikal as a Trading Center: Why It Rose and Fell, Paper Presented at the XLIII International Congress of Americanists, Vancouver.

JONES, C., W. ASHMORE, AND R. J. SHARER

1983   The Quirigua Project: 1977 Season, *Quirigua Reports III*, pp. 1–38, Museum Monographs, University Museum, Philadelphia.

JONES, G. D.

1977   Ed., *Anthropology and History in Yucatan*, University of Texas Press, Austin.

1979   Southern Lowland Maya Political Organization: A Model of Change from Protohistoric through Colonial Times, *Actes du XLIII Congres International des Americanistes, Congres du Centenaire* 8: 83–94, Paris.

1982   Agriculture and Trade in the Colonial Period Southern Lowlands, in K. Flannery, Ed., *Maya Subsistence*, pp. 275–293, Academic Press, New York.

1983   The Last Maya Frontiers of Colonial Yucatan, in M. MacLeod and R. Wasserstrom, Eds., *Spaniards and Indians in Southeastern Mesoamerica: Essays on the History of Ethnic Relations*, pp. 64–91, University of Nebraska Press, Lincoln.

JONES, G. D. AND R. KAUTZ

1981a   Archaeology and Ethnohistory on a Spanish Colonial Frontier, Presented at Symposium on Arqueologia Historica en el Area Maya, XVII Mesa Redonda de la Sociedad Mexicana de Antropologia, San Cristobal, Chiapas.

1981b   Post-Conquest Native Elites: Postclassic Continuities in the Southern Maya Lowlands, Paper presented to the Annual Meeting of the American Anthropological Association, Los Angeles, California.

JONES, G. D., D. S. RICE, AND P. M. RICE

1981   The Location of Tayasal: A Reconsideration in Light of Peten Maya Ethnohistory and Archaeology, *American Antiquity* 46: 530–547.

KAUFMAN, T.

1976   Archaeological and Linguistic Correlations in Mayaland and Associated Areas of Meso-America, *World Archaeology* 8: 101–118.

KELLEY, D. H.

1962   Glyphic Evidence for a Dynastic Sequence at Quirigua, Guatemala, *American Antiquity* 27: 323–35.

1976   *Deciphering the Maya Script*, University of Texas Press, Austin.

KIDDER, A. V.

1954   Miscellaneous Archaeological Specimens from Mesoamerica, *Notes on Middle American Archaeology and Ethnology*, No. 117, Carnegie Institution of Washington, D.C.

KIDDER, A. V., J. D. JENNINGS, AND E. M. SHOOK

1946   Archaeological Investigations at Kaminaljuyu, Guatemala, *Proceedings of the American Philosophical Society* 105: 559–570.

KIRCHOFF, P.

1950   The League of Mayapan and Its Thirteen Calendars: An Historical Geographical Interpretation, Abstract of Paper Presented to the Supper Conference for Anthropologists, Viking Fund.

KUBLER, G.

1976   Mythological Dates at Palenque and the Ring Numbers in the Dresden Codex, *Segunda Mesa Redonda de Palenque*, Vol. III.

KURJACK, E. B.

1974   *Prehistoric Lowland Maya Community and Social Organization: A Case Study at Dzibilchaltun, Yucatan, Mexico*, Middle American Research Institute, Tulane University, Publication 38, New Orleans.

KURJACK, E. B. AND E. W. ANDREWS V

1976   Early Boundary Maintenance in Northwest Yucatan, Mexico, *American Antiquity* 41(3): 318–25.

KURJACK, E. B. AND S. GARZA T.

1981   Pre-Columbian Community Form and Distribution in the Northern Maya Area, in W. Ashmore, Ed., *Lowland Maya Settlement Patterns*, pp. 287–309, University of New Mexico Press, Albuquerque.

LEHMANN, H.

1968 *Mixco Viejo: Guia de las Ruinas de la Plaza Fuerte Pokoman*, Tipografia Nacional, Guatemala.

LINCOLN, C. E.

n.d. The "Total Overlap Model" of Ceramic Chronology at Chichen Itza: A Review of the Literature, in J. Sabloff and E.W. Andrews V, Eds., *Late Lowland Maya Civilization: Classic to Postclassic*, University of New Mexico Press, Albuquerque.

LIZARDI RAMOS, C.

1939 Exploraciones Arqueologicas en Quintana Roo, Mexico, *Revista Mexicana de Estudios Antropologicas* 3: 46–53.

LOPEZ DE COGOLLUDO, D.

1867–68 *Historia de Yucatan*, 3rd. edition, 2 Vols., Merida.

1971 *Tres Siglos de la Dominacion Espanola en Yucatan o sea Historia de esta Provincia*, Akademische Druck-u, Verlagsanstalt, Graz, Austria (originally published 1688).

LOTHROP, S. K.

1924 *Tulum, An Archaeological Study of the East Coast of Yucatan*, Carnegie Institution of Washington, Publication 335, Washington, D.C.

1952 *Metals from the Cenote of Sacrifice Chichen Itza, Yucatan*, Memoirs of the Peabody Museum of Archaeology and Ethnology, Vol. 10(2), Harvard University, Cambridge.

MACKIE, E. W.

n.d. Excavations on Mamey Hill, Pomona, Stann Creek District, Unpublished Manuscript, Hunterian Museum, University of Glasgow.

MACNEISH, R. S., J. WILKERSON, AND W. NELKEN-TERNER

1980 *First Annual Report of the Belize Archaeological Reconnaissance*, Peabody Foundation, Andover, Mass.

MAJEWSKI, T.

1980 Excavations at Chjuyub and Chitinamit, El Quiche, Guatemala, in K. Brown, Ed., *Quiche Basin Archaeology: A Report on the Field Investigations and Artifact Studies*, The Institute for Mesoamerican Studies, Albany.

MALER, T.

1910 Explorations in the Department of Peten Guatemala and Adjacent Regions: Motul de San Jose; Peten Itza, *Memoirs of the Peabody Museum of American Archaeology and Ethnology*, Vol. 4(3), pp. 131–174, Harvard University.

MARCUS, J.

1973 Territorial Organization of the Lowland Classic Maya, *Science* 180: 911–916.

1976 *Emblem and State in the Classic Maya Lowlands*, Dumbarton Oaks, Washington, D.C.

MATHENY, R. T.

1970   *The Ceramics of Aguacatal, Campeche, Mexico*, Papers of the New World Archaeological Foundation, No. 27, Provo.

MAYER, P.

1977   Cancun: Informe Preliminar, *XV Mesa Redonda, Sociedad Mexicana de Antropologia*, Tomo II: 207–213, Guanajuato.

MEANS, P. A.

1917   *History of the Spanish Conquest of Yucatan and of the Itzas*, Papers of the Peabody Museum of Archaeology and Ethnology, No. 7, Harvard University, Cambridge.

MEGGERS, B. J.

1954   Environmental Limitation on the Development of Culture, *American Anthropologist* 56(5): 801–824.

MENDIZABAL, M. O. DE

1929   *Influencia de la Sal en la Distribucion Geografica de los Grupos Indigenas de Mexico*, Imprenta del Museo Nacional de Arqueologia, Historia, y Etnografia, Mexico.

MICHELS, J. W.

1979   *The Kaminaljuyu Chiefdom*, The Pennsylvania State University Press Monograph Series on Kaminaljuyu, No. 5, Pennsylvania State University Press, University Park.

MILLER, A. G.

1974   West and East in Maya Thought: Death and Rebirth at Palenque and Tulum, in M. G. Robertson, Ed., *Primera Mesa Redonda de Palenque*, Pt. II, pp. 45–49, The Robert Louis Stevenson School, Precolumbian Art Research Institute, Pebble Beach, California.

1977a   Captains of the Itza: Unpublished Mural Evidence from Chichen Itza, in N. Hammond, Ed., *Social Process in Maya Prehistory*, pp. 197–225, Academic Press, London.

1977b   The Maya and the Sea: Trade and Cult at Tancah and Tulum, Quintana Roo, Mexico, in E. Benson, Ed., *The Sea in the Pre-Columbian World*, pp. 97–138, Dumbarton Oaks Research Library and Collections, Trustees for Harvard University, Washington, D.C.

1982   *On the Edge of the Sea: Mural Painting at Tancah—Tulum*, Dumbarton Oaks, Washington, D.C.

MILLER, A. G. AND N. FARRISS

1979   Religious Syncretism in Colonial Yucatan: The Archaeological and Ethnohistorical Evidence from Tancah, Quintana Roo, in N. Hammond and G. R. Willey, Eds., *Maya Archaeology and Ethnohistory*, pp. 223–240, University of Texas Press, Austin.

MILLON, R.

1955   When Money Grew on Trees: A Study of Cacao in Ancient Mesoamerica, Ph.D. Dissertation, Department of Anthropology, University of Michigan.

MOHOLY-NAGY, H.

1963   Shells and Other Marine Material from Tikal, *Estudios de Cultura Maya* 3: 65–83, Mexico.

MORLEY, S. G.

1911   The Historical Value of the Books of Chilam Balam, *American Journal of Archaeology* 15: 195–214.

1935   *Guide Book to the Ruins of Quirigua*, Carnegie Institution of Washington, Supplementary Publication No. 16, Washington, D.C.

1937–38   *The Inscriptions of Peten*, Carnegie Institution of Washington, Publication 437, Washington, D.C.

1947   *The Ancient Maya*, Stanford University Press, Stanford.

MORLEY, S. G. AND G. W. BRAINERD

1956   *The Ancient Maya* (3rd edition), Stanford University Press, Stanford.

MORLEY, S. G., G. W. BRAINERD, AND R. J. SHARER

1983   *The Ancient Maya* (4th edition), Stanford University Press, Stanford.

MORRIS, E. H., J. CHARLOT, AND A. A. MORRIS

1931   *The Temple of the Warriors at Chichen Itza, Yucatan*, Carnegie Institution of Washington, Publication 406, Washington, D.C.

MULLER, F.

1959   *Atlas Arqueologico de la Republica Mexicana 1: Quintana Roo*, Instituto Nacional de Antropologia e Historia, Mexico City.

NAVARRETE, C.

1966   *The Chiapanec History and Culture*, Papers of the New World Archaeological Foundation, Brigham Young University, No. 21, Provo.

1974   Material Ceramico de la Cueva de Xelha, Quintana Roo, *Notas Antropologicas* 1(8): 53–57, Universidad Nacional Autonoma de Mexico, Mexico.

1976   Algunas Influencias Mexicanas en el Area Maya Meridional Durante el Postclasico Tardio, *Estudios de Cultura Nahuatl*, pp. 345–382.

NELSON, F. W. AND D. A. PHILLIPS, JR.

n.d.   X-ray Fluorescence Analysis of Obsidian Blades from Cozumel, Quintana Roo, Mexico (1979).

NELSON, F. W. , D. A. PHILLIPS, F. ROBLES, P. MAYER, AND A. BARRERA RUBIO

n.d.   Results of Analysis of Obsidian Artifacts from Coba, Cancun, and Tulum, Quintana Roo, Mexico, unpublished data (1979).

NICHOLSON, H. B.

1955   Native Historical Traditions of Nuclear America and the Problem of Their Archaeological Correlation, *American Anthropologist* 57: 594–613.

1960   The Mixteca-Puebla Concept in Mesoamerican Archaeology: A Re-Examination, in A. F. C. Wallace, Ed., *Men and Cultures*, International Congress of Anthropological and Ethnological Sciences, University of Pennsylvania, Philadelphia.

1961   The Use of the Term "Mixtec" in Mesoamerican Archeology, *American Antiquity* 26: 431–433.

NIE, N. H., C. H. HULL, J. G. JENKINS, K. STEINBRENNER, AND D. H. BENT
1975   *SPSS: Statistical Package for the Social Sciences*, 2nd edition, McGraw-Hill; New York.

NOGUERA, E.
1940   Ceramica de Quintana Roo: Expedicion Cientifica Mexicana 1937, *El Mexico Antiguo* 5: 9–40, Mexico.
1975   *La Ceramica Arqueologica de Mesoamerica*, Instituto de Investigaciones Antropologicas, U.N.A.M., 2nd edition, Mexico.

NUTTALL, Z.
1902 (1975) Ed., *The Codex Nuttall: A Picture Manuscript from Ancient Mexico*, The Peabody Museum of American Archaeology and Ethnology, Harvard University, Cambridge (republished by Dover Press).

OCHOA, L. AND L. CASASOLA
1978   Los Cambios del Patron de Asentamiento en el Area del Usumacinta, in L. Ochoa, Ed., *Estudios Preliminares Sobre los Mayas de las Tierras Bajas Noroccidentales*, Universidad Nacional Autonoma de Mexico, Mexico, D. F.

PAGDEN, A. R.
1971   Trans. and Ed., *Hernan Cortes—Letters from Mexico*, Grossman, New York.

PENDERGAST, D. M.
1967   Occupacion Post-Clasica en Altun Ha, Honduras Britanica, *Revista Mexicana de Estudios Antropologicos* 21: 213–224.
1969   Altun Ha, British Honduras (Belize), the Sun God's Tomb, Royal Ontario Museum, *Art and Archaeology Occasional Paper* 19, Toronto.
1970   Tumbaga Object from the Early Classic Period, Found at Altun Ha, British Honduras (Belize), *Science* 168: 116–118.
1975   The Church in the Jungle, *Rotunda* 8: 32–40.
1977   Royal Ontario Museum Excavation: Finds at Lamanai, Belize, *Archaeology* 30: 129–131.
1979   *Excavations at Altun Ha, Belize, 1964–1970*, Vol. 1, Royal Ontario Museum, Toronto.
1981a   Lamanai, Belize: Summary of Excavation Results, 1974–1980, *Journal of Field Archaeology* 8(1): 29–53.
1981b   The 1980 Excavations at Lamanai, Belize, *Mexicon* 2(6): 96–99.
1981c   Lamanai, Belize: 1981 Excavations, *Mexicon* 3(4): 62–63.
1982a   *Excavations at Altun Ha, Belize, 1964–1970*, Vol. 2, Toronto, Royal Ontario Museum.
1982b   Ancient Maya Mercury, *Science* 217: 533–535.
n.d.a   Stability through Change: Lamanai, Belize, From the 9th through 17th Century, in J. Sabloff and E. W. Andrews V, Eds., *Late Lowland Maya Civilization: Classic to Postclassic*, University of New Mexico Press, Albuquerque.
n.d.b   *Excavations at Altun Ha, Belize, 1964–1970*, Vol. 3, in preparation.

PHILLIPS, D. A.

1979a Material Culture and Trade of the Postclassic Maya, Ph.D. Dissertation, University of Arizona, Tucson.

1979b Pesas de Pesca de Cozumel, Quintana Roo, *Boletin de la Escuela de Ciencias Antropologicas de la Universidad de Yucatan*, Ano 6, No. 36: 2–18, Merida.

PINA CHAN, R.

1968   *Jaina: La Casa en el Agua*, Instituto Nacional de Antropologia e Historia, Mexico.

POLLOCK, H. E. D.

1980   *The Puuc: An Architectural Survey of the Hill Country of Yucatan and Northern Campeche, Mexico*, Memoirs of the Peabody Museum of Archaeology and Ethnology, Vol. 19, Harvard University, Cambridge.

POLLOCK, H. E. D., R. L. ROYS, T. PROSKOURIAKOFF, AND A. L. SMITH

1962   *Mayapan, Yucatan, Mexico*, Carnegie Institution of Washington, Publication 619, Washington, D.C.

POTTER, D. F.

1977   *Maya Architecture of the Central Yucatan Peninsula*, Middle American Research Institute, Tulane University, Publication 44, New Orleans.

PRICE, H. W.

1899   Excavations on Sittee River, British Honduras, *Proceedings of the Society of Antiquaries* 17: 339–344.

PRING, D.

1973   Op 8—Santa Rita, in N. Hammond, Ed., *British Museum—Cambridge University Corozal Project, 1973 Interim Report*, pp. 62–67, Centre of Latin American Studies, University of Cambridge.

1976   Outline of Northern Belize Ceramic Sequence, *Ceramica de Cultura Maya* 9: 11–52.

PROSKOURIAKOFF, T.

1950   *A Study of Classic Maya Sculpture*, Carnegie Institution of Washington, Publication 593, Washington, D.C.

1951   Some Non-Classic Traits in the Sculpture of Yucatan, in S. Tax, Ed., *The Civilizations of Ancient America, Selected Papers of the 29th International Congress of Americanists*, pp. 108–118, University of Chicago Press, Chicago.

1955   The Death of a Civilization, *Scientific American* 192: 82–88.

1962a Civic and Religious Structures of Mayapan, in H.E.D. Pollock et al., Eds., *Mayapan, Yucatan, Mexico*, pp. 87–163, Carnegie Institution of Washington, Publication 619, Washington, D.C.

1962b The Artifacts of Mayapan, in H.E.D. Pollock et al., Eds., *Mayapan, Yucatan, Mexico*, pp. 321–438, Carnegie Institution of Washington, Publication 619, Washington, D.C.

1974   *Jades from the Cenote of Sacrifice, Chichen Itza, Yucatan*, Mem-

oirs of the Peabody Museum of Archaeology and Ethnology, Vol.
10(1), Harvard University, Cambridge.

PULESTON, D. E.

1973 Ancient Maya Settlement Patterns and Environment at Tikal,
Guatemala, Ph.D. Dissertation, Department of Anthropology, University of Pennsylvania.

RANDS, R. L.

1952 Some Evidences of Warfare in Classic Maya Art, Ph.D. Dissertation, Columbia University, New York.

1954 Artistic Connections between Chichen Itza Toltec and the Classic
Maya, *American Antiquity* 19: 281–282.

RATHJE, W.

1975 Last Tango at Mayapan: A Tentative Trajectory of Production-
Distribution Systems, in J. A. Sabloff and C. C. Lamberg-Karlovsky,
Eds., *Ancient Civilization and Trade*, University of New Mexico
Press, Albuquerque.

REED, N.

1964 *The Caste War of Yucatan*, Stanford University Press, Stanford.

REINA, R. E.

1962 The Ritual of the Skull of Peten, Guatemala, *Expedition* 4(4):
26–36.

RELACIONES DE YUCATAN

1898–1900 *Relaciones de Yucatan*, Coleccion de documentos ineditos
relativos al descubrimiento, conquista y organizacion de las antiguas posesiones espanolas de ultramar, 2nd series, vols. 11 and 13
(I, II), Madrid.

RICE, D. S.

1974 *The Archaeology of British Honduras: A Review and Synthesis*,
Katunob Occasional Publications in Anthropology, Archaeology Series, No. 6, University of Northern Colorado, Museum of Anthropology, Greeley.

1976 The Historical Ecology of Lakes Yaxha and Sacnab, El Peten,
Guatemala, Ph.D. Dissertation, Pennsylvania State University.

1981 Zacpeten: A Postclassic Center in Central Peten, Guatemala, Paper
presented at the 46th Annual Meeting of the Society for American
Archaeology, San Diego.

n.d. The Peten Postclassic: A Settlement Perspective, in J. Sabloff and
E. W. Andrews V, Eds., *Late Lowland Maya Civilization: Classic to
Postclassic*, University of New Mexico Press.

RICE, D. S. AND D. E. PULESTON

1981 Ancient Maya Settlement Patterns in the Peten, Guatemala, in
W. Ashmore, Ed., *Lowland Maya Settlement Patterns*, pp. 121–156,
University of New Mexico Press, Albuquerque.

RICE, D. S. AND P. M. RICE

1979 Preliminary Report, Proyecto Lacustre, First Field Season, 1979,
manuscript prepared for National Science Foundation.

1980a The Northeast Peten Revisited, *American Antiquity* 45(3): 432–454.

1980b Proyecto Lacustre: Second Preliminary Report: Second Season, 1980, manuscript prepared for National Science Foundation.

1981   Muralla de Leon: A Lowland Maya Fortification, *Journal of Field Archaeology* 8(3): 271–288.

1982   Proyecto Lacustre: Project Summary Report: 1979, 1980, and 1981 Seasons, manuscript prepared for National Science Foundation.

1984a Lessons from the Maya, *Latin American Research Review* 19(3): 7–34.

1984b Collapse to Conquest: Postclassic Archaeology of the Peten Maya, *Archaeology* 37(2): 46–51.

RICE, P. M.

1979   Ceramic and nonceramic artifacts of Lakes Yaxha-Sacnab, El Peten, Guatemala, Part I, The Ceramics, Section B, Postclassic Pottery from Topoxte, *Ceramica de Cultura Maya* 11: 1–86.

1980   Peten Postclassic Pottery Production and Exchange: A View from Macanche, in R. Fry, Ed., *Models and Methods in Regional Exchange*, pp. 67–82, Occasional Papers 1 of the Society for American Archaeology.

n.d.a The Peten Postclassic: Perspectives from the Central Peten Lakes, in J. Sabloff and E. W. Andrews V, Eds., *Late Lowland Maya Civilization: Classic to Postclassic*, University of New Mexico Press, Albuquerque.

n.d.b Macanche Island, El Peten, Guatemala: Excavations and Pottery Type Descriptions, unpublished manuscript.

RICHARDSON, F. B.

1940   Non-Maya Monumental Sculpture of Central America, in C. L. Hay et al., Eds., *The Maya and Their Neighbors*, pp. 395–416, New York.

RICKETSON, O. AND E. RICKETSON

1937   *Uaxactun, Guatemala: Group E—1926–1931*, Carnegie Institution of Washington, Publication 477, Washington, D.C.

ROBERTSON, D.

1970   The Tulum Murals: The International Style of the Late Post-Classic *Verhandlungen des XXXVIII Internationalen Amerikanistenkongresses* 2: 77–88.

ROBLES CASTELLANOS, F.

1976   Ixil, Centro Agricola de Coba, *Boletin de la Escuela de Ciencias Antropologicas de la Universidad de Yucatan* 4(20): 13–43, Merida.

1977   Secuencia Ceramica Preliminar de la Region de Coba, Quintana Roo, Tesis Profesional, Escuela Nacional de Antropologia e Historia, Mexico.

1978   Proyecto Xelha, Unpublished manuscript.

1980   La Secuencia Ceramica de la Region de Coba, Quintana Roo, Tesis Profesional, Escuela Nacional de Antropologia e Historia, Mexico.

ROVNER, I.

1975   Lithic Sequences from the Maya Lowlands, Ph.D. Dissertation, Dept. of Anthropology, University of Wisconsin, Madison.

ROYS, L. AND E. W. SHOOK

1966   *Preliminary Report on the Ruins of Ake, Yucatan*, Society for American Archaeology Memoirs 20.

ROYS, R. L.

1933 (1967, 1976) *The Books of Chilam Balam of Chumayel*, Carnegie Institution of Washington, Publication 505, Washington, D.C. (republished by the University of Oklahoma Press, Norman).

1943 (1972) *The Indian Background of Colonial Yucatan*, Carnegie Institution of Washington, Publication 548, Washington, D.C. (reprinted University of Oklahoma Press, Norman).

1957   *The Political Geography of the Yucatan Maya*, Carnegie Institution of Washington, Publication 613, Washington, D.C.

1960   The Maya Katun Prophecies of the Books of Chilam Balam, Series I, *Contributions to Anthropology and History*, Vol. 12(57), pp. 1–60, Carnegie Institution of Washington, Publication 606, Washington, D.C.

1962   Literary Sources for the History of Mayapan, in H. E. D. Pollock et al., Eds., *Mayapan, Yucatan, Mexico*, pp. 25–86, Carnegie Institution of Washington, Publication 613, Washington, D.C.

1965   Lowland Maya Native Society at Spanish Contact, in R. Wauchope, Ed., *Handbook of Middle American Indians*, Vol. 3, pp. 659–678, University of Texas Press, Austin.

1966   Native Empires in Yucatan: The Maya-Toltec Empire, *Revista Mexicana de Estudios Antropologicos* 20: 153–177, Mexico.

RUPPERT, K.

1935   *The Caracol at Chichen Itza, Yucatan, Mexico*, Carnegie Institution of Washington, Publication 454, Washington, D.C.

1952   *Chichen Itza: Architectural Notes and Plans*, Carnegie Institution of Washington, Publication 595, Washington, D.C.

RUPPERT, K. AND J. H. DENNISON

1943   *Archeological Reconnaissance in Campeche, Quintana Roo, and Peten*, Carnegie Institution of Washington, Publication 543, Washington, D.C.

RUZ LHUILLIER, A.

1969   *La Costa de Campeche en los Tiempos Prehispanicos*, Instituto Nacional de Antropologia e Historia, Vol. 18, Mexico.

SABLOFF, J. A.

1973   Continuity and Disruption during Terminal Late Classic Times at Seibal: Ceramic and Other Evidence, in T. P. Culbert, Ed., *The Classic Maya Collapse*, pp. 107–131, University of New Mexico Press, Albuquerque.

1977   Old Myths, New Myths: The Role of Sea Traders in the Development of Ancient Maya Civilization, in E. Benson, Ed., *The Sea in the Pre-Columbian World*, pp. 67–88, Dumbarton Oaks Research

Library and Collections, Trustees for Harvard University, Washington, D.C.

SABLOFF, J. A. AND D. A. FREIDEL

1975   A Model of a Pre-Columbian Trading Center, in J. A. Sabloff and C. C. Lamberg-Karlovsky, Eds., *Ancient Civilizations and Trade*, pp. 369–408, University of New Mexico Press, Albuquerque.

SABLOFF, J. A. AND W. L. RATHJE

1973   A Study of Changing Pre-Columbian Commercial Patterns on the Island of Cozumel, Mexico, *Atti del XL Congresso Internazionale degli Americanisti*, Vol. 1, pp. 455–463, Roma.

1975a   Eds., *A Study of Changing Pre-Columbian Commercial Systems: The 1972–1973 Seasons at Cozumel, Mexico*, Monographs of the Peabody Museum of Archaeology and Ethnology, No. 3, Harvard University, Cambridge.

1975b   The Rise of a Maya Merchant Class, *Scientific American* 233: 72–82.

SABLOFF, J. A. AND G. R. WILLEY

1967   The Collapse of Maya Civilization in the Southern Lowlands: A Consideration of History and Process, *Southwestern Journal of Anthropology* 23(4): 311–336.

SANCHEZ DE AGUILAR, P.

1937   *Informe contra Idolorum Cultores del Obispado de Yucatan*, 3rd Ed., Imprenta Triay, Merida.

SANDERS, W.

1956   The Central Mexican Symbiotic Region, in G. Willey, Ed., *Prehistoric Settlement Patterns in the New World*, pp. 115–127, Viking Fund Publications in Anthropology, Vol. 23, Wenner-Gren Foundation for Anthropological Research, New York.

1960   *Prehistoric Ceramics and Settlement Patterns in Quintana Roo, Mexico*, Contributions to American Anthropology and History, Vol. 12(60), Carnegie Institution of Washington, Publication 606, Washington, D.C.

1966   Review of "Desarrollo Cultural de los Mayas", E.Z. Vogt and A. Ruz Lhuillier, Eds., *American Anthropologist* 68: 1068–1071.

1971   Cultural Ecology and Settlement Patterns of the Gulf Coast, in G. F. Ekholm and I. Bernal, Eds., *The Handbook of Mesoamerican Indians*, Vol. 2, pp. 543–557, University of Texas Press, Austin.

SANDERS, W. T. AND B. J. PRICE

1968   *Mesoamerica: The Evolution of a Civilization*, Random House, New York.

SANDERS, W. T., J. R. PARSONS, AND R. S. SANTLEY

1979   *The Basin of Mexico*, Academic Press, New York.

SATTERTHWAITE, L.

1937   Identification of Maya Temple Buildings at Piedras Negras, in D. S. Davidson, Ed., *Philadelphia Anthropological Society, Twenty-fifth Anniversary Studies*, University of Pennsylvania Press, Philadelphia.

1943–54 *Piedras Negras Archaeology*, 6 parts, University Museum, Philadelphia.
1956 Radiocarbon Dates and the Maya Correlation Problem, *American Antiquity* 21: 416–419.
1958 The Problem of Abnormal Stela Placements at Tikal and Elsewhere, *Tikal Reports*, No. 3, Museum Monographs, University Museum, Philadelphia.

SATTERTHWAITE, L., AND W. R. COE
1968 The Maya-Christian Calendrical Correlation and the Archaeology of the Peten, in *Actas y Memorias*, Vol. 3, pp. 3–19, 37th International Congress of Americanists, Buenos Aires.

SATTERTHWAITE, L. AND E. K. RALPH
1960 New Radiocarbon Dates and the Maya Correlation Problem, *American Antiquity* 26: 165–184.

SAVILLE, M.
1892 Vandalism among the Antiquities of Yucatan and Central America, *Science* 20(517).

SCHELE, L.
1976 Accession Iconography of Chan-Bahlum in the Group of the Cross at Palenque, in M. Greene Robertson, Ed., *Segunda Mesa Redonda de Palenque*, Part III, Robert Louis Stevenson School, Pebble Beach, California.

SCHOLES, F. V. AND R. L. ROYS
1948 (1968) *The Maya Chontal Indians of Acalan-Tixchel*, Carnegie Institution of Washington, Publication 560, Washington, D.C. (republished by University of Oklahoma Press, Norman).

SCHOLES, F. V. AND J. E. S. THOMPSON
1977 The Francisco Perez *Probanza* of 1654–1656 and the *Matricula* of Tipu (Belize), in G. Jones, Ed., *Anthropology and History in Yucatan*, pp. 43–68, University of Texas Press, Austin.

SELER, E.
1902 *Gesammelte Abhandlungen zur Amerrikanischen Sprach- und Aterthumskunde*, 5 Vols., Berlin.
1963 *Codice Borgia*, Fondo de Cultura Economica, 3 Vols., Mexico.

SHARER, R. J.
1977 The Maya Collapse Revisited: Internal and External Perspectives, in N. Hammond, Ed., *Social Process in Maya Prehistory*, pp. 532–552, Academic Press, London.
1978 Archaeology and History at Quirigua, Guatemala, *Journal of Field Archaeology* 5: 51–70.
1979 Classic Maya Elite Occupation in the Lower Motagua Valley, Guatemala: A Preliminary Formulation, Paper Presented at the Ethnohistory Workshop, University of Pennsylvania.
1982 Did the Maya Collapse? A New World Perspective on the Demise of Harappan Civilization, in G. Possehl, Ed., *Harappan Civilization*, pp. 367–383, New Delhi.

SHARER, R. J., W. ASHMORE, E. M. SHORTMAN, P. A. URBAN, J. L. SEIDEL, AND
D. W. SEDAT
1983   The Quirigua Project: 1978 Season, *Quirigua Reports II*, pp. 39–54,
       Museum Monographs, University Museum, Philadelphia.
SHARER, R. J. AND A. F. CHASE
1976   New Town Ceramic Complex: New Town Ceramic Sphere, in J.
       Gifford, *Prehistoric Pottery Analysis and the Ceramics of Barton
       Ramie in the Belize Valley*, pp. 288–315, Memoirs of the Peabody
       Museum of Archaeology and Ethnology, Vol. 18, Harvard Univer-
       sity, Cambridge.
SHARER, R. J. AND W. R. COE
1979   The Quirigua Project: Origins, Objectives and Research in 1973 and
       1974, *Quirigua Reports I*, pp. 1–11, University Museum Mono-
       graph 37, Philadelphia.
SHARER, R. J., C. JONES, W. ASHMORE, AND E. M. SHORTMAN
1979   The Quirigua Project: 1976 Season, *Quirigua Reports I*, pp. 45–73,
       University Museum Monograph 37, Philadelphia.
SHARP, R.
1981   *Chacs and Chiefs: Iconography of Mosaic Stone Sculpture in Pre-
       Conquest Yucatan, Mexico*, Dumbarton Oaks, Washington, D.C.
SHEEHY, J. J.
1977   1976 Excavations at Travesia: A Preliminary Report, Paper Pre-
       sented at the 42nd Annual Meeting of the Society for American Ar-
       chaeology, New Orleans.
SHEETS, P. D.
1978   Artifacts, in R. Sharer, Ed., *The Prehistory of Chalchuapa, El Sal-
       vador*, Vol. 2, Museum Monographs, Philadelphia.
SHEPARD, A.
1948   *Plumbate—A Mesoamerican Trade Ware*, Carnegie Institution of
       Washington, Publication 573, Washington, D.C.
SHERMAN, W. L.
1978   *Forced Native Labor in Sixteenth-Century Central America*, Uni-
       versity of Nebraska Press, Lincoln.
SHUMAN, M.
1977   Archaeology and Ethnohistory: The Case of the Lowland Maya,
       Ethnohistory 24(1): 1–18.
SIDRYS, R.
1976   Mesoamerica: An Archaeological Analysis of Low-Energy Civiliza-
       tion, Ph.D. Dissertation, University of California, Los Angeles.
1983   *Archaeological Excavations in Northern Belize, Central America*,
       Monograph 17, Institute of Archaeology, University of California,
       Los Angeles.
SIMMONS, M. P. AND G. F. BREM
1979   The Analysis and Distribution of Volcanic Ash-Tempered Pottery
       in the Lowland Maya Area, *American Antiquity* 44(1): 79–91.

SMITH, A. L.

1950 *Uaxactun, Guatemala, 1931–1937*, Carnegie Institution of Washington, Publication 588, Washington, D.C.

1955 *Archaeological Reconnaissance in Central Guatemala*, Carnegie Institution of Washington, Publication 608, Washington, D.C.

1961 Types of Ball Courts in the Highlands of Guatemala, in S. K. Lothrop et al., Eds., *Essays in Pre-Columbian Art and Archaeology*, pp. 100–125, Harvard University Press, Cambridge.

1962 Residential and Associated Structures at Mayapan, in H. E. D. Pollock et al., Eds., *Mayapan, Yucatan, Mexico*, Carnegie Institution of Washington, Publication 619, Washington, D.C.

1972 *Excavations at Altar de Sacrificios: Architecture, Settlement, Burials, and Caches*, Papers of the Peabody Museum of Archaeology and Ethnology, No. 62(2), Harvard University, Cambridge.

1977 *Patolli* at the Ruins of Seibal, Peten, Guatemala, in N. Hammond, Ed., *Social Process in Maya Prehistory*, pp. 349–363, Academic Press, London.

SMITH, R. E.

1955 *Ceramic Sequence at Uaxactun, Guatemala*, Middle American Research Institute, Publication 20, 2 vols., Tulane University, New Orleans.

1958 The Place of Fine Orange Pottery in Mesoamerican Archaeology, *American Antiquity* 24: 151–160.

1971 *The Pottery of Mayapan*, Papers of the Peabody Museum of Archaeology and Ethnology, No. 66, Harvard University, Cambridge.

SPINDEN, H. J.

1924 The Reduction of Mayan Dates, in *Papers of the Peabody Museum of Archeology and Ethnology* No. 6(4), Harvard University, Cambridge.

STEWART, R.

1977 Classic to Postclassic Period Settlement Trends in the Region of Santa Cruz del Quiche, in D. Wallace and R. Carmack, Eds., *Archaeology and Ethnohistory of the Central Quiche*, pp. 68–81, Institute for Mesoamerican Studies, No. 1, Albany.

STOLTMAN, J. B.

1978 Lithic Artifacts from a Complex Society: The Chipped Stone Tools of Becan, Campeche, Mexico, *Middle American Research Institute, Tulane University, Occasional Paper*, No. 2, New Orleans.

STREBEL, H.

1885–89 *Alt Mexiko Archeologische Beitrage zur Kultgeshichte seiner Bewohner*, 2 Vols., Hamburg and Leipzig.

STRICKTON, A.

1965 Hacienda and Plantation in Yucatan: An Historical-Ecological Consideration of the Folk-Urban Continuum in Yucatan, *America Indigena* 25(1): 35–63.

STROMSVIK, G., H. POLLOCK, AND H. BERLIN

1955   Exploration in Quintana Roo, *Carnegie Institution of Washington Current Reports*, Vol. 2, pp. 169–178, Washington, D.C.

STRONG, W. D.

1935   *Archaeological Investigations in the Bay Islands, Spanish Honduras*, Smithsonian Miscellaneous Collections, Vol. 92, No. 14, Washington, D.C.

STRONG, W. D., A. KIDDER II, AND A. J. D. PAUL JR.

1938   *Preliminary Report on the Smithsonian Institution–Harvard University Archaeological Expedition to Northwestern Honduras, 1936*, Smithsonian Miscellaneous Collections, Vol. 97, No. 1, Washington, D.C.

STUCKENRATH JR., R., W. R. COE, AND E. K. RALPH

1966   University of Pennsylvania Radiocarbon Dates IX, *Radiocarbon* 8: 348–385.

TERRAY, E.

1974   Long-Distance Exchange and the Formation of the State: The Case of the Abron Kingdom of Gyaman, *Economy and Society* 3(3): 315–345.

1975   Classes and Class Consciousness in the Abron Kingdom of Gyaman, in Bloch, Ed., *Marxist Analyses and Social Anthropology*, pp. 85–135, John Wiley, New York.

THOMAS JR., P. M.

1981   *Prehistoric Maya Settlement Patterns at Becan, Campeche, Mexico*, Middle American Research Institute, Publication 45, Tulane University, New Orleans.

THOMPSON, J. E. S.

1927   A Correlation of the Mayan and European Calendars, *Field Museum of Natural History*, Publication 241, *Anthropological Series*, Vol. 17, No. 1, Chicago.

1937   Maya Chronology: The Correlation Question, *Contributions to American Archaeology* No. 145, pp. 51–104, Carnegie Institution of Washington, Publication 456, Washington, D.C.

1938   Sixteenth and Seventeenth Century Reports on the Chol Mayas, *American Anthropologist* 40: 584–604.

1939   *Excavations at San Jose, British Honduras*, Carnegie Institution of Washington, Publication 506, Washington, D.C.

1941a   Dating of Certain Inscriptions of Non-Maya Origin, *Theoretical Approaches to Problems* 1, Carnegie Institution, Washington, D.C.

1941b   A Coordination of the History of Chichen Itza with Ceramic Sequences in Central Mexico, *Revista Mexicana de Estudios Antropologicos* 5(2–3): 97–109, Mexico.

1942   Representations of Tezcatlipoca at Chichen Itza, *Notes on Middle American Archaeology and Ethnology, No. 12*, Carnegie Institution of Washington Division of Historical Research, Cambridge.

1945   A Survey of the Maya Area, *American Antiquity* 11(1): 2–24.

1950 (1971) *Maya Hieroglyphic Writing: An Introduction*, University of Oklahoma Press, Norman.

1951 The Itza of Tayasal Peten, in *Homenaje al Doctor Alfonso Caso*, pp. 389–400, Mexico.

1953 A Stela at San Lorenzo, Southeastern Campeche, *Notes on Middle American Archaeology and Ethnology*, No. 115, Carnegie Institution of Washington, Washington, D.C.

1954 A Presumed Residence of the Nobility at Mayapan, Carnegie Institution of Washington, *Current Reports*, Vol. 1, No. 19, Washington, D.C.

1966 *The Rise and Fall of Maya Civilization*, 2nd Edition, University of Oklahoma Press, Norman.

1970 *Maya History and Religion*, University of Oklahoma Press, Norman.

1972 *The Maya of Belize: Historical Chapters since Columbus*, The Benex Press, Belize.

1977 A Proposal for Constituting a Maya Subgroup, Cultural and Linguistic, in the Peten and Adjacent Regions, in G. Jones, Ed., *Anthropology and History in Yucatan*, pp. 3–42, University of Texas Press, Austin.

TOZZER, A. M.

1913 A Spanish Manuscript Letter on the Lacandones in the Archives of the Indies in Seville, *18th International Congress of Americanists, Acta*, Vol. 2, pp. 497–509, London.

1941 *Landa's Relacion de las Cosas de Yucatan*, Papers of the Peabody Museum of Archaeology and Ethnology, No. 18, Harvard University, Cambridge.

1957 *Chichen Itza and Its Cenote of Sacrifice: A Comparative Study of Contemporaneous Maya and Toltec*, Memoirs of the Peabody Museum of Archaeology and Ethnology, Vols. 11 and 12, Harvard University, Cambridge.

TURNABAUGH, W. A.

1979 Calumet Ceremonialism as a Nativistic Response, *American Antiquity* 44: 685–691.

TURNER, B. L. II

1974 Prehistoric Intensive Agriculture in the Maya Lowlands, *Science* 185: 118–124.

U.S. DEPARTMENT OF STATE

1919–20 *Mediation of the Honduran-Guatemalan Boundary Question*, 2 Vols., U. S. Government Printing Office, Washington, D.C.

URBAN, P. A.

1980 Proyecto Valle de Sula 1978, Instituto Hondureno de Antropologia e Historia, Tegucigalpa.

VAILLANT, G. C.

1935 Chronology and Stratigraphy in the Maya Area, *Maya Research* 2: 119–143.

VALENTINI, P. J.

1880   The Katunes of Maya History, *Proceedings of the American Anti-quarian Society*, No. 74, pp. 71–117.

VAUGHAN, H. H.

1979   Prehistoric Disturbance of Vegetation in the Area of Lake Yaxha, Peten, Guatemala, Ph.D. Dissertation, Department of Botany, University of Florida.

VELAZQUEZ VALADEZ, R.

1974   Informe de Trabajo: Comprede los Trabajos de Campo en la Zona Arqueologica de Tulum, Quintana Roo; los Dias 11 al 14 de Noviembre y del 21 y 22 del Mismo Mes, del Ano de 1974, Unpublished Manuscript.

1976   Informe de la Exploraciones Arqueologicas y Trabajos de Mantenimiento en la Zona de Tulum, Quintana Roo, *Cuadernos de los Centros*, No. 27, pp. 19–83, Mexico.

VELIZ, R. V.

1977   Proyecto Valle de Sula 1978, Instituto Hondureno de Antropologia e Historia, Tegucigalpa.

VILLA ROJAS, A.

1945   *The Maya of East Central Quintana Roo*, Carnegie Institution of Washington, Publication 559, Washington, D.C.

VILLAGUTIERRE SOTO MAYOR, DON DE

1933 (1701)   *Historia de la Conquista de la Provincia de el Itza, Guatemala*.

VOKES, A. W.

1978   They Don't Make Them Like They Used To, Paper Presented at the Forty-Third Annual Meeting of the Society for American Archaeology, Tucson.

VON EUW, E.

1978   *Corpus of Maya Hieroglyphic Inscriptions, Volume 5, Part 1, Xultun*, Peabody Museum of Archaeology and Ethnology, Harvard University, Cambridge.

WALLACE, A. F. C.

1969   *The Death and Rebirth of the Seneca*, Random House, New York.

1970   *Culture and Personality* (2nd edition), Random House, New York.

WALLACE, D. T.

1977   An Intra-site Locational Analysis of Utatlan: The Structure of an Urban Site, in D. Wallace and R. Carmack, Eds., *Archaeology and Ethnohistory of the Central Quiche*, pp. 20–54, Institute for Mesoamerican Studies, Albany.

WAUCHOPE, R.

1947   An Approach to the Maya Correlation Problem through Guatemalan Highland Archaeology and Native Annals, *American Antiquity* 13: 59–66.

1948   *Excavations at Zacualpa, Guatemala*, Middle American Research Institute, Publication 14, New Orleans.

1949   Las Edades de Utatlan e Iximche, *Instituto de Antropologia e Historia de Guatemala, Revista* 1(1): 10–22.

1970   Protohistoric Pottery of the Guatemala Highlands, in W. R. Bullard
        Jr., Ed., *Monographs and Papers in Maya Archaeology*, Papers of the
        Peabody Museum of Archaeology and Ethnology, No. 61, pp.
        89–244, Harvard University, Cambridge.

1975   *Zacualpa, El Quiche, Guatemala: An Ancient Provincial Center of
        the Highland Maya*, Middle American Research Institute, Publica-
        tion 39, Tulane University, New Orleans.

WEAVER, M. P.

1972   *The Aztecs, Mayas, and Their Predecessors*, Academic Press, New
        York.

WEBSTER, D. L.

1976   *Defensive Earthworks at Becan, Campeche, Mexico: Implications
        for Maya Warfare*, Middle American Research Institute, Publication
        41, Tulane University, New Orleans.

1979   *Cuca, Chacchob, Dzonot Ake—Three Walled Northern Maya Cen-
        ters*, Occasional Papers in Anthropology, No. 11, Department of
        Anthropology, Pennsylvania State University, University Park.

WEEKS, J. M.

1977   Evidence for Metalworking on the Periphery of Utatlan, in D. Wal-
        lace and R. Carmack, Eds., *Archaeology and Ethnohistory of the
        Central Quiche*, pp. 55–67, Institute for Mesoamerican Studies,
        No. 1, Albany.

WEITZEL, R. B.

1931   The Books of Chilam Balam as a Tradition, *The Archaeological In-
        stitute of America* 35: 319–23.

WEST, R. C., N. P. PSUTY, AND B. G. THOM

1969   The Tabasco Lowlands of Southeastern Mexico, *Coastal Studies
        Series No. 27*, Coastal Studies Institute, Louisiana State University,
        Baton Rouge.

WILKERSON, S. J. K.

1979   In Search of the Mountain of Foam: Human Sacrifice in Eastern
        Mesoamerica, Paper presented at the conference on Human
        Sacrifice in Pre-Columbian America, Dumbarton Oaks, Washing-
        ton, D.C.

WILLEY, G. R.

1972   *The Artifacts of Altar de Sacrificios*, Papers of the Peabody Mu-
        seum of Archaeology and Ethnology, No. 64(1), Harvard University,
        Cambridge.

1973a   Certain Aspects of the Late Classic to Postclassic Periods in the
        Belize Valley, in T. P. Culbert, Ed., *The Classic Maya Collapse*, pp.
        93–106, University of New Mexico Press, Albuquerque.

1973b   *The Altar de Sacrificios Excavations, General Summary and Con-
        clusions*, Papers of the Peabody Museum of Archaeology and Eth-
        nology, No. 64(3), Harvard University, Cambridge.

WILLEY, G. R., W. R. BULLARD JR., J. B. GLASS, AND J. C. GIFFORD

1965   *Prehistoric Maya Settlements in Belize Valley*, Papers of the Peabody Museum of Archaeology and Ethnology, No. 54, Harvard University, Cambridge.

WILLEY, G. R. AND D. SHIMKIN

1973   The Maya Collapse: A Summary View, in T. P. Culbert, Ed., *The Classic Maya Collapse*, pp. 457–502, University of New Mexico Press, Albuquerque.

WILLEY, G. R. AND A. L. SMITH

1969   *The Ruins of Altar de Sacrificios, Department of Peten, Guatemala: An Introduction*, Papers of the Peabody Museum of Archaeology and Ethnology, No. 62(1), Harvard University, Cambridge.

WILLEY, G. R., A. L. SMITH, G. TOURTELLOT III, AND I. GRAHAM

1975   Introduction: The Site and Its Setting, in *Excavations at Seibal: I*, Memoirs of the Peabody Museum of Archaeology and Ethnology, Vol. 13(1), Harvard University, Cambridge.

WONDERLEY, A. W.

1981   *Late Postclassic Excavations at Naco, Honduras*, Latin American Studies Program Dissertation Series 86, Cornell University, Ithaca.

n.d.   Structures of Authority and Acquisition in the Late Postclassic Maya Lowlands, in P. J. Netherly and D. Freidel, Eds., *Pathways to Power: New Models for the Political Economy of Pre-Columbian Polities*, Cambridge.

WOOD, G. A. R.

1975   *Cocoa*, 3rd Edition, Longman, London.

WOODBURY, R. B. AND A. TRIK

1953   *The Ruins of Zaculeu, Guatemala*, 2 Vols., United Fruit Co., New York.

WRIGHT, A. C. S., D. H. ROMNEY, R. H. ARBUCKLE, AND V. E. VIAL

1959   *Land in British Honduras*, D. H. Romney, Ed., Report of the British Honduras Land Use Survey Team, Her Majesty's Stationery Office, London.

Subject Index

Author Index